How Policies Make Interest Groups

How Policies Make Interest Groups

Governments, Unions, and American Education

MICHAEL T. HARTNEY

THE UNIVERSITY OF CHICAGO PRESS   CHICAGO AND LONDON

The University of Chicago Press, Chicago 60637
The University of Chicago Press, Ltd., London
© 2022 by The University of Chicago
Published 2022
Printed in the United States of America

31 30 29 28 27 26 25 24 23 22   1 2 3 4 5

ISBN-13: 978-0-226-82088-0 (cloth)
ISBN-13: 978-0-226-82090-3 (paper)
ISBN-13: 978-0-226-82089-7 (e-book)
DOI: https://doi.org/10.7208/chicago/9780226820897.001.0001

Library of Congress Cataloging-in-Publication Data

Names: Hartney, Michael T., author.
Title: How policies make interest groups : governments, unions, and American education /
    Michael T. Hartney.
Description: Chicago ; London : The University of Chicago Press, 2022. |
    Includes bibliographical references and index.
Identifiers: LCCN 2022007608 | ISBN 9780226820880 (cloth) | ISBN 9780226820903 (paperback) |
    ISBN 9780226820897 (e-book)
Subjects: LCSH: Teachers unions—Political aspects—United States. | Pressure groups—
    United States. | Labor policy—United States. | Education—Political aspects—
    United States.
Classification: LCC LB2844.53.U6 H27 2022 | DDC 331.88/113711123/eng/20220—dc02
LC record available at https://lccn.loc.gov/2022007608

♾ This paper meets the requirements of ANSI/NISO Z39.48-1992 (Permanence of Paper).

TO SHERYL AND MICHAEL

Contents

Abbreviations

AARP	American Association of Retired Persons
AEA	Alabama Education Association
AFT	American Federation of Teachers
ABA	American Bar Association
AMA	American Medication Association
ANES	American National Election Studies
BMLC	Ballot Measure Legislative Crisis program
CB	Collective bargaining
CBA	Collective bargaining agreement
CTA	California Teachers Association
DOE	Department of Education
ESSA	Every Student Succeeds Act
FEC	Federal Election Commission
ISTA	Indiana State Teachers Association
MEA	Michigan Education Association
NAEP	National Assessment of Educational Progress
NCLB	No Child Left Behind Act
NCTQ	National Council on Teacher Quality
NGA	National Governors Association
NEA	National Education Association
NJEA	New Jersey Education Association
NLRA	National Labor Relations Act
NRA	National Rifle Association
NRTWC	National Right to Work Committee

NSBA	National School Boards Association
PAC	Political action committee
PTA	National Parent Teacher Association
RttT	Race to the Top
RTW	Right-to-work (law)
TWP	Teacher workforce policies
UFT	United Federation of Teachers
UniServ	Unified Staff Service Program
VEA	Virginia Education Association
WEA	Washington Education Association
WEAC	Wisconsin Education Association Council
WFT	Wisconsin Federation of Teachers

Preface

More than a decade ago, I began to study teachers unions in American politics and their influence on American education more generally. Then a doctoral student at the University of Notre Dame, I was warned by a number of scholars about the risks of writing about such a controversial topic. Their concerns have proved to be well founded.

Few unions or education reform advocacy organizations were willing to share data with me. Given the highly charged political timing—which included the rise of the Tea Party and the Great Recession—many of the teachers and elected officials whom I attempted to survey were understandably guarded. In Wisconsin, where a gubernatorial recall was being waged over the curtailment of union rights, teachers were more than eager to share their views, yet many feared I was an undercover operative working for either a pro- or anti-labor group. And whenever I presented my findings—no matter how persuasive or measured—someone was displeased that those findings might be used to advance a policy agenda with which they disagreed.

What I have come to learn is that no aspect of American education is as polarizing as the nation's teachers unions. According to one former US Education Secretary, the National Education Association (NEA)—America's largest union of public employees—is a "terrorist" organization.[1] Not to be outdone, in 2014, then-NEA president Lily Eskelsen García blasted education reformers' support for tying teachers' evaluations to their students' progress on standardized tests as "the mark of the devil"![2]

Of course, as humorist Finley Peter Dunne once wrote, "politics ain't beanbag." Insofar as teachers unions are central to the politics of American public education, we should expect hard-hitting rhetoric. Yet despite their deeply entrenched and polarized perspectives, teachers union supporters and critics both agree about two basic facts: first, the unions are unquestionably the most politically active and organized interest in education politics; and second, researchers have paid far too little attention to them.

Ultimately, it was the combination of these two factors—the unparalleled activism of teachers unions paired with scholarly inattention to them—that convinced me to pursue this project. The final product is a study that helps to explain how one of the most important interest groups in postwar American politics amassed political power, leveraged it into policy influence, and fought back to regain its strength after an unexpected period of labor retrenchment.

A lot has happened since I first embarked on this project in the late aughts. The Great Recession, the Obama-era coalition of Democrats for Education Reform, and the rise of the Tea Party led some observers to begin writing the teachers unions' obituary.[3] For a brief time, I too grew concerned that the project might not reflect the current political reality. But a funny thing happened in the final eighteen months or so leading up to the book's completion—*teachers unions made an impressive comeback*. In Wisconsin and New Jersey, anti-union governors Scott Walker and Chris Christie were put out to pasture, replaced by union allies in Tony Evers and Phil Murphy. Several states rolled back the controversial teacher tenure and evaluation reforms they had adopted during the Obama years, after the federal and foundation dollars that had incentivized states to undertake that work dried up and disappeared.[4] Meanwhile, in 2020, Virginia Democrats used their first governing trifecta in over two decades to make Old Dominion the first southern state to authorize teacher bargaining in half a century.[5]

At the federal level, teachers unions reclaimed their traditional VIP status within the Democratic Party, as President Biden made it clear that he would tack away from his former boss's school reform agenda. Biden even gave serious consideration to appointing a union president to run his department of education (DOE).[6] While he ultimately pulled back from that decision, in just the first few months of his presidency, Biden appointed several teachers union officials to important education posts, hosted the presidents of both the NEA and the American Federation of Teachers (AFT) at the White House, and made certain that the Centers for Disease Control and Prevention (CDC) consulted closely with the unions before updating their scientific guidance on reopening schools during the pandemic.[7]

Speaking of COVID-19, it strikingly revealed—in a way that nothing else could—just how little influence teachers unions had lost during the challenging decade of the 2010s. During the pandemic, several studies showed that elected officials' decisions about when and how much to reopen public schools were influenced more by teacher-union resistance than by scientific or public health considerations.[8] By the time I had wrapped up the book, I realized that it contained the answer to a puzzle that I could not possibly have anticipated when I first set out to write it. Namely, it helps explain how teachers unions could bounce back from such a challenging decade to quickly regain their footing after so many people had written them off for good.

Before turning to the substance of the book, I should say a word about my choice of words and the multiple connotations that words can have. While I have chosen my words carefully, in such a charged policy area even attempts to be neutral can be read as masking value judgments. For instance, some may object to my use of the phrase "subsidized interests" to describe American teachers unions' relationship with subnational governments after the onset of public-sector collective bargaining. Even though patronage is a classic theme in the study of interest groups, some readers may mistakenly assume that by describing teachers unions as subsidized, I am somehow suggesting that they *should not* be subsidized. This is not my intent. In a democracy, politicians decide what sort of relationship the state will enter into with various groups of citizens. The relationship between government and teachers is no different. A social scientist's task is far more modest. My aim is to document the consequences for American education of the relationship that politicians have chosen to forge with organized teacher interests. To that end, readers should grapple with my argument about union subsidization on scientific and analytic grounds, not normative ones.

Still, I am not naive about the political divisiveness of the issues addressed in this book. For example, during this project's early stages, a former NEA executive director encouraged me to contact the NEA's research division to obtain some information I had been seeking about an affiliate's endorsement of school-board candidates in a particular state. Soon thereafter, I received a rather curt note declining my request. Apparently, someone was displeased with an article that I had written showing that states where the NEA had made more political campaign contributions were less likely to enact "reforms" that the union opposed.[9] Initially, I was dumbfounded. A political advocacy organization was upset because someone had demonstrated that they were effective advocates!

Later on, however, I realized that I needed to do more to clarify what policy scholars mean when they use terms like "reform" and "status quo" in their work. Let's start with what those terms do not mean in this particular context. It is *not* the case that education reforms are inherently "good" and that existing schooling policies are "bad." Rather, these terms are meant to distinguish between whether a policy proposal represents a major, minor, or non-departure from existing policy. No more, no less.

Just like everyone else, school reformers tend to view their own ideas in a favorable light. For reformers, only meaningful and even uncomfortable departures from the status quo will improve outcomes for kids. But whether a particular reform works is an empirical question, not a normative one, and this book is not intended to be an exercise in cheerleading for any specific reforms. Even when I turn to the controversial issue of union power and student achievement in chapter 8, I make no claim that raising standardized test scores should be the only, or even the primary, mission of public education. It is essential to recognize that the purposes of public schooling in a democratic society are both varied and contested. Indeed, the goals of education—what outcomes society should value most—have been vigorously debated since the earliest days of the republic.[10] While raising student achievement and closing test-score gaps between subgroups of students may be the overarching concern of today's policymakers, this was not the case for most of American history. These normative sorts of questions about the purposes of schooling, while profoundly important, are not the focus of this book. I encourage readers interested in such debates to look elsewhere.[11]

Despite these earnest pleas, I still anticipate that readers' normative views about teachers unions, and labor unions more generally, will color their assessment of both the arguments and evidence that fill the pages that follow. Nevertheless, I tried to be mindful of two distinct audiences while writing the book. One is those who feel strongly that teachers unions play a positive and valuable role in American education while also acting as an important bulwark against conservatives' efforts to "privatize" public education and weaken labor unions in the United States. The other is those who believe that teachers unions present a significant obstacle to reforming and improving the nation's schools. These two groups of readers are, it turns out, in good company. Polling data consistently reveal that the public are closely divided along these very same lines when it comes to assessing the role that unions play in American education.[12]

While my book will not bridge this divide, I believe that its argument and evidence offer something for readers in both camps. In many ways, this is a textbook example of a policy problem seen through the old adage "where you sit is where you stand." For teacher-union advocates, my findings will amplify their urgency to elect leaders who will promote policies that enable unions to remain a powerful voice for workers' rights and strong advocates for their vision of public schooling. For union opponents, on the other hand, my findings will signal that the kind of labor retrenchment undertaken in Wisconsin and elsewhere can modestly reshape the politics of education for the better.

In the end, irrespective of how one approaches teachers unions in particular and education policy more generally, I hope that all readers will come away persuaded that the policies governments enact—even seemingly arcane components of labor law—often have significant and enduring implications for interest group politics, citizens' political participation, and, ultimately, the distribution of power in American education.

CHAPTER ONE

Governments, Teachers Unions, and Education Policy

Today, teachers unions are the single most important actors in American education.[1] Yet, prior to the 1970s, teachers in the United States were completely disengaged from politics, and their interest groups possessed few resources and little to no policy influence. This book examines how that all changed. Specifically, it demonstrates how teachers became a potent force in American politics and how their historical rise to power affects education today.

The book's core argument, put most simply, is that the nature of the relationship that governments enter into with teachers unions matters immensely. More specifically, *How Policies Make Interest Groups* develops what I call the *subsidy hypothesis*: that beginning in the late 1960s and throughout the 1970s, state and local governments adopted new systems of labor relations that subsidized and strengthened the power of teachers unions in American politics.[2]

Although no one seems to dispute that teachers unions are effective at mobilizing their members for political activity, it is less clear how the unions first became and today remain the leading organized interest in education politics. Remarkably, teachers spent the better part of the 1950s and 1960s as disorganized, irrelevant actors in American politics. Teachers' fortunes quickly changed, however, after state governments adopted favorable labor policies and practices that made it easier and less costly for unions to recruit and mobilize educators in politics. These new policies and practices simultaneously empowered teachers to build strong, federated interest-group organizations that were especially well-suited to compete in education politics.

After detailing how governments helped foster organized teacher political power, I ask: what are the consequences for America's schools?
Scholars have often drawn contrary conclusions about the effects that
unions have on education outcomes, especially student achievement. I
argue that much of this ambiguity stems from the failure to focus on the
political power of teachers unions as interest groups in *subnational* politics. Many prominent scholars have rightly insisted that interest groups
return to the center of the study of American politics since such groups
are central to the policymaking process.[3] However, far too little attention has been paid to studying interest-group influence in state and local
politics, the arenas where education policy is made.[4] My book responds by
putting the most active and organized education interest group—rather
than voters or elected officials—at the center of the study of education
politics and policy. It shows how the advantages that teachers unions wield
in subnational politics often enable them to block or dilute the types of
education reform they most oppose.

The book also speaks directly to why teacher-union power and influence
persists even after a decade in which public-sector unions lost some highly
publicized political battles. The unions' setbacks were induced by an unusual focusing event (the Great Recession) that temporarily enabled
anti-union forces to make common cause with an eclectic liberal coalition
of school reformers led by a pro-reform Democrat in the White House
(Obama).[5] During this unusual time period, some states enacted new laws
upending the pro-union equilibrium in public-sector labor law that had,
since the late 1970s, granted the majority of teachers collective-bargaining
rights.[6] Since I argue that teacher-union political power is rooted in the
friendly relationships forged between governments and unions in those
earlier decades, examining the fallout from these recent setbacks is essential for understanding what the future of union power will look like in
American education.

In fact, these dynamics became even more relevant when, in 2018, the
US Supreme Court handed down its controversial 5–4 decision in *Janus v.
American Federation of State, County, and Municipal Employees, Council 31,
et al.* In *Janus*, the court narrowed the power of public-sector unions by
overturning a forty-year precedent which allowed them to charge fees to
nonmembers. Many experts anticipate that by eliminating unions' access
to agency fees, *Janus* will reduce the incentive for teachers to join and pay
union dues. This new landscape would presumably entail less revenue for
unions and fewer members for them to mobilize in politics. Although the

consequences of *Janus* are just beginning to materialize, the nation's largest teachers union has already taken some steps to adapt. The National Education Association (NEA) responded to the ruling by trimming millions of dollars from its annual operating budget. It even created a new membership category for non-educators—a first in the organization's 160-year history—to try and mitigate the lost agency-fee revenue through a new source of income.[7]

Politics, of course, lies at the very center of these recent changes. In 2008, Barack Obama unexpectedly defeated staunch union ally Hillary Clinton for the Democratic nomination. As president, Obama pushed his party to embrace charter schools and teacher accountability. By staking out these unorthodox positions (for a Democrat), Obama, along with his education secretary, Arne Duncan, put teachers unions on the political defensive. Meanwhile, the economic collapse that happened before President Obama took office made his political party especially vulnerable in the 2010 midterm elections. That year, an anti-union and pro-austerity political movement called the Tea Party helped Republicans win twenty state governing trifectas, including several victories in states that were not traditional bastions of GOP control (e.g., Maine, Michigan, Ohio, Pennsylvania, and Wisconsin).[8] Even in the Democratic and union stronghold of New Jersey, in 2009, Republican Chris Christie was elected governor on a platform that openly promised to fight the state's powerful teachers unions.

The biggest waves of all were made in Wisconsin in 2011. A few months into his first term in office, Republican governor Scott Walker and his conservative allies in the legislature enacted Act 10, a law that sharply curtailed the collective-bargaining rights of teachers. Among other things, the law imposed a new requirement that teachers unions win annual union-recertification elections, simply to maintain their representational rights. To add irony to insult, Wisconsin had been the very first state to adopt a teacher bargaining law way back in 1959! Tensions over the new law boiled over so much that by mid-February forty school districts were forced to close when thousands of teachers called out sick to protest at the state capitol. Soon thereafter, the state's largest union, the Wisconsin Education Association Council (WEAC), led an effort to recall Walker. When the dust had settled, not only had WEAC lost the recall and its court challenges to Act 10, but in 2018, the Supreme Court's *Janus* decision came down, handing teachers unions their biggest political defeat to date.[9]

In the intervening years, teachers unions have been actively working with their allies in state governments around the country to enact new

laws to soften the blow of losing access to agency-fee revenue. Lawmakers in upwards of fifteen states adopted measures intended to blunt the
impact of the court's decision. Some states expanded unions' access to
school employees to aid union recruitment efforts; still others ensured
that school districts would deduct union dues; while other states simply
reduced the time window for teachers to opt out of paying their union
dues.[10] One state (Virginia) even granted teachers collective-bargaining
rights for the very first time.[11] In Wisconsin, teachers eventually managed
to oust Scott Walker, but the fallout from his tenure is likely to shape the
power of their unions there for years to come.

Irrespective of one's views surrounding these contentious issues, in order to understand the fundamentals that shape American education, it
is essential to study the role of teachers and their unions in politics. *But
that's not what scholars do*. Not even close. In fact, outside of one notable
exception discussed below, social scientists who study education rarely
put teacher-union political power at the center of their theories or analyses. This book represents an effort to correct that imbalance. It focuses
squarely on the role of teachers in education politics.

Why Teacher Political Activism Matters

Understanding the causes and consequences of organized teacher political power in the United States is important for several reasons.

Teacher Compensation Drives Education Costs

First, as a practical matter, the fiscal costs that state and local governments
incur to provide public education are driven almost entirely by employee
compensation. Schooling is an intensely human capital affair. America's
teachers are hardly paid exorbitant salaries, yet nearly 80 cents out of every dollar that Americans spend on their schools goes to paying teachers'
salaries and benefits.[12] All told, roughly 25 percent of the average state's
general-fund budget goes to compensating school employees, the majority of whom are classroom teachers.[13]

This fact matters immensely because decisions over how to allocate
compensation are not simply technocratic. Determining how teachers
should be paid is among the most politically charged issues in education. No matter what elected officials decide to do, there will be winners

and losers. For example, modestly raising all teachers' salaries across the board may come at the expense of policymakers investing in a class-size reduction plan that requires putting resources into hiring a larger number of teachers. Similarly, dramatically increasing starting teacher salaries to attract a greater number of talented early-career applicants reduces the funds that are available to give veteran educators or those who have recently earned an advanced degree pay-bumps of their own. The basic point is that decision-making in the absence of consensus about these trade-offs will need to be resolved by politics. Teachers and their unions have some of the strongest incentives to be active in these debates over who will get what, when, and how.

Effective Teachers Are Essential

A large body of research now confirms that teacher quality is the most important school-level factor impacting student achievement.[14] Access to or denial of effective teachers can make or break a child's future.[15] However, there is significant variation in teacher effectiveness within and across schools.[16] Since many existing teacher workforce policies (TWPs), including tenure and seniority-based hiring and assignment rules, can sometimes result in low-income and racial minority students being assigned to less effective teachers, during the Obama years many education policymakers began to make reforming these TWPs a top concern.[17]

As former Clinton White House advisor and Harvard education professor Tom Kane argued in the aftermath of a 2012 lawsuit challenging California's teacher-tenure law:

> Teachers have large and lasting impacts on the lives of children. The negative impact of an ineffective teacher is as large and lasting as the positive impact of a great teacher. It makes no sense to make tenure automatic after 18 months on the job. And it is indefensible for schools to be forced to lay-off great young teachers to make space for ineffective teachers with more seniority. Such laws are not in the interest of students, and hurt disadvantaged minority students disproportionately. I welcome the [trial court] judge's ruling.[18]

Kane is hardly alone in his thinking. In fact, in recent years, education reform has largely centered on how to reform TWPs to (1) increase students' access to more effective teachers and (2) ensure that access is equitable across student populations. This focus on TWPs represents a significant shift in the tone and substance of education-reform debates in the United States. Students of American education will recall that after the federal government released its groundbreaking 1983 report *A Nation at Risk*, a majority of states raised their academic standards and Washington ultimately adopted a highly prescriptive accountability system for enforcing those standards under the 2002 No Child Left Behind Act (NCLB). Despite wide agreement that attracting and retaining better teachers is the key to improved student learning, however, these prior reform efforts largely failed to focus on teacher effectiveness.

One reason that policymakers' attention to teacher quality initially lagged behind this new research consensus is that reforming the teaching profession is highly contentious. Politically, it had been one thing to say under NCLB that states, school districts, or even schools should be held accountable for improving student learning. But a few years after NCLB, many education reformers had begun to embrace a far more controversial idea. They now insisted that *individual teachers* should be held accountable for how much their students learned.

The tight budgets and fiscal pain that accompanied the global economic downturn in 2007 presented these school reformers with a rare policy window to push their ideas into the political mainstream. Many politicians, especially those in subnational governments, were suddenly receptive to arguments that traditional TWPs like defined-benefit pension plans, tenure and seniority rules, and step-and-lane pay systems had outlived their usefulness.[19] In 2008, for example, the nonpartisan National Governors Association (NGA) released a report entitled *Building a High-Quality Education Workforce: A Governor's Guide to Human Capital Development*. While the NGA report acknowledged "lingering resistance to embracing [teacher pay reforms] among teacher unions," the governors nonetheless concluded that, to improve teacher effectiveness, states would need to embrace "new and sustainable investments in the way teachers and principals are recruited, trained, and compensated," including reforming rigid salary schedules in favor of more flexible, differentiated, and performance-based pay systems.[20]

Understandably, the nation's teachers unions responded to this new reform environment by vigorously defending their members' existing benefits and job protections. For example, reacting to gubernatorial proposals to overhaul teacher tenure, then-NEA president Dennis van Roekel questioned, "Why aren't governors standing up and saying, 'In our state, we'll devise a system where nobody will ever get into a classroom who isn't competent?' Instead they are saying, 'Let's make it easy to fire teachers.' That's the wrong goal."[21] Striking a similar tone, AFT president Randi Weingarten has explained that the debate over teacher accountability has caused many teachers to feel "under attack."[22] Whether one views these sorts of reform proposals as legitimate and necessary steps to improve American education, or takes the position that they are motivated by good old-fashioned union bashing, it is undeniable that the fallout from these policy debates will represent an important battle line between teachers unions and school reformers in the United States for years to come.

Teachers and the Public Often Disagree about Teacher Policy

Although the public is overwhelmingly fond of individual teachers—seeing them as underpaid and altruistic public servants—most Americans are far more supportive of experimenting with bold education reform proposals than the teachers whom they so admire. A few years ago, a group of scholars at Harvard University's Program on Education Policy and Governance (PEPG) carried out an extensive analysis gauging how teachers and the (non-teacher) public felt about many of the aforementioned education reforms. In 2014, the PEPG research team compiled their findings into a short book, which they called *Teachers Versus the Public*.[23]

The authors' title underscored their key finding: teachers and the public hold sharply different views about reform. On the most salient TWP reform proposals—from adopting performance-based pay to eliminating tenure and linking educator evaluations to student learning—teachers and the public stand far apart. On the whole, teachers (understandably) tend to view these reforms as threatening, whereas the public is inclined to favor broader experimentation. This divide between teachers and the public is important because, although we tend to think about teachers narrowly as instructors, they are also "street-level" bureaucrats who influence how education policy is implemented on the ground.[24] In other words, teachers occupy a critical space where policy and practice meet and where the success or failure of implementing school reform ultimately lies. As a result, policymakers will struggle when they attempt to implement education reforms that provoke significant resistance and pushback from teachers.

American Education Is Not Working Especially Well

American education—and by extension the teaching workforce that delivers it—is expected to play a unique role in American political, social, and

economic life. Public education is the largest social policy aimed at promoting economic mobility for all Americans that commands broad public
support.[25] Moreover, teachers serve important public aims by training future citizens to participate in and become guardians of their democracy.[26]

Yet Americans have good reason to worry that their schools are not
up to the challenge. Despite public education's lofty goal of providing all
citizens with the chance to achieve equal political and economic standing, America's schools are by all accounts failing to achieve the far more
modest aim of ensuring that all children graduate with basic literacy and
numeracy skills.[27] Even America's upper-class and academically gifted
students tend to lag far behind their advantaged peers around the globe,[28]
which could jeopardize US competitiveness in an increasingly global
economy. According to a McKinsey and Company study cited in the
aforementioned NGA report, "what separates the world's top-performing
K-12 school systems from low-performing ones in the United States is
[America's] well-documented, comparative inability to attract and retain
highly effective teachers."[29]

Clearly, it is essential to understand the role that teachers unions play
in shaping and constraining the boundaries of school reform in the United
States. But before we can hope to understand these larger dynamics in
American education, we first need to identify the specific roots of teachers
unions' power and influence in American politics.

Special and Vested Interests

My core argument is that favorable government policies helped make
teachers unions an unrivaled political force in American education. This
claim builds on two key insights in the work of Stanford University's Terry
Moe.[30] To date, Moe is the lone political scientist to develop a complete and
parsimonious theory of the organizational incentives of teachers unions.[31]
Specifically, he argues that teachers unions are *special* and *vested* interests.

First, he proposes, teachers unions should be analyzed as a special interest group, in the very same way that one would study the political advocacy efforts of chambers of commerce, the National Rifle Association
(NRA), or AARP. Society may rightly view individual teachers as altruistic and apolitical public servants, but that fact cannot obscure the reality
that, in organizational terms, "teachers unions represent the job-related
interests of their members, and these interests are simply not the same as

the interests of children."[32] The raison d'être of teacher-union organizations is to prioritize and represent those job-related interests, irrespective of whether such interests uniformly align with the needs or preferences of other education stakeholders.[33]

Second, teachers unions are the quintessential example of vested interests. "What is distinctive about vested interests," Moe explains, "is not solely that they are special interests or that they express 'differential intensities of preference,' but rather that *they arise from the very institutions whose stability and change we want to explain*."[34] The United States spends well over 700 billion dollars a year on its K–12 schools. With nearly 80 percent of those expenditures going to compensate school employees, teachers have unambiguous vested interests in growing and defending those fiscal commitments. Combined, they help fund some six million jobs in public education.

Once teachers are rightly conceptualized as special and vested interests, three important implications for the politics of education follow. First, teachers unions will tend to *resist* education reforms that alter existing policies and practices that benefit their members. Even if a majority of citizens agree that schools need to be reformed and restructured, as vested interests unions will tend to resist radical reforms on the grounds that:

> when people and organizations have vested interests in a given institutional system, they will tend to see transformative change—involving major alterations in public programs, and not just an expansion or strengthening of what exists—as disruptive to the sources of their benefits. Real change threatens a future in which their benefits are reduced or eliminated or there is considerable uncertainty about what their benefits will be.[35]

To be clear, this does *not* mean that teachers unions will always resist change. Unions routinely lobby for improved teacher working conditions through, for example, better teacher salaries and benefits, additional support staff, and smaller classes. Later in the book, I discuss how, under certain circumstances, these efforts can also benefit students. The key point here, however, is that we should expect teachers unions to typically resist any reforms that threaten their members' interests, even if those changes *could* benefit other education stakeholders.

To state this and to formally label teachers unions "vested interests" is *not* to demean or criticize them. Even scholars who are far more sympathetic to the unions than Moe acknowledge the basic reality of these incentives. In *The Color of School Reform*, for example, political scientist Jeffrey Henig and his colleagues firmly acknowledge that "professional educators are not likely to support reforms perceived either to threaten jobs or to radically change the favored way of doing things."[36] Political scientist Lorraine Mc-Donnell has made similar arguments.[37] In his seminal book *The One Best System*, decorated education historian David Tyack bluntly describes teachers unions as "the group with the greatest power to veto or sabotage proposals for [education] reform."[38] Suffice it to say, there is nothing surprising or nefarious about teachers unions promoting and defending their members' occupational interests. To do so is part and parcel of their job as an interest group in the democratic political process.

Second, teachers unions will play an active and enduring role in education politics. Unlike other groups of citizens that are only episodically engaged, organized teacher interests can be uniquely counted on to be a permanent fixture in education debates. The incentive for school employees to remain politically active is never-ending. In contrast, their opponents—even well-financed reform coalitions—will struggle to match the unions' intensity in the long run.

For example, a foundation's commitment to school reform can suddenly be eclipsed by a newfound interest in global climate change, pandemic prevention, or racial justice. Recently, after his foundation had spent hundreds of millions of dollars encouraging states to evaluate teachers based on student learning outcomes, Bill Gates raised the white flag and abandoned the project entirely. According to the *Washington Post*, Gates said "he would no longer directly invest in developing models to evaluate teachers. His other models—which pushed districts to use test scores to size up teacher performance—*were often controversial among educators*." The *Post* went on to explain that "60 percent [of the foundation's future contributions] would go to traditional public schools . . . to let schools and educators drive the process."[39] Gates is not alone. The Los Angeles-based Eli and Edythe Broad Foundation has made a similar pivot in recent years.[40] In fact, according to a major survey of grant makers, by the late 2010s the entire field of education philanthropy had moved away from funding Obama-era teacher-quality reforms. Instead, funders are now focusing more on "whole learner" investments, early childhood education, and "diversity, equity, and inclusion" initiatives.[41]

The shifting priorities of foundations and business executives have significant implications for the basic structure of education politics. Reform groups that rely on corporate or foundation support to compete with teachers unions can catch lightning in a bottle, but the permanence of employee interests will often mean that reform victories are episodic and tepid (at best). As Wilbur Rich's case studies of large urban school districts in *Black Mayors and School Politics* revealed, vested interests usually ensure that the system reverts to the status quo once the unusual political climate that briefly allowed for reform to blossom fades away. Nat Malkus and R. J. Martin highlight this same dynamic in the long-troubled Newark, New Jersey school system:

> [In 2019], Newark's school district and local teachers union agreed on a contract that eliminates a key part of one of the most ambitious, and tumultuous, education reform overhauls of the past decade: merit pay for teachers. The uncommon alignment of three factors—state control of Newark schools, energetic support from then-Mayor Cory Booker and then-Gov. Chris Christie, and $200 million in philanthropy led by Facebook CEO Mark Zuckerberg—brought hope that Newark could radically reimagine teacher pay by aligning compensation with student success. This game-changing chance at reform, announced on The Oprah Winfrey Show and celebrated in national media institutions like The New York Times, brought unions on board and established merit pay to Newark. Less than 10 years later, all three ingredients that fueled those reforms have gone away, and now, so has merit pay. Instead, *Newark is retreating to the same system it had before.*[42]

Third and finally, teachers unions will tend to be successful when they seek to block the education reforms they oppose, even if they cannot achieve all their own policy objectives. Unlike school reformers—who face the daunting challenge of having to *overcome* power and alter existing policy arrangements—teachers unions (just like all vested interests) benefit from a veto-rich American political system. They only need to "win" once in the long chain of the policymaking process: a committee vote, executive veto, or court decision. Moreover, as I explain later in the book, the fact that American education governance is fragmented and decentralized further enhances the influence of teachers unions by making more of these veto points available to the unions when they play political defense.

Government's Role in Teacher-Union Power

Teachers unions, as special and vested interests, are clearly at the forefront of the politics of education in the United States. However, it is essential to

recognize that their political power and influence are themselves a consequence of past policy enactments. "Policies and institutions," Moe notes,
"give rise to constituencies that benefit from their existence, have vested
interests in seeing them maintained, and use their political power to prevent change."[43] Yet this fact raises a more fundamental, first-order question, one that is the primary focus of this book: *how did America's teachers
unions obtain sufficient political power to prevent change in the first place?*

The answer cannot simply be that teachers unions are a vested interest.
After all, not all vested interests are powerful. Consumers of education—
parents, employers, homeowners, taxpayers, and students—all have vested
interests in America's schools. Yet compared to the teachers unions, these
other actors are disorganized and, as I show later in the book, far weaker
players in education politics than teachers.

This power imbalance is no accident. In fact, my subsidy hypothesis
provides a simple explanation for it. Teacher-union power is rooted in
the fact that government policies have long subsidized and assisted their
efforts to accumulate and maintain political power. Unlike other education interests, the unions' efforts to raise money, recruit members, and
mobilize their supporters in politics have all been aided by public policies
that make those tasks easier and less costly.

The political power of teachers unions in New Jersey, for example, can
be traced to a series of choices made by state lawmakers over several
decades. In 1968, New Jersey made a fundamental change to its system
of public-employee labor relations when it mandated that school districts
bargain collectively with teachers unions. Collective bargaining agreements (CBAs) between school districts and teachers unions quickly spread
across the state, making it far easier for unions to organize and mobilize
teachers for collective action. A decade later, New Jersey gave teachers
unions the right to charge agency fees to nonmember teachers, thereby
making membership recruitment easier and less costly. Finally, New Jersey
requires all of the state's public schools to close for a two-day period each
year so members of the state's largest union, the New Jersey Education
Association (NJEA), can attend the union's annual convention in Atlantic City.[44] Altogether, New Jersey's system of labor relations transformed
Garden State teachers unions from mere special and vested interests into
state-*subsidized interests.*

Do these subsidies make teachers unions more influential in politics? If
one prominent New Jersey lawmaker is to be believed, the answer would
certainly appear to be yes. In his book *Government Against Itself,* CUNY

political scientist Daniel DiSalvo recounts the following story relayed by the beat reporter who had been assigned to cover statehouse politics in Trenton. In the 1990s, New Jersey Senate president Carmen Orechio refused to support an education bill that he'd been inclined to favor because the bill was fiercely opposed by the NJEA. "Look, I'm in a swing district," Orechio explained to the reform supporter. "Can you give $10,000 to my campaign and give me five knowledgeable people to help with my campaign?" When the bill's supporter said that he couldn't, Orechio responded: "The NJEA can."[45]

Orechio's tale perfectly aligns with the reasons interest-group scholars give to explain why some advocacy groups are more politically powerful than others. Groups that have clout tend to be highly organized. Once organized, they can use grassroots lobbying to their advantage, mobilizing their supporters to contact and pressure elected officials in government. Finally, organizations that can recruit lots of members and raise large sums of money hold key resource advantages in politics. The fact that teachers unions combine the ability to do all three of these things gives them rare power and influence. The NEA's longtime general legal counsel, Robert Chanin, put it this way in his retirement speech at the union's 2009 convention:

> [Teachers unions] are effective advocates because we have power. And we have power because there are more than 3.2 million people who are willing to pay us hundreds of millions of dollars in dues each year because they believe that we are the unions that can most effectively represent them, the unions that can protect their rights and advance their interests as education employees.[46]

An analogy drawn from America's Pastime nicely illustrates the intuition behind my subsidy hypothesis. During the first decade of the 2000s, Major League Baseball was rocked by a doping scandal. The steroids era is best remembered for the home-run records that were broken. The players who broke those records were talented hitters even before they began doping. Steroids don't turn a church softball-league player into Barry Bonds or Mark McGwire. With superior hand-eye coordination and athleticism, these pros started out with plenty of advantages. *But steroids made their power otherworldly.* As one former all-star and steroid user put it, "It's still a hand-eye coordination game, but the difference is the ball is going a little farther. Some of the balls that would go to the warning track [become home runs with steroids]. That's the difference."[47]

Like pro athletes without steroids, teachers unions come to the plate with several structural advantages in education politics. As special interests, they have unique incentives to pursue the occupational interests of their members. As vested interests that arise from within the education system itself, they benefit from a veto-rich political system that enables them to outlast their political opponents and fight off threatening reforms. As special and vested interests, teachers start from a relative position of strength. But when governments intervened in the 1960s and 1970s to subsidize teacher-union interest groups, they fundamentally altered the balance of interest-group power in education politics, creating a uniquely powerful triple threat.

A Theory of Subsidized Teacher Interests

Political scientists have long recognized the important role that governments play in subsidizing the formation and maintenance of interest groups.[48] Policy-feedback scholars have likewise built a large literature detailing how government policies can affect who participates in politics.[49] However, little attention has been given to understanding how these two processes reinforce one another. This lack of attention is surprising when we consider that interest groups, including those that rely on governments for support, are at the forefront of recruiting citizens to participate in politics.[50] Combining these two insights, I hypothesize that interest groups that are *better-subsidized* become interest groups that can *better organize* and *better mobilize* their supporters in politics.

Government patrons, for example, can provide critical resources to newly formed interest groups—resources that help groups sustain their momentum in their early stages of development. Such subsidies can operate exclusively at the organizational level. For example, favorable policies might enhance an interest group's ability to become more financially secure. A prominent example is the case of the National Rifle Association (NRA). In the aftermath of World War II, a federal law required that NRA members have exclusive rights to buy US Army surplus rifles at a discount. This benefit boosted NRA membership from a mere seventy thousand in 1946 to over a million by 1968.[51] In turn, this favorable government policy provided the NRA with an early organizing advantage, enabling it to gain members and revenue that could be used to strengthen its subsequent political advocacy efforts.

However, the policy-feedback effects of governmental subsidy need not occur exclusively at the organizational level. Rather, I argue that government policies can impact the political behavior of individual citizens by changing the nature of the relationship between those citizens and the interest group itself. For example, interest groups that receive government support may find that those benefits make it easier or less costly for them to mobilize potential and existing group members to participate in various forms of collective action. Groups can put these subsidies to use internally by promoting member involvement within the interest group organization itself. Alternatively, groups can use these subsidies to mobilize participation in external arenas, such as in electoral politics or grassroots lobbying.

Applying this logic to the politics of education, I argue that the policy-feedback effects of public-sector labor laws gave rise to teacher-union power and influence in American education. Specifically, teachers unions' membership recruitment, political fundraising, and electoral mobilization efforts have each been aided by government policies that made those tasks easier and less costly, thereby enabling teachers to become a potent force in education politics. My argument focuses on how the labor policies and practices arising out of states' public-sector labor laws made it far easier for teachers unions to secure organizational resources and more effectively mobilize individual educators to participate in politics. In turn, the emergence of union interest groups with superior resources and greater political-mobilization capacity altered the overall balance of power in American education.

The events that set these processes in motion began in the 1960s. At that time, subnational governments faced a crisis of public employee militancy. With a record number of strikes across the country, state lawmakers—including many Republican politicians—agreed to adopt new labor laws that promoted collective bargaining between subnational governments and their workers.[52] To implement this revolution in public-sector labor relations, states turned to the federal government's private-sector labor law—the 1935 National Labor Relations Act (NLRA)—for guidance. In fewer than two decades' time, a majority of states had adopted public-sector labor laws modeled on the NLRA. That decision proved to be enormously consequential because federal labor law had long relied on the principle of *exclusivity*. Exclusivity is simply the legal requirement that a single union—the "exclusive representative" union—be given the sole right to represent all the workers in a collective bargaining unit.

Why did state governments choose to codify exclusivity into their own labor-relations regimes? Advocates of exclusivity argue that it helps stabilize labor relations, simplifying collective bargaining and promoting "labor peace" between government and its employees. Since governments were adopting these new laws during an era of labor strife, such arguments appealed to political moderates and a strike-weary public. A single employer, negotiating with a single union that speaks for all employees, was framed as the simplest and most efficient possible arrangement for government employers. The final report issued by New York governor Nelson Rockefeller's Committee on Public Employee Relations, for example, advanced these very same arguments in favor of exclusivity, just prior to the state adopting its public-sector bargaining law, better known as the Taylor Law, in 1967.

> We find a number of advantages in the use of the principle of recognizing a majority organization as exclusive representative for all employees in the unit. There are advantages in the elimination of the possibility that the executives of an agency will play one group of employees or one employee organization off against another. There are advantages in the elimination, for a period, of interorganizational rivalries. There are advantages in discouraging the 'splitting off' of functional groups in the employee organization in order to 'go it on their own.' There are advantages in simplifying and systematizing the administration of employee and personnel relations. There are advantages in an organization's ability to serve all the employees in the [bargaining] unit.[53]

On the other hand, public-sector unions and their closest political allies in state government favored exclusivity for far more strategic reasons.[54] Giving teachers unions a statutory monopoly on the right to represent all workers would greatly promote their power in collective bargaining and also, as I will show, in politics.[55]

An "Exclusive" Set of Powers

Collective bargaining promoted the teachers unions' political power in two basic ways. First, because exclusive recognition meant that teachers unions would represent all of the teachers in a school district (both union members and nonmembers alike), many states adopted laws that provided unions with security provisions to discourage free riding and ensure that unions had sufficient financial resources to bargain. In public-sector labor relations, union-security provisions take three basic forms.[56] First, under "dues checkoff" arrangements, the school district agrees to deduct union dues and fees from each teacher's paycheck, giving the union greater financial security. Second, "maintenance of membership" clauses require that members remain in the union for the duration of the bargaining agree-

ment, providing certainty and stability to the union. Finally, prior to the Supreme Court's recent *Janus* decision, unions could negotiate "agency shop"
provisions, requiring nonmembers to pay fees to the union to help cover
the union's costs of representing them. As I demonstrate in chapter 5, these
security provisions played an important role outside the collective bargaining process. They provided newly emerging teacher-union interest groups
organizational subsidies that enabled them to more easily recruit members, raise revenue, and ensure long-term group maintenance and survival.

Second, exclusive recognition incentivized school-district governments
to provide teachers unions with other subsidies that, while not intended
as such, would be useful for organizing and mobilizing teachers in politics.
These subsidies, referred to as "Association rights" provisions in CBAs,
arise from the fact that exclusive collective-bargaining regimes *institutionalize* private union interest groups as formal public actors in school
district governments. In an important US Supreme Court decision that I
discuss in detail in chapter 2, when a teachers union becomes the exclusive
representative, under American labor law that union is said to "[assume]
an official position in the operational structure" of a school district.[57]

That official position requires that the union oversee and coordinate
the relationship between all teacher employees and the district employer.
As a practical matter then, this state of affairs led school districts to confer
a variety of exclusive rights and privileges upon the union. Many districts,
for example, provided teachers unions with communications platforms so
the union could quickly, cheaply, and reliably correspond with teachers
throughout the district. Similarly, unions gained access to physical meeting space and supplies, making it easier for them to organize and hold impromptu meetings with teachers to discuss union business. Unions also secured the contact information for all new employees (potential members).
Finally, some districts agreed to pay part of the union president's salary
while he or she took leave to work full time on union business. Of course,
these sorts of contract provisions are rarely the cause of labor strife. Nor
are they likely to garner any news coverage during labor negotiations.
However, my argument is that these seemingly mundane provisions became extremely valuable to union interest groups because they made it
easier and less costly for those groups to mobilize teachers in politics.

Figure 1.1 lays out the basic theoretical framework of my subsidy hypothesis. American labor law begins by designating a teachers union as
the "exclusive representative." Exclusivity then creates and sustains the
rationale for government to provide the union with security provisions.
Those provisions help the union solve its collective-action problems,

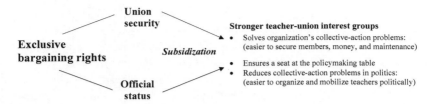

FIGURE 1.1 How labor law subsidizes teachers unions in politics

enabling it to recruit members, raise money, and ensure group maintenance and survival. At the local level, exclusivity gives the teachers union
a formal seat at the policymaking table. At the other end of that table is
the school-district employer. It negotiates CBAs that frequently provide
the union with strong Association rights provisions. These provisions provide all sorts of practical benefits that make it easier and less costly for the
union to organize and mobilize teachers in politics.

E. E. Schattschneider famously declared that "new policies create a
new politics."[58] This insight helps explain how America's teachers went
from disengaged bystanders to formidable political activists. Before state
governments enacted strong teacher labor laws, union interest groups
were hard pressed to locate, coordinate, and mobilize teachers—who
were scattered across districts and schools—to engage in political action.
And, like all membership associations, teachers unions faced significant
collective-action problems in recruiting teachers to join their ranks and
pay dues. Collective bargaining changed all of this. It bolstered the political recruitment and mobilization capacity of teachers unions, which in
turn altered the balance of power in American education, stabilizing education politics in a pro-union direction.

Plan of the Book

This book is divided into two parts. Part I first tests the explanatory power
of the subsidy hypothesis as the key antecedent to the rise in teacher political activism that began in the 1970s. In part II, I explore the consequences
of teacher-union political power for American education policy.

Chapter 2 begins with a puzzle: prior to the 1970s, the majority of the nation's teachers were completely disengaged from politics. To obtain power
and influence in education, teachers unions needed to convince individual

educators to get off the sidelines and participate. Drawing on the theory of subsidized interests outlined in this chapter, chapters 2 and 3 show how governments helped unions realize their potential as political recruitment organizations.

Chapters 4 and 5 pivot to focus on how these same government policies helped strengthen the political power of teacher-union interest groups. These chapters focus on the rise of most powerful interest group in American education: the National Education Association (NEA). Drawing on both qualitative and quantitative data from the NEA's archives, I show how government policies helped the NEA secure the three resources interest groups covet most: members, money, and organizational maintenance.

After demonstrating how teachers unions used favorable government policies to mobilize teachers in politics and build strong interest groups, chapters 6–8 shift gears to consider the consequences of these developments for the modern American education-reform movement. Chapter 6 focuses on the influence of teachers unions in state politics. This influence is important since, in America's federalist system, education reform often hinges on the decisions of state officials. Chapter 7 explores the role of teachers unions in local school politics. Together these chapters reveal how the advantages that unions wield in *subnational* politics give them unrivaled influence in shaping education policy. Chapter 8 considers whether union political power constrains policymakers' efforts to raise student achievement. By drawing on newly available measures of student achievement that are more comparable across states and analyzing recent changes in certain states' teacher labor laws, I find some suggestive evidence that too much union power can reduce the academic performance gains that states make.

Finally, the Great Recession-era wave of labor retrenchment has led some to forecast a decline in teacher-union power. In contrast to this view, chapters 9 and 10 conclude by providing evidence that teachers unions are (at worst) "down, but not out." Specifically, I show that unions have remained powerful because their setbacks—although significant in recent historical terms—do little to undo the deeper roots of their power. By the time President Joe Biden took the oath of office in January of 2021, the revitalization of the nation's teachers unions was well underway, and things were once again looking up for them.

Meetings, Mailboxes, and Mobilization

In 1993, the California Teachers Association (CTA) organized the single-largest volunteer phone bank in the history of American state politics. The CTA recruited over 10 percent of the state's entire teacher workforce to make nearly a million calls urging voters to reject Proposition 174, a school-voucher initiative. More impressive still, over one hundred thousand of the calls were made on a single day—the Monday of election eve—when research shows this sort of outreach is most effective.[1]

Two decades after teachers helped defeat vouchers in the Golden State, tens of thousands of Wisconsin educators helped mobilize the first gubernatorial recall election in Badger State history. Surveying over four thousand Wisconsin teachers during that campaign, I found that over 15 percent made phone calls, 25 percent circulated petitions, and six out of ten urged their colleagues to vote. More generally, 75 percent of the teachers whom I surveyed said they almost always take the time to discuss the candidates' positions on education issues with their colleagues before an election. A majority said those discussions took place at school.[2]

On the surface, this sort of grassroots political activism may seem unremarkable. The previous chapter made clear that teachers, as government employees, have unique incentives to participate in education politics. Based on their occupational incentives and high levels of education, we should expect teachers to be far more politically active than the average American. As the *New York Times* once put it, "[The teacher] constituency is a natural one to organize . . . [Teachers] are articulate, well-educated, interested in public affairs and have the flexible schedules and time to engage in political activity."[3]

TABLE 2.1 **Teacher political participation in the 1950s**

Political activity	Percentage of teachers saying teachers *should not* do this	Percentage of teachers reporting they *did* this
Represent a political party as an official conducting an election	63.0	4.0
Volunteer for a political party (electoral organizing work)	68.0	4.4
Volunteer for a presidential candidate/campaign	77.0	2.9
Volunteer for a school-board candidate/campaign	78.0	3.8
Influence the vote of others in a school-board contest	63.0	19.7
Run for public office	n/a	2.9

Source: NEA Research Division, "Status of the American Public School Teacher," *NEA Research Bulletin* 35, no. 1 (February 1957).

It is surprising then that *until the mid-1970s, the majority of the nation's teachers were completely disengaged from politics.* The political activism demonstrated by California and Wisconsin teachers would have been literally unimaginable to their colleagues in earlier decades. Throughout the 1950s and into the 1960s, most teachers declined to participate in politics, even when they were asked by their professional associations to engage on behalf of education issues.

Just how inactive were the nation's teachers? In 1956, the National Education Association (NEA) surveyed a representative sample of the American teacher workforce and found that two-thirds believed that teachers should not participate in *any* form of political activity beyond voting.[4] Table 2.1 highlights the full extent of teacher disengagement across a broad range of political activities. Only one out of five educators, for example, said that teachers should volunteer on behalf of a presidential candidate. Two-thirds said that teachers should not volunteer for a political party. Fewer than one in twenty teachers indicated that they had ever done so. Finally, when asked if they had ever run for public office, fewer than 3 percent of teachers said that they had. This finding is striking when one thinks back just a few years to the 2018 midterm elections, when the NEA reported that nearly 1,800 educators ran for political office as part of a grassroots educator movement that organizers called #RedForEd.[5]

Even when the NEA queried teachers about their involvement in *local* school politics in the 1950s—the political arena with the most direct impact on teachers' daily lives—just one in five said that they had ever

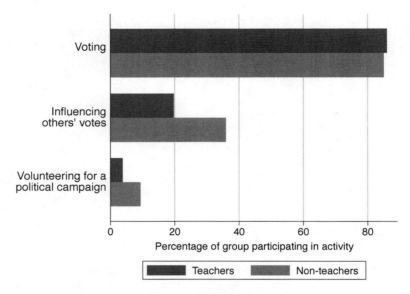

FIGURE 2.1 Political participation by teachers and non-teachers in the 1950s

Notes: Figure shows the percentage of teachers and non-teachers who reported that they participated in three separate political activities: (1) voting, (2) trying to influence the vote of others, or (3) working for a political party or campaign. The non-teacher sample is confined to college-educated female respondents.

Source: The data for teachers is from an NEA survey carried out in 1956, whose results were published in NEA Research Division, "Status of the American Public School Teacher," *NEA Research Bulletin* 35 (1957). The data for non-teachers is from the American National Election Studies (1956–1960), https://electionstudies.org/.

tried to persuade a colleague to support a specific school-board candidate. What's more, two-thirds of teachers deemed it inappropriate for their colleagues to hold private "off the record" conversations about which school-board candidates deserved teachers' support. As we will see, these earlier patterns of teacher disengagement in local politics are remarkable. Today, teachers are considered the most active group in school-board elections and teachers union–endorsed candidates win the majority of all contested school-board races.[6]

America's teachers weren't simply rejecting politics alongside their fellow citizens in the 1950s. Rather, teacher apathy during this earlier era stood in stark contrast to the robust levels of political engagement recorded by demographically comparable non-teacher citizens. In figure 2.1, for example, I draw on data from the American National Election Studies (ANES) to make comparisons between teachers and non-teachers on three separate political activities: (1) voting, (2) influencing or persuading others how to vote, and (3) volunteering for campaign or party work. Because teachers are more educated and disproportionately female than the American electorate as a whole (especially in the 1950s), I compare teachers in the NEA survey with non-teachers in the ANES who reported that they were college-educated women.[7]

The data display a dichotomy. Teachers were always reliable voters. But in the 1950s, they did little else in the political arena, especially when we compare their levels of political participation to demographically similar non-teacher citizens of that era. For example, non-teachers were nearly twice as likely to report that they had tried to influence their friends or family to support a particular candidate for political office (36 percent of non-teachers did this compared to just 20 percent of teachers). Non-teachers were also over three times more likely to volunteer for a political candidate or undertake unpaid volunteer work for a political party (9 percent of non-teachers did this versus just 3 percent of teachers). In sum, beyond fulfilling their civic duty to vote, teachers were less likely than their fellow citizens to get involved in political endeavors.

An Extraordinary Transformation

The bottom line is that, at the dawn of the 1960s, teachers were woefully disengaged from the nation's political affairs, and their nascent unions were ineffective political mobilizers. However, these circumstances all changed in short order. Teachers would soon move to the head of the political class. Indeed, the political ascent of organized teacher interests would come about in rapid, unparalleled fashion. By no later than the mid-1970s, members of the nation's two largest school-employee unions began a longstanding tradition of sending the largest share of delegates to the Democratic Party's national convention (DNC). In most years, teachers union–affiliated delegates would go on to achieve more representation at the DNC than the entire state of California had.

Teachers' plunge into subnational politics was even more impressive. Whereas fewer than five NEA state affiliates had dedicated political-action units in 1965, by 1980, all fifty had established political action committees (PACs). Many of these PACs quickly became top contributors in state politics.[8] Individual teachers also began to seek and win elective office at a torrid pace: whereas in 1956, only 3 percent of teachers reported that they had ever been candidates for public office, by 1975, over four hundred educators were serving in state legislatures, with the median statehouse boasting 10 percent teacher-members.[9] Interest-group scholars and state capitol insiders began to take note. The teachers unions' state affiliates were now, for the very first time, being ranked among the most powerful organized interests in state politics, sharing this distinction with America's venerable business lobby.[10]

Meanwhile, rank-and-file teachers also became heavily involved in local school politics. In the early 1980s, local school superintendents indicated that teachers were the constituency group that had most steadily increased their political demands on the superintendent.[11] As Wirt and Kirst observed, "In an open-ended question about what aspect had most changed since starting their [superintendent] career, the answer was overwhelmingly, 'politics,' often written with exclamations."[12] At the same time, a majority of the nation's school-board members began 'to classify teachers as the most politically active and influential group in their districts. Board members reported that teacher groups outflanked both parent and business interests.[13]

It is difficult to convey just how unusual it is to observe any group of citizens accomplish what teachers did in the 1970s: transform from disengaged bystanders and political unknowns into an active and powerful constituency group and a key member of a major political party's electoral coalition. Yet this transformation was as essential as it was unlikely. Organized teacher interests would only go on to gain power and influence in American education if they could find a way to reliably mobilize large numbers of teachers to participate in electoral politics, especially at the state and local levels.

To succeed, teachers unions needed to overcome several practical challenges that are inherent in any collective organizing effort. First, they needed a way to locate, contact, and organize individual teachers for political recruitment. Second, they needed to convince teachers to abandon their political apathy and agree to take part in coordinated political advocacy. Finally, they needed to solve the basic collective-action problem that all groups confront: the incentive for individual teachers to free ride on the efforts of their colleagues.

Here and in the next chapter, I detail how governments helped teachers unions realize their full potential as political recruitment organizations, enabling them to bring individual teachers off the sidelines and turn them into reliable and committed political activists. More specifically, these chapters showcase the powerful policy-feedback effects that public-sector collective-bargaining laws had on boosting teachers' political participation. In particular, I show how these laws helped ease the collective-action challenges facing America's teachers unions as they sought to mobilize educators for coordinated political action.

The remainder of this chapter is organized as follows. I first lay out some basic theoretical expectations about the relationship between citizens' political participation, interest groups' mobilization efforts, and the effects that public-sector labor laws had on these two related phenomena for teachers. I then briefly discuss how the revolution in public-sector bargaining enhanced the status of teachers unions in education politics. I conclude by providing historical evidence that the subsidies teachers unions obtained from state and local governments at the onset of teacher bargaining helped position them to begin organizing and mobilizing teachers in politics at the start of the 1970s.

Why Citizens Engage in Politics

To begin, it is helpful to review the general factors that lead some citizens to participate in political activity and others to forgo it altogether. Verba, Schlozman, and Brady's (VSB) "Civic Participation Model" offers an especially useful starting point.[14] These authors identify three reasons why citizens do *not* participate: they don't want to, they don't know how to, or nobody asked them. In other words, people are unlikely to participate when they lack sufficient motivation, resources, and mobilization networks for recruitment. VSB's Civic Participation Model points us to the reason why collective bargaining would be so instrumental in leading teachers out of the political wilderness during the 1970s. To see how it did so, we can apply the Civic Participation Model to teachers during the 1950s, *before* they became an active and influential constituency group in American politics.

Motivation. As public employees, teachers have always had strong occupational incentives to participate in politics.[15] As the California Teachers Association's former executive director Carolyn Doggett was fond of saying when she led the CTA in the middle of the first decade of the 2000s, "Teachers will stay out of politics when politicians stay out of the classroom."[16] Yet her insight was every bit as true between 1950 and 1970 (when teachers weren't participating) as it was during her leadership tenure (when they were). Doggett wasn't the first union leader to stress these same incentives. Former NEA president George Fischer reminded teacher delegates at the NEA's 1970 annual meeting that "since every decision which we live by, teach by, is a political decision determined by elected politicians, we must begin to influence the forces which control our functions, our finances and our futures."[17] Simply put, teachers have always been keenly aware of the political nature of their occupation. There is no clear reason, therefore, to pin their unimpressive rates of political participation in the 1950s and early 1960s on the absence of a strong motivation for them to engage.

Resources. Another unlikely culprit is a lack of resources or civic skills. Whereas many citizens lack the know-how to organize a meeting or lead a volunteer operation, teachers have always been among the most highly educated Americans. As noted in the *New York Times* article cited earlier, teachers also enjoy several other advantages that make them a natural constituency to organize in politics. Compared to other citizens, teachers have relatively greater job security and more-flexible work schedules—especially during the summer months when primary elections are held and much of the groundwork is being laid for general elections in the fall. In sum, if any group of citizens can be said to possess the sorts of civic skills and resources that are a precondition for political involvement, it would be teachers. Based on their high levels of educational attainment alone, insufficient resources or civic skills would appear to be an unsatisfactory explanation for the low rates of teacher participation registered prior to the 1970s.

Mobilization. By a process of elimination, teachers' transformation must somehow be related to the last explanatory factor: mobilization networks. In the Civic Participation Model, the term *mobilization networks* refers to the propensity of some citizens to be more securely embedded in social networks where they are more likely to receive political recruitment requests. In other words, certain citizens are more reliably solicited to participate in political activity, which in turn increases the likelihood that they will participate. "We cannot understand the process of political activation," VSB explain, "without considering the role played by requests for participation."[18]

It is important to recognize, however, that teacher disengagement in the 1950s and 1960s cannot be blamed on the absence of any existing organizational *effort* to try and mobilize them to participate. To the contrary, the NEA had already made recruiting teachers into politics a significant priority. For example, the organization routinely asked teachers to contact and lobby their representatives in Congress to support the association's efforts to procure federal education dollars. The NEA even doubled down on these efforts after it became concerned about teacher apathy in its own membership surveys. Specifically, it overhauled its Citizenship Committee in the late 1950s, putting more resources directly into teacher political mobilization. As Shotts reports in her study on the founding of the NEA's political action committee, NEA-PAC:

> As early as 1956–57 the NEA sought . . . to bring about a change in [teacher political disengagement] . . . The Citizenship Committee sought to convince teachers that they were citizens as well as teachers and as such should be participants in the political process . . . Beginning in 1963, [the NEA] began a series . . . of regional political clinics which continued through 1970, "to get teachers interested in politics and to see their proper role."[19]

However, these outreach efforts largely failed to move the needle in the 1960s. To successfully recruit teachers into politics, a far more powerful and enduring exogenous change would be required. That profound sort of change came when state governments oversaw a dramatic revolution in their public-sector labor relations regimes. Specifically, state governments began to enact public-sector bargaining laws requiring local school districts to bargain collectively with teachers unions.

Recruiting Teachers into Politics

The timing of this explanation fits. In the final quarter of the twentieth century, teacher unionization rates soared in the wake of these new laws guaranteeing public employees the right to bargain collectively with their government employers. In 1959, Wisconsin became the very first state to enact such a law. By 1980, twenty-nine states had followed suit. As Terry Moe observes:

> All things considered, the most reasonable conclusion is that the breakthrough came about because, beginning around 1960 and continuing into the 1970s, governments began passing new labor laws. These laws were specifically *sought* by unions (and their allies) to overcome their collective action problems, they were specifically designed to promote unionism and collective bargaining—and in large measure, they were successful.[20]

Moe's argument about why unions sought bargaining rights—to solve their collective action problems—is a useful starting point to explain how these labor laws spurred teachers' new foray into politics.

Prior to collective bargaining, unions were challenged to locate, co-ordinate, and mobilize individual educators—who were scattered across districts and schools—to engage in collective action. The institutionalization of teacher bargaining helped remedy these organizing challenges. Specifically, these new labor laws enhanced the organizational capacity of unions to mobilize teachers to take part in collective action. While the immediate focus was on putting this organizational capacity to use for collective action at the bargaining table (to negotiate higher wages and better working conditions), it would also be extremely useful for organizing and mobilizing teachers in politics. For example, organizing all the teachers in a school district into a single employee-bargaining unit made it both logistically easier and financially less costly for unions to recruit teachers to participate in politics. As discussed below, this process was aided and abetted by American labor law's unique reliance on the principle of *exclusive representation* in collective bargaining.[21]

In labor law, exclusivity means that employers (here school district governments) are required to recognize and bargain with just a single labor union: the one chosen by a majority of teachers. This requirement was important because it meant that all formal interactions between school districts and their teacher employees—no matter how minute—would henceforth need to be channeled through the union that a majority of teachers had designated as their exclusive representative. As a practical matter, school districts in states that had adopted these new bargaining regimes were thereby prompted to confer an assortment of valuable "Association rights" to the newly empowered exclusive-representative union. These rights quickly became institutionalized in collective bargaining agreements (CBAs) and teacher labor law more generally, literally redefining the nature of the relationship between school-district governments and teachers unions.

Many districts, for example, agreed to provide the exclusive-representative union with communications platforms so that the union could quickly, cheaply, and reliably correspond with all teachers throughout the district. In essence then, teachers unions obtained the equivalent of Congressional "franking" privileges, enabling them to more easily communicate with their teacher "constituents" for free. In fact, in many CBAs, it became common to include the local teachers union's off-site headquarters on the school district's daily mail route so that union mailings could be distributed to teachers at work. Similarly, many unions were now, for the first time, given access to physical meeting space and the use of school office supplies, making it more convenient for them to organize and hold impromptu meetings with teachers at low or no cost. At the start of each new school year, districts now began to provide the union with detailed contact information for all new hires (potential union members). Additionally, space on the agenda at faculty meetings and new employee orientations would also be reserved for the union. Finally, some school districts agreed to subsidize a portion of the local union president's salary so that she could focus her efforts on union business.

Drawing on examples from a sample of teacher CBAs that unions negotiated in the nation's largest school districts during the middle of the first decade of the 2000s, table 2.2 provides some specific examples of the most common Association-rights provisions that districts began granting unions after the onset of teacher bargaining in the United States. These examples serve to illustrate how this new system of exclusive and mandatory teacher bargaining provided unions with a broad assortment of subsidies (formal and contractual) that could be used to solve their collective-action problems and more easily organize and mobilize teachers to engage in politics.

It is important to acknowledge that school districts did not necessarily set out to negotiate CBAs that would strengthen teachers unions as political recruitment organizations. Many district leaders no doubt saw the extension of favorable Association-rights provisions as a low-cost way to pacify their local teachers union. Moreover, by granting strong Association rights to a single employee organization, elected officials and school administrators could minimize the threat of rival unionism and promote labor peace in their districts. Finally, since district leaders wanted a stable employer-employee relationship, they could argue that these concessions would help ensure that the district would have a reliable and respected partner at the bargaining table.

This is not to say that Association-rights provisions have gone entirely unnoticed over the years. During the Great Recession, for example, many political conservatives aggressively scrutinized these sorts of provisions, characterizing them as taxpayer giveaways to special interest groups. For example, in response to a *Denver Post* analysis from 2011 that showed Colorado taxpayers had "spent more than $5.8 million [over a five year period] to subsidize the activities of local teachers unions," the state's

Association-rights "subsidy"	Relevant language in CBA	District/Year
A. *Free use of buildings for meetings:* Contract ensures free use of school facilities for conducting union business/meetings	*"The Association shall be allowed the use of school buildings for Association meetings during regular school days so long as arrangements have been made with the principal of the building."*	Washoe, NV (2005, 12)
B. *Free use of equipment:* Contract gives union the right to use school equipment for union business	*"The Association shall have the right to use school audiovisual and specified business equipment when such equipment is not otherwise in use, and reservations have been made with the supervising administrator or central office."*	Rockford, IL (2002, 12)
C. *Use of mailroom/mailboxes:* Contract ensures union access to district's pony mail system and/or employee mailboxes	*"The Federation shall have the right to place material in the mailboxes of teachers and other professional employees. Placement will be made by the authorized representative of the Federation or her/his designee."*	Hartford, CT (2006, 10)
D. *Bulletin-board use:* Contract stipulations ensure union access to and use of bulletin boards in school buildings	*"A bulletin board shall be provided in the main office and in teachers' workrooms, where feasible, on which the CTU [Cleveland Teachers Union] shall be permitted to post notices and materials. The CTU Chapter Chairperson or designee shall have the exclusive responsibility for posting and removing CTU notices subject to reasonable regulations issued by the CEO."*	Cleveland, OH (2000, 6)
E. *Employee directory/contact information:* Contract ensures union has access to employee names and/or contact information	*"The Board agrees to furnish the Union . . . at the start of the school year, a current list of new teachers . . . The Board shall provide to VTO, on a monthly basis, a computerized listing . . . of all bargaining unit personnel . . . which shall include their name, address, phone number, payroll dues deduction status, date of birth, unique identifier, hire date, start date, seniority date, job role/title, school email address, and school/work assignment."*	Volusia, FL (2006, 7–8)
F. *Presentation time at faculty orientation:* Contract provisions ensuring union is able to address new employees at faculty orientations	*"The Association shall be provided time on the agenda of the general orientation programs for new certificated employees."*	Lincoln, NE (2003, 3)
G. *Presentation time at faculty meetings:* Contract provisions ensure union is able to address employees at faculty meetings	*"Association Representatives shall be allowed to make brief announcements during faculty meetings and/or through e-mail. Upon adjournment of regular faculty meetings, an Association representative will be given an opportunity to meet with faculty members."*	Escambia, FL (2004, 11)

TABLE 2.2 **(continued)**

Association-rights "subsidy"	Relevant language in CBA	District/Year
H. Release time for union business: Contract provisions grant release time to either teachers or union officers/leaders for the purpose of conducting union business	*"The president and executive vice-president of the SEA [Seattle Education Association] shall be provided leave for the school years for which he/she is elected, without loss of salary, stipend, or fringe benefits, subject to full monthly reimbursement to the SPS [Seattle Public Schools]."*	Seattle, WA (2004, 67)
I. District pays for release time: Contract provisions hold that (at least some of) the costs associated with the granting of Item H (union release time) are paid for by the district itself	*"The President of the Association may be released from teaching duties up to full time, and the Association will pay monthly seventy-five percent of the appropriate portion of the salary and benefits including [Public Employees' Retirement Association pension obligations], paid on behalf of the President. Specific arrangements for the release time will be mutually agreed upon by the president and building principal involved, with the District responsible for paying the cost of the classroom replacement."*	Cherry Creek, CO (1999, 82)

Republican treasurer Walker Stapleton bristled, "It's a shame the money isn't getting into the classrooms and to students."[22]

After Colorado's flagship newspaper found that a majority of the school districts whose contracts it had analyzed paid at least part of the local union president's salary and benefits, Beverly Ingle, then-president of the Colorado Education Association, countered that "people don't understand the value of our role in helping the [school] district function."[23] In a similar vein, one local union president argued that release time enabled her to "'advocate for those in the classroom' and resolve problems before they blow up. 'I think both the district and the association see the value' in release time, she said."[24]

Irrespective of these more recent debates, one thing is clear about the adoption and entrenchment of strong Association-rights provisions during the early days of teacher bargaining. Whereas school districts at that time tended to view these provisions as inexpensive giveaways to be traded off against unions' demands for better salaries and benefits, the historical record indicates that teachers unions both prioritized and placed immense value on them. In fact, union leaders predicted early on that securing strong Association rights would help their unions achieve greater political power and assure organizational strength over the long run. Moreover, despite any contemporary controversy over characterizing Association rights as "subsidies," the unions themselves characterized them this way—openly contending that these subsidies would strengthen and ensure their organizational survival.

In 1970, for example, NEA attorneys Robert Chanin and Donald Wollet coauthored *The Law and Practice of Teacher Negotiations*. According to the NEA, this treatise was drafted to provide teacher-union organizers across the country with "practical advice on collective bargaining, drafting and implementing [labor] statutes, and model [CBA] contract language."[25] In the book, Chanin and Wollet provide clear instructions for teacher-union organizers about the significance of obtaining strong Association-rights provisions in their CBAs. After making specific mention of the importance of obtaining the very same Association-rights provisions outlined in table 2.2, these authors concluded by admonishing union staff to remember that

> the CBA serves as a means for strengthening the [union] . . . in its relationship with its [teacher] constituents. This last objective . . . is illustrated by the article [on Association rights], which is concerned with the privileges and rights extended to the [union]. The article provides for *school district subsidy of organizational activities* by, among other things, giving negotiators, [union] officers, and [union] building representatives time off without loss of pay to perform [union] business and permitted the [union] to use school property and equipment free of charge.[26]

Further testament to the importance unions placed on these Association-rights subsidies is the significant resources they devoted to defending them in federal court. In the 1970s, minority unions, dissident nonunion teachers, and anti-union groups like the National Right to Work Committee (NRTWC), challenged the constitutionality of allowing school districts to grant exclusive benefits to private teacher-union organizations. In 1976, the US Supreme Court clarified that there were some limits to what districts could grant to the union. In *City of Madison Joint School District 8 v. Wisconsin Employment Relations Commission*, the court overturned an order that had prohibited a teacher who was not a union member from speaking out in opposition to the union's policy position at a public school-board meeting.[27]

Although *City of Madison* clearly revealed that there was a ceiling on the rights that school districts could grant to the exclusive-representative union, the court went on to set that ceiling quite high.[28] For example, in 1977, it ruled that unions that had won exclusive recognition could charge fees to teachers who were not union members to support the union's collective bargaining activities.[29] A few years later, the court concluded that exclusive-bargaining regimes did not violate nonmembers' rights when they empowered a single union to represent and speak for all employees (including those who wished not to be represented or spoken for).[30]

A lesser known, though equally important, decision in this line of cases was the justices' 5–4 decision in *Perry Education Association (PEA) v. Perry Local Educators' Association (PLEA)*. In *Perry*, the Supreme Court settled a 2–1 split that had divided the federal circuit courts over the question of whether school districts could grant a single union the exclusive right to use public resources like the school district's internal mail system.[31] In affirming the right of school districts to subsidize a single union, the court lifted the curtain and exposed just how much public-sector bargaining had changed the education landscape:

> The [district's mail] system was properly opened to PEA [the union], when it, pursuant to [Indiana labor law] was designated the collective bargaining agent for all teachers in the Perry schools. *[The union] thereby assumed an official position in the operational structure of the District's schools*, and obtained a status that carried with it rights and obligations that no other labor organization could share.[32]

An "Exclusive" Seat at the Table

Perry is important because it reveals how public-sector labor law "institutionalizes" private teacher-union interest groups as formal public actors in American education. Enabling teachers unions to "assume an official position in the operational structure" of school-district governments significantly influences the balance of power in education politics.

Whereas the fortunes of most interest groups tend to ebb and flow in response to shifts in the broader political winds, public-sector labor law virtually assures that teacher interests will have a permanent seat at the policymaking table. As Sarah Anzia observes, "in districts with mandatory collective bargaining, teacher unions automatically get a place at the table: District officials are required to negotiate and reach agreement with teacher unions on salaries, benefits, and work rules."[33] Political scientists have long recognized that political influence is predicated on access.[34] Regardless of

whether we characterize such access as gaining entree to a policy monopoly, an iron triangle, or an issue network, what's clear is that interest
groups will be more influential when they have access to the policymaking
venues that have authority over the issues they care about. For education
interests, those institutions are clearly state and school-district governments. The revolution in public-sector collective bargaining that occurred
in the late 1960s and 1970s ensured that teachers unions would have a
permanent reservation at those tables.[35]

There is also profound irony in the precedent that was established by
the Supreme Court in *Perry*. In pushing back on the dissenting justices'
position that the school district's mail system should have been treated as
a public forum that was accessible to other advocacy groups, the majority argued that if Indiana's labor law did not allow local school districts
to confer subsidies solely to the exclusive representative teachers union,
the law would implicitly require that districts grant those same rights to
"any other citizen's group or community organization with a message
for school personnel—[from] the Chamber of Commerce, right-to-work
groups, or any other labor union . . ."[36]

The court's reasoning sets up an interesting historical counterfactual.
Perry was decided in 1983. That same year, the federal government's *A
Nation at Risk* report was released, giving rise to the modern education-
reform movement. One consequence of that movement has been the proliferation of new education-reform advocacy groups.[37] Many of these groups
forthrightly position themselves as a political counterweight to teachers unions. Imagine an alternative scenario in which the *Perry* court had
rejected exclusivity and instead accepted the minority justices' public-
forum analysis. The result might well have been the abolishment of these
subsidies for teachers unions, or, at least, the extension of them to *other*
education-advocacy groups.

In other words, the stakes of institutionalizing teachers unions as formal actors in American education goes far beyond an abstract legal debate. If one were to ask a sample of interest-group policy entrepreneurs
what sort of startup assistance would be most useful in organizing and recruiting potential supporters, the types of subsidies that became accessible
to teachers unions in collective bargaining would no doubt rank highly on
almost every list.[38] In sum, the *Perry* case underscores how public-sector
bargaining uniquely advantages teachers unions as political advocacy organizations. This advantage is especially evident when one compares the
organizing challenges facing teachers with the much steeper hurdles faced

by other education stakeholders. When most other education stakeholders attempt to overcome their collective action challenges by building the
requisite organizational infrastructure to mobilize their constituents in
education politics, they do so without the same benefit of having been
designated an official actor in school governance. Getting organized looks
very different under such circumstances.

Parents offer an especially interesting case for comparison.[39] A number
of observers have drawn attention to recent efforts to organize and mobilize parents in education politics.[40] An illustration of the numerous challenges that parent activists face is depicted in the 2012 Hollywood film
Won't Back Down (starring Maggie Gyllenhaal and Viola Davis). Loosely
based on real-world events related to California's "parent trigger law,"
Gyllenhaal plays a low-income single mother who is trying to mobilize
parents to pressure the school board into converting her child's chroni-
cally low-performing school into a charter school. Setting aside the happy
(and unrealistic) Hollywood ending, the film shows Gyllenhaal struggling
to recruit and mobilize parents to support her cause because she lacks
the exact sort of resources that collective bargaining made available to
teachers unions. For example, she has to take unpaid leave from her job to
engage in door-to-door canvasing. Without contact information for all the
parents in her child's school, she has a difficult time tracking them down
and getting signatures. Likewise, there is no cheap and easy way for her
to contact and communicate reliably with parents (no district-provided
parent mailboxes or email listservs). Before she can make any progress,
Gyllenhaal discovers that the teachers union has counter-mobilized the
district's employees against her cause.

While it is unfortunate (and unnecessary) that the movie frames these
events as a hero-villain morality tale, its general depiction of the challenges that parents face in trying to organize themselves is on target. In
fact, it dovetails with what research on parent organizing has shown about
the difficulty of mobilizing parents in education politics and sustaining an
organized coalition of parent activists.[41] For example, efforts to organize
so-called "parents unions" have mostly tended to fail in the long run. A
2012 *Education Week* story noted that "many parents' unions are still in
their infancy, and can count few outright successes or failures in trying to
shape policy."[42] But if parents unions were still in their "infancy" in 2012,
what explains the litany of news reports and research studies *from the
1970s and 1980s* discussing the "rise" of "new" parents unions?[43] What the
historical record actually reveals is a graveyard of these sorts of parent

advocacy groups. They tend to emerge in response to an unexpected or unusual and controversial event,[44] only to fade away into obscurity when members, money, and enthusiasm dry up. Many different groups of citizens have a vested interest in the public schools. But unlike teachers unions, these other stakeholders cannot count on a formal set of government policies to strengthen their organization and political-mobilization efforts. Likewise, their interests in education are not formally recognized with an official seat at the policymaking table.

Evaluating the Subsidy Hypothesis

If my basic hypothesis is correct—that public-sector labor law helped give rise to subsidies that made political mobilization easier and less costly for teachers unions—three observable implications should follow.

First, the sort of subsidies shown earlier in table 2.2 should have become common in the CBAs negotiated right at the onset of the revolution in public-sector labor relations. Not only should we begin to observe CBAs containing strong Association-rights provisions in the early days of teacher bargaining, we should also find that these provisions became more common (and entrenched) in CBAs over time. Second, we should find evidence that rank-and-file teachers began to participate more reliably in politics after their state enacted a mandatory teacher-bargaining law spurring the spread of operational subsidies in CBAs. Third, an increase in teacher participation should be associated with an increase in the number of political recruitment requests unions send to teachers. In other words, there should be a linkage between the subsidies arising out of mandatory bargaining laws and increases in successful mobilization by the unions who now had access to subsidies that made recruitment easier and less costly.

Figures 2.2 and 2.3 provide some descriptive historical evidence in support of the first expectation. Namely, shortly after the onset of mandatory teacher-bargaining laws in the 1960s and early 1970s, teachers unions successfully negotiated the exact sort of Association-rights provisions that I have argued made organizing and mobilizing teachers in politics easier and less costly. The data shown in figure 2.2, for example, which are drawn from a series of historical reports commissioned by the NEA's Research Division, highlight—for the 1970–71 school year—the total percentage of teacher CBAs in operation nationwide that contained several different Association-rights subsidies. The data reveal a few interesting patterns about the prevalence of union subsidies in CBAs at the onset of teacher bargaining.

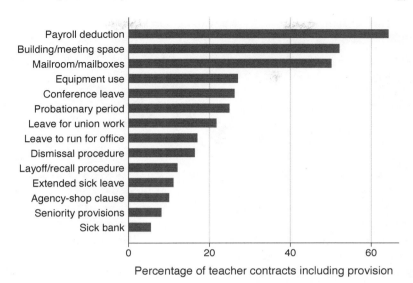

FIGURE 2.2 Provisions in teacher collective bargaining agreements (CBAs) in the early 1970s

Notes: Figure shows the percentage of CBAs containing each type of contract provision. The data include 1,529 CBAs covering 54 percent of all teachers working under a CBA in 1970.

Source: Author's analysis of data reported in the November 1971 issue of the NEA publication *Negotiation Research Digest.*

First, school districts in the early days of teacher bargaining were, on the whole, quite willing to grant teachers unions a variety of low-cost Association rights. For example, 64 percent of districts agreed to provide payroll deduction services for the union to more easily collect member dues (and in some cases PAC contributions). Another 52 percent of districts ensured that the teachers union would have access to school buildings (space) to hold union meetings with teachers in a convenient location at low (or no) cost. About half of school districts agreed to provide their union with various communication platforms that could be used to cheaply and quickly deliver the union's literature to all the district's teachers.

Districts were also far more willing to part with Association-rights items than they were to grant expensive union-favored benefits related to compensation and working conditions. Unlike Association-rights subsidies— provisions that cost the district very little in fiscal terms—school boards were far less willing to include sick-leave privileges (11 percent), seniority clauses (8 percent), or layoff protections (12 percent), which we tend to think of as the core items of concern for labor unions and their members today.

This pattern, whereby districts granted subsidies more willingly than bread-and-butter benefits, is indicative of two things. First, the unions had every incentive to formalize strong Association rights that would help them solve their organizing challenges. Consistent with the afore-mentioned Chanin and Wollet field manual, the teachers unions' first or-der of business was to secure Association rights that would enshrine and protect their organization's seat at the table vis-à-vis their school-district employer. Second, unions knew that school boards had little incentive to fight their efforts to obtain strong Association rights because these sorts of provisions carry no or only minor direct fiscal costs to school districts.[45] What matters most, of course, is the fact that these data provide strong evidence that Association rights proliferated in CBAs during the early days of teacher bargaining, just prior to the time in which teachers would begin to get active in electoral politics. In other words, the timing is en-tirely consistent with my subsidy hypothesis.

Not only did such Association rights subsidies proliferate at the onset of teacher bargaining in the early 1970s, but they also grew more common in CBAs over time. Figure 2.3 draws on more recent CBA data—a database of CBAs from the nation's largest districts in the first decade of the 2000s—to establish the second historical piece of evidence in favor of my subsidy hy-pothesis.[46] Specifically, the introduction of Association-rights provisions that began in earnest in the 1970s grew to become an increasingly common and enduring feature of the CBAs negotiated in subsequent decades, as teach-ers became increasingly active and influential in politics. Looking at four specific subsidies that were tracked in both the 1970s NEA contract data-base and the more recent CBA database from the first decade of the 2000s, we see clear evidence that Association rights became increasingly common in CBAs in later years. For example, whereas just 22 percent of CBAs pro-vided subsidized leave time for union presidents and officers in the early 1970s, three decades later, nearly half of the sampled CBAs provided this subsidy. Similarly, access to communication platforms like teacher mail-boxes increased from 50 percent to 63 percent between the two samples.

Altogether, then, the proliferation of strong Association rights in CBAs was not an idiosyncratic practice that emerged for a limited duration during the onset of teacher bargaining in the 1970s. Rather, the rise of mandatory teacher-bargaining laws led to a permanent sea change in the relationship between unions and school districts, with such subsidies becoming an en-trenched institutional benefit that unions could call upon to aid their politi-cal organizing and mobilizing efforts in the decades that followed. Thanks to the revolution in American public-sector labor law that took place in the

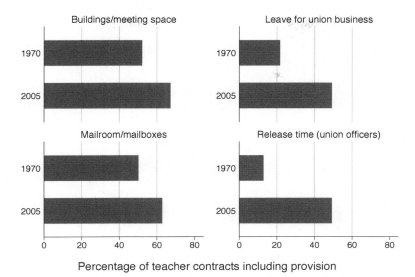

FIGURE 2.3 Growth in Association-rights provisions (subsidies) since the 1970s

Notes: Figure shows the percentage of CBAs containing each type of contract provision, during two separate time periods.

Source: Author's analysis of CBA provisions comes from two sources. Data from the 1970s is from the November 1971 issue of the NEA publication *Negotiation Research Digest.* Data from the 2000s is from the National Council on Teacher Quality, https://www.nctq.org/contract-database.

1960s and 1970s, teachers unions had, to quote the *Perry* Supreme Court majority, "assumed an official position in the operational structure of [thousands of local school districts]" around the country. In the next chapter, we will empirically assess the consequences of these policy changes for the teachers unions' efforts to turn out teachers in electoral politics.

Chapter Appendix

2012 Wisconsin Teacher Recall Survey (WTRS)

The WTRS was a survey of public school teachers administered online during the weeks leading up to and shortly after the June 2012 statewide recall election in Wisconsin. The project was approved as exempt by the Institutional Review Board (IRB) at the University of Notre Dame on May 25, 2012. The survey's target population was the entire K–12 public school teacher workforce in Wisconsin (N=67,353). Teachers were invited to participate via personal email invitations sent to their (school)

TABLE A2.1 **Descriptive statistics from the 2012 Wisconsin Teacher Recall Survey (WTRS)**

Teacher demographics

	Average age	Female	White	Average years of teaching experience (in current local district)	Average years of teaching experience (total)	Advanced degree	Average teacher compensation (salary and benefits)
Respondents	44.2	75%	98%	11.9	14.6	63%	$70,977
Nonrespondents	42.9	76%	95%	11.8	13.9	57%	$67,785

School-district demographics

	Average district enrollment	Poor students	White students	English learners	Obama vote	Median income	Bachelor's degree
Respondents	2,882	38%	79%	5%	52%	$67,503	28%
Nonrespondents	5,621	41%	74%	5%	53%	$65,124	28%

School-district demographics (*excludes Milwaukee*)

	Average district enrollment	Poor students	White students	English learners	Obama vote	Median income	Bachelor's degree
Respondents	2,635	38%	79%	5%	52%	$67,777	28%
Nonrespondents	2,708	37%	80%	5%	52%	$68,434	29%

Note: Author's analysis of data provided by the Wisconsin Department of Public Instruction, https://dpi.wi.gov/cst/data-collections/staff/published-data.

employee email address through the survey platform Qualtrics. A total of 4,763 teachers located in 379 of Wisconsin's 424 school districts completed (at least a portion of) the survey, for a response rate of 7 percent. The actual response rate, however, is likely much higher than 7 percent. Since districts varied in the transparency and/or accuracy of the employee email addresses they made available, many teachers could not be reached. Certain districts, for example, were more effective at blocking outside emails, resulting in some teachers not receiving an invitation to participate. Since I primarily use the WTRS to carry out a series of survey experiments (in chapters 6 and 8), even if it is not perfectly representative of the Wisconsin teacher workforce, the internal validity of these experiments is not a major concern. However, I took additional steps to examine the overall representativeness of the WTRS sample.

First, I compared the demographic characteristics of the teachers who responded to the WTRS to those who did not. Second, I compared the demographic (community) characteristics of the school districts where respondents and nonrespondents worked. Table A2.1 displays these comparisons. On the whole, respondents look quite similar to those teachers who either chose not to respond or were unreachable. Overall, there is no evidence to suggest that the WTRS sample is significantly unrepresentative of Wisconsin's teacher workforce in 2012. The only major difference between respondents and nonrespondents is district size. The districts that are represented in the WTRS are (on average) smaller. However, this discrepancy is partly attributable to the fact that the state's largest district—Milwaukee Public Schools (MPS)—had an employee email system that proved far less accessible. The survey's inability to reach a large number of MPS teachers makes it appear as though the WTRS sample is disproportionately drawn from smaller school districts. However, as the bottom panel of Table A2.1 shows, when Milwaukee is excluded these demographic differences between respondents and nonrespondents narrow. That said, since MPS is the state's largest school district, and it is not well represented in the WTRS, it is fair to say that the survey is not perfectly representative of the state's teacher workforce. On the other hand, there is one positive factor associated with this particular bias. It undoubtedly makes the WTRS sample much *less* pro-union and *less* politically liberal. In other words, to the extent that one might worry that the timing of the survey—amid a hotly contested recall of a controversial Republican governor—encouraged political liberals and pro-union teachers to respond more fervently, the absence of robust participation from teachers in politically liberal MPS would help mitigate this bias.

CHAPTER THREE

Turning Out Teachers

We can now begin to directly assess whether and how teacher collective bargaining enabled teacher-union interest groups to increase political participation among rank-and-file educators. Recall that for my subsidy hypothesis to be true, I must first show that individual teachers became more politically active *after* their state adopted public-sector labor laws that gave rise to the type of collective bargaining agreements (CBAs) discussed in the previous chapter (i.e., those with strong Association-rights provisions).

Labor Laws and Teacher Political Participation

My first test of the subsidy hypothesis relies on using small differences in the timing (year) when states implemented mandatory teacher collective-bargaining laws (hereinafter CB laws) to isolate the effects of these laws on the propensity of teachers to participate in politics. The specific year that states adopted CB laws varies significantly, and often idiosyncratic factors drove the timing.[1] These tiny differences in the timing of law adoptions across states are helpful because they allow me to more credibly identify whether, once fully implemented, these laws *caused* teachers to participate more reliably in electoral politics. In other words, by relying on *within-state* variation in CB laws over time, I can better determine whether the laws themselves led to higher rates of teacher participation independent of any unrelated and unobserved differences across states that are constant over time.

To measure variation in states' teacher CB laws over time, I rely on a database originally constructed by scholars Richard Freeman and Robert Valletta that codes states' CB laws for different classifications of public employees beginning in 1955, four years before Wisconsin adopted the nation's first teacher-bargaining law in 1959.[2] When compiled together, for every year from 1956 to 2004, each state is assigned a score from zero to six to classify the strength of its CB law. However, because there is little theoretical or substantive difference between most of these categories, to simplify things, I use a simple 0–1 binary measure where 1 = state/election years in which a mandatory teacher CB law had been fully implemented in a given state, and 0 = state/election years in which it had not.

To measure citizens' political participation—my main outcome variable of interest—I use the American National Elections Studies (ANES) study and pool survey responses from each November even-year election survey between 1956 and 2004, yielding a combined sample of over 1,300 teachers and 29,000 non-teachers.[3] I focus on citizens' political participation in electoral or campaign-related activities separate and apart from voting for two reasons. First, the literature treats voting separately, and efforts to explain voting behavior are often theorized as distinct from other forms of participation.[4] More importantly, voting is not related to the central puzzle that I am seeking to explain: the fact that teachers eventually became active in electoral politics whereas they once resisted it. Remember, teachers were *always* reliable voters, but they rejected other forms of political participation. With such little variation in teacher voter turnout (it typically exceeds 80 percent each year in the ANES data), there is simply little to explain regarding voting.

In contrast, the rates of teacher participation in nonvoting electoral activities varies significantly across the ANES time series. The ANES has been asking a consistent battery of political-participation questions for over fifty years. Specifically, each respondent is scored on an additive (0–5) participation index using five survey items that asked respondents whether they engaged in the following activities: (1) trying to influence the vote of others by talking with them, (2) working for a political campaign, (3) displaying a button or sign in support of a particular candidate, (4) donating money to a candidate's political campaign, and (5) attending a meeting or rally in support of a particular candidate. Across the entire ANES time series, teachers' mean score on the five-item participation index is 0.91 with a standard deviation of 1.21. By way of comparison, non-teachers participated (unsurprisingly) at lower rates, with a mean of 0.54 on the index and a standard deviation of 0.94.

I first examine some simple descriptive patterns in the raw ANES data, looking for any obvious changes in the rate of political participation before and after the adoption of a CB law in a citizen's state. To that end,

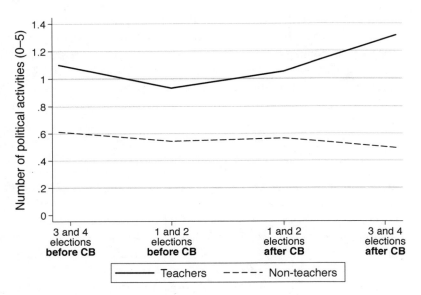

FIGURE 3.1 Political participation before and after mandatory teacher bargaining

Notes: Figure shows the average number of political activities that teachers and non-teachers reported undertaking in the elections before and after their state implemented a mandatory teacher bargaining law.

Source: Author's analysis of the American National Election Studies Cumulative File (1956–2004), https://election studies.org/.

figure 3.1 displays the average number of political acts on the five-item participation index separately for teacher and non-teacher respondents before and after their state had fully implemented a CB law.[5] The figure reveals a clear and consistent pattern. In the two subsequent elections following the implementation of a mandatory CB law—but especially by the third and fourth elections after such a law had fully gone into effect—teachers increased their levels of political engagement. By contrast, the rate of participation reported by *non-teacher* respondents does not appear to be influenced by changes in their state's CB law status. This finding is important because it suggests that the timing of the adoption of CB laws is plausibly exogenous to other unobserved state-level factors that could have led to higher rates of political participation across the whole state electorate.

A very similar pattern emerges when I examine teachers' involvement in political-campaign volunteer work. Recall that in 1956, fewer than 3 percent of teachers indicated that they had ever volunteered for a campaign. At that time, 75 percent of teachers said that educators should never get involved in such work. Yet, in my analysis of the raw ANES data, I find that teachers jumped headfirst into campaign work in the elections immediately following the implementation of a mandatory CB law in their state. For example, prior to the implementation of such a law, teachers and non-teachers reported similar rates of campaign volunteerism—a mere 4 percent participation. However, in subsequent elections—after the new CB law had gone into effect—teachers, *but only teachers*, reported a large increase in their willingness to engage in campaign work, with 14 percent of teachers reporting that they had volunteered for a political campaign.

To evaluate these descriptive patterns in the ANES data more rigorously, I use regression analysis to model the number of political activities that a teacher reported engaging in as a function of whether a mandatory CB law had been implemented in their state during an election year, along with a host of other demographic control variables. Specifically, I control for union status, the intensity of a teacher's political partisanship, level of education, income, age, gender, and racial/ethnic background.[6]

To make the strongest possible case that CB laws *caused* teacher participation to rise, my analysis relies on a statistical technique that social scientists call unit fixed effects. This technique simply means that I include a dummy variable for each state to control for any time-invariant differences across states that influence a respondent's level of political involvement. The inclusion of these state fixed effects helps to account for all of the important ways in which states are different from one another that are constant over time (e.g., history, culture, electoral institutions), thereby helping to better isolate the effect of a state's newly adopted CB law on teachers' participation.[7]

Table 3.1 presents the results of four separate regression models. The model in column 1 focuses on teacher respondents in the ANES. Consistent with my theoretical expectations, the coefficient on the mandatory teacher CB law variable is positive and statistically significant, indicating that teachers reported participating in politics at higher rates in elections held *after* their state had fully implemented a CB law. Simply put, a mandatory CB law boosts subsequent political participation among teachers. The control variables all behave as expected. Most notably, teachers who are union members participate at higher rates than nonmembers, and teachers who are partisans participate at higher rates than nonpartisans.

If mandatory CB laws also boosted participation among non-teachers in the ANES sample, then it is likely that the boost in teacher participation observed in column 1 is caused by some other unobserved state-level

TABLE 3.1 **Effect of mandatory CB laws on teachers' political participation**

	Political participation (ANES index)			
	Teachers (after CB law change) (1)	Non-teachers (after CB law change) (2)	Teachers (one election cycle before CB law change) (3)	Teachers (two election cycles before CB law change) (4)
Mandatory CB law	0.347**	−0.030	0.130	0.004
	(0.137)	(0.045)	(0.155)	(0.174)
Union member	0.244***	0.089***	0.244***	0.245***
	(0.093)	(0.028)	(0.094)	(0.094)
Partisan strength	0.268***	0.310***	0.263***	0.261***
	(0.046)	(0.012)	(0.046)	(0.046)
Education	0.083	0.190***	0.082	0.082
	(0.051)	(0.007)	(0.051)	(0.051)
Income	0.064	0.137***	0.064	0.063
	(0.048)	(0.011)	(0.049)	(0.048)
Age	0.019	0.017***	0.019	0.019
	(0.015)	(0.004)	(0.015)	(0.015)
Age^2	−0.000	−0.000***	−0.000	−0.000
	(0.000)	(0.000)	(0.000)	(0.000)
Female	−0.047	−0.194***	−0.055	−0.055
	(0.090)	(0.022)	(0.091)	(0.091)
African American	−0.301**	−0.011	−0.317**	−0.318**
	(0.151)	(0.038)	(0.152)	(0.152)
Hispanic	−0.081	−0.171***	−0.098	−0.102
	(0.204)	(0.058)	(0.205)	(0.205)
Other race	−0.186	−0.115*	−0.212	−0.218
	(0.194)	(0.064)	(0.195)	(0.195)
Average # of acts for non-teachers in state-year	0.357	—	0.339	0.326
	(0.229)		(0.229)	(0.230)
Constant	−2.959***	−2.158***	−2.890***	−2.869***
	(0.684)	(0.158)	(0.682)	(0.683)
State fixed effects	Yes	Yes	Yes	Yes
Year fixed effects	Yes	Yes	Yes	Yes
Pseudo R^2	0.05	0.06	0.05	0.05
Observations	1,133	28,979	1,133	1,133

Notes: Cell entries are negative binomial regression coefficients, with standard errors adjusted for clustering by state-year reported in parentheses. *p<0.1, **p<0.05, ***p<0.01.

factor that I have not accounted for. However, if a mandatory CB law has no effect on the participation of non-teachers, that would provide greater confidence that the positive effect I have uncovered for teachers is not spurious. Column 2 of table 3.1 reports the results of my non-teacher analysis, confirming that CB laws had no discernable impact on the participation rates of non-teachers (the coefficient is negative, though insignificant). This null result for non-teachers provides additional confidence that the effect of CB laws observed for teachers is not spurious and *is* fully consistent with my subsidy hypothesis: that teacher CB laws helped spur greater political mobilization among the nation's teachers.

Substantively, the effect of a mandatory CB law on teachers' political participation is large. Figure 3.2 displays the predicted change on the five-item ANES participation index for teacher respondents when manipulating several independent variables of interest and holding all other control variables at their mean value. The middle row of the figure reveals that, for teachers, the implementation of a CB law leads to a predicted increase of 0.27 additional political activities on the five-item index. By comparison, as the figure shows, this difference is equal to or larger than the difference between a teacher who is not a union member and one who is, between a teacher with some college and one with an advanced degree, and between a teacher in the lowest income quintile and one in the highest quintile. The effect of a mandatory CB law on teacher participation is also nearly as large as the difference between a teacher who is nonpartisan compared to a teacher who identifies with a political party. In sum, when compared to what are often considered the most influential predictors of political

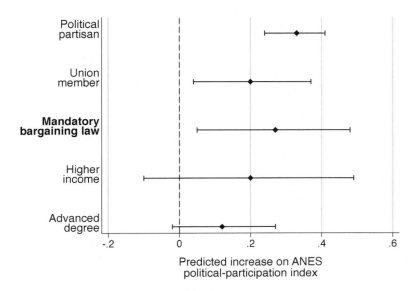

FIGURE 3.2 Substantive effects of a CB law on teachers' political participation

Notes: Figure plots the predicted change (with 95 percent confidence intervals) on the 0–5 ANES participation index when varying the independent variable as specified and holding all other variables at their mean values.

participation, the effect of a mandatory CB law on teachers' political activity is substantively large and meaningful.

I have argued that mandatory CB laws helped spark greater political participation among rank-and-file teachers. However, an alternative interpretation of the findings presented so far is that the causal arrow runs in the opposite direction. Specifically, it is plausible that individual teachers ratcheted up their participation to try and convince elected officials in their state to enact a teacher CB law. In other words, the boost in teacher participation that I have observed could simply be a cause (and not an effect) of changes in states' public-sector labor laws.

To examine this possibility, I first reran the analysis of teachers presented in column 1 of table 3.1 with one minor change. Instead of coding the presence of a mandatory CB law after it actually went into effect, I artificially "led" the timing of the CB-law variable so that it entered the model one (column 3) and then two (column 4) election cycles before the law had been fully implemented in a teacher's state. The results of this robustness check reveal that teacher participation did *not* increase in the election years during and immediately leading up to the enactment of a CB law. These results can be taken as evidence that the implementation of CB laws temporally *preceded* the rise in teacher participation. Simply put, there is no evidence that teachers were increasingly active in the elections prior to their state adopting a CB law.

Even though CB laws do not appear to arise in response to higher rates of teacher participation, it is still possible that these laws arose (and were thus endogenous to) strong and influential teacher-union interest groups. This concern would be problematic for my argument that these laws increased political activity among rank-and-file teachers by conferring important organizational advantages upon unions that helped them mobilize rank-and-file teachers in politics.

To investigate this concern, I examined a survey of state legislators conducted by political scientist Wayne L. Francis in 1963. In the survey, legislators were asked, "One hears a lot these days about the activities of interest groups and lobbies. Which would you say are the most powerful organizations of this kind in your state?" and could rank up to six different groups in order of their influence. I calculated (1) the average ranking of teacher groups in each state, (2) the percent of legislators in each state mentioning a teacher group at all, and (3) the percent of legislators in each state that ranked a teacher group as most powerful. I then separately used each of these measures as independent variables in three separate regression models predicting whether a state adopted a mandatory CB law in the remainder of the decade (before 1970). In all three analyses, I find no relationship between legislators' evaluations of the strength of teacher groups in their state and the likelihood that a CB law was enacted in the near future. These findings suggest that CB laws led to an increase in political activity among teachers and not that such laws were enacted in response to already-powerful teacher-union interest groups.[8]

Up to this point, I have shown that the political activity of individual teachers increased in the elections following the implementation of a CB law. I also performed several robustness checks to ensure that these relationships were not spurious, and I offered evidence that because CB laws are plausibly exogenous to other causes of participation that the results presented thus far can be interpreted as causal. Yet an important question remains: namely, *why* did teacher political participation increase after the enactment of mandatory CB laws?

My subsidy hypothesis contends that these laws made it easier and less costly for unions to organize and recruit teachers to take part in politics. In other words, I have suggested that teachers began to participate more in politics in part because they were increasingly recruited by their unions to do so. To evaluate this claim, I re-examine the ANES data to see whether mandatory CB laws increased the likelihood that teachers reported being recruited to participate in politics. The ANES has regularly and separately asked respondents whether one of the two major political parties or an outside "nonparty" group recruited them to participate. Relying on the very same empirical approach that I have used throughout this chapter, I examine whether (1) teachers were more likely to report receiving a political recruitment request and (2) which groups were more likely to make requests after the implementation of a mandatory CB law in their state.[9] The results of these analyses are shown in table 3.2.

Interestingly, neither political party became more likely to recruit teachers after they had been organized under a mandatory CB law. The coefficient on the CB law variable is not a significant predictor of either increased Democratic (column 1) or Republican (column 2) party contact. This finding is important because it eliminates the possibility that the law-participation boost is being driven by a Democratic Party–Labor coalition story. Instead, the subsidy hypothesis is premised on the notion that teachers unions are doing the mobilization work. And, in fact, that is precisely what I find evidence for in the model shown in column 3. Here, the positive and significant coefficient on the CB-law variable indicates

TABLE 3.2 **Effect of mandatory CB laws on union recruitment of teachers into politics**

	Source and target of political recruitment request (ANES)			
	Democrats contact teachers (1)	Republicans contact teachers (2)	Nonparty group contacts teachers (3)	Nonparty group contacts non-teachers (4)
Mandatory CB law	0.144	−0.261	4.226***	0.065
	(0.235)	(0.202)	(0.472)	(0.175)
Union member	0.132	−0.020	0.241	0.140***
	(0.122)	(0.140)	(0.160)	(0.042)
Partisan strength	0.053	−0.030	−0.112	0.019
	(0.053)	(0.054)	(0.071)	(0.015)
Education	0.106*	0.022	0.036	0.074***
	(0.062)	(0.065)	(0.081)	(0.009)
Income	0.113**	0.111*	0.200**	0.039***
	(0.057)	(0.063)	(0.080)	(0.015)
Age	0.033*	0.047**	−0.005	0.014***
	(0.017)	(0.020)	(0.025)	(0.005)
Age^2	−0.000	−0.000*	0.000	−0.000*
	(0.000)	(0.000)	(0.000)	(0.000)
Female	−0.003	0.115	0.136	0.001
	(0.103)	(0.119)	(0.147)	(0.030)
African American	0.404**	−0.367**	0.011	−0.043
	(0.158)	(0.169)	(0.243)	(0.052)
Hispanic	0.353	−0.213	0.591**	−0.012
	(0.241)	(0.316)	(0.264)	(0.073)
Other race	−0.290	−0.596*	0.122	0.058
	(0.244)	(0.305)	(0.306)	(0.075)
Average percentage of non-teachers contacted in state-year	3.012***	2.983***	1.530	—
	(0.577)	(0.646)	(0.952)	
Constant	−3.252***	−3.680***	−1.614*	−1.534***
	(0.660)	(0.740)	(0.972)	(0.302)
State fixed effects	Yes	Yes	Yes	Yes
Year fixed effects	Yes	Yes	Yes	Yes
Pseudo R^2	0.11	0.14	0.12	0.04
Observations	976	1,018	638	14,809

Notes: Dependent variable listed above each column. Cell entries are probit coefficients, with standard errors adjusted for clustering by state-year reported in parentheses. *p<0.1, **p<0.05, ***p<0.01.

that there is a strong relationship between CB laws and the frequency with which teachers receive political recruitment requests from a nonparty (outside) group. Descriptively, 18 percent of teachers in states with CB laws reported contact from an outside group, compared to only 11 percent of teachers in states without such laws. Although the ANES's question wording does not specify the identity of the outside nonparty group doing the recruiting, we can surmise that for most teacher respondents this contact is coming from their union. One way to validate that assumption is through a "placebo" test that replicates this same analysis for non-teacher respondents. The results of that analysis, shown in column 4 of table 3.2, show that non-teachers were not more likely to be contacted by a nonparty group after the enactment of a mandatory CB law. Instead, such an effect is confined only to teachers.

Collective Bargaining and Union Political Mobilization

So far, we have seen that the adoption of mandatory CB laws helped transform teachers into more committed political activists. First, such laws led teachers to engage in more electoral activities during November even-year elections. Second, teachers began to receive more recruitment requests from nonparty-based organizations after their state had put a CB law in place. Although these findings are consistent with my subsidy hypothesis, it would be helpful to obtain some more granular evidence that teachers unions used the subsidies arising out of CB laws to more easily mobilize teachers to participate in union-sponsored political activities. Whereas the strength of the ANES data is that it enables us to observe teacher political participation over time, its key weakness lies in the limited sample size of teachers and the lack of specific information about CB in each teacher's school district.

To address these limitations, I draw on a large, nationally representative survey of public school teachers carried out by Terry Moe in 2003. The Moe survey has many strengths that make it ideally suited for performing additional tests of my subsidy hypothesis. For example, the survey includes detailed information on the characteristics of each teacher's school district, including whether a teacher's district engages in CB with a union. It also asked teachers whether they participated in *union-sponsored* political activities and whether, for each activity, the union had recruited them to participate. In short, these data enable us to examine when and where teachers unions' political mobilization efforts are successful as well as how mobilization success varies in relation to the presence of CB in a teacher's district.

I begin by looking at the patterns of union political recruitment reported by teacher respondents. Figure 3.3 reveals significant variation in how frequently teachers reported being asked to participate in politics by their union. Teachers working in CB districts, for example, were far

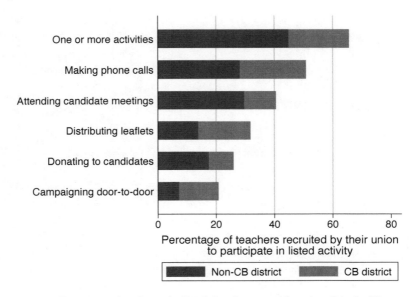

FIGURE 3.3 Percentage of teachers asked by their union to participate in politics, by CB status

Notes: Figure shows the percentage of teachers who reported being asked by their union to participate in various political activities. Results are displayed separately by the collective bargaining status of each teacher respondent's school district.

Source: 2003 Harris "Survey of Educators," commissioned by Terry Moe. For details, see Terry M. Moe, *Special Interest: Teachers Unions and America's Public Schools* (Washington, DC: Brookings Institution Press, 2011).

more likely than teachers in non-CB districts to report that their union had asked them to get involved in a range of different political activities. Specifically, two-thirds of teachers in CB districts received at least one political recruitment request, whereas fewer than half of teachers in non-CB districts reported that they had been asked to engage in at least one activity. Across all five union-sponsored political activities, teachers in CB districts were far more likely to find themselves on the receiving end of a political recruitment request. Teachers in CB districts were 36 percent more likely to be asked to attend a political meeting and more than twice as likely to be asked to go door to door and canvas for a union-backed candidate or cause.

Do higher rates of union political recruitment requests in CB districts translate into higher rates of actual teacher political participation (i.e., successful mobilization)? Consistent with a large literature on the importance of political recruitment in boosting citizens' participation,[10] the answer is an emphatic yes. Figure 3.4 displays the difference in the percentage of teachers who were successfully mobilized to participate in each of the aforementioned political activities separately for CB and non-CB districts. As the figure shows, the mobilization advantage in CB districts is significant. For example, while fewer than one in four teachers in non-CB districts was mobilized by their union to participate in at least one political activity, over one in three teachers in CB districts responded favorably to their union's recruitment request.

One might worry that teachers who are more likely to participate in politics choose to work in school districts where the local teachers union is more politically active. One way to address this concern is to examine whether teachers in CB districts were more likely to engage in union-sponsored activities "spontaneously," meaning they participated without the union having asked them to do so. As it turns out, there is actually very little difference in the levels of political participation among teachers in CB and non-CB districts when we focus on self-directed participation. In

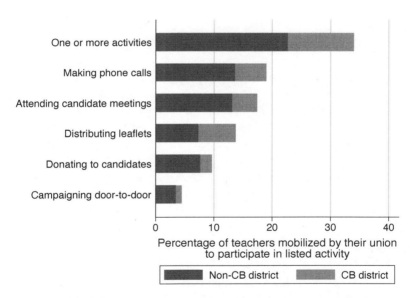

FIGURE 3.4 Percentage of teachers mobilized by their union to participate in politics, by CB status

Notes: Figure shows the percentage of teachers who, having been asked by their union to participate, reported that they had heeded the recruitment request and participated in the specific activity they had been asked by their union to do. Results are displayed separately by the collective bargaining status of each teacher respondent's school district.

Source: 2003 Harris "Survey of Educators," commissioned by Terry Moe. For details, see Terry M. Moe, *Special Interest: Teachers Unions and America's Public Schools* (Washington, DC: Brookings Institution Press, 2011).

CB districts, 8 percent of teachers reported participating without having been asked to do so, compared to 7.5 percent of teachers in non-CB districts. In other words, the differences in participation that arise between teachers in CB and non-CB districts are confined to mobilized forms of participation: those that follow from receiving a recruitment request.

Still, there are probably many unobserved factors that correlate with a school district's CB status that also influence the patterns of mobilization observed in figures 3.3 and 3.4. To address these concerns, I estimate a series of regression models that control for a wide array of both individual- and school-district-level factors that one would expect to influence the ability of teachers unions to mobilize teachers to participate in politics. To keep the analysis as simple as possible, I model the likelihood that a teacher participated in *any* of the above political activities (1=some participation; 0=no participation).

My main independent variable of interest is a simple binary indicator for whether a teacher's school district bargains collectively. In addition to basic demographic controls (e.g., age, education, gender, income, partisanship, and race), I include several other variables that should influence a teacher's likelihood of responding favorably to their union's political recruitment requests. First, I include a measure of each teacher's overall level of satisfaction with their local union. Since a district's collective bargaining status tends to correlate with other district-level factors that could influence teacher participation, I also include variables that account for the size, poverty rate, and type of locale (i.e., urban or rural) where a teacher works. Finally, I control for whether teachers report that their local union is active in district politics. In other words, this measure helps account for the level of interest and effort that each teacher's union puts into politics. The inclusion of this control variable is important because it allows me to better isolate the effect of a union having access to CB on that union's *ability* to mobilize teachers, even after accounting for the effort it puts forward in *trying* to mobilize them.

Table 3.3 presents the results of three separate regression models. The model in column 1 focuses on recruitment, estimating the likelihood that a teacher was asked to engage in a union-sponsored political activity. Holding all other control variables at their mean value, teachers in CB districts were significantly more likely—*14 percentage points more likely*—to be contacted and asked to participate in politics by their union. Next, the model in column 2 examines whether teachers were successfully mobilized (i.e., whether they heeded the recruitment request and participated). Even

TABLE 3.3 **Effect of collective bargaining on union recruitment and mobilization efforts**

	Teacher recruited to participate (1)	Teacher mobilized to participate (2)	Teacher mobilized to participate (controlling for union recruitment) (3)
CB district	0.369***	0.182**	0.032
	(0.071)	(0.072)	(0.077)
Teacher recruited	—	—	1.368***
			(0.080)
Teacher satisfied	−0.006	0.194***	0.222***
	(0.031)	(0.032)	(0.034)
Active union	0.251***	0.242***	0.153***
	(0.039)	(0.040)	(0.041)
Constant	−1.246***	−2.022***	−2.520***
	(0.240)	(0.237)	(0.245)
Pseudo R^2	0.05	0.07	0.22
Observations	2,232	2,232	2,232

Notes: Cell entries are probit coefficients, with standard errors adjusted for clustering by school district reported in parentheses. All models control for a teacher's income, education, partisanship, ideology, sex, and race. Models also control for the size, poverty, and geographic locale of a teacher's school district. *$p<0.1$, **$p<0.05$, ***$p<0.01$.

after controlling for an extensive array of individual-level and district-level factors, including a teacher's level of satisfaction with their union and that union's baseline level of political involvement, teachers in CB districts were 6 percentage points more likely to be successfully mobilized to participate. These are large and substantively meaningful effects. They are comparable, for example, to the difference that a union experiences in trying to mobilize teachers who are Democratic partisans compared to teachers who are political independents.

The model in column 3 replicates the model shown in column 2 while adding an indicator for whether a teacher received a union recruitment request on the right-hand side of the model (i.e., makes recruitment an independent variable). Here is where we can begin to see concrete evidence in support of the subsidy hypothesis. Specifically, after controlling for whether a teacher is asked to participate by their union, the CB variable becomes *insignificant* in the model while the recruitment variable remains positive and significant. These findings indicate that higher levels of teacher participation are driven by CB *through* the mechanism of increased union recruitment requests.[11] In other words, once union recruitment requests are accounted for, CB is no longer a strong predictor of whether a teacher is mobilized to participate. A formal mediation analysis confirms that the effects of CB on teacher participation is, in fact, strongly mediated through the more numerous union recruitment requests that are made in CB districts.[12]

I conduct one final analysis using the Moe survey data, putting the subsidy hypothesis to its toughest test yet. Specifically, I conclude by examining whether teachers who work in districts where the local CBA contains stronger Association-rights provisions are more likely to be mobilized to participate in politics. In other words, I move beyond the dichotomous CB/no-CB approach used up to this point and instead directly analyze variation in the actual subsidy provisions found in teachers' CBAs. To obtain information on the subsidies available to the unions representing teacher respondents in the Moe survey, I drew upon the National Council on Teacher Quality (NCTQ)'s database of CBAs from the early to middle years of the first decade of the 2000s. I further supplemented NCTQ's database by obtaining CBAs for districts where there were at least three teacher respondents in the Moe survey. Altogether, this effort yielded 144 CBAs covering approximately eight hundred teacher respondents in the survey.

I then performed an extensive content analysis of each CBA to record whether a school district provided each of the nine separate Association-rights subsidies shown in table 2.2 in the previous chapter.[13] All nine items were coded in a simple binary fashion. For example, in assessing whether districts provided unions with access to their internal mail system, CBAs that expressly did so were coded (1=yes; no or silent=0). Overall, 66 percent of the 144 sampled CBAs provided the mailbox subsidy compared to one-third that did not. In other areas, Association-rights subsidies were far less common. Only a quarter of districts guaranteed their union an opportunity to address new teachers at faculty orientations, and just 30 percent put the union on the agenda at faculty meetings. Since my interest is in measuring the overall degree to which local CBAs subsidize a union's ability to mobilize teachers in politics, I condense these separate items into a single measure through a statistical technique known as principal components analysis (PCA).[14] Higher values indicate that a district provides more Association rights and lower values mean that a district's CBA provides fewer subsidies.

Even with a significantly reduced sample size of teacher respondents, I nevertheless find a strong and positive relationship between the rate at which teachers are politically mobilized and the prevalence of more generous subsidies in their union's CBA. Controlling for all of the same individual- and district-level factors accounted for in the analyses presented in table 3.3, I find that the number of subsidies in a teacher's CBA has a positive and statistically significant impact on the likelihood that they are successfully mobilized to participate in union-sponsored political activities. The effect sizes range from teachers being 3 percentage points more likely to participate (in the case of a one-standard-deviation increase in the Association-rights provisions of their CBA) to 13 percentage points more likely to participate (when moving from the least-subsidized districts in the sample to the most-subsidized ones). Considering the limited sample size of this analysis, these are meaningful effect sizes.

A Final Test of the Subsidy Hypothesis

So far, the subsidy hypothesis appears to be strongly supported by both the ANES and the Moe survey data. However, a few worries remain. While the ANES provides a lengthy time series gauging teacher participation before and after collective bargaining, the sample size of teacher respondents is less than ideal. In contrast, the Moe survey offers the opportunity to examine the political behavior of a large sample of teachers, but only at a single point in time. This constraint limits my ability to make strong causal claims.

Therefore, I round out my evaluation of the subsidy hypothesis by examining the decisions of over fifty thousand teachers about whether to contribute to their union's political action committee (PAC). These data—which come from the Washington State Public Disclosure Commission (PDC)—include all donations made to any registered PAC in Washington State. Like all state NEA affiliates, the Washington Education Association (WEA), works hard to raise PAC funds, soliciting donations from teachers organized into approximately 270 separate school-district bargaining units across the Evergreen State. In fact, the WEA goes to great lengths to publicize the success rate of its local affiliates in PAC fundraising, encouraging each union local to meet or exceed a 50 percent participation rate.

Using the PDC database, I match each unique teacher-contributor to their official employee record maintained by the state's department of education (Office of Superintendent of Public Instruction, or OSPI). This leaves me with a simple binary indicator where 1= a teacher who made at least one official contribution to WEA-PAC and 0= a teacher who never donated. Across the population of public school teachers in Washington State, I find that approximately 45 percent contributed to WEA-PAC at least once between 2007 and 2016.

If my subsidy hypothesis is correct, teachers should be more likely to make PAC contributions when their local union operates with the advantage of a subsidy-rich collective bargaining agreement (CBA). To test this expectation, I first needed a way to measure differences in the Association-rights provisions embedded in CBAs across Washington school districts.

I am fortunate to have a valid and reliable measure of the strength of Association-rights provisions negotiated by each WEA local during the years for which I observe teacher PAC giving. In the early 2010s, economist Dan Goldhaber and his colleagues completed a multi-year project analyzing the entire population of teacher CBAs in Washington State.[15] Unlike the basic content analysis that I performed in my own CBA analysis using the NCTQ contract data, Goldhaber's team employed a more sophisticated technique known as the Partial Independence Item Response method (PIIR). In short, PIIR measures the degree of "restrictiveness" in each CBA across specific issue dimensions.[16] One of the topics that his team scored CBAs on was *Association-rights* provisions like the ones shown in table 2.2 in the previous chapter. Additionally, CBAs were scored on each of the following separate subject provisions: *teacher evaluation*, *grievance*, *layoffs*, *benefits and leave*, *hiring and transfers*, and *workload*. This scoring enables me to directly test whether the CBA provisions that are the most theoretically relevant to my subsidy hypothesis— Association rights—predict higher rates of teacher PAC giving.

Using the PAC contributions data set and detailed information on the strength of Association-rights (and other) provisions in each teacher's CBA, I estimate five separate regression models, the results of which are shown and discussed in table A3.2 of the chapter's appendix. In all five models, the coefficient on my main explanatory variable of interest—the strength of Association-rights provisions—is positive and statistically significant, indicating that teachers working in school districts where the local union has more Association rights are much more likely to make a PAC contribution.

The substantive effect of a teacher working in a district with strong Association rights is both large and meaningful. Figure 3.5 plots the likelihood that a teacher will make a PAC donation when manipulating several independent variables of interest and holding all other control variables at their mean value. Moving from a teacher who works in a district that is one standard deviation below the mean in Association-rights provisions to one standard deviation above it is associated with an 8-percentage-point increase in the likelihood of a PAC donation. This effect is nearly as large as moving from a teacher paid $38,000 to one paid $62,000 (one stan-

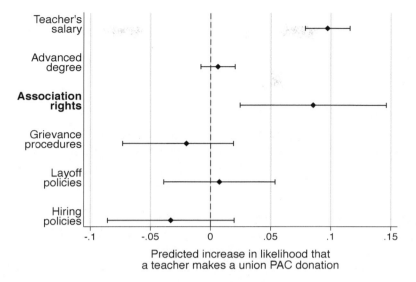

Predicted increase in likelihood that
a teacher makes a union PAC donation

FIGURE 3.5 Stronger Association rights help increase teacher PAC giving

Notes: Figure plots the marginal effects of each independent variable on the likelihood that a teacher donated to their union's political action committee (PAC). Except for the indicator denoting whether a teacher has an advanced degree, all of the other variables can be interpreted as the effect of shifting one standard deviation below a variable's mean value to one standard deviation above it. For example, the positive 0.08 value on Association rights can be interpreted as follows: a teacher who works in a district where Association-rights provisions are one standard deviation above the state mean (compared to one standard deviation below it) is 8 percentage points more likely to make a PAC contribution. The effects shown in figure 3.5 are derived from the regression model presented in column 3 of table A3.2 in the chapter appendix.

dard deviation below the mean salary to one standard deviation above it). Since income is usually one of the strongest predictors of political giving, I conclude that Association-rights provisions are an especially powerful tool for promoting higher rates of union political mobilization.

Finally, since unobserved differences across school districts that correlate with stronger Association-rights provisions could account for these higher rates of teacher PAC giving, I perform two additional robustness tests. These tests are shown and discussed in columns 4 and 5 of table A3.2 in the chapter appendix. The first test uses a two-stage (instrumental variables) model while the second examines how teacher PAC giving is affected when a teacher changes jobs and enters a different school district altogether (i.e., one with higher/lower Association-rights provisions in their CBA). In both cases, I find that teachers working under CBAs with stronger Association rights are more likely to make union PAC contributions. In sum, a wide variety of evidence suggests that unions find it much easier to mobilize teachers to support their political advocacy efforts when they operate with the advantage of strong Association rights.

The Bigger Picture

E. E. Schattschneider once famously declared that "new policies create a new politics."[17] In this chapter, I have presented a similar policy-feedback story to explain how America's teachers went from disengaged bystanders to committed political activists in less than a decade. To test my subsidy hypothesis—that governments helped awaken teachers politically by enhancing their unions' capacity to organize and mobilize them—I provided three separate strands of evidence. Each piece of evidence showed that interest groups that are *better subsidized* become interest groups that can *better mobilize* their supporters in electoral politics.

This finding has broad implications for the politics of education and the study of political advocacy groups more generally. First, it is important to recognize that politics is not a unidirectional contest in which governments respond to the policy demands of politically active citizens. Instead, government policies can and often do serve as a springboard for groups to better organize and mobilize their supporters for political action. Rosenstone and Hansen once famously argued that "the strategic choices of political leaders—their determination of who and when to mobilize—determine the shape of political participation in America."[18] Yet such choices are hardly determinative. Relentless effort and sound strategy are no guarantee of success. Throughout the 1950s and much of the 1960s, nascent teacher-union interest groups routinely tried and failed to mobilize educators in politics. But only after state governments institutionalized public-sector bargaining regimes did their efforts to locate, recruit, and politically mobilize teachers bear fruit. The lesson here is that the state can play a decisive role in helping interest groups recruit and mobilize their supporters in politics.

Consider Andrea Campbell's work on the effects of the social security program on the political behavior of America's seniors.[19] Much like teachers, seniors were once politically disengaged, participating at lower rates than non-elderly citizens. Seniors, like teachers, had not evolved into a group that politicians sought out for support. For both teachers and seniors, favorable government policies would help reverse these trends. However, the similarities between the two groups mostly end there. The feedback effects that Campbell uncovered focused on the provision of material resources to *individual* seniors, which in turn led them to participate more faithfully as higher-status citizens. These social welfare programs then spurred the creation of interest groups that could represent a "senior lobby," composed of individual seniors who were incentivized to protect the resource benefits provided by these new programs.

In the case of teachers, however, the feedback effects operated through already-established *interest groups*. Recall, both the NEA and the AFT existed well before the end of the 1970s, the time by which the majority of states had enacted CB laws. In fact, these groups had long been active in politics, lobbying at both state and federal levels. Apart from voting, however, their individual constituents (teachers) were not highly engaged. So whereas Social Security created a senior constituency ripe for mobilization and indirectly led to the creation of groups like the American Association of Retired Persons (AARP), it did not confer special organizational benefits to AARP in the same way that teacher-bargaining laws did for union interest groups. With renewed attention to the role of groups in American politics, participation scholars would do well to expand their focus on policy feedback beyond the individual.[20] Significant payoffs could be realized by giving greater attention to understanding how policies both subsidize and, by extension, institutionalize interest-group power in American politics.

Finally, an emerging narrative in education is that the political power of teachers unions is in decline. Careful attention to the results from this chapter, however, suggest otherwise. Much of the narrative that unions have been weakened focuses on the fact that the Supreme Court's *Janus* decision no longer allows teachers (and other public-sector) unions to collect fees from nonmembers. Though *Janus* is a clear setback, the unions' ability to mobilize educators in politics is, I have shown, mostly related to the benefits that flow from having exclusive collective-bargaining rights. It is these policies that provide them with an advantage in political organizing and an official seat at the policymaking table. Teachers unions can take solace in the fact that *Janus* does nothing to eliminate these rights. Even as they now enter a new post-agency-fee environment, most teachers unions have shown little interest in trading their exclusive bargaining rights for a members-only system of teacher representation.

Teachers unions recognize that there are enormous benefits to retaining exclusivity, even without the ability to collect agency fees. In fact, a variety of evidence suggests that teachers unions today are re-emphasizing the importance of securing the sort of Association rights that this chapter showed were so instrumental to their early mobilizing success. The NEA, for example, has released two recent publications highlighting the importance of all the following Association rights for recruiting and organizing members in a "post–agency fee" world: securing a place for the union on the agenda at new employee orientations, obtaining access to school work sites and employee meetings, having access to member information and communications platforms with members, securing release time for association business, and having access to payroll deduction.[21]

On the other side, the behavior of political conservatives indicates that they know *Janus* is an important but limited victory. Just as unions have set out to secure strong Association rights after the loss of agency fees, conservative activists have sought to eliminate these policies. With support from conservative think tanks, in December 2018—a few months after the *Janus* decision was handed down—several nonunion teachers filed lawsuits challenging exclusivity on First Amendment grounds. In *Uradnik v. Inter Faculty Organization*, Kathleen Uradnik, a professor at St. Cloud State University (SCSU) in Minnesota, objected to the union that represents her in collective bargaining having the sole right to represent faculty at SCSU. Had the courts ruled in her favor, exclusivity—and along with it the chief justification for providing unions with an official seat at the table—would have vanished. However, on April 29, 2019, the US Supreme Court refused to hear the case.[22] For the time being, America's teachers unions have managed to preserve exclusivity and all the benefits that flow from it.[23]

When it comes to these ongoing and future battles over public-sector labor law, my findings are a reminder that the policies governments enact have the power to shape the participatory behavior of citizens in the political sphere. In helping to "turn out teachers," governments played an important role in the creation and maintenance of one of the largest and most active coalition groups in American politics today. Although these laws help explain the onset of higher rates of (individual) teacher political activism, my findings raise other questions related to the emergence of teachers unions as powerful interest-group advocacy organizations—questions that I attend to in the chapters that follow.

Chapter Appendix

TABLE A3.1 **Likelihood of states where organized teacher interests were stronger in the early 1960s to have enacted a mandatory teacher CB law by 1970.**

	(1)	(2)	(3)
Average state-legislator ranking of teacher group power	−0.160 (0.208)	—	—
Percentage of state legislators mentioning a teacher group	—	−1.003 (1.132)	—
Percentage of state legislators ranking teacher group as most powerful	—	—	−1.358 (1.490)
Constant	−0.149 (0.252)	−0.116 (0.261)	−0.167 (0.221)
Pseudo R²	0.01	0.01	0.01
Observations	49	49	49

Notes: In all three models the dependent variable is a binary indicator for whether a state enacted a mandatory CB law that applied to teachers by the year 1970 (0=no, 1=yes). Wisconsin is excluded from the analysis because it had already enacted a mandatory CB law for teachers in 1959. Cell entries are probit coefficients, with standard errors reported in parentheses. *p<0.1, **p<0.05, ***p<0.01.

Table A3.2 presents five separate regression models that each estimate the likelihood that a teacher donated to WEA-PAC (1=contributed, 0=did not contribute).

Column 1 presents the simplest model, controlling only for teachers' demographic characteristics (e.g. age, education, income, race).

Column 2 adds contextual variables to the model to account for the fact that teacher giving may be influenced by the size and demographic makeup of their local school community.

Column 3 adds the six additional CBA provisions (i.e., those unrelated to Association rights). Importantly, even after controlling for these other dimensions of CBA restrictiveness, only the subcategory of Association rights predicts higher rates of teacher PAC giving. This finding suggests that the positive relationship between higher rates of teacher PAC giving and stronger Association rights is not simply an artifact of teachers unions comprised of more politically active teachers negotiating stronger CBAs. Rather, the connection between CBA strength and teacher PAC giving is isolated to the Association-rights provisions of the contract, just as the subsidy hypothesis would predict.

Since it is possible that unobserved differences across districts that correlate with Association rights could account for higher rates of teacher PAC giving, I carry out two additional robustness checks in columns 4 and 5.

TABLE A3.2 **Relationship between Association-rights strength and rates of teacher PAC giving**

	Baseline model (1)	Add district controls (2)	Add other contract provisions (3)	Two-stage model (instrumental variable) (4)	Teachers switching districts (5)
Association rights	0.151*** (0.039)	0.083* (0.044)	0.133*** (0.049)	0.556*** (0.032)	0.400*** (0.044)
Teacher salary (log)	0.371*** (0.043)	0.390*** (0.042)	0.410*** (0.040)	0.151*** (0.012)	
Experience	−0.007*** (0.001)	−0.007*** (0.001)	−0.007*** (0.001)	−0.003*** (0.000)	
Advanced degree	0.032* (0.019)	0.021 (0.019)	0.015 (0.018)	0.004 (0.006)	
Female	0.220*** (0.016)	0.211*** (0.015)	0.210*** (0.015)	0.078*** (0.006)	
African American	−0.019 (0.051)	-0.054 (0.059)	−0.041 (0.048)	−0.028 (0.031)	
Hispanic	0.020 (0.039)	0.062 (0.040)	0.070* (0.040)	0.099*** (0.016)	
District size		0.084*** (0.029)	0.088*** (0.028)	−0.055*** (0.007)	
District poverty		−0.408*** (0.155)	−0.431*** (0.149)	−0.149*** (0.015)	
Evaluation rights			−0.063* (0.033)	−0.005 (0.004)	−0.236*** (0.032)
Grievance rights			−0.033 (0.029)	−0.003 (0.003)	−0.018 (0.024)
Layoff rights			0.009 (0.029)	0.025*** (0.004)	0.153*** (0.029)
Benefits rights			0.030 (0.037)	−0.069*** (0.006)	−0.067** (0.027)
Hiring/transfers			−0.055 (0.044)	−0.182*** (0.012)	−0.029 (0.043)
Workload rights			−0.044 (0.045)	−0.127*** (0.008)	−0.101*** (0.039)
Constant	−4.310*** (0.450)	−4.978*** (0.496)	−5.207*** (0.481)	−0.889*** (0.128)	—
Teacher fixed effects	No	No	No	No	Yes
Year fixed effects	No	No	No	No	Yes
Pseudo R^2/R^2	0.01	0.02	0.02	0.30	—
Observations	54,108	54,108	52,738	44,290	22,563

Notes: Cell entries are probit (Columns 1–3), OLS (Column 4), and logit (Column 5) coefficients, with standard errors clustered by school district below in parentheses. The dependent variable is whether a teacher contributed to their state union's PAC (1 = yes; 0=no). *p<0.1, **p<0.05, ***p<0.01.

The model in column 4 employs a statistical technique called *instrumental variables regression*. Specifically, I use the fact that teachers unions in Washington were organized into regional "UniServ" units back in the 1970s. UniServ staff help local unions in their region negotiate CBAs, leading to a high degree of similarity in the contract items negotiated in each region. Because these boundaries were first established in the 1970s, it is unlikely that a district's assignment to its original UniServ region has any bearing on the tendency of teachers to make PAC contributions today. Therefore, I instrument for the strength of a district's Association-rights provisions by using the average strength of the same Association-rights provisions in neighboring districts (i.e., those that share the same UniServ boundaries). The intuition is straightforward. There should be no relationship between the CBA provisions in the districts outside of a teacher's own district and that teacher's PAC giving, other than through the mechanism of a shared UniServ negotiator bargaining for similar provisions in the region. The results of this robustness check (presented in column 4) confirm the positive and significant relationship between stronger Association rights and higher rates of teacher PAC giving.[24]

Finally, the model in column 5 examines teachers who moved across school districts. By following the same teachers over time, I can observe their political giving when they enter a new district, one with stronger or weaker Association rights than the district they left. This analysis narrows its focus to the teachers who moved districts and can be observed more than once in the PAC contributions data set. Specifically, I use unit (teacher-specific) fixed effects that capture each teacher's overall tendency to donate, thereby isolating the effect of a teacher's exposure to a new CBA environment on giving. Once again, I find that teachers working under CBAs with stronger Association rights are more likely to make PAC contributions. Even after introducing the high bar of individual teacher fixed effects, the effect of Association rights is substantively large. For example, when a teacher moves out of a district that is one standard deviation below the mean in Association rights to one standard deviation above it, I estimate that the likelihood of a teacher making a union PAC contribution in their new district rises by 14 percentage points (22 percent to 36 percent).

CHAPTER FOUR

Creatures of the State

This [teachers] union under California law is a State entity.[1]
–Supreme Court Justice Sonya Sotomayor

B y the mid-1970s, America's revolution in public-sector labor relations
had led many educators to become politically active for the very first
time in their lives. Although this was a necessary change for teachers to
gain greater influence in American education, it was hardly sufficient.
Teacher political activism—like any form of citizen activism—is far more
influential when individuals are well organized and represented by strong
interest groups. Whereas the previous two chapters showed how government policies helped boost political participation among *individual* teachers, here and in the next chapter, I turn my attention to the effects of those
policies on the strength and durability of teacher-union political advocacy
organizations.

The vast majority of organized teacher political activity in the United
States today is coordinated by the National Education Association (NEA).
The NEA is a massive federated interest group. Anchored in Washington
but composed of fifty separate state and fourteen thousand–plus local
affiliates, the NEA is the single largest union of public employees in North
America. To fully understand organized teacher power in American education, then, one must account for the strength of the NEA as an interest
group in American politics.

By 1980, the NEA had firmly established itself as the most dominant
interest group in American education. It was also a powerhouse in American politics more generally.[2] Consider that no other organization, of any
kind, has sent more delegates to the Democratic Party's nominating convention than the NEA. During the 1980 Democratic presidential primary

campaign, Vice President Walter Mondale and his rivals acknowledged, "If you want to go anywhere in national politics these days, you better get the NEA behind you!"[3] The *New Republic* described the NEA's ascent to power by simply asking:

> What's the most powerful special interest group in Washington? If you think it's the oil companies, the steel industry, or the AFL-CIO [American Federation of Labor and Congress of Industrial Organizations], think again. Almost overnight, and almost unnoticed, these veteran power brokers have been pushed aside by a relative newcomer to the hurly-burly of capital politics—the National Education Association, the biggest organization of teachers in America.[4]

In subsequent decades, the nation's largest teachers union only grew wealthier and more powerful. By the early 1990s, just a few years after *A Nation at Risk* sparked the rise of the modern education-reform movement, the NEA and its affiliates were already a billion-dollar interest group.[5] The *New York Times'* characterization of the NEA's tepid response to this new reform environment read like a textbook political-science lesson on vested interests. As the 1980s came to a close, the Gray Lady observed that the NEA remained "solidly against proposals for major changes that [were] gathering increasing support from parents and politicians . . . [including] merit pay for teachers and expanding parental and student choice."[6]

The timing and sequence of these two events—the rise of the NEA followed by the onset of the excellence movement—would prove to be highly consequential for American education. The simple fact that teachers got politically organized well *before* education reform made it onto the nation's agenda put teachers unions in a far stronger position than reform groups. Whereas reform groups would need to *overcome* union power and win at each stage of the policymaking process, teachers unions only needed to play defense. They could preserve their power and influence in education politics and policy simply by blocking, diluting, or weakening the implementation of the reform movement's agenda.

In other words, the NEA did not even need to meet the *New Republic's* hyperbolic criteria of "strongest interest group in America" to remain the most influential actor within education politics. Organized teacher interests aren't really in competition with the powerful business interests in Washington. Instead, most key education decisions in the United States turn on the policy choices made by state and local officials. And, as I will show in chapters 6 and 7, it is precisely within these two levels of government where teachers unions are most politically effective. At the subnational level, teachers unions face less direct political competition; they also benefit from multiple veto points that allow them to block or influence reforms that require coordinated implementation from the state to the local level. Finally, and most importantly, they have the advantage of holding, as the Supreme Court's *Perry* majority put it, "an official position in the operational structure" of school-district governments.

That is not to say that teachers unions face no political competition from other education stakeholders in subnational politics, especially in the larger arena of state politics. But as Sarah Anzia astutely observes, teachers unions focus "almost exclusively on education [issues], whereas for businesses and billionaire philanthropists, education policy is *one* of many policy arenas they might try to influence."[7] At the end of the day, all that really matters is how powerful teachers unions are on a *relative* basis when they seek to influence education issues at the state and local levels. Here, the unions are almost always much better organized than other stakeholders, including those groups that care deeply about education issues (e.g., parents, civil rights groups, school reformers). Part of the explanation for teachers' superior organization in subnational politics stems from the fact that, during the late 1960s and early 1970s, teachers strategically fashioned the NEA into a strong federated interest group—embracing a structure that, as I will show, was tailor-made for winning political battles at the state and local levels.

Yet the NEA wasn't always a juggernaut interest group in subnational politics. For decades, the organization was both poorly organized and significantly under-resourced. It had also struggled to coordinate and maintain a unified program of teacher political advocacy across states and school districts. Between 1960 and 1980, teachers radically remade the NEA, transforming it from an administrator-dominated "education lobby" into a strong and effective public employee union interest group.

There is significant analytic value to be had in stepping back to identify the factors that enabled teachers to build and maintain such a formidable interest group. First, as Terry Moe has argued, the rise of organized teacher interests is responsible for shifting the power center in American education—taking authority away from elected officials and school administrators and giving it to organized education employees.[8] Second, since American education is so deeply shaped by federalism and localism, teachers could only become influential by getting politically organized across vast geographies and at multiple levels of government. For that very reason, the NEA's ability to unify millions of teachers under the banner of a single well-financed federated interest group ranks among its most consequential and enduring achievements. Finally, the NEA's quick rise to power is itself something of a puzzle. Right at the time teacher organizing flourished, the flagship occupational associations representing physicians and attorneys—the American Medical Association (AMA) and American Bar Association (ABA)—were entering a period of permanent decline. The growth of organized teacher interests thus stands apart as a unique success story when juxtaposed with the deterioration of other membership associations during this period of contraction in American civic life.[9]

So, what accounts for the NEA's divergent success?

I argue that a specific set of government policies helped subsidize the formation and maintenance of teacher-union interest groups in the United States. Specifically, I trace the NEA's meteoric rise in politics to the effects of strong teacher labor laws; these new laws enabled teacher groups to obtain three crucial resources that all interest groups covet: *members*, *money*, and a reliable means of ensuring organizational *maintenance*. In short, my findings suggest that, without state support, teachers would not have obtained their own equivalent of what gun-rights advocates and seniors have in the NRA and AARP.

Before outlining my argument about how government policies provided important forms of organizational subsidy to newly emerging teacher-union interest groups, I should say a brief word about my decision to focus mostly on the NEA. There are two reasons why I emphasize the NEA far more than the nation's other major union of school employees, the American Federation of Teachers (AFT). First, the NEA has long been the larger of the two groups. Not only is the NEA numerically larger, but its organizational footprint is found in all fifty states. In contrast, outside of New York and Illinois, the AFT's strength tends to be confined to a smattering of large urban school districts. The second reason is data availability. The NEA maintains a series of historical reports (including transcripts of its annual meetings) that enable researchers to closely track a variety of information about the organization's annual membership and revenue growth, including at the state level, as far back as the 1940s. Unfortunately, the AFT maintains no comparable set of publicly available records. Although these two factors ultimately make the NEA the better case for theory testing, the core argument that I develop here, and in chapter 5, should apply equally to the rise of the AFT as an important political-pressure group and influential actor in American education. In fact, aside from a unique federal charter that was given to the NEA by Congress in 1906 (discussed in chapter 5), the NEA and the AFT have both benefitted from the same set of government policies.

How Governments Strengthened Organized Teacher Interests

What makes America's teachers unions influential in education politics? Recall what the NEA's longest-serving general counsel, Robert Chanin, once said about the roots of teachers unions' political power in the United States. "NEA and its affiliates . . . have power because there are more than 3.2 million people willing to pay us hundreds of millions of dollars in dues each year."[10] In other words, teachers unions gained clout by recruiting and organizing millions of dues-paying members. Dues revenue could be deployed in both collective bargaining and politics to help ensure the unions' longevity, or what interest-group scholars call "organizational maintenance." Members, money, and maintenance are the lifeblood of political organizations. Without them, citizens' interests remain unorganized and advocacy groups struggle to survive.

However, securing these sorts of resources isn't easy. If it were, all citizens with shared interests—in less pollution, affordable housing, and access to health care, for example—would be well represented by wealthy interest groups promoting and defending their collective interests in politics. Yet this type of interest-group representation is the exception, not the rule.

The problem is that forming and maintaining strong interest-group organizations requires overcoming huge collective-action problems. Potential group members have strong incentives to shirk and free ride, either avoiding the costs of funding the group's startup or getting involved for a brief time but abandoning ship when continued involvement consumes too much time, effort, or money.[11] Maintaining group strength also poses a regular and persistent challenge. It requires ensuring that members and money flow into the organization year after year. As James Q. Wilson put it, "An organization may be formed in a burst of member enthusiasm or purposive commitment, but enthusiasm tends to wane and commitments to falter."[12] Despite these obstacles, not only did America's teachers manage to get highly organized, but they also successfully overcame their collective-action problems and built the NEA into a political powerhouse in a mere decade.[13]

Strangely, most existing accounts of the teachers unions' rise to power focus on individual teachers. Demographic changes in the composition of the postwar teacher workforce and the broader political and social upheaval of the 1960s have been said to have caused teachers to become more "militant."[14] Accordingly, the sudden surge in teacher political activism and interest-group organizing that followed were, simply put, the product of an idea whose time had come.[15] In contrast to these sorts of atheoretical and exclusively bottom-up explanations, I will show that favorable government policies were the key factor that enabled individual teachers to get organized and build strong political advocacy organizations that would last for generations to come. Again, as Terry Moe put it, "the key event that promoted [teacher] unionization and collective bargaining is that the laws changed."[16]

My theory takes the need to focus on changes in public-sector labor laws as its starting point.[17] Recall the discussion in the previous two chapters about American labor law's unique reliance on the principle of exclusivity. When US public-sector labor law grants teachers the power to select a union to represent them in collective bargaining, the union that wins majority support is empowered to represent all teachers in a given school district, even those who oppose the majority-favored union. In legal parlance, the union becomes the "exclusive representative"; it has a statutory duty to represent all teachers, union member and nonmember alike.[18]

Advocates of exclusivity argue that it helps stabilize labor relations, simplifying collective bargaining and promoting "labor peace." A single employer negotiates with a single union that is empowered to speak for all employees. However, decades of contentious litigation reveal that exclusivity greatly complicates the relationship between public-sector unions and dissenting nonmembers. A union's duty to represent both members (who pay dues) and nonmembers (who do not) costs money. Since American labor unions can't force employees to become members, US labor law embraced a compromise: unions can negotiate union-security provisions to ensure they have sufficient resources to perform the duty of fair representation.

As discussed in chapter 1, union-security provisions take three basic forms. First, under dues-checkoff arrangements, the employer agrees to deduct union dues and fees from each employee's paycheck, giving the union greater financial security. Second, maintenance-of-membership clauses require that union members pay dues for the duration of the collective bargaining agreement (CBA), providing unions with financial stability. Finally, unions negotiate "agency shops," requiring nonmembers to pay union fees.[19]

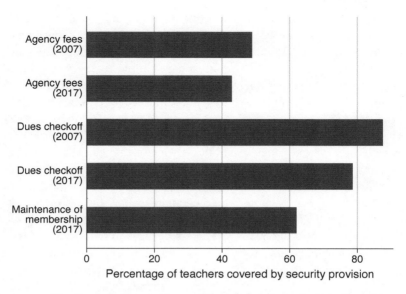

FIGURE 4.1 Prevalence of union-security provisions before and after the Great Recession

Notes: Figure shows the percent of K–12 public school teachers working in states where public-sector labor law either (1) mandates or (2) allows for each type of security provision. Data on maintenance-of-membership provisions is specific to Pennsylvania and denotes the percentage of school districts there that include this provision in their local CBA.

Source: Author's analysis of data provided in 2000 and 2017 NEA reports entitled *Collective Bargaining Laws Manual State Summaries.* Data on maintenance-of-membership provisions is from the Commonwealth Foundation database "School District Teacher Contract Overview," accessed August 1, 2020, https://datawrapper.dwcdn.net/Fix49/8/.

How common are these sorts of security provisions? Figure 4.1 shows the share of the American teacher workforce who work in states where public-sector labor law allows unions to negotiate various union-security provisions.

Prior to the Great Recession, in 2007, about half of all teachers worked in states where unions were authorized to charge fees to nonmember teachers. At that same time, roughly 90 percent of all teachers worked in states that allowed dues checkoff. These numbers declined slightly after the wave of conservative Tea-Party lawmaking that occurred during the economic downturn. Just prior to the Supreme Court's *Janus* decision in 2018, teachers unions were able to negotiate agency fees in twenty states that employed over 40 percent of the nation's teachers. Even after the *Janus* ruling, about 80 percent of teachers continue to work in states that mandate or permit school-district governments to facilitate the collection of union dues, and in some cases, the collection of teachers' contributions to their union's political action committee (PAC).[20] To account for the lack of nationwide data on the prevalence of maintenance-of-membership provisions in CBAs, I examine the incidence of this type of security provision across all five hundred of Pennsylvania's school districts. Despite its reputation as a prolabor state, Pennsylvania's teacher labor law was not especially strong when it was first enacted in 1970. The law prohibited agency fees until 1988, and maintenance of membership was seen as a compromise. Nonetheless, well over 60 percent of districts in the Keystone State included these provisions in their CBAs as of 2017.[21] In sum, union-security policies are ubiquitous, and even after *Janus* remain a cornerstone of teacher labor law in the United States.

Despite this widespread use and the overall significance of security provisions in US labor laws, social scientists have paid little attention to how these provisions strengthen unions as political advocacy organizations.[22] Yet careful attention to the legal rationale behind these security provisions makes their political implications much more explicit.

Consider the following exchange between Justice Sonya Sotomayor and an appellate attorney during oral arguments in *Friedrichs v. California Teachers Association*, the agency-fee case that preceded *Janus*. Here, Justice Sotomayor is addressing an attorney whose teacher-client objected to the provision of California's teacher labor law that required her to pay an agency fee to the National Education Association-California Teachers Association (NEA-CTA). Sotomayor invokes the exclusivity principle, which she explains transforms the private teacher-union interest group, the NEA-CTA, into an official organ of the state. California, she reasoned, had merely used its power as employer to subsidize the union.

SOTOMAYOR: We've already permitted subsidization of bar associations, of government programs. We've permitted assessments on a lot of different levels, so why can't the government, as employer, *create a State entity*? Because this union under California law is a State entity.

RESPONDENT-ATTORNEY: No.

SOTOMAYOR: I beg to differ. Hold on, I'll get you the section. [Our court's precedent] says, "When recognized as the exclusive bargaining representative, a union assumes an official position in the operational structure of a school" . . . meaning the State is creating the union . . .[23]

In other words, as a byproduct of the government's interest in stable labor relations, the state, Sotomayor argues, is entitled to act as a partner and patron for the union, subsidizing the union's *private* organizational needs for the purpose of serving broader *public* policy aims. But whereas lawyers are quick to identify and debate the constitutional and legal issues of subsidization, political scientists should recognize that such subsidies are likely to have profound policy feedback effects on the strength of unions as political advocacy organizations. For example, scholars have long recognized the important role that patrons play in subsidizing the formation and maintenance of private organized interests.[24] As John Mark Hansen observes, "the key to understanding which [interest] organizations form . . . is understanding which groups get *subsidized* and when."[25]

In chapter 1, for example, I alluded to a case in which the federal government subsidized the National Rifle Association (NRA) in the aftermath of World War II. Shortly after the war, federal authorities adopted a law that provided NRA members with exclusive rights to purchase Army surplus rifles at a discounted rate. In a special investigative report for the *Philadelphia Inquirer* written in 1979, journalist Aaron Epstein recounted the significant effects this favorable federal policy had on the NRA's growing organizational strength:

> The phenomenal growth of the National Rifle Association (NRA) from a small-bore organization to a high-powered national pressure group of more than one million members was made possible primarily by the Defense Department, according to an NRA internal report. The document . . . attributes the biggest growth in NRA membership since World War II to periodic sales of surplus Army rifles to NRA members at cost . . . The report . . . shows that the NRA grew only slightly during World War II. Then, in late 1945, the Army's director of civilian marksmanship released Springfield rifles for sale to NRA members — and the membership rolls soared . . . There is no doubt that this assisted in the two membership campaigns — to reach the half-million members in 1962 and the one-million membership campaign in June 1968.[26]

Thanks to this early government subsidy, the NRA gained significant financial resources that it later poured into its political advocacy efforts. Specifically, Epstein's investigative report went on to detail several prominent political-lobbying expenditures that the NRA made during the ensuing years when it had grown larger and wealthier — thanks, in part, to this favorable government policy. Sam Fields, director for the National Coalition to Ban Handguns, argued that it was simply unfair for government to pick winners and losers in the interest-group marketplace, with his interest group clearly being the loser. "To require NRA membership to purchase rifles through the Defense Department," he complained to Epstein, "makes no more sense than to require membership in the Democratic Party to be eligible for food stamps."[27]

In the case of teachers unions and American education policy, I argue that favorable public-sector labor laws directly subsidized the ability of their newly emerging interest groups to gain members and money, and to secure their long-term organizational maintenance. These expectations are laid out schematically in table 4.1 below. Each row in the far left-hand column lists the specific organizational resources that the NEA needed to gain power in education politics. The table then links each of these resource needs to specific strategies that the union would use to obtain those resources (middle column). Finally, the far-right column highlights the specific government policy or policies (state subsidies) that made the NEA's solution possible. In other words, my claim is that without these favorable government policies the NEA would have had far fewer resources at its disposal, rendering teacher interests much less effective in interest-group politics and in turn less powerful in American education.

For example, in the early 1970s, to recruit more members the NEA mandated unification, a new requirement that any teacher wishing to join one level of the association join all three branches: national, state, and local (row 1, column 2). In theory, unification should have caused many teachers to flee the NEA on account of having to pay more dues to the organization. But just the opposite occurred. The NEA's unification strategy worked, and membership rose. The first row of the far-right column lists

TABLE 4.1 **Ways in which government policies help subsidize teacher-union interest groups**

Organizational need	Strategy used by the NEA to achieve this need	Government policies that made the NEA's strategy viable
Members	Mandate unified membership	Strong mandatory CB laws with union security (i.e., no RTW laws)
Money	(1) Raise members' dues (2) Solicit dues and PAC contributions via payroll deduction (3) Add special assessments to dues	Agency-fee provisions Dues-checkoff privileges Property-tax exemption
Maintenance (organizational)	Use a revenue-sharing model	Affiliated representation

the elements of American labor law that helped the NEA's unification strategy succeed. Specifically, strong mandatory teacher-bargaining laws created incentives for teachers to abide by the NEA's more costly unified membership requirements and join all three levels of the newly unified, federated union interest group.

In the next chapter, I present three historical case studies—one on membership, one on money, and one on maintenance—each testing the explanatory power of my subsidy hypothesis against the empirical evidence of the NEA's organizational growth in the postwar era. For each case study, the reader is encouraged to refer to the framework outlined here in table 4.1.

Before proceeding to chapter 5 and the tests of my theory, it is important to establish a key conceptual point about teacher-union interest groups' revenue and expenditures. Outside of one narrow exception,[28] union revenue should almost always be understood as a fungible resource. In other words, whenever teachers unions spend money to engage in various forms of organized advocacy, those expenditures are paid for by revenue dollars that are *interchangeable*. Fungibility is an important concept for my broader argument about the important role of the state in strengthening teacher-union interest groups. The logic here is fairly straightforward. In each and every instance where a government policy eliminates or reduces the cost of an expenditure that teachers unions would otherwise need to incur (i.e., to pay lobbyists, hire staff, or conduct research), the organization can redirect those revenue savings to some other activity.

To illustrate the mechanics of fungibility, consider the clash between former Wisconsin governor Scott Walker and the state's teachers unions over Act 10 in 2011. While most attention was paid to how the law restricted what unions could bargain for, Act 10 also had the de facto effect of sending a new "hidden" invoice to Wisconsin's teachers unions. Specifically, Act 10 added a provision to Wisconsin labor law requiring that teachers unions win annual recertification elections, simply to maintain their status as the exclusive-representative union in a given school district. Prior to this change in law, once a majority of teachers had selected their union—whether that vote took place in 1979 or 2009—the result of the inaugural certification election was essentially permanent. Since contesting certification elections costs the union both time and money, the new law ensured that teacher-union interest groups would have to shift valuable resources to secure a benefit that the state's prior labor law had given them free of charge since 1959. That is the essence of fungibility.

CHAPTER FIVE

Members, Money, and Maintenance

As Harvard social scientist Robert Putnam points out, every year over the last two decades millions of Americans have withdrawn from the affairs of their communities. Participation in many civic organizations has also dropped dramatically. PTA membership dipped from more than 12 million in 1964 to 7 million today. Obviously, *the NEA has bucked this trend.* Our membership growth has been strong and has been steady. In 1964 we numbered 330,000. And now we are over 2.2 million strong.[1] —Keith Geiger, NEA President (1990–96)

Over the course of its 165-year history, the NEA has existed as three completely different entities: an education lobby, a proto-union, and a federated public-employee union interest group. The organization was founded in 1857. However, up until 1962, it was an administrator-dominated "school lobby," only coincidentally involved in representing teachers' interests. When the NEA lobbied government on behalf of America's teachers, it mostly did so as a byproduct of seeking additional government aid for education.[2]

Starting in the early 1960s, however, teachers gained greater power inside the NEA. Two external factors pushed the NEA to prioritize teachers' interests within the association. First, President Kennedy's executive order extending collective-bargaining rights to federal workers gave new legitimacy to public-sector unionism. Meanwhile, the NEA began to face stiff competition from the AFL-CIO-affiliated American Federation of Teachers (AFT). Things came to a head in New York City in 1961. Following a series of strikes, Mayor Robert F. Wagner Jr. agreed to hold an election for teachers to select a union to represent them. When the more militant AFT handily defeated the NEA in that inaugural representation election, the NEA was steadily forced to embrace more-aggressive forms of teacher advocacy in order to compete with its organizational rival.[3] By the mid-1970s, the NEA had unabashedly embraced teacher unionism.[4]

The complex relationship between these external factors and the NEA's internal reorganization has been studied extensively by others,[5] and they are not my focus here. I only wish to emphasize that, although teachers ended the 1960s on a high note (having successfully deposed the administrators who had long controlled the association), there was still no guarantee that they would be able to turn the NEA into an organized and powerful new force for teacher political advocacy. Teachers still faced many daunting challenges. Anyone who has ever tried to recruit someone to join and financially support an organization can attest to the difficulty of recruiting members and raising money. It is especially difficult to do so year after year. Interest groups engaged in political advocacy are no exception. These challenges are especially pronounced for advocacy groups whose central purpose is the pursuit of what economists call a "nonexcludable" good: a cleaner environment, safer roads, or, in the case of the NEA, more-favorable teaching conditions throughout the United States. Why pay the costs when you'll benefit from the group's effort either way?[6]

More problematic still, a new trend in American civic life was working against the NEA's recruitment efforts. Specifically, the country's mass-membership associations had entered what would prove to be a steep and permanent period of decline by the end of the 1960s. Robert Putnam, for example, found that Americans weren't just leaving their fraternal lodges and bowling leagues; they were also dropping out of professional associations that represented citizens' occupational interests.[7] As figure 5.1 shows, despite the fact that the American Medical Association (AMA), the American Bar Association (ABA), and the NEA began the 1970s with relatively similar levels of membership density, only the NEA was able to grow and maintain its membership base in the ensuing decades. By the 2000s, while the ABA and the AMA struggled to keep just one in five attorneys and physicians as dues-paying members, the NEA retained seven out of every ten American teachers as association members.

The argument of this book, of course, is that organized teacher interests held a decisive and unusual advantage over these other professional groups. Mandatory collective-bargaining laws that began to spread across the American states in the 1960s and 1970s helped subsidize the NEA's ability to recruit and retain more teachers as members. Two specific factors converged to produce and preserve these large membership gains for the NEA: the organization's unification movement, which would be aided and abetted by the growth of strong teacher labor laws across the states.[8]

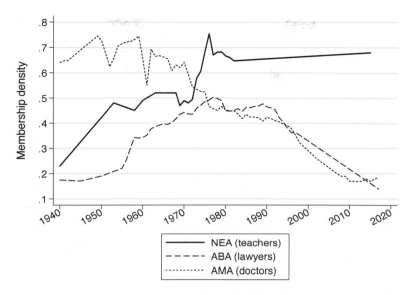

FIGURE 5.1 Membership in professional associations before and after the collapse in civic life

Notes: Figure shows the percentage of teachers, lawyers, and doctors who were members of the national arm of their respective professional associations (at various yearly intervals) between 1940 and 2017.

Source: Author's analysis of Robert Putnam's *Bowling Alone* data, along with NEA membership statistics reported in annual editions of the *NEA Handbook* (Washington, DC: National Education Association).

Unification

Because the NEA was founded as a federation of fully autonomous state and local associations, prior to the 1970s most of America's teachers opted *not* to join the national branch of the organization.[9] In 1958, for example, the year before Wisconsin passed the nation's first teacher collective-bargaining law, 90 percent of teachers belonged to their state and local associations, but just 45 percent were national dues-paying NEA members.[10] *Unification changed all this.* It required that any teacher who wished to join or remain a member of their state or local teachers association henceforth also join and contribute financially to the NEA.[11]

Mandating unification strengthened the NEA in two important ways. First, in the short term, it dramatically boosted membership in the national organization. Second, it helped the NEA better coordinate its political advocacy efforts both inside and outside Washington. In other words, it enabled the NEA to become a formidable federated interest-group organization.

Since education policy is shaped by all three levels of government in the United States, effective teacher political advocacy requires strategic coordination across states and local school districts. In short, teachers have to be able to raise and deploy resources (e.g., staff and money) to engage in political battles from the nation's capital all the way to its tiniest rural school district. Before unification, however, the NEA's efforts were disorganized and disjointed. As the association's president complained to a reporter in 1971, "We spend $150 million a year in local, state and national dues, but [up until now it's been] *uncoordinated*."[12]

To address these organizational deficiencies and establish a more coherent and coordinated system of teacher political advocacy, in 1970 the NEA announced that it would establish a new program called the Unified Staff Service Program, better known today as "UniServ." Once fully implemented, UniServ would enable the NEA to build and maintain strong local union affiliates that were directly tied to the national organization. Thanks to unification, UniServ would eventually make it so that NEA affiliates across the country could regularly draw on thousands of professional staff who were trained to help teachers coordinate and mobilize politically in the trenches.[13] Even recently, during the "red state" teacher strikes of 2018, some reports indicated that the NEA sent UniServ organizers to West Virginia and Kentucky to assist its local affiliates there. According to the NEA's bylaws, "UniServ staff members will be available . . . for up to ten days each [year] to provide on-site assistance to NEA affiliates and Active members in other states in connection with representational challenges, collective bargaining crises, training programs, and/or other special needs situations . . ."[14] The key point is that, had the NEA failed to unify in the 1970s, teachers would never have gained the strong federated political machinery that helped make them a highly organized and potent political force in American education today. But while unification was undoubtedly the right strategy to make the NEA more politically effective, implementing unification would prove immensely difficult. In fact, the NEA had tried to unify as far back as 1944.[15] But those early efforts failed. By the end of the 1950s, just six states had agreed to unify.

One problem was that state associations shunned unification because they feared losing their own members if they were suddenly forced to require teachers to pay dues to the national organization. Since membership in state associations was already high, state leaders had everything to lose (and little to gain) by making state and local membership contingent on national membership. Even the more militant teachers who began to take control of the NEA in the late 1960s knew that unification was risky. An internal survey revealed that 40 percent of the NEA's own members opposed unification. As the *National Journal* explained rather bluntly, "[unification] met with resistance because [teachers] did not relish paying triple dues."[16]

The NEA also knew that unification was risky because it had watched as another membership association—the American Medical Association—tried and then failed to unify.[17] Between 1950 and 1970, thirteen state medical societies mandated that their members also join the AMA. For a brief period, the strategy worked. However, the move ultimately backfired; by the early 1970s, the AMA lost $1.25 million in revenue when state medical societies suddenly dropped their unification requirements after the AMA raised dues and doctors fled the organization.[18] Unless the NEA could somehow ensure that teachers would join and remain NEA members after unification, such a strategy might backfire on the teachers unions too.

Unlike the AMA, the NEA had access to a subsidy—a government policy—that could keep unification from undermining its recruitment and retention capabilities. Strong public-sector collective-bargaining (CB) laws would decrease the risks unification posed to the NEA's effort to recruit and retain teacher members. Specifically, as more teachers began to work in states where labor laws encouraged union organizing and membership growth, the NEA gained more members and revenue. The NEA could then use that revenue to help subsidize its own state affiliates who were struggling to unify on their own. For example, during the 1960s, the NEA agreed to compensate any state affiliate that lost members as a result of unification.[19]

Additionally, unification would become more palatable to the NEA's state affiliates once they were able to secure a strong teacher CB law in their state. Recall from the previous chapter how the exclusivity principle in American labor law led many states to adopt mandatory CB laws that empowered teachers unions to negotiate union-security provisions in their labor contracts. These security provisions incentivized teachers to both join unions and remain members. Consequently, state affiliates that were in the process of obtaining strong CB laws had less reason to fear that unification would make it harder for them to recruit and retain members. In contrast, the NEA's affiliates in states without CB laws, and those where CB laws were accompanied by a "right-to-work" (RTW) law, would find it more difficult to unify without losing members.

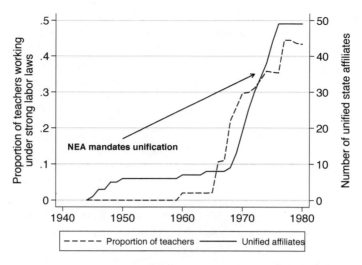

FIGURE 5.2 Strong teacher labor laws helped to accelerate the NEA's unification project

Notes: Figure displays the total share of US public school teachers working in states with a mandatory teacher CB law and without an RTW law (dashed line) each year from 1944 to 1980. The solid black line shows the total number of state NEA affiliates that had unified with the national organization by the start of each fall school year (over the same time period).

Source: Information on unification was compiled from Allan M. West's book *The National Education Association: The Power Base for Education* (New York: Free Press, 1980) and confirmed in NEA archival sources consulted by the author.

If my expectation is correct, we should find that the number of NEA state associations agreeing to unify increased after more teachers began working under strong CB laws. Second, we should also find that NEA headquarters resisted mandating unification (i.e., threatening to disaffiliate their state and local affiliates who refused to unify) until a sufficient number of states enacted strong CB laws. Figure 5.2 is instructive. The dashed line shows the proportion of all teachers working in states with mandatory teacher CB laws and no RTW statute between 1944 and 1980 (left y-axis). The solid black line (right y-axis) then shows the cumulative number of state NEA affiliates that unified each year during this time frame. The relationship between these two variables provides support for my hypothesis. Although the NEA had made unification a top organizational priority starting in 1944, the figure clearly shows that unification did not gain real momentum until strong teacher CB laws began to spread across the American states. Likewise, the NEA did not act to mandate unification (with the threat of disaffiliation) until *after* a critical mass of teachers were working under state labor laws that incentivized more teachers to become dues-paying members in the newly unified federated interest group.

If the willingness of state governments to adopt strong teacher CB laws helped lower the costs that unification imposed on the NEA's state affiliates, we should expect to find that affiliates that gained access to strong CB laws unified more quickly than affiliates in states with weaker labor laws. To augment the descriptive evidence from figure 5.2, I test this hypothesis more formally by analyzing the speed with which the NEA's state affiliates unified with their (parent) national organization. Using an event-history framework, I employ a statistical procedure that models the time it took for an affiliate to unify as a function of the presence of a strong CB law in an affiliate's state during a given year. This analysis confirms that the presence of a strong CB law increased the likelihood that a state affiliate voluntarily unified with the NEA. I find that as the proportion of teachers in a non-RTW state who were covered by collective bargaining increased by 10 percentage points, the likelihood that the state affiliate unified during this time period increased by 7 percentage points. The full results of these estimations are shown in table A5.1 in the chapter appendix.[20]

In sum, the NEA faced a dilemma when it came to unification. It was the ideal strategy to rapidly grow the organization's membership, but it was divisive for many teachers and had already backfired on the nation's premier physician's association (the AMA). Yet the NEA was uniquely able to make unification work because a growing number of states had adopted favorable public-sector bargaining laws that helped the union soften the risks that unification posed to its affiliates. By mandating unification, the NEA was able to create a strong federated interest group that would be well equipped to advocate for teachers in the decades to come.

Teacher Labor Laws and NEA Membership Growth

After the NEA solved its unification problem in the mid-1970s, the nascent union interest group continued to benefit from the fact that more states were enacting and strengthening their teacher CB laws. These laws would be an essential tool in helping the NEA to recruit and retain members in the ensuing decades. The reason is that CB laws empower teachers unions to seek exclusive representation rights and, in the absence of RTW laws, make it easier for them to negotiate security provisions that incentivize teachers to join unions and remain members.[21] For the NEA, then, I expect that the willingness of state governments to enact strong CB laws in the 1960s and 1970s decreased the incentives for teachers to free ride and *increased* NEA membership.

How certain can we be that favorable government labor policies helped teachers unions boost their membership rolls? Prior studies examining the relationship between labor laws and union membership rates have consistently uncovered higher rates of teacher-union membership in states with stronger CB laws. In one study, Terry Moe found that even after controlling for a variety of alternative explanations, the presence of a strong CB law remained a powerful predictor of a teacher's propensity to join a union.[22] While Moe's study suggests that CB laws play an important role in encouraging union membership today, it is unclear whether and how much these laws *caused* unions to recruit more members in the early days of teacher organizing. The problem with prior research is the inability to analyze membership trends before and after states enacted their labor laws in the 1960s and 1970s. Since states that adopted stronger laws likely had more pro-union cultures than states that did not, it is difficult to know how important these new laws were for boosting membership. In other words, the absence of historical data on teacher-union membership over time—what scholars refer to as *longitudinal data*—has rendered such an analysis impossible until now.

Fortunately, by digitizing historical materials from the NEA's archives in Washington DC, I was able to build a new, longitudinal data set measuring NEA membership across all fifty states in each year from 1945 to 2007. I use these membership numbers to create two dependent variables of interest. First I create a measure of each state's annual *membership density*: a simple ratio of NEA members to K–12 teachers in each state/ year.[23] My second outcome of interest, *membership growth*, measures the annual percentage change in membership density in a state.

I model variation in these two measures of union membership as function of the presence of a strong CB law in each state during a given year. This approach mirrors the one used in chapter 3, where I examined how teacher political-participation rates varied over time in response to changes in states' labor laws. Similarly, this analysis involves using those same small differences in the timing of state CB-law implementation to carefully isolate the effects of a strong CB law on teacher-union membership across states over time.

In addition to my key independent variable of interest—a strong teacher CB law—I include a handful of other state-level factors in my analysis that

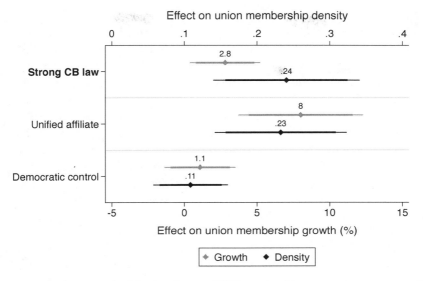

FIGURE 5.3 Strong teacher labor laws increased NEA membership

Notes: Figure plots the coefficients for three independent variables of interest in two separate regression models. The full estimates are shown in table A5.2 of the chapter appendix. The dependent variable in the first regression model (shown at the top of the x-axis) is NEA membership density in each state between 1944 and 2007. The dependent variable in the second regression model (shown at the bottom of the x-axis) is the annual percentage growth in each state's NEA affiliate's membership density over the same time period.

could also account for differences in teacher-union membership across the American states. Specifically, I include (1) an indicator for whether a state union affiliate was (in a given year) unified with the national NEA, (2) a measure of citizen ideological liberalism in each state to account for shifts in a state's political culture,[24] and (3) an indicator for Democratic Party control of state government. I also include an indicator for whether a state NEA affiliate had merged with its state AFT counterpart in a given state/year (to account for the large membership gains that naturally accompany these rare but important events). Finally, I include state fixed effects to account for all the important ways in which states are different from one another that are constant over time.[25] Crucially, unlike the methodology used in prior studies, this technique enables me to better isolate the causal effect of strong CB laws on teacher-union membership across states.

Figure 5.3 displays the results of these two regression analyses, examining the impact of a strong CB law on teacher-union membership. The model estimating the effect of CB laws on membership density is listed along the top of the x-axis in the figure. In contrast, the model where the outcome of interest is membership growth is shown along the bottom of the x-axis.[26]

Starting with the union-membership density outcome, the point estimates on the CB-law variable (denoted by the solid black diamond) show that the adoption of a strong CB law had a positive and statistically significant impact on teacher-union membership density. This effect is substantively meaningful as well. The coefficient (0.24) corresponds to an increase of two-thirds of a standard deviation in a state's NEA-membership rate. Likewise, I find that the adoption of a strong CB law leads to higher rates of year-over-year membership growth. The coefficient (2.8) on the CB-law variable (denoted by the solid gray diamond) indicates that the adoption of a strong CB law is associated with an increase of nearly 3 percent in a state's annual rate of union membership growth. Taken together, these findings demonstrate that if the NEA has power because more than 3.2 million teachers pay NEA dues, the genesis of that power was rooted, in part, in the decision of state governments to enact strong teacher CB laws.

Money

Having detailed the powerful role that state labor laws played in helping the NEA recruit and retain more members, I now transition to discuss what California Assembly Speaker Jesse Unruh famously described as "the mother's milk of politics": *money*. In what follows, I outline the specific strategies that teachers unions used to amass greater financial resources, the bulk of which could be spent in politics. At each step along the way, I demonstrate how government policies made those organizational strategies possible for the burgeoning interest group and its state affiliates.

Teacher Labor Laws and Dues Revenue

There are just two ways for membership groups like teachers unions to raise more dues revenue: (1) recruit more members or (2) increase the rate each member pays. Unfortunately for group leaders, most members are cost sensitive. For example, professional associations like the AMA and the ABA have been forced to reduce or alter their dues policies to try and reverse the large membership declines they have experienced in recent decades.[27] Other issue-based advocacy organizations like the NRA, the National Parent Teacher Association (PTA), and AARP have each tended to lose members the year after increasing their dues.[28] It's a tradeoff. Membership growth helps an organization gain more revenue. But if membership growth is flat or in decline, the only way to increase revenue is to ask current members to pay more. Unfortunately, that only works if members don't respond by leaving the organization when asked to pay more.

In 2005, however, the California Teachers Association (CTA) challenged this basic law of economics. That year, the union spent over fifty million dollars to fight several ballot measures backed by then-governor Arnold Schwarzenegger. The CTA's opposition campaign was wildly successful: all four measures were defeated.[29] To fund this massive political advocacy effort, the CTA increased each one of its three hundred thousand–plus members' dues by over 10 percent, or $60 per teacher for three consecutive years.[30] That's the kind of dues increase that, in theory, would lead a group to lose a significant number of members. For most groups, the quantity of memberships purchased varies inversely with the price charged. *But the CTA simply defied this law of demand.*

What made the CTA different was that it operated, as noted earlier by Justice Sotomayor, with an organizational subsidy provided by the state of California. Prior to the 2018 *Janus* decision, California law had authorized (since 1976) and later mandated (since 2000) that all school districts automatically deduct fees from their teachers' paychecks on behalf of the CTA. Teachers who considered resigning over the CTA's dues increase would still have been obligated to pay the union a fee equal to about 65 percent of full membership dues.[31] But as nonmembers, those teachers would have lost their liability-insurance coverage, members-only benefits, and the right to vote and participate in their local association's affairs. Given these countervailing incentives, it is not terribly surprising that the CTA didn't feel a pinch after it aggressively raised dues. In fact, it went on to enjoy tremendous membership growth.

This anecdote provides a useful motivating example that can help us begin to unpack the relationship between government policies and the ability of teachers unions to raise large sums of revenue for political advocacy. Let's begin by examining how the national branch of the NEA has consistently generated large and steady sums of dues revenue over the past several decades.

NEA Dues: A Case Study

For most of the NEA's history, delegates to its annual Representative Assembly (RA) decided how much teachers would have to pay each year in national membership dues. Over that time span, the NEA faced the same basic tension that all membership groups face between raising dues and growing membership. While teachers had clearly become more politically active in the intervening years, they were still in no mood to part with more of their hard-earned money. A 1967 survey, for example, found that one-third of NEA members opposed the association's proposal to enact a much needed five-dollar dues increase that year. One in ten teachers even threatened to leave the organization if the NEA went through with the increase.[32]

Eventually, the NEA found a way to overcome this perennial struggle and balance its members' sensitivity to higher costs with the organization's need for more revenue. That solution came about in 1978 when delegates to the annual RA meeting narrowly agreed to change the organization's bylaws so that *dues would automatically be set as a percentage of the average annual teacher salary in the United States* (as determined by the association).[33] In other words, instead of requiring that its elected delegates take unpopular votes to raise dues every few years when the NEA needed more revenue, the NEA simply adopted what it called a self-adjusting "ratio" dues policy that could keep dues ticking upward, thereby ensuring that the national union had a predictable and reliable stream of revenue.

As figure 5.4 shows, after this new dues policy was fully implemented in 1979, the NEA experienced a steadier year-over-year increase in revenue. This new self-adjusting dues policy was also helpful in combating the highly inflationary 1970s. As reflected by the volatility that appears early on in the time series shown in figure 5.4, before the NEA switched over to its new dues policy, the ad hoc dues increases it enacted in 1968 (from $10 to $15) and 1970 (from $15 to $25) were quickly diluted by inflation. Only after the NEA pegged teachers' dues to a fixed percentage of the nation's average yearly teacher salary was the national organization able to secure a reliable annual revenue stream. It's also important to emphasize that the NEA's revenue grew *both* because it raised membership dues and because it did an effective job retaining the teachers it had recruited in the decades prior to adopting the new dues policy. As figure 5.1 showed earlier in the chapter, between 1960 and 1980 the NEA experienced tremendous membership growth. But it also maintained the majority of its members over the ensuing decades, even after its (more expensive) ratio-based dues policy went into effect. In other words, asking teachers to pay these higher dues rates did *not* have a significant negative effect on the union's membership recruitment. Or, as we shall see, *at least not in all states.*

The NEA was only able to thread this needle, however, because of the new and favorable changes in teacher labor law that many states had

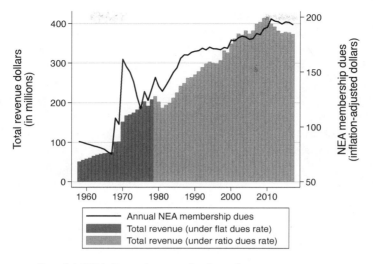

FIGURE 5.4 Growth in NEA dues and revenue (1958–2017)

Notes: The solid black line displays the national dues rate that the NEA charged full-time (active professional) members each year from 1958 to 2017. The corresponding bars show the organization's total annual revenue (in millions of dollars) over the same time period. Both measures are adjusted for inflation (using 2017 dollar values). The dark gray bars indicate years where the NEA's dues were set as a flat rate. In contrast, the lighter gray bars show the trajectory of revenue during the years after the NEA had switched to a self-adjusting ratio dues policy.

enacted in the intervening years. These laws made it less likely that teachers would leave the NEA when they were asked to pay more in dues. Specifically, as more teachers began working in states where local NEA affiliates could negotiate and levy agency fees on nonmembers, dues could be raised more liberally without causing the NEA to worry that members would exit. To show how government policies helped underwrite the NEA's ability to increase members' dues and raise more revenue for the national organization, I begin by examining the historical period leading up to the organization's decision to adopt its ratio-based dues policy in 1979, tracing the timing and sequence of that decision to an important development in teacher labor law.

The story begins in 1965 in Michigan. The NEA's state affiliate there, the Michigan Education Association (MEA), had recently begun to operate under a strong mandatory teacher CB law. The original law said nothing explicit about unions being able to charge fees to nonmembers; in practice, however, because Michigan did not have an RTW law, the number of teachers unions that could obtain agency-fee revenue grew steadily. By 1968, 20 percent of locals had obtained agency fees, and that number rose to over 50 percent by 1972.[34] In 1972, the Michigan Supreme Court ruled against agency fees, and they very briefly became illegal. However, the state immediately reversed course as the legislature amended the state's CB law to explicitly allow for them. This legal ping-pong set the stage for the US Supreme Court's landmark *Abood v. Detroit Board of Education* decision in 1977. In *Abood*, the high court ruled that states were allowed to include agency-fee provisions in their public-sector CB laws—a major victory for teachers unions and public-sector unions in the United States more generally.

Abood was handed down on May 23, 1977. That date is important because the ruling was issued a mere forty days before the NEA's 1978 annual RA meeting was to take place. If my argument—that the spread of agency fees legitimized by *Abood* induced the NEA to raise dues—is correct, we would expect the NEA to have acted immediately, raising dues just after the court had ruled in its favor. However, the NEA had a longstanding requirement that any changes in the organization's bylaws (which included enacting a dues increase) needed to be submitted in writing at least 120 days in advance of each year's annual RA meeting. Having narrowly missed the window for 1977, the NEA then waited until the earliest moment allowable under its bylaws to propose that increase: its July 1978 annual meeting.

According to the transcript of that 1978 RA meeting, the proposal to raise dues and peg them to a percentage of the average teacher's salary was highly controversial, passing by only the slimmest margin (3,856 delegates voted yes while 3,746 voted no). In addition to the suggestive post-*Abood* timing, the transcript from the 1978 annual meeting provides more evidence that the NEA's delegates were acutely aware of the relationship between strong union-security provisions in CB laws and the organization's flexibility to raise membership dues during these early days of teacher organizing. Although a handful of delegates from strong labor-law states expressed some concerns about raising members' dues, the transcript reveals that most of the skepticism came from delegates who were leaders of NEA affiliates in RTW states, where agency fees would never be allowed as a means of incentivizing membership. Remarks from delegates in Nebraska and North Carolina (two RTW states) capture these predictable concerns:

NEBRASKA DELEGATE: I would urge you to vote no! You should not support a rapidly escalating dues rate ... Don't give NEA a blank check. With the index factor you will have an increase each year. I know the 1,600 teachers that I represent will not support a large, continuous increase in dues ... and it will cost NEA membership.

NORTH CAROLINA DELEGATE: If this dues increase passes, NEA will find itself in the same position as our colleagues from California. We will have our Proposition 13, but this time it is going to be led by the [exiting] members back home![35]

In sum, NEA members from states without agency fees invoked arguments about the need to be sensitive to the potential for exit—of membership losses in state and local affiliates that could not take advantage of the *Abood* ruling by negotiating for agency fees. These members were right to be concerned. In 1979, the average teacher salary in RTW states was a mere $13,039. In non-RTW states, the average teacher salary was $15,300. In other words, under the NEA's new dues policy, teachers in RTW states would be asked to pay more in national union dues (as a percentage of their actual salary) than their colleagues in non-RTW states, giving delegates from RTW states even more reason to fear a membership revolt back home.

Altogether, then, the historical record strongly suggests that the willingness of state governments and the federal courts to enshrine the agency shop in teacher labor law enabled teacher-union interest groups to increase their dues and, in turn, their revenue. As figure 5.5 shows, the NEA increased its dues rates most aggressively precisely at the point in time when a critical mass of states' labor laws turned in a pro–agency fee direction: the percent of teachers working in states allowing fees rose from 0 percent to 40 percent of the nation's teacher workforce by 1980.

It's also noteworthy that the nation's other major teachers union, the AFT, responded in a similar way after the *Abood* decision became law. At its 1979 convention, the AFT raised membership dues by over 35 percent. The nation's two largest teachers unions, then, both enacted major national dues increases—with one, the NEA, embracing an entirely more liberal dues policy—on the immediate heels of a major favorable change in the way American labor law treated union security in public-sector collective bargaining. Altogether, there can be little doubt that by making dues increases possible, these government policies helped subsidize the national teachers unions' organizational needs as interest groups to secure more revenue.

Raising Dues Revenue for State Political Advocacy

It is a bit of a misnomer that teachers (and other) unions cannot spend dues money on politics. Though *federal* law expressly prohibits labor unions from using their general treasury funds to donate to federal candidates

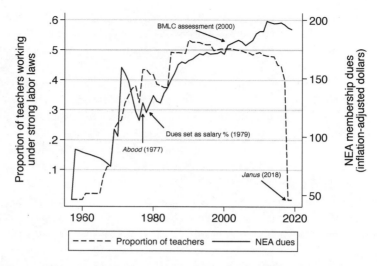

FIGURE 5.5 NEA dues grew as the share of teachers working under strong CB laws grew

Notes: Figure plots the total share of teachers working in states with a mandatory CB law and no prohibition against agency fees (dashed line) against the dues rate that the NEA charged full-time (active professional) members (solid black line). Both data points are shown annually from 1957 to 2019. The *Abood* and *Janus* decisions denote the years in which the US Supreme Court authorized (in 1977) and later took away (in 2018) unions' access to agency fees. "BMLC Assessment" denotes the year (2000) when the NEA added this assessment to each member's dues to fund political advocacy. The assessment increased members' dues above and beyond the "ratio" dues rate that had taken effect in 1979. The BMLC is discussed in more detail later in the chapter.

or parties, teachers unions are free to spend their dues revenue on PAC administration and solicitation, lobbying, independent expenditures, ballot initiative or referenda campaigns, rallies, protests, and member communication and voter mobilization drives. More importantly, many *state* governments set no limits whatsoever on the use of union dues money in subnational politics.

This spending freedom is important because one of the arguments I have made throughout this book is that government policies helped strengthen teacher-union interest groups at the state and local levels—the institutional arenas where they *need* to be politically influential to shape K–12 education policy. If it could be shown that by enacting strong CB laws, states made it easier for union interest groups to raise more dues revenue, that would provide additional evidence that state subsidies helped strengthen organized teacher interests in *state* politics.

To determine whether the sorts of changes in teacher labor law that enabled the national NEA to raise more dues revenue also benefitted state unions in the same way, I built two additional longitudinal data sets. First, I gathered information on the annual dues rate charged by each NEA state affiliate between 1957 and 2003.[36] State affiliates varied significantly in the rate they charged over this time period. For example, the average NEA affiliate required teachers to pay 0.52 percent of the average teacher salary in the state. The highest dues were set by the NEA's Michigan affiliate in 1994 (1.04 percent), with the lowest set by Missouri in 1966 (0.06 percent).

Are these differences in teachers unions' dues rates related to the strength of the security provisions authorized in their states' labor laws? Specifically, did teachers unions in states that authorized them to charge nonmembers fees have an easier time raising dues without sacrificing membership gains? To answer this question, I first identified the specific year that each state (twenty-four in total) authorized agency fees. Using the same statistical approach employed in my earlier analysis of union membership density,[37] I examine how NEA state affiliates' dues rates vary over time in response to state governments authorizing teachers unions to negotiate agency fees. This analysis reveals that the adoption of agency fees had a positive and statistically significant effect on the level of dues that state teacher-union affiliates were able to levy on their members. Specifically, NEA affiliates that gained access to agency fees subsequently set dues rates 10 percent higher than affiliates who did not explicitly allow for such fees. The full results of this analysis are presented in column 1 of table A5.3 in the chapter appendix.

Clearly, teachers unions were able to raise their members' dues as a consequence of gaining agency fees in state labor laws. However, an equally important and related question is whether strong union-security provisions inoculated teachers unions from losing members when the union did raise dues. Recall that membership associations typically lose members after they institute dues increases. However, union-security provisions should make teacher-union interest groups different. To investigate whether teachers unions in states with strong security provisions are less likely to lose members when they raise dues, I carried out two additional analyses.

In both analyses, my outcome of interest is each state NEA affiliate's membership density (the same membership indicator used earlier in the chapter). The key independent variable of interest is an interaction between each state affiliate's dues rate and the availability of union-security provisions under the state's teacher labor law. The results of the first analysis are presented in column 2 of table A5.3. In this model, I interact an affiliate's dues rate with an indicator for whether agency fees are legal in an affiliate's

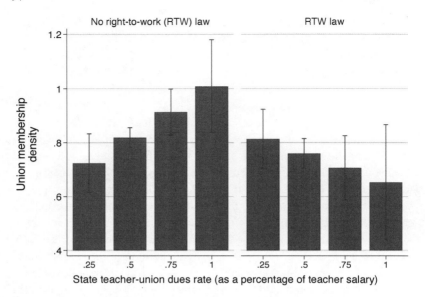

FIGURE 5.6 Raising union dues does not reduce union membership in states with strong labor laws

Notes: Figure plots the marginal effects of an NEA state affiliate's dues rate on each state's overall membership density, separately by states with and without RTW laws. Dues are measured as the percentage of the average teacher salary in each state. The full regression model is shown in column 3 of table A5.3 in the chapter appendix.

state. As an alternative approach, the model presented in column 3 interacts an affiliate's dues rate with an indicator for whether there is an RTW law in effect in the affiliate's state. If my hypothesis is correct, we should observe that state NEA affiliates with agency fees have an easier time maintaining membership density even after they raise dues. In contrast, affiliates in RTW states—where teachers have no similar financial incentive to remain members—should struggle to keep members when dues rise.

Figure 5.6, which is based on the model shown in column 3 of table A5.3, confirms this expectation. Specifically, when affiliates in RTW states raise teacher-union dues from 0.25 percent to 1 percent of the average teacher's salary, the union's membership density declines from 0.81 to 0.65, or almost half a full standard deviation in the average state's teacher-union membership density. In contrast, state NEA affiliates that are not constrained by RTW laws benefit from union-security provisions, which help blunt any membership losses. In fact, as the left side of the figure shows, higher dues rates are accompanied by *higher* membership density in non-

RTW states. In sum, agency fees provided a critical subsidy to organized teacher interests in the early days of teacher organizing, enabling them to lock in higher dues rates and grow revenue, all while maintaining membership in ways that most ordinary membership associations cannot. One obvious question that arises, then, is whether *Janus* will reverse these trends and keep teachers unions from aggressively raising dues in years to come. I address the *Janus* question more extensively in chapter 9.

Financing Political Advocacy

The NEA's foray into federal political action was also aided and abetted by government policy, mainly through a security provision known as "dues checkoff." Dues checkoff refers to the practice of states either requiring or authorizing teachers unions to have access to their school district's payroll-deduction program to collect members' dues. However, since unions usually solicit teachers for political action committee (PAC) contributions at the same time that they pitch membership, payroll deduction can often serve a dual purpose, simplifying and making it less costly for unions to raise PAC funds in one fell swoop.

When the NEA initially created its federal PAC, NEA-PAC, in the early 1970s, it predictably struggled to convince teachers to contribute.[38] As is common in the early stages of interest-group formation, a handful of entrepreneurs had to step up and subsidize the startup costs of the group's new political advocacy program. In 1972, several NEA board members cobbled together a few thousand dollars to seed NEA-PAC. Initially, however, the NEA's effort to obtain support from rank-and-file educators fizzled. Even though the NEA had only asked teachers to donate $1 per year, few funds were raised in the early going.[39]

To address the problem, delegates at the NEA's 1973 annual RA meeting were asked to adopt a new PAC solicitation procedure known as "reverse checkoff." Then-NEA president Helen Wise implored the delegates to adopt this policy, whereby all current NEA members would automatically contribute $1 to NEA-PAC. Teachers could make a separate written request asking not to contribute, but the *default* arrangement was that all members would donate. The reverse checkoff is effective because of the human tendency toward inertia. A large research literature in behavioral economics has shown that people are far more likely to participate in an activity when the default arrangement passively opts them into participating, rather than requiring that they actively opt in to participate of their own accord.[40]

How important was the reverse-checkoff procedure to NEA-PAC's fundraising success? After raising a mere $30,000 in 1972, NEA-PAC took in $700,000 in teacher contributions in 1976—*after* it had fully implemented the reverse-checkoff procedure.[41] Clearly, the combination of a reverse–dues checkoff in conjunction with the union-security provision of payroll deduction proved to be a tremendous boon for the NEA's political-fundraising efforts. Unfortunately for the NEA, in 1978 the Federal Election Commission (FEC) ruled that the reverse-checkoff procedure violated federal campaign-finance law. It is noteworthy that the NEA's chief legal counsel at that time, Robert Chanin, argued that the combination of payroll deduction and reverse checkoff helped subsidize the union's political-fundraising efforts. He explained to the presiding federal district court judge:

> It is well recognized that if you take away the mechanism of payroll deduction you won't collect a penny from these people [teachers], and it has nothing to do with voluntary or involuntary. I think it has to do with the nature of the beast, and the beasts who are our teachers who are dispersed all over cities who simply don't come up with money regardless of the purpose.[42]

Ultimately, the NEA's loss of the reverse-checkoff procedure proved to be only a minor setback. As I discuss in the next chapter, the FEC's ruling only applied to the NEA's solicitation of PAC funds for federal elections. Many state PACs, subject only to state campaign-finance laws, continued to use the reverse-checkoff procedure in subnational politics. In any event, the national NEA eventually made a strategic decision to focus more on issue-based political advocacy—advocacy that can be funded with general treasury revenue (members' dues) rather than PAC money. Specifically, in 2000, the NEA adopted a new targeted assessment called the Ballot Measure Legislative Crisis (BMLC) program.

Prior to 2000, the NEA was still using the policy it had adopted in 1979 whereby members paid 0.28 percent of the average teacher's salary in national NEA dues. Yet a careful look at figure 5.5 from earlier in the chapter reveals that, beginning in 2000, the NEA suddenly began to charge teachers more in dues. Using the NEA's own data on teacher salaries, I calculate that the NEA's dues rate increased from 0.28 percent of the average teacher's salary in 1999 to 0.32 percent by 2011. Given that the NEA's bylaws required adhering to the 0.28 percent dues rate, how was the union able to obtain these additional funds for political advocacy? The reason is that the NEA's delegates—although reluctant to raise dues—have been far more willing over the years to adopt ad hoc "targeted assessments"—fees that are charged on top of dues. The NEA's BMLC program is by far the most important such assessment. The BMLC add-on was initially set at just $5.00. In other words, starting in 2000, $5.00 was added to each member's dues ($123 that year). However, over time, the BMLC assessment ticked upward. The union raised it to $10 and then to $20 per member in 2011. In 2015, the NEA officially made the BMLC a permanent part of members' dues.

The BMLC program is important because it has allowed the NEA to raise and spend tens of millions of dollars for political advocacy each year *without soliciting any members for political donations.* While the BMLC fund cannot be used to donate to federal candidates, it can be spent liberally in state politics. For example, the NEA has frequently relied upon the BMLC program to help its state affiliates defeat state ballot measures that would have adopted voucher programs, as well as charter, teacher pay, tenure, and evaluation reforms (to name just a few). The BMLC program was made possible, in part, because of strong union-security provisions in states' teacher CB laws. For example, prior to the *Janus* decision in 2018, the NEA lost members when it increased the BMLC assessment, but those losses occurred in states that had RTW laws that prohibited agency fees. In other words, the decision of states to maintain strong labor laws with favorable union-security provisions allowed the NEA to raise more money for political advocacy (by increasing the rate of its BMLC assessment) without suffering membership losses in its largest state affiliates.

Other Miscellaneous Revenue Subsidies

Finally, in addition to union-security provisions, other state subsidies helped the NEA maximize revenue to enhance its political advocacy efforts. Among the most unique subsidies any private interest-group organization has ever received, the NEA benefitted for decades from a rare property-tax exemption on its Washington, DC headquarters.[43] Prior to it becoming a labor union in the early 1900s, Congress granted the NEA a rare federal charter for the purpose of promoting education.[44] One of the benefits of the federal charter was being shielded from paying any taxes on property owned in the District of Columbia. From an organizational revenue perspective, these benefits proved to be enormous. Combining historical records on commercial property-tax rates in the District of Columbia with several decades of LM-2 reports that the NEA filed with the Department of Labor (reporting the value of its real estate holdings), I estimate that the union retained an additional $40 million in revenue between 1970 and 1998 on account of this charter. According to FEC records, that revenue would have offset a nontrivial share of the NEA's total PAC spending in federal elections between 1972 and 2000.

Only when House Republicans threatened to eliminate the NEA's entire charter in the aftermath of the 1994 GOP takeover of Congress did the NEA's leadership voluntarily relinquish the tax exemption. Yet even in giving up this benefit, the NEA was able to use the giveback for political gain. The union warned congressional Republicans that it would fight to keep its exemption if lawmakers included a school-voucher program for the District of Columbia in its annual budget.[45] The important point is that the property-tax exemption provides yet another example of the unique relationship that governments (here the federal government) have entered into with teachers unions. Although the original point of the federal charter was to support the NEA's role in promoting the cause of education, the NEA continued to enjoy the benefits of the charter long after it had evolved into a labor union. During the critical time, then, when the NEA was becoming a major interest group, it benefitted from the government's conferral of a significant cost-savings advantage—savings that, owing to the principle of fungibility discussed at the end of chapter 4, could be directed elsewhere, including spending on issue-based political advocacy.

Revenue Summary

The teachers who took the reins of the NEA at the end of the 1960s found an organization that was in poor fiscal shape; it ended the decade $180,000 in the red, a significant shortfall in those days.[46] But the union was able to solve its financial difficulties by raising members' dues and later by levying and making permanent targeted special assessments. It was a risky strategy that, absent favorable government policies, would almost certainly have failed.

Membership associations that frequently raise dues to solve their fiscal challenges lose members who, over time, become resistant to parting with more of their money. In the universe of education-advocacy groups, the National Parent Teacher Association (PTA) offers a compelling case in point. In 2019, delegates to the PTA's annual convention voted down a trivial $1.50 dues increase—*from $2.25 to $3.75!*—over concerns that many parents would leave the organization (a not-unreasonable fear given that the PTA had lost millions of members over the past half century).[47] Yet thanks to favorable public policies, teacher-union interest groups could raise dues and fees without having to worry about these same sorts of concerns.

First, both the NEA and the AFT waited until after the US Supreme Court held that teachers unions could charge fees to nonmembers before these unions raised their national dues. Similarly, the NEA's own state affiliates increased their state dues rates after agency-fee provisions were added to teacher labor laws in their states. And finally, when the national organization needed additional revenue—beyond what its bylaws allowed it to charge in dues—it levied a targeted assessment, the BMLC, on its members. Teachers in states with RTW laws—where nonmembers could not be charged union fees—responded to these dues and fee increases by leaving the union. In contrast, teachers in states with strong teacher labor laws were more likely to remain members and simply pay the higher costs.

Altogether then, government policies played a foundational role in helping America's teachers build their unions into strong and financially stable interest groups. These policies ultimately enabled teachers to secure the necessary revenue to engage in organized political advocacy. The ability to raise money through dues revenue was and remains central to the political strength of teachers unions in the United States. As the NEA's former secretary-treasurer John T. McGarigal explained to delegates at the organization's 1976 annual meeting, "[the NEA's financial reports] may be difficult to read [and] they may have the appearance of being dull. But please remember, [*the union's*] *financial capability is the major source of our political power*."[48]

Maintaining Power

By 1980, the NEA had gained sufficient members and money to become, as Theda Skocpol put it, a "stalwart in state and local as well as national Democratic Party politics." However, the union still faced one final challenge: organizational maintenance. Political scientists are keenly aware that interest groups can only remain effective if they are able to maintain themselves year after year. As a federated interest group, the NEA faces a unique challenge when it comes to organizational maintenance: it has to maintain strength throughout a network of affiliates that each operate under very different state labor laws. Some affiliates have enjoyed the benefits of favorable laws that promote membership and revenue growth, whereas other affiliates were left to struggle under weak or nonexistent laws that did just the opposite.[49]

Unfortunately for the teachers unions, the expansion of teacher bargaining laws stalled by the mid-1980s. When the dust had settled, sixteen states, mostly southern and border states, refused to pass mandatory bargaining laws.[50] The NEA first tried to solve this problem by appealing to their allies in Congress to enact a nationwide public-sector CB law.[51] When that effort failed, the NEA needed to identify an alternative solution to take care of its most vulnerable state affiliates. Today, the organization's leaders remain acutely aware of this ongoing challenge. "[Since] we're only as strong as our weakest link . . . almost a third of our budget goes directly into [our] affiliates," the NEA's chief financial officer, Michael McPherson, explained in 2006 to an *Education Week* reporter. The reporter further noted that: "Often that means a redistribution of money to affiliates struggling to build numbers in so-called 'right to work' states, where nonmembers pay no dues."[52]

The NEA's strategy to ensure organizational maintenance and survival is a product of unification and federalism: the national organization ensures that revenue is shared between its state affiliates. Again, this fact speaks to why the unification movement—aided by the favorable expansion of state public-sector labor laws in the 1970s—has been and remains so valuable to the NEA's power as a political advocacy organization.

The basic advantage of organizing as a unified federated group is the flexibility the national branch has over the organization's finances, including its decisions to target support to needy state affiliates.[53] As the previous discussion of revenue showed, the NEA's affiliates in strong–labor law states consistently found it easier to charge teachers higher membership dues and adopt bigger budgets. But state affiliates needn't rely solely on these internally generated dues funds for revenue. They can also turn to their national parent union in Washington for support. If the NEA engages in organizational maintenance by, as McPherson put it, "redistributing money to affiliates struggling," then we should expect to find that NEA state affiliates without strong labor laws rely disproportionately on

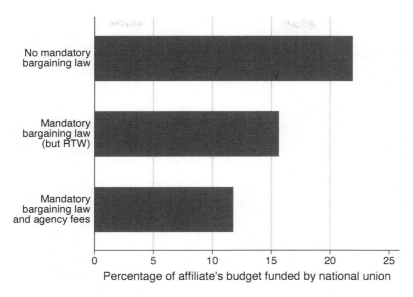

FIGURE 5.7 Percentage of affiliates' budgets funded by the NEA, by labor law environment

Notes: Figure displays the percentage of state affiliates' total revenue that came from the NEA between 2005 and 2011.

Source: Author's analysis of NEA LM-2 (Department of Labor) and (Internal Revenue Service) 990 financial reports from 2005–2011. DOL data is available at https://www.dol.gov/agencies/olms/public-disclosure-room; 990 data can be found at https://www.guidestar.org/.

the national union to fund their operations. In other words, they rely on the national union for organizational maintenance and survival.

Figure 5.7 shows evidence of precisely that reliance. From 2005 to 2011, NEA affiliates in states with the strongest CB laws funded almost 90 percent of their own operations. In contrast, affiliates in states with the weakest labor laws relied on the NEA to fund nearly a quarter of their budgets.

In a study on this topic, Leslie Finger and I demonstrate the NEA's widespread use of this kind of revenue sharing—what we call "financial solidarity"—between teacher-union affiliates within the NEA's federated network.[54] By examining how the NEA responded to the wave of anti–labor retrenchment laws enacted in the aftermath of the Great Recession, we found that the national union redistributed significant resources back to vulnerable state affiliates to help them maintain their operations and fund political fightback campaigns. After a state weakened its teacher labor law, for example, the NEA was nearly 25 percentage points more likely to make a financial contribution in state politics to support its newly embattled affiliate.

TABLE 5.1 **NEA support for its state affiliates in key ballot-initiative campaigns**

NEA state affiliate	Labor law environment	Election year	NEA's (national) contribution	State affiliate's contribution	Contribution ratio (national to state)
California (CTA)	Mandatory CB Mandatory fees	2005	$2,500,000	$54,740,885	0.1
Ohio (OEA)	Mandatory CB Negotiable fees	2011	$4,078,566	$6,562,364	0.6
Idaho (IEA)	Mandatory CB Fees banned	2012	$3,029,458	$728,593	4.2
Colorado (CEA)	No mandatory CB	2008	$3,849,613	$526,477	7.3

Source: Author's analysis of data provided by the National Institute on Money in State Politics

Recall how the California Teachers Association levied a large special assessment on its members to fight a series of anti-union ballot proposals in 2005. To fund its opposition to Governor Schwarzenegger's proposed reforms, the CTA simply raised each of its members' dues $60 dollars to generate some $50 million in political advocacy revenue. Compare the ease with which the CTA (operating at that time with a *mandatory* agency-fee law) raised money, to the approach taken by the NEA's state affiliates in Colorado, Ohio, and Idaho—states that each faced similar anti-union ballot measures in 2008, 2011, and 2012. Without the benefit of California's exceptionally strong labor law, these comparatively weaker state union affiliates had to rely more on their parent union (the NEA) for financial support.

Table 5.1 shows (1) the amount of money the NEA distributed in national dues revenue to fund opposition to each set of ballot initiatives, (2) the amount each state affiliate was able to self-fund, and (3) (in the far right-hand column) the ratio of national NEA dollars to state dollars spent fighting these measures. For example, both California and Colorado affiliates faced hostile ballot initiatives that proposed to institute a "paycheck protection" law making it harder for their unions to raise money in politics. Similarly, California and Idaho both faced measures that would have weakened teacher tenure. Finally, Idaho and Ohio were each facing a ballot initiative that proposed to curtail teachers' collective-bargaining rights. Across a host of similar measures, the stronger the affiliate's labor-law environment, the less it had to rely on the NEA to fund the opposition campaign. Conversely, the weaker the affiliate's legal environment, the more it had to rely on the national union to bankroll its opposition campaign. The most important takeaway, of course, is that thanks to the federated structure of the NEA, no affiliate was left without a significant amount of money to fend off the proposed measures.

How has American labor law subsidized the NEA's ability to engage in this sort of revenue sharing, which in turn helps ensure the organizational survival of all its affiliates? It turns out that the union's revenue-sharing policies are not simply a matter of internal union affairs. The strategy ultimately required the federal judiciary to intervene and declare that—as a matter of law—the dues and fees teacher-employees owe to their exclusive-representative union also must include dues and fees to the state and national parents with which the local union affiliates. That intervention formally took place in a US Supreme Court case called *Lehnert v. Ferris Faculty Association*. In *Lehnert*, the court was asked to strike down a provision of Michigan's public-sector bargaining law that required objecting nonunion teachers to pay fees to both the national NEA and its state affiliate, the Michigan Education Association (MEA).

Crucially, in *Lehnert*, the objecting nonunion educator was not a K–12 teacher, but rather a postsecondary faculty member at Ferris State University. The plaintiff objected to the fact that his compelled agency-fee payments to the NEA and MEA, respectively, were being spent on behalf of K–12 public school teachers who, all parties conceded, shared no direct bargaining interests with the dissident Ferris State faculty member. Nevertheless, in upholding the NEA's right to use the professor's agency fees on interest-group activities unrelated to his college faculty union's bargaining unit, the Supreme Court held that (emphasis added):

> A local bargaining representative may charge objecting employees for their pro rata share of the costs associated with otherwise chargeable activities of its state and national affiliates, even if those activities were not performed for the direct benefit of the objecting employees' bargaining unit. *Because the essence of the affiliation relationship is the notion that the parent union will bring to bear its often considerable economic, political, and informational resources when the local is in need of them*, that part of a local's affiliation fee which contributes to the pool of resources potentially available to it is assessed for the bargaining unit's protection, even if it is not actually expended on that unit in any particular membership year.[55]

In subsequent years, the court has continued to reaffirm the core holding of *Lehnert*.[56] The principle of affiliated representation, therefore, continues to be an important component of teachers unions' efforts to ensure the organizational maintenance of their state and local union affiliates throughout the United States. Had the federal judiciary taken public-sector labor law in a much different, less pro-union direction— construing the operational definition of the exclusive-representative union more narrowly—federated teacher-union interest groups would have lost significant revenue and been far more constrained in sharing and spending revenue throughout their affiliate network. In sum, without the courts' assent and willingness to make affiliated representation a core plank of American labor law, teachers unions would be in a significantly worse position to aid their embattled affiliates.

Chapter Summary

Politics is ultimately a contest that hinges on the strength of organized groups. Education is no different. Teachers are influential because—far more than any other education interest group—they are represented by a massive federated interest group capable of coordinating political action in fifty states and thousands of local school districts. Importantly, though, my findings show that teachers were only able to build that kind of organizational strength because of state patronage.

Membership. First, union-security provisions helped the NEA gain millions of members. Favorable labor laws also enabled the NEA to build a unified interest group, binding millions of teachers together under a single powerful organization. As former NEA executive director Don Cameron put it, "unification provided NEA with the financial stability it had never before experienced."[57] Unification also allowed the NEA to build and maintain its UniServ program, the heart and soul of its political advocacy efforts today. As then-NEA federal policy manager Randall J. Moody explained in 2003, "Politics move our policy. We work through UniServ."[58]

Money. Political advocacy requires money. To expand and sustain its revenue base, the NEA linked national dues to growth in teacher salaries, ensuring steady revenue increases year after year. At the state level, agency fees enabled affiliates to increase dues without sacrificing membership. State support helped the NEA raise money in other ways too. A rare property-tax exemption based on a federal charter granted prior to its evolution into a labor union saved the NEA tens of millions of dollars. The NEA could also rely on a reverse dues-checkoff system, buoyed by state labor laws that authorized school districts to deduct NEA members' dues and PAC contributions on behalf of the organization. When the FEC later ruled the reverse checkoff illegal at the federal level, the NEA regrouped. It began to levy a new special assessment to obtain more money that could be spent in politics. Again, subsidies proved helpful here since these assessments were essentially dues increases that the NEA could safely enact thanks to the fact that half their members worked in states where strong labor laws reduced the threat of member exit.

Maintenance. Finally, the NEA came to rely on the labor-law principle of affiliated representation to ensure the organizational maintenance and survival of its affiliates. Specifically, the NEA's strength as a unified federated interest group means that the national organization can engage in revenue sharing by moving resources it disproportionately draws from its strongest affiliates to underwrite the political needs of its weakest ones.

Far from being a spontaneous product of 1960s social consciousness or a labor-oriented social movement, the origins of organized teacher political power in the United States are partly a product of state support. As this chapter and the preceding ones showed, at both the individual and organizational levels, government policies subsidized organized teacher interests, helping them rise to the top of the political class. The key question that remains is: What have been the effects of organized teacher political power on American education? It is to this question that I turn in the remainder of the book.

Chapter Appendix

TABLE A5.1 **Relative likelihood of NEA affiliates in states with stronger teacher labor laws to unify ahead of the national NEA's unification mandate**

	(1)	(2)	(3)	4)
CB law and no RTW	0.623*	—	0.660*	—
	(0.327)		(0.341)	
Percentage of teachers covered by CBA and no RTW	—	0.007*	—	0.008*
		(0.003)		(0.004)
Pseudo R^2	—	—	0.34	0.33
Observations	1,108	1,108	1,108	1,108

Notes: Models 1 and 2 are Cox proportional-hazard models. Models 3 and 4 are piecewise poisson regression models where the hazard changes year over year. All models report results as coefficients, with standard errors clustered by state in parentheses. Data span 1944–1976 (the time period before the NEA began to disaffiliate its noncompliant affiliates for failing to unify). *p<0.1, **p<0.05, ***p<0.01.

TABLE A5.2 **Effect of strong teacher labor laws on NEA membership density and growth**

	Membership density (1)	Membership growth (2)
Strong CB law	0.240***	2.799**
	(0.050)	(1.203)
Unified	0.233***	7.999***
	(0.045)	(2.133)
Merged	0.467***	46.167
	(0.111)	(38.898)
Democratic control	0.108***	1.073
	(0.026)	(1.217)
Mass liberalism	0.157	-1.213
	(0.100)	(4.834)
Constant	0.738***	27.847***
	(0.041)	(4.537)
State fixed effects	Yes	Yes
Year fixed effects	Yes	Yes
R^2	0.74	0.13
Observations	3,052	3,052

Notes: Cell entries are OLS regression coefficients, with standard errors clustered by state reported in parentheses. The dependent variable in column 1 is a state-year measure of NEA membership density. In contrast, column 2 models the effect of a strong CB law on each state's annual percentage growth in NEA membership. *p<0.1, **p<0.05, ***p<0.01.

TABLE A5.3 **Effect of stronger labor laws on teachers unions' ability to raise dues and keep members**

	NEA state affiliate dues rate (1)	Overall state NEA membership density (2)	(3)
Agency fees	0.053**	-0.198	—
	(0.021)	(0.212)	
Unified	0.021	0.282***	0.240***
	(0.024)	(0.044)	(0.053)
Merged	-0.016	0.498***	0.498***
	(0.036)	(0.125)	(0.120)
Democratic control	0.002	0.074***	0.088***
	(0.009)	(0.026)	(0.026)
Mass liberalism	-0.122***	0.199**	0.184*
	(0.042)	(0.097)	(0.095)
Agency fees * dues	—	0.674**	—
		(0.304)	
Dues rate	—	-0.055	0.379**
		(0.148)	(0.180)
RTW law * dues	—	—	-0.593***
			(0.214)
RTW law	—	—	0.238**
			(0.116)
Constant	0.146***	0.859***	0.674***
	(0.018)	(0.051)	(0.073)
State fixed effects	Yes	Yes	Yes
Year fixed effects	Yes	Yes	Yes
R^2	0.89	0.78	0.75
Observations	2,183	2,183	2,183

Notes: Cell entries are OLS regression coefficients, with standard errors clustered by state in parentheses. The dependent variable in column 1 is the dues rate charged by each state NEA affiliate (measured as the percentage that that amount equates to using the average teacher salary in each member's state during a given year). The dependent variable in columns 2 and 3 is NEA membership density. The key independent variable of interest in column 2 is the interaction term Agency fees * dues. The positive and significant coefficient on this interaction term indicates that dues increases are associated with higher membership growth in states where teachers unions could collect agency fees from nonmembers. Similarly, the key independent variable in column 3 is the interaction term RTW law * dues. Here, however, the coefficient on the interaction term is negative and significant, indicating that when NEA state affiliates increased dues in RTW states, membership declined. *p<0.1, **p<0.05, ***p<0.01.

Teachers Unions in State Politics

I've been in the Legislature for 18 years and dealt with every kind of pressure group. But I had never seen anything like it when the teachers found out someone was going to fool around with their [pensions]. When I went to the post office, they were there. They were at church. When I went home, I couldn't find a parking place in my yard. Now that gets your attention![1]
— Alabama state legislator, 1972

There are only three things I fear: God, my redheaded wife, and the CTA.[2]
— California state legislator Charles Chapel

If you ask the average American why the National Rifle Association (NRA) is such a force in American politics, you will probably hear something about money. Political scientists know better.[3] It's not that money doesn't matter. But the NRA's influence isn't a product of buying legislators' votes. Rather, elected officials listen to the NRA because of its massive membership. Members are organized and easily mobilized on gun-related issues.[4]

What about the NRA's opposition? Former New York City mayor Michael Bloomberg, lead voice for the gun-control lobby, also has deep pockets. In fact, Bloomberg's group, Everytown for Gun Safety, often outspends the NRA.[5] A majority of Americans' views on guns are closer to Bloomberg's than the NRA's. Yet serious gun reform remains a pipe dream in the United States.

What makes the NRA so effective is precisely what makes Bloomberg and his allies politically weak. Compared to the NRA, Bloomberg's base of support is a mile wide and an inch deep. After each mass shooting, people convince themselves that this will be the event that changes everything. Americans tell pollsters they favor gun reform. The NRA remains out of touch with public sentiment. And nothing much changes, because everyone knows that—unlike their opponents—NRA members will put the gun issue at the center of their political universe. It motivates when and how they participate. NRA members will prioritize gun issues, even if it means discounting other policy concerns.[6]

In the remainder of the book, I argue that the movement to reform America's schools has followed a remarkably similar script. To understand how and why teachers unions have been so influential at thwarting the modern education-reform movement's broader policy goals and ambitions, it is helpful to begin with a brief historical overview of American education.

A Brief History of American Education

Nearly all advanced democracies make large investments in their elementary and secondary education systems. But as Terry Moe and Susan Wiborg explain, the most consequential investments have typically unfolded during two distinct time periods: an early era of *institutional formation*, which is then followed (usually many decades later) by an era of *performance-based* reform.[7]

In the United States, the era of institutional formation came at the turn of the twentieth century (1890–1930) when Progressive-Era reformers eliminated patronage politics from the public schools.[8] A century later, their handiwork remains visible. Political authority is vested primarily in state governments, but that authority is highly fragmented.[9] State boards of education and state superintendents—some elected, others appointed—operate alongside governors and state legislators. Local school districts also retain important powers, particularly when it comes to implementing federal and state policy. Districts are governed by school boards composed of amateur politicians who run for office in low-turnout, nonpartisan elections that are often held at odd times of the year when few voters are paying attention.[10]

The progressives succeeded in many ways. Their reforms eliminated political corruption from the schools. They also helped the United States become the twentieth century's global leader in high-school enrollment and graduation.[11] But the system the progressives left behind also had serious limitations. Schools were governed by a tangled web of different political authorities—a messy system that combined elements of both centralization and decentralization. The simple fact is that, although they were ambitious reformers for their day, the progressives had no reason to anticipate that the nation would one day desire an education system that could graduate each and every student from high school ready for college or a career.

That work would fall to a future group of reformers that, by 1983, had united under the banner of "the excellence movement." That year, the performance-based era in American education officially began when the federal government released *A Nation at Risk*—a report that shined an unflattering light on the state of academic achievement in America's high schools.[12]

Unlike many government reports that do little more than gather dust in an archive, this one mattered. It helped put school reform front and center on the nation's political agenda.[13] In prior decades, education poli-cymakers had focused more on issues related to racial integration and fed-eral school aid. Suddenly, politicians were focusing more narrowly on how to raise student academic achievement. The excellence movement cham-pioned school accountability and financial incentives to improve school performance. In this new era, performance would no longer be judged on traditional input-based measures like funding, staffing, and enrollments. Rather, schools would be evaluated based on measurable student learning outcomes.[14]

The excellence movement started out with some significant political ad-vantages. It was bipartisan and popular, and it made education reform more salient among the public.[15] Presidents, governors, and legislators all jumped on the reform bandwagon. The movement's proposed solutions—standards and accountability, performance incentives, and school choice—were, on the whole, appealing in an apple-pie sort of way to the average American.[16]

However, several obstacles stood in the way. First, these reformers were not starting with a blank slate. Instead, their proposals had to be made to fit within the existing system's institutional arrangements, the ones be-queathed by the progressives. For example, reformers had to ensure that their proposed changes meshed with the nation's tradition of local con-trol. They would also have to deal with fragmented political authority. To bring reform to scale, a variety of state and local officials—each with his or her own political incentives—would need to be persuaded to enact and implement policy change.

Throughout it all, vested interests—the teachers unions being the most important—could be counted on to push back against reforms that threat-ened to undo features of the existing education system that benefitted them. In practice, this reality meant that the most consequential reform proposals—those that called for schools and educators to be held meaningfully accountable for student learning—would be vigorously contested and resisted. Fragmentation and localism make blocking reform easier by multiplying the number of veto points where unions and other establishment interests can resist reformers' efforts to enact radical change.

Timing also favored the unions. As I have shown, they rose to power in the late 1960s and 1970s on the heels of government subsidization, giving them more than a decade's head start on the reformers in the excellence movement. Before the ink was dry on *A Nation at Risk*, teachers unions had mastered the complexities of education politics. For example, they learned how to use oddly timed, low-turnout school-board elections to help elect sympathetic board members.[17] Meanwhile, teachers unions had also become key players in state politics.

These advantages would prove pivotal in their effort to stave off the excellence movement's most threatening reform proposals. After all, most key education policies are made by elected officials in subnational governments. Even though reform hinges on the decisions of state and local officials, most research to date has not followed through on this insight. Preoccupied with studying organized interests in Washington, scholars have, as Sarah Anzia explains, "looked for influence in all the wrong places."[18] To identify how organized teacher interests influence American education, subnational governments (states and school districts) need to be the focus of our attention.

The remainder of this book does just that, focusing on the political activity and influence of teachers in subnational politics. This chapter begins by examining the role of organized teacher interests in state education politics, asking three specific questions:

(1) How politically active are teachers and their unions in state politics?
(2) Do teachers prioritize their occupational interests in state politics?
(3) Finally, are teachers unions able to use their clout in state politics to defeat education reforms they oppose, a dynamic Terry Moe labels "the politics of blocking"?

Organized Teacher Interests in State Politics

Buoyed by the subsidizing benefits of collective bargaining, America's teachers unions entered the 1980s having convinced once-disengaged teachers to

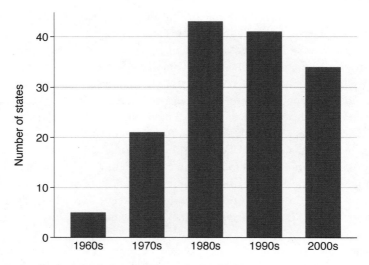

FIGURE 6.1 Number of states where teachers were rated the top pressure group, by decade

Notes: Author's analysis of several different surveys where elites (e.g., academics, legislators, statehouse insiders) rated the most-influential interest groups in their state.

Source: Data for the 1960s comes from Wayne L. Francis, *Legislative Issues in the Fifty States: A Comparative Analysis* (Chicago: Rand McNally, 1967). Data for the 1970s comes from Sarah McCally Morehouse, *State Politics, Parties, and Policy* (New York: Holt, Rinehart & Winston, 1981). Data for the 1980s and 2000s comes from Anthony J. Nownes, Clive S. Thomas, and Ronald J. Hrebenar, "Interest Groups in the States," in *Politics in the American States: A Comparative Analysis*, ed. Virginia Gray and Russell L. Hanson (Washington, DC: CQ Press, 2008): 98–126. Data for the 1990s comes from Clive Thomas and Ronald J. Hrebenar, "Interest Groups in the States," in *Politics in the American States: A Comparative Analysis*, 7th ed., ed. Virginia Gray, Russell L. Hanson, and Herbert Jacob (Washington, DC: CQ Press, 1999).

participate in politics. But to influence education policy, they would need to mobilize teachers in the less-glamorous arena of state politics and build clout in statehouses around the country. Figure 6.1 offers some evidence that teachers unions made significant gains in state politics beginning in the 1970s, but especially by the dawn of the 1980s. Whereas few state legislators and political insiders rated them influential in the 1960s, teachers unions' state affiliates emerged as the single most influential pressure group in over 80 percent of statehouses by the 1980s.

Why did state legislators begin to regard teachers as politically influential? One possibility is that unions were able to show them that teachers were becoming active in state elections. As underscored by the chapter epigraphs, elected officials are prone to pay more attention to interest groups that apply grassroots pressure. If teachers prioritize state politics and their unions are more likely to mobilize them to participate in state elections, the implications are profound and straightforward. State officials will have strong electoral incentives to heed teachers' policy preferences. In turn, teachers unions will be well-positioned to influence state education policymaking.

To evaluate whether teachers prioritize state politics, I examine how their political participation varies in relation to the types of offices that are being contested in a given election. A variety of idiosyncratic factors have led some states to hold their gubernatorial and/or state legislative elections separately from federal even-year elections. While the majority of states hold at least some state elections in November of even years, this is not the case in all states. Moreover, differences in electoral cycles have even varied over time within the same state. Kentucky, for example, held all of its state legislative elections in odd years prior to 1986.[19] Today, a handful of states still hold their state legislative elections in odd years.[20] Finally, differences in the length of legislators' terms, combined with variation in gubernatorial election cycles that date back to the timing of each state's constitution, mean that some states do not vote for any state offices during certain November even-year elections.

. To see whether variation in these patterns affects teachers' political participation, I return to the American National Election Study (ANES) used previously in chapter 3. Recall that the ANES provides a clean and consistent measure of Americans' political participation over half a century. Figure 6.2 shows the participation rates for teachers and non-teachers on ANES's five-item index depending on the types of state offices that were on the ballot during each survey year. Specifically, the figure reports the mean number of political activities that both teachers and non-teachers undertook in three different electoral environments: (1) elections where no state offices were on the ballot, (2) elections where either a gubernatorial or state legislative race was on the ballot, and finally (3) elections in which both state legislative seats and the governor's mansion were up for grabs.

As the figure shows, state officials would be foolish to overlook the policy preferences of their teacher constituents. Compared to other citizens, teachers more reliably prioritize state elections. Teacher participation surges when state offices are up for election. The average teacher, for example, undertakes one political act when state elections are on the ballot compared to just 0.63 acts in elections where only federal offices are at stake. These differences remain strong even when they are subjected to more elaborate statistical models (i.e., using state and year fixed effects to exploit changes in states' election cycles over time, as in the case of Kentucky).

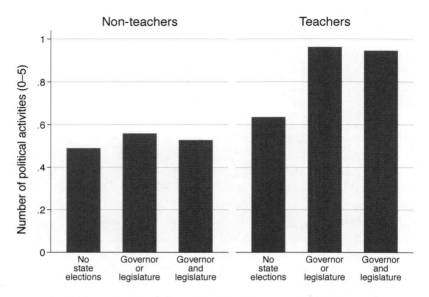

FIGURE 6.2 Teachers prioritize elections when state offices are on the ballot

Notes: Figure shows the average number of political activities (0–5) that teachers and non-teachers reported doing based on the state political offices that were on the ballot in their state during the year in which they were surveyed by the ANES.

Sources: Author's analysis of the ANES cumulative file (https://electionstudies.org/), paired with information on each state's electoral calendar taken from Carl Klarner's "State Partisan Balance Dataset" (https://dataverse.harvard.edu /dataset.xhtml?persistentId=hdl:1902.1/20403).

In other words, teachers living in the same state are more likely to participate in politics in elections with state-level races on the ballot.

What about non-teachers? As the left-hand side of the figure clearly shows, they are not especially motivated in gubernatorial or state legislative election years. Non-teacher participation rates remain similar across all three types of elections. And yet, the behavior of non-teachers reveals something interesting about *teachers*. Given their high levels of education, we should expect teachers to participate more reliably than non-teachers, regardless of what is on the ballot. Yet the data do not support this expectation.

On average, teachers performed 0.63 political acts when only federal offices were at stake. This result compares to 0.5 acts for non-teachers in a federal-only electoral context. These are minor differences. In other words, when elections involve choosing politicians who will make state education policy, teachers are highly active. But if only federal offices are at stake, teachers behave more like the average American, participating minimally. This finding fits nicely with what Terry Moe has shown regarding how teachers participate in school-board elections.[21] Just as occupational incentives are required to bring teachers to the polls in low-turnout school-board elections, teachers are strategically involved in state elections that have direct implications for education policymaking.

While the ANES data show that rank-and-file teachers get more involved in state elections, it would be useful to know whether teachers unions also ratchet up their involvement at such times. Since elected officials are more likely to be responsive to grassroots lobbying that is organized, we want to know whether the uptick in teacher participation observed in figure 6.2 is, in fact, the result of coordinated efforts by teachers unions. A good way to gauge whether unions are the driving force behind teachers' higher levels of participation in state politics is to revisit the ANES question from chapter 3 that asked respondents whether they received any political-recruitment requests from a nonparty (outside) group. Figure 6.3 displays respondents' answers to this political-recruitment question, separately for teachers and

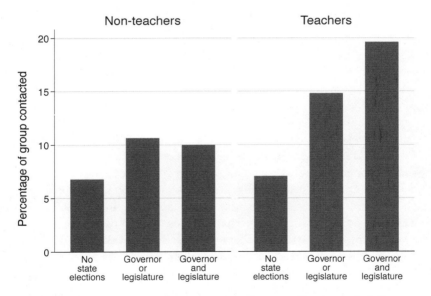

FIGURE 6.3 Teachers unions mobilize teachers more when state offices are on the ballot

Notes: Figure shows the percentage of teachers and non-teachers who reported being contacted and asked to participate in politics by a nonparty group, based on the state political offices that were on the ballot in their state during the year in which they were surveyed by the ANES.

Sources: Author's analysis of the ANES cumulative file (https://electionstudies.org/), paired with information on each state's electoral calendar taken from Carl Klarner's "State Partisan Balance Dataset" (https://dataverse.harvard.edu /dataset.xhtml?persistentId=hdl:1902.1/20403).

non-teachers, and broken out by each respondent's state-specific election environment.

The results confirm that union mobilization is indeed very likely behind the higher rates of teacher participation in state politics. As figure 6.3 shows, teachers are much more likely to report being contacted to participate by a nonparty group—presumably their own union—when governors and state legislators are running for office. For example, nearly 20 percent of teachers reported receiving a political-recruitment request when their state's electoral calendar was full, compared to just 7 percent who were asked when only federal offices were at stake. It is also worth noting that teachers reported no differences in the rate of recruitment requests sent by either the Democratic or Republican parties based on the offices that were up for election. Instead, the only uptick in teacher political recruitment occurs via nonparty groups in election cycles where state offices are on the ballot.

Teacher-Union Money in State Politics

Recruiting teachers to participate in politics requires money. Like all large membership groups, unions need revenue to finance their political operations. As we saw in chapter 5, favorable state labor laws are helpful. They allow unions to obtain dues revenue that can be used to fund various types of political activity. However, they have one major limitation. At the federal level, and in many states, unions and corporations are prohibited from using dues revenue to make contributions to candidates. For this reason, beginning in the 1970s, political action committees (PACs) became central to unions' electioneering efforts. PACs are segregated funds that allow interest groups to raise money that is specifically earmarked for candidate donations, or so-called hard-money contributions.

In recent years, a string of federal court decisions has given unions and corporations greater freedom to spend their general funds on political-issue advocacy.[22] Still, PACs remain an important tool of interest groups' electioneering efforts.[23] For one thing, unlike writing a check from their general treasury, union PAC dollars are raised from individual members. These dollars signal to elected officials that an interest group's members are committed to the cause. Organizations that garner little support from their rank-and-file members are more easily dismissed as "Astroturf" groups. For example, when the Washington Education Association

(WEA) asks its members to contribute to its PAC, the union tells a story of a legislator who told the union's lobbyist, "Fewer than 10,000 of your 75,000 members contribute to WEA-PAC. You don't represent the teachers. I don't have to listen to you."[24] In contrast, elected officials are more likely to perceive groups whose members reliably contribute as authentically powerful. Recall the story in chapter 1 about the former New Jersey State Senate president, Carmen Orechio, who refused to disappoint New Jersey's largest teachers union because it had provided him with real grassroots support, including a large PAC donation.[25]

On the whole, teachers unions have been highly successful at raising PAC revenue. Three specific features of union PAC operations show why teachers are primed to be influential in state electioneering. First, the unions raise and contribute far more money in state politics than do education reform groups. Second, teachers are strategic; they contribute disproportionately to state (rather than federal) elections. Third, many states have enacted payroll-deduction laws that make it relatively easy for teachers unions to solicit and raise PAC funds.

Data on teacher-union PAC giving was hard to come by before the first decade of the 2000s. However, in recent years, nonprofit organizations like the National Institute on Money in Politics have created databases that allow researchers to quantify the size and scope of teacher-union spending in state elections. Three studies—each from a different decade—reveal that teachers unions hold a consistent advantage over other education interests in state political giving. In one early study, Eugenia Toma and colleagues examined the proportion of PAC dollars contributed by teacher-unions state affiliates compared to all contributions from state education interests during the 1990s. She found that, on average, teachers unions accounted for more than 90 percent of all PAC contributions made by education-advocacy groups in the states.[26] A decade later, Terry Moe's analysis of teacher-union PAC giving confirmed that the 1990s were no fluke. Looking at two election cycles in the late aughts, Moe compared teachers unions' contributions in state politics with the contributions of all other interest groups. In most states, he found that teachers unions were ranked first or among the top handful of contributors. Even when Moe compared teachers unions to business interests, the unions came out on top in most states.[27]

By 2010, the emerging consensus was that teachers unions had lost power. The Great Recession emboldened conservative governors to challenge public-sector unions. And even in states where the Tea Party wasn't in power, unions had to contend with a Democratic president (Obama) whose signature education initiative induced states to adopt reforms that they opposed. Yet even in this challenging decade, teachers unions maintained their longstanding advantage in state political giving. Political scientists Sarah Reckhow and Leslie Finger examined how much various education groups contributed to state politics before (2000–2003) and after the Great Recession (2014–2017). Even in an era of labor retrenchment, they calculated that teachers unions accounted for 92 percent of all the contributions made by education-advocacy groups in state politics between 2014 and 2017—a mere 7-percentage-point decline compared to the pre–recession era period they examined.[28]

What has allowed teachers to maintain this advantage in state politics even in more challenging times? Perhaps teachers prioritize their unions' state political advocacy efforts.

To examine the factors that motivate teachers to contribute, I collected original data on NEA members' annual state and federal PAC donations between 1980 and 1998. These data were gleaned from a series of reports known as *Profiles of State Associations*, commissioned by the NEA and the National Council of State Education Associations. The *Profiles* data provide a unique opportunity to analyze teacher PAC giving. Prior studies of union PAC giving have been limited to looking at the aggregate amount that unions give to a specific candidate or cause. However, the *Profiles* data report the average dollar amount that members of each NEA state affiliate contributed to their union's PACs each year over the course of two decades. I examine two separate measures of teacher PAC giving: (1) the number of dollars (per member) that members of each NEA state affiliate contributed to the *NEA's federal PAC (NEA-PAC)*, and (2) the number of dollars (per member) that members contributed to their *state union's PAC*. This distinction is important because teachers' contributions to state PACs are spent on state political causes, whereas NEA-PAC funds are earmarked for federal elections.

Figure 6.4 displays the average per-member PAC contribution rates from 1980 to 1998. Over these two decades, teachers always contributed significantly more to their state union's PAC than to the NEA's federal PAC. On average, across all fifty state affiliates, NEA members contributed $5.81 each toward state political causes compared to a paltry $1.29 to federal ones. The importance of this difference cannot be overstated. State officials have strong incentives to pay attention to the policy preferences of teachers on education issues. State legislators know that teachers

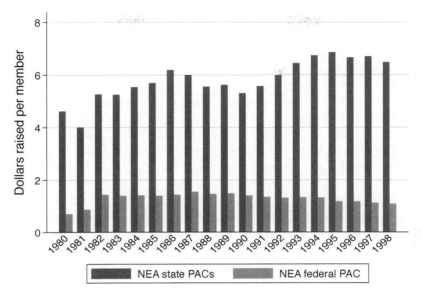

FIGURE 6.4 Teachers contribute more to their unions' state political efforts

Notes: Each bar shows the number of dollars raised per member by (1) the average NEA state affiliate's PAC and (2) the federal NEA-PAC, separately by year. All values are in 1998 dollars (inflation adjusted).

Source: Author's analysis of PAC contributions data reported by the NEA and the National Council of State Education Associations in a series entitled *Profiles of State Associations*, published annually between 1968 and 1998.

prioritize state political activity. Other citizens may pay more attention to what happens in Washington, but teachers keep their eyes (and their wallets) focused on state politics.

What makes teachers unions such successful fundraisers in state politics? On the one hand, teacher activism in state politics is partly a story of motivation. It is easier to convince teachers that their money is being put to good use when it stays close to home to defend their occupational interests in the state. However, there is another reason why the unions' state affiliates have been so effective at raising PAC funds. The answer takes us back, full circle, to the main argument of the book: the power of governmental subsidy.

The story begins in the 1970s. Back then, teachers unions were struggling — like all membership groups tend to do — to convince teachers to make separate PAC contributions on top of their membership dues. Low member-contribution rates sent precisely the wrong signal to elected officials. It suggested that teachers unions lacked authentic grassroots support and that, when push came to shove, teachers wouldn't support their union's political advocacy agenda.

Two NEA state affiliates—the Indiana State Teachers Association (ISTA) and the Alabama Education Association (AEA)—serve as telling examples. While both ISTA and AEA's state PACs would eventually become top fundraisers in their respective states by the 1980s, each union fell victim to the power of the collective-action problem in their early years. ISTA relied on a mere 1.5 percent of its membership to fund a little under half of the union's entire state PAC budget.[29] As for the AEA, in 1980, it asked each member to make a $5 contribution. Members responded by contributing, on average, just 90 cents each.

What could be done? Recall the story of NEA-PAC told in the prior chapter. At the national level, the NEA had struggled to raise money when it launched its federal PAC in 1970. However, the union quickly found success by turning to a solicitation procedure known as the *reverse checkoff*. Under the reverse checkoff, unions collect PAC contributions automatically unless a member affirmatively objects. In other words, unless a member opts out, their membership form automatically opts them in as a contributor. Their contribution is then made through their employer's payroll-deduction system and continues until such time as a member affirmatively dissents.

The process works like this. Suppose a teacher's union dues are $100 and the union's suggested PAC contribution is $20. Under the reverse-checkoff procedure, the union instructs the school district's payroll department to deduct $120 from each teacher-member's paycheck and forward it directly to the union. Although the teacher can get the $20 back, they have to take the additional step of opting out. Those steps could range from the simple (i.e., navigating some fine print) to the onerous (i.e., acquiring additional forms from the union and mailing them back to the union by a certain date). By design, the reverse checkoff makes it easier for the union's PAC to raise money because the *default* arrangement presumes that each member wants to contribute. Passivity, not activity, results in a contribution. No affirmative activity is necessary to donate. Anyone who has ever had a subscription service—especially that rarely used gym membership paid on an automatic credit card—can understand the power of inertia in human behavior.[30]

By 1980, the teachers unions' state affiliates held a key advantage. The Federal Election Commission (FEC) had dealt a blow to the NEA's federal PAC by ruling the reverse checkoff illegal.[31] However, at the subnational level, things evolved differently. A majority of states were in the midst of adopting new labor laws that encouraged teacher organizing. Many Democratic state legislators stood to gain political support if teachers unions grew more powerful. With clear incentives to strengthen the unions' political power, sympathetic legislators pushed for laws that gave teacher groups access to school districts' payroll-deduction systems. In doing so, these lawmakers reduced the costs for unions of raising PAC contributions. Moreover, almost no states followed the FEC's ruling against the reverse checkoff. Opt-out methods were permitted by most state campaign-finance laws—the laws that mattered most for the unions' state affiliates.[32]

Consider the case of Alabama and the AEA. Although the AEA secured a dues-checkoff law in 1973, in 1983 the Alabama legislature went even further to boost the AEA's fundraising capabilities. At the urging of the AEA's then-executive director Paul Hubbert, Alabama adopted a law requiring all school districts to automatically deduct PAC contributions from each AEA member's paycheck. According to Hubbert, "the legislation was the most important bill [the AEA] ever got passed."[33] But just how important could an obscure payroll-deduction law be for a liberal interest group in a politically conservative state like Alabama?

As figure 6.5 shows, the returns to the AEA's PAC "A-VOTE" were substantial. Teacher contributions spiked from $2 to $8 and then to nearly $10 per member by the end of the following decade. The spike came immediately after the reverse-checkoff law was implemented. Moreover, as the flat dashed line of the figure shows, AEA members were no more likely to donate to the NEA's *federal* PAC, NEA-PAC, after the 1983 payroll-deduction law took hold. Remember, the FEC prohibited the reverse-checkoff from being used for federal PAC contributions. Since few Alabama teachers took affirmative steps to donate, contributions made by Alabama teachers to NEA-PAC never exceeded $2 per AEA member. This finding is important because it shows that *state subsidies* directly strengthened teacher-union interest groups in *state politics*. It was not simply the case that teachers in Alabama became general political activists. Rather, their political activism was geared specifically toward state elections.

Though Alabama represents an especially pronounced case of subsidy, most legislatures simply left it to unions to work out contribution forms with their local school districts. Since most states had laws either permitting or requiring dues checkoff for public employees by 1980, and states also

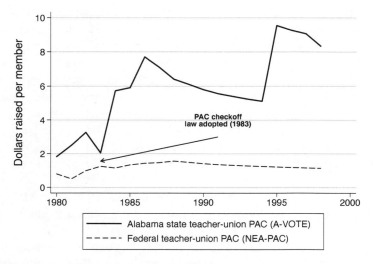

FIGURE 6.5 How government policies help teachers unions raise PAC funds

Notes: Solid line shows the number of dollars that AEA members contributed each year, on a per-member basis, to their union's state PAC (A-VOTE). Dashed line shows the average number of dollars these same AEA members contributed to the federal NEA-PAC. All values are in 1998 dollars (inflation adjusted).

Source: Author's analysis of PAC contributions data reported by the NEA and the National Council of State Education Associations in a series entitled *Profiles of State Associations*, published annually between 1968 and 1998.

had less-stringent campaign-finance laws than the FEC, teachers unions had a great deal of flexibility in identifying effective solicitation procedures for their state PACs. ISTA, the NEA's state affiliate in Indiana, took advantage of that flexibility by adopting an opt-out state solicitation system in the mid-1980s.[34] It helped boost per-member PAC contributions from $2 in the early 1980s to over $6 by 1988.

The payoff of using the reverse-checkoff procedure proved significant for teachers unions across the country. Using the *Profiles* data, I compared the PAC fundraising success of state affiliates using the reverse checkoff to affiliates that required members to affirmatively opt in when making contributions. Not surprisingly, there are large and statistically significant fundraising advantages for unions using an opt-out system with employer payroll deduction. Specifically, between 1980 and 1998, opt-out union affiliates raised an average of $8.40 per member for their state PAC compared to just $4.46 per member in states with opt-in procedures. These differences are robust to a more sophisticated analysis that uses changes over time in states' solicitation procedures to identify the causal effects of the reverse-checkoff system on teacher PAC giving. All told, the procedure is responsible for netting the average state teacher-union PAC an addition $2–3 dollars per member.

This increase is a significant boon for teachers unions' state electioneering efforts. A typical affiliate with fifty thousand members can count on an additional $100,000–$150,000 simply because the combination of payroll-deduction laws and the reverse checkoff make it cheaper and easier to keep more members contributing to their union's state PAC. Again, it is worth emphasizing that there is no difference in how much teachers donate to the NEA's federal PAC based on the type of solicitation procedure that a state affiliate uses. This finding suggests that favorable PAC checkoff policies are a *cause* of higher rates of teacher giving in state politics, not simply a consequence of teachers being more politically active in states with favorable checkoff policies.[35]

Teachers as an Issue Public in State Politics

If the first secret to succeeding in politics, as in life, is simply showing up, the evidence so far suggests that teachers are primed to be influential in state politics. Educators prioritize state elections. They donate disproportionately to their unions' state PACs, and they participate reliably in state elections. Showing up, however, is just a first step. For teachers to maximize their influence, they need to show state officials that they prioritize education issues.

The durability of the postwar Democratic Party–Labor coalition means that unionized teachers are more likely to identify as Democrats.[36] Since party identification remains the strongest predictor of citizens' voting behavior,[37] we might expect these teachers to reliably support Democrats in state politics. However, in recent years, neither political party has walked in lockstep with teachers unions. Prior to the election of Donald Trump, and especially during the Bush-Obama years, a growing number of Democrats broke ranks with teachers unions, supporting reforms that a majority of teachers oppose (e.g., teacher pay and evaluation reform, and the expansion of charter schools).[38] Although Republicans have long favored these reforms, their constituents are often quite apathetic about them. Therefore, Republicans have little electoral incentive to push for school reforms that teachers intensely oppose.

This shifting political terrain raises an important question about whether teachers unions are an effective *issue public* in state politics: a group of voters

TABLE 6.1 **State-candidate election experiment**

Name: Bill Glass	Name: Tom Jones
Party: Republican	Party: Democratic
Key Issue Positions	*Key Issue Positions*
• **Supports merit pay for teachers**	• **Opposes merit pay for teachers**
• Opposes a woman's right to choose	• Supports a woman's right to choose
• Supports faith-based organizations	• Opposes faith-based organizations
• Favors tax cuts for small business	• Opposes tax cuts for small business
• **Supports tying teacher tenure to student learning outcomes**	• **Opposes tying teacher tenure to student learning outcomes**
Biography	*Biography*
• Running for: State senate	• Running for: State senate
• Prior experience: State assembly	• Prior experience: State assembly
• Race/ethnicity: White	• Race/ethnicity: White
• Family: Married with children	• Family: Married with children

Notes: The experimental condition shown here is pro-union Democrat vs. anti-union Republican. Bold font denotes the issue positions that were varied across the four different experimental conditions.
Source: Author's original survey of Wisconsin public school teachers.

who are "more alert, attentive, interested and informed about a given issue."[39] Just like the NRA strives to ensure that its members "vote the gun issue," teachers unions face a somewhat similar challenge. State officials have little reason to respect teachers unions as a voting bloc if most teachers do not prioritize their occupational interests at the ballot box. For example, if teachers simply vote based on party labels, paying little or no specific attention to education issues, teachers unions stand to be less formidable. However, if elected officials know that teachers will rally behind their union and withhold their support from anti-union candidates in their own party, then state officials have strong incentives to listen to teachers and support them on education issues.

To determine whether teachers prioritize partisanship or occupational self-interest in state politics, I carried out an experiment on a large sample of Wisconsin teachers during the weeks leading up to the state's recall election in 2012.[40] In the survey, I included a question that presented teacher respondents with a hypothetical matchup between two candidates vying for a seat in the state legislature. One of the matchups that respondents saw is displayed in table 6.1.

After being shown a pair of competing candidates, teachers were then asked to briefly assess the candidates' issue positions and note which candidate, if either, they would support. Teachers were assigned to one of four possible experimental conditions. Each condition presented a different configuration of the candidates' issue positions. With one exception, the candidates were always shown holding policy positions that aligned with their party's orthodox stance on the issues. For example, the Republican candidate always supported tax cuts while the Democratic candidate was always shown opposing them. Similarly, the Republican candidate was always shown opposing abortion while the Democratic candidate was always pro-choice on abortion. The *only* issue positions that varied across each of the four experimental conditions were the candidates' *relative* positions on the teacher workforce policies (TWPs) having to do with pay and evaluation reform. Candidates who were shown supporting these TWP reforms oppose the union's position. In contrast, candidates who were shown opposing these TWP reforms are supportive of the union. The four different experimental conditions were as follows:

(1) Only the Republican candidate supports the union position:
    The Republican candidate opposes TWP reforms
    The Democratic candidate supports TWP reforms
(2) Both candidates oppose the union position:
    Both candidates support TWP reforms
(3) Both candidates support the union position:
    Both candidates oppose TWP reforms
(4) Only the Democratic candidate supports the union position:
    The Democratic candidate opposes TWP reforms
    The Republican candidate supports TWP·reforms

Because each teacher was randomly assigned to one of these four experimental treatment conditions (i.e., to a different pair of candidate vignettes), we can be certain that, on average, teachers assigned to each condition are identical on both observable and unobservable characteristics. The only difference in each condition is in the relative positions taken by the pair of candidates on TWP reforms, so any differences in who teachers say they will vote for can be directly attributed to the candidates' positions on merit pay and teacher evaluation.[41] My outcome of interest is the share of teachers in each of four different experimental conditions who said they would refuse to vote for their own party's candidate for the state senate.

What do teachers do when their partisan and occupational interests come into conflict? Figure 6.6 graphs the percentage of teachers in each of the four experimental conditions who said they would refuse to support their own party's candidate, with results shown separately for Republican and Democratic teachers in the sample.

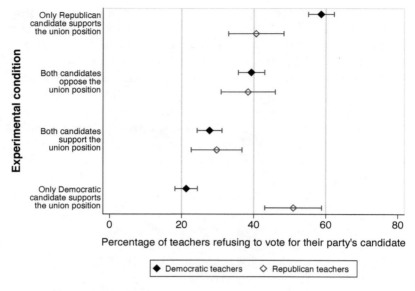

FIGURE 6.6 Many teachers prioritize occupation over party in state politics

Notes: Figure displays the percentage of teachers (in each of the four separate experimental conditions) who said they would *not* vote for their party's candidate for state legislature, separately by teacher's party.

Source: Author's original survey of Wisconsin public school teachers (discussed in the chapter 2 appendix).

Let's begin by examining the behavior of Democratic teachers who composed the majority of the Wisconsin sample. The group of teachers shown at the very bottom of the figure were forced to choose between a pro-union Democrat and an anti-union Republican candidate. Unsurprisingly, 80 percent of teachers who identified as Democrats indicated they would vote for the Democratic candidate in this scenario (only about 20 percent said they would defect).

But what happens if Democratic teachers are asked to choose between a pro-union Republican and an anti-union Democrat? These results are shown at the very top of the figure. Here we can begin to see that occupational interests will trump partisanship for teachers in state politics. Nearly 60 percent of Democratic teachers said they would *not* vote for their fellow Democrat when their party's candidate took anti-union positions on teacher pay and evaluation reform and the Republican candidate took a pro–teachers union stance. Where exactly do these disaffected Democratic teachers go? A quarter of them defect to support the pro-union Republican. Another 36 percent abstain from supporting either candidate.

What about Republican teachers? Although they composed a smaller share of the overall sample, they also prioritized occupation over party. Over 50 percent said they would *not* vote Republican when the GOP candidate took anti-union positions on pay and evaluation reform and the Democratic candidate ran on a pro-union platform (denoted by the hollow diamond at the bottom of figure 6.6). That said, the responses of Republican teachers in Wisconsin were more complicated. For example, 40 percent said they would abandon their party when forced to choose between a pro-union Republican and an anti-union Democrat; yet just 30 percent said they would jump ship when both parties' candidates took pro-union positions (the difference is not statistically significant). On the one hand, this finding suggests that there were probably a nontrivial number of Republican teachers in Wisconsin who supported Scott Walker's agenda and who favored merit pay and evaluation reform. Though we can't know for sure, it is plausible that this committed minority of Republicans abandoned the Republican candidate in the experiment when he was shown taking pro-union stances (such a circumstance would explain the higher support for the Republican candidate when both parties' candidates ran on a pro-union platform). Still, on the whole, the experiment provides clear evidence that a majority of teachers in both parties prioritize their occupational interests over their partisan allegiances in state politics. In sum, teachers easily meet the threshold for being an active and informed issue public in state politics, and they are a group that elected officials will need to take seriously when making state education policy.

Teachers Unions and the Politics of Blocking

So far we have seen that teachers unions hold some key advantages in state politics. First, they have significant financial resources. Dues money can both support inside lobbying activities and fund grassroots advocacy efforts. Teachers unions' large sums of state PAC revenue enable them to be major players in state electioneering. Finally, teachers unions are highly effective at mobilizing rank-and-file educators to participate in politics where it matters: state elections. In those state elections, teachers are willing to prioritize their occupational interests, punishing politicians who propose education reforms they oppose. Taken together, these advantages send a clear message to state officials: pursue policies that threaten teacher interests and you will be met with stiff political resistance.

Altogether, this state of affairs should create a basic equilibrium in state education politics—an equilibrium in which the status quo tends to prevail. Major reforms, especially ones that threaten teachers' occupational interests, will usually be kept at bay.

This equilibrium exists in part because of the unique political incentives facing state lawmakers in each party. For their part, Democrats in state government have obvious reasons not to antagonize teachers. They are an important component of the party's electoral coalition.[42] The resources that teachers unions can usually bring to bear in state politics are simply too valuable for most Democrats to resist. It would be a major gamble for them to alienate teachers when their unions can fund a primary opponent or withhold support in a general-election campaign. Here, it is important to emphasize that while teachers are firmly in the Democratic Party's electoral coalition, they are hardly captured by them.[43] For example, teachers unions have been known to punish powerful incumbent Democratic state officeholders that they had previously endorsed when those Democrats abandoned them on education issues.[44]

Republicans, on the other hand, are not so obviously constrained by teacher-union power. Yet neither do these Republicans have straightforward incentives to robustly champion controversial education reforms. Many GOP lawmakers, especially those representing affluent suburban constituents, have little reason to spend time and political capital on an issue that is not a priority for the majority of their constituents. As Frederick Hess has observed:

> While just 18% of the public gave American schools overall an A or a B, a sizable majority thought their own elementary and middle schools deserved those high grades. The implication is that most Americans, even those with school-age children, currently see education reform as time and money spent on other people's children. This makes school reform a losing vote for suburban legislators—one that they can take because it's the right thing to do, but that is calculated to burn rather than win political capital.[45]

Many Republicans then, have nothing to gain politically—and quite possibly something to lose—by alienating teacher constituents who might support them on other issues. As the candidate experiment in Wisconsin showed, Republican teachers will withhold their support from GOP candidates who throw their support behind teacher pay and evaluation reforms that teachers steadfastly oppose. Since these same Republican candidates know that they are unlikely to be supported by the low-income voters whose schools are most in need of reform, there is little upside for them to become reform crusaders. Politicians like Scott Walker and Chris Christie are somewhat atypical. Both men had presidential ambitions and came to power at a time when an extreme economic downturn made public employees in their states an easy scapegoat. During more normal times, the average GOP state official has little reason to directly antagonize teachers in pursuit of reforms about which their other constituents are mostly apathetic.

The exception to this general equilibrium was a rare moment of extraordinary political upheaval. The Great Recession and the willingness of President Obama to break with teachers on some issues opened a brief policy window where teachers unions were dealt some setbacks. The administration's Race to the Top (RttT) program, for example, encouraged states to reform TWPs in certain ways that unions opposed.[46] What is important to keep in mind, though, is that these moments are both unusual and temporary. When the Obama administration no longer had the power and authority to use federal grants and NCLB compliance waivers to push states to embrace TWP reforms, many states predictably reverted to the status quo. For example, several states retreated from the new teacher-evaluation systems they had adopted.[47] Others went through the motions, adopting watered-down evaluation systems that rarely identified and removed low-performing teachers.[48] Ironically, the Tea Party's antagonism of public-sector unions that began in 2010, combined with the unexpected election of Donald Trump, helped bring education politics back into equilibrium by 2018. During the 2020 primary election, for example, most of the Democratic Party's presidential contenders worked hard to assure teachers that they would not return the country to the school-reform agenda of the Obama era.[49]

Terry Moe has long argued that this basic equilibrium—in which the status quo almost always prevails—is kept in place because of the teachers unions' political power to block reform.[50] He argues that teachers unions will usually be able to block or dilute major education reforms they oppose for two simple reasons. First, because they are almost always *relatively* more powerful than their opponents in education politics. Second, because when they are playing defense, unions benefit from the fact that the American political system makes it far easier to block reforms than to enact and sustain them.

Moe's theory has much intuitive appeal. Clearly, the political incentives facing elected officials in state government render the pursuit of controversial reforms a risky exercise. The presence of multiple veto points provides numerous opportunities for unions to block reform. In turn, the politics of education reform comes to resemble the type of client politics described by political scientist James Q. Wilson in the early 1970s.[51] The costs of maintaining the policy status quo (e.g., traditional salary schedules or defined benefit pensions) are diffuse, passed on to all of society. Yet the benefits are mostly, if not entirely, accrued by education employees. Since reformers are trying to enact policy changes that would result in widely shared public benefits for many different education stakeholders, it is difficult for them to convince most citizens to pay the costs of supporting reform advocacy. It would, for example, require asking the average voter to behave like education employees, putting education issues at the center of their political universe. Since this is inherently unlikely to happen, it's no accident that the education reform movement has, over the years, had to rely heavily on policy entrepreneurs, like corporate philanthropists, to underwrite the costs of their political advocacy.[52]

While we've seen that teachers unions hold some major resource and participation advantages in state politics, what ultimately matters most is whether they can turn those advantages into policy influence on the issues they care about. In the remainder of the chapter, therefore, I assess whether teachers unions are more effective at blocking the reforms they oppose in states where they have more organizational resources to allocate to state politics.

Reforming States' Teacher Workforce Policies

It would be impossible to examine the politics of union blocking for every education-reform issue that has arisen since the excellence movement first began in the 1980s. Instead, I carry out a more focused case study that examines the teachers unions' efforts to block teacher workforce policy (TWP) reforms their members oppose. TWPs broadly refer to the policies that states use to recruit, deploy, reward, evaluate, and retain teachers. In what follows, I pay special attention to the education-reform movement's attempt to reform teacher pay and evaluation policies.

I examine TWPs for a variety of reasons. First, they are a substantively important education-policy issue. As noted in chapter 1, TWPs matter because research shows that improving the quality of the teacher workforce is a key driver of student achievement.[53] Second, even though standards and accountability were the initial focus of the excellence movement, many state policymakers have sought to reform their TWPs for quite some time. This fact is important because it means that unions and reformers have clashed over these issues in very different political climates. This variation is helpful on analytic grounds because it means that I can evaluate how effective unions have been at blocking TWP reforms in political environments that were both favorable and unfavorable to them (e.g., the Great Recession).

Finally, TWPs offer a tough test of the blocking hypothesis because proposals to reform teacher pay and evaluation tend to be relatively popular with the public. Support for teacher performance pay, for example, has always been much higher among the public than with teachers. In 1958, a Gallup poll asked whether teacher pay raises "should be based on teaching ability or the length of service." Seven out of ten Americans said ability.[54] This result was no fluke. In four separate Gallup polls conducted since 1970 (one in each decade), more Americans said they would prefer to see teachers paid based on their performance rather than for their experience and credentials alone.[55] Pay reform has also attracted support from politicians across the political spectrum. In the early 1980s, several state and national reports, including *A Nation at Risk*, argued that pay reform should be part of a bipartisan education-reform agenda. Thomas Toch summarized the state of the debate at the end of the 1980s:

> . . . The single-salary schedule was never attacked the way it has been since the onset of the excellence movement [1983]. The major reform reports all have urged its end, as have corporate leaders, the nation's governors, a congressional task force, the U.S. secretary of education, and the president. [In response] the NEA has waged its toughest campaign against attempts to pay and promote teachers on the basis of performance.[56]

In the intervening decades, teachers unions have mostly maintained their opposition to performance-based pay and their support for the traditional salary schedule that pays teachers based on their years of experience and education. This position makes good theoretical sense. In contrast to the aforementioned surveys showing strong public support for pay reform, most surveys of teachers show the opposite: teachers are more risk averse and thus tend to prefer fixed, as opposed to variable, compensation.[57] In 2019, for example, the NEA declared that "the single salary schedule is the most transparent and equitable system for compensating

education employees." Moreover, "[the NEA] opposes providing additional compensation to attract and/or retain education employees in hard
to recruit positions ... and further believes that merit pay or any other system of compensation based on an evaluation of an education employee's
performance are inappropriate."[58]

Altogether then, the debate over TWPs, and especially over retooling
the single-salary schedule, has been politically salient, attracted bipartisan
and public support, and been strongly opposed by a majority of teachers. All these dynamics have been true from the onset of the excellence
movement in the 1980s through today. Evidence that TWP reforms have
failed to gain traction in states where teachers unions are politically stronger would provide empirical support for the blocking hypothesis. After
all, if unions are able to block relatively *popular* education reform proposals, they will almost certainly be able to defeat ones that only have
narrow support. Finally, the fact that the education-reform movement
has enjoyed politically favorable periods for reforming TWPs (e.g., the
Great Recession; the Obama presidency) would seem to make this issue
a tough one for unions to successfully block, unless they really are pivotal
in state education politics. In what follows, I present two empirical case
studies: one on the decades-long quest by governors to reform their states'
teacher-pay policies, and one that explores the politics of reforming states'
TWPs during the Great Recession.

Unions, Governors, and Teacher-Pay Reform

Since the early 1980s, the nation's governors have shown a voracious ap-
petite for education reform. As political executives who represent broad
political constituencies, governors tend to see a clear linkage between
education quality and economic growth in their states. Over the last several decades, then, governors have frequently wrestled with the issue of
teacher pay. Traditional pay systems—those typically favored by unions
and teachers—rely on a standardized salary schedule that pays teachers
based on their years of service and formal educational credentials. While
standardization ensures fairness and equity, it also fails to recognize differences in performance, the difficulty of particular teaching assignments,
and the demand for certain skills and subject-matter expertise. Consequently, after the release of A Nation at Risk, governors in both political parties came to believe that the salary schedule was making it more

difficult to improve the quality of their states' teaching forces. Changing labor-market conditions, especially the fact that their states' most talented female graduates were no longer pushed into teaching careers, only heightened this concern.[59] In response, governors like Lamar Alexander (R-TN), Dick Thornburgh (R-PA), and Bob Graham (D-FL) all proposed to de-emphasize the single-salary schedule. Their proposals ranged from "career ladder" programs that would recognize and reward "master teachers" to performance-pay programs that would reward top-performing teachers with individual bonuses. As Thomas Toch explains, this flurry of pay-reform proposals was met with stiff resistance from teachers unions, especially state NEA affiliates, which resisted efforts to undo the single-salary schedule because of their concerns about pay equity and fairness. For example, Florida's NEA affiliate explained its opposition to Florida governor Bob Graham's performance-pay proposal by noting, "There is no objective means to establish who is a meritorious teacher, it's a flawed concept."[60]

How did gubernatorial efforts to reduce reliance on the traditional salary schedule pan out over the past four decades? To assess whether and where teachers unions were effective at blocking performance pay, I began by content-analyzing every gubernatorial state-of-the-state address (SOS) from 1980 to 2019 (1,535 speeches in total). As in the case of presidents making State of the Union addresses, governors use their SOS speeches to lay out their policy agendas for both the legislature and the public. Researchers have regularly used SOS speeches, therefore, to measure a governor's policy priorities and track his or her positions on specific issues.[61] These speeches are also useful because they help to reveal which policies are kept off a state's education agenda. This information provides a window into the political power of teachers unions to block the education reforms they most oppose by keeping such proposals off their state's policy agenda altogether.

After reading each SOS speech, I coded it for whether a governor in a given year called on the legislature to either enact teacher performance pay or expand an existing merit-pay program (1=yes; 0=no). Overall, I found that only a minority of governors proposed performance-pay reforms. However, support varied over time. In the 1980s, about one in ten governors proposed merit pay (13 percent); however, after the exuberance surrounding *A Nation at Risk* wore off and opposition from teachers unions ramped up, just one in twenty governors came out in favor of performance pay during the 1990s (5.9 percent). Support ratcheted back up in the first decades of the 2000s after the Great Recession put teachers unions on the political defensive. From 2000 to 2019, 13 percent of governors proposed performance-based pay in their SOS addresses. Gubernatorial support for performance pay also varied by party. I observe 154 Republican and 135 Democratic governors over these four decades. A little over 40 percent of Republicans proposed performance pay at least once during their tenure in office. In contrast, fewer than 15 percent of Democratic governors did so.

How much can the presence of more-powerful teachers unions explain the fact that performance pay was frequently kept off the political agenda? To assess the relationship between gubernatorial support for performance-pay reform and the strength of states' teachers unions, I estimate the probability that a governor proposed performance pay as a function of teachers unions' political resources in each state during the year preceding a governor's speech. I focus on two measures of the unions' political resources across states: (1) each NEA state affiliate's total revenue per teacher and (2) the number of dollars contributed per NEA member to each state affiliate's PAC. Finally, my analysis controls for other factors—apart from union strength in a governor's state—that are likely to influence whether governors propose performance pay in a given year. Specifically, I include controls for a governor's party, Democratic control of the state legislature, and the ideological liberalism of the state's electorate. Year fixed effects are also incorporated into the model since governors may, as a general matter, be more or less likely to propose teacher pay reform in certain years.

Figure 6.7 graphs the marginal effects of three different independent variables of interest on the likelihood that a governor proposed performance pay in their SOS speech. The marginal effects of the two variables shown in the upper half of the figure are my two state-level measures of teacher-union resources that can be allocated to state politics. As these two panels in the figure clearly show, as the political strength of unions in *state* politics increases, the likelihood that performance pay is proposed declines significantly. For example, governors from states where the average teacher-union affiliate had access to upwards of $1,000 in revenue per teacher and $10 per member in state PAC money have only a 5 percent probability of coming out in support of merit pay. In contrast, governors hailing from the weakest union states, where unions generate little revenue per teacher and few state PAC contributions, are three times more likely to propose performance pay. Remember, these effects are observed

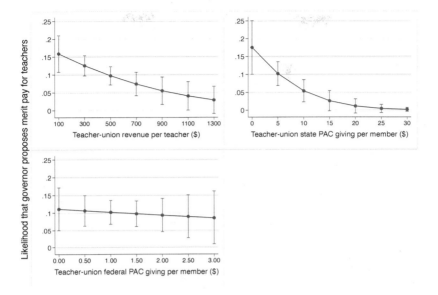

FIGURE 6.7 Governors are less likely to propose merit pay reforms when teachers unions have more resources to spend in state politics

Notes: Figure shows the marginal effects of three different measures of union strength across states on the likelihood that a governor proposes performance-based pay reform. Source: Author's analysis of gubernatorial state-of-the-state speeches from 1980 to 2019.

after accounting for a governor's party, the party that controls the legislature, and the ideology of the state electorate.

In the bottom left quadrant of the figure, I show the marginal effects of a "placebo" measure of teacher-union political power across states: the amount of *federal* NEA-PAC dollars contributed (per member) by teachers in each state. As the figure shows, unlike the other two state-level measures of union resources that can be allocated to state politics, this placebo measure is completely unrelated to a governor's propensity to propose merit pay in their state. While contributions to NEA-PAC capture the general level of political activism among teachers in each state, this measure cannot influence state education policymaking in any meaningful sense because federal PAC money is targeted to federal elections. In short, the results of this placebo test indicate that it is not the case that more politically active teachers in federal politics reduce the likelihood of performance pay getting on the agenda. Rather, we see that governors are specifically sensitive to the theoretically and politically relevant measures of teacher-union power in their states: the power that unions bring to bear in *state* politics.

In sum, teachers unions appear to be effective at keeping performance-based pay reforms that their members find threatening off their state's political agenda. Given the initial enthusiasm of governors toward TWPs in the aftermath of *A Nation at Risk*, combined with the public's willingness to endorse pay reform, these findings are a reminder that what often counts most in interest-group politics is not the size of a constituency but the priority, commitment, and organizational resources that a group is able to devote to its cause.

Unions, Reformers, and the Great Recession

I now turn to examine teacher-union influence in state education politics during the Great Recession. To do so, I draw on a 2011 survey of approximately two hundred policymakers and education insiders across all fifty states who were asked to assess the power and influence of teacher-union interest groups in their states.[62] The respondents ranged from governors' education-policy advisors, legislators serving on education committees, members of state boards of education, state superintendents, state charter-school associations, journalists covering the flagship state newspaper's education beat, and leaders of state education-advocacy organizations. Importantly, each state had a good cross section of these different types of respondents.

Above all, the timing of this survey makes it ideally suited to testing the hypothesis that teachers unions are effective at blocking state education reforms they oppose. Because respondents were asked to evaluate the influence of teachers unions in their state during the aftermath of the Great Recession—a period when unions were at their weakest—the survey arguably provides a lower bound of teacher-union power in state education policymaking.

Before turning to the set of questions pertaining to union influence in states' TWP reform debates during the Great Recession, it is worth highlighting some of the more general patterns of union influence in state education politics that respondents identified. The survey began by showing participants a list of different state education interest groups and asking them to rank order the "five most important entities" in their state "in terms of their influence in shaping education policy over the last three years" (i.e., 2008–2011).[63] Even in the immediate aftermath of the Great

Recession—a time when teachers unions were on the political defensive—most respondents still placed them among the most influential interest groups in their state: 25 percent rated unions the single most influential group, 22 percent put them second, and 20 percent rated them third. Only 33 percent of respondents ranked teachers unions outside of the top three and fewer than 15 percent failed to put them in their top five.

What about the unions' political competition? Although education-reform advocacy groups and the business community have been portrayed by some as more influential in education politics in recent years, neither group outgunned teachers unions. For example, just 7 percent of respondents ranked business groups the most influential entity in their state and just 14 percent put education reform advocacy groups on top. Although respondents often mentioned both business and reform groups as influential, many also left them out of their top five altogether. Whereas just 15 percent of respondents ranked unions outside of the top five groups in state education politics, half of all respondents failed to rank business and reform groups among the top five.

Even though state policymakers and education insiders regarded teachers unions as more influential than all other groups, this perception does not mean that teachers unions get everything they want in state education policymaking. Most respondents (64 percent) agreed that teachers unions in their state have to "compromise with policymakers to ensure that their preferred policies are enacted at the state level." Instead, respondents seemed to vouch more for the politics-of-blocking thesis. They said teachers unions were far more capable of *blocking* the education reforms they opposed than they were of setting the education agenda and winning all the reforms they favored. For example, respondents were asked whether they agreed or disagreed with the statement, "Teacher unions/teacher associations in my state are effective in warding off education-reform proposals with which they disagree." Most agreed. Specifically, 54 percent said teachers unions in their state were effective blockers whereas just 32 percent said they were not (the remainder were neutral). In contrast to the broad agreement that the unions are effective at blocking reforms they oppose, only 33 percent of respondents said that education policies in their state "often" or "always" reflect the teachers unions' own priorities. Instead, most respondents (50 percent) said education policies "sometimes" reflect union priorities.

What we really want to know, however, is whether state education policymakers say that teachers unions are more influential in states where

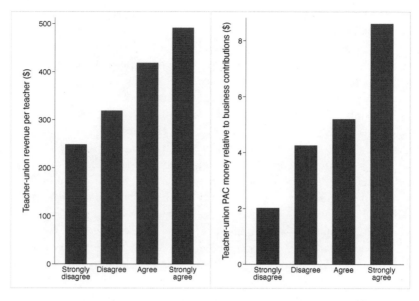

FIGURE 6.8 Well-resourced teachers unions deemed more effective at blocking reform

Notes: Figures show the breakdown in responses from nearly two hundred state education officials and education-policy insiders to the statement "Teacher unions/teacher associations in my state are effective in warding off education-reform proposals with which they disagree," in relation to two different measures of union resources in a respondent's state.

the unions have more resources to deploy in state politics. I used two different measures to capture variation in teachers unions' resource advantages across states in the years leading up to the survey in 2011: (1) each state NEA affiliate's total revenue per teacher and (2) the ratio of teacher-union to business contributions in state elections (the higher the ratio, the more money teachers unions contribute relative to business in a state). Figure 6.8 shows how these two union resources vary in relation to the answers that respondents gave when they were asked whether they agreed or disagreed that unions in their state were effective in warding off education-reform proposals with which they disagreed. As the figure shows, perceptions of union influence were strongly related to the level of resources that teachers unions could bring to bear in state politics. For example, respondents who strongly agreed that unions are capable of warding off reforms came from states where, on average, the unions raised $500 of revenue per teacher and contributed eight times more to state politics than business groups. In comparison, respondents who disagreed that unions were effective at blocking reform came from states where teachers unions raised a more modest $300 dollars of revenue per teacher and contributed four times more to state political causes than business groups.

It is important to recognize too that vested interests can wield political power in two very different ways. Although it is difficult to study, political scientists recognize that there are two faces of interest-group power.[64] With the first face, interest groups show their power directly when they defeat or visibly influence policy proposals during the legislative process. This form of power is easy to observe since scholars can, for example, compare legislators' votes or state policy adoptions and then analyze these policy outcomes in relation to interest groups' resources. But the second face of power is not so easily observed. With the second face of power, vested interests are powerful because they can keep issues off the government's agenda altogether. Unfortunately, these dynamics are rarely observable since there are few ways to measure nondecision points that are not reflected in official roll-call votes or formal signing statements. In rare instances, scholars find clever ways to observe the second face of power. Terry Moe, for example, used a natural experiment—Hurricane Katrina—to observe how elected officials responded when they were given the opportunity to redesign the New Orleans public school system free from the power of vested-interest opposition. Even in a traditionally "weak" union state like Louisiana, Moe deduced that teachers unions had used the second face of power to keep radical education reforms off the agenda in New Orleans prior to Katrina. After the storm and unburdened by union power, the same policymakers who had shown no interest in radical reform suddenly became cage-busting school reformers.[65]

Although it is difficult to study the second face of power, we cannot assess the politics of education without accounting for the possibility that unions are able to keep the policies they oppose off the agenda. With these dynamics in mind, I carried out two additional analyses using data from the survey gauging education policymakers' perceptions of teacher-union influence in their state during the Great Recession. Since my focus is on TWPs, I examined a series of questions that were posed to these respondents about their states' specific efforts to adopt Obama Race to the Top-inspired TWPs during the 2010–11 legislative session. Specifically, respondents were asked about the extent to which teachers unions in their state impacted policy outcomes for each of the following six TWP reform issues:

(1) **Merit pay.** Performance-based pay policies
(2) **Differential pay.** Other forms of differential pay (e.g., bonuses for teaching in high-need areas such as science or math, or in high-need schools)

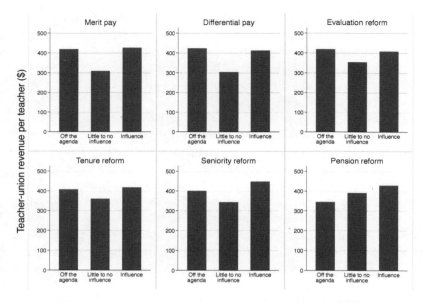

FIGURE 6.9 Well-resourced teachers unions deemed more influential in state education reform policymaking during the Great Recession

Notes: Figures show the breakdown in responses from nearly two hundred state education officials and education-policy insiders asked about the "extent to which teacher unions/teacher associations impacted policy outcomes for each issue during the latest legislative session," in relation to the amount of revenue (per teacher) raised by teachers unions in a respondent's state.

(3) *Evaluation reform.* Teacher-evaluation reform (e.g., inclusion of value-added measures in teacher evaluations)

(4) *Tenure reform.* Teacher-tenure reform (e.g., eliminating tenure or lengthening the time period before tenure is awarded)

(5) *Seniority reform.* "Last in, first out" policies in layoff decisions (e.g., examining teacher effectiveness in addition to or in place of seniority)

(6) *Pension reform.* Reforms related to teacher retirement benefits (e.g., changes in pension plans, increases in health insurance contributions, etc.)

In an approach similar to the one taken in figure 6.8, here I assess how respondents characterize their state union's ability to influence policymaking based on the size of the revenue (figure 6.9) and state campaign-contribution advantages (figure 6.10) that teachers held in their state. The only difference in these figures is that respondents were able to mention whether an issue was "kept off the agenda" in their state (consistent with the second face of power). If unions are more effective at blocking TWPs where they have large resource advantages, we should observe a U-shaped pattern in the graphs. Politically stronger unions should either be able to defeat TWPs by (1) keeping them off the agenda (left-hand bar) or (2) "influencing them a great deal" (right-hand bar). In contrast, the middle bar in each figure denotes the average level of union resources in the states where respondents said that teachers unions only exhibited limited influence over the issue. In other words, the middle bar in each figure represents states where respondents said teachers unions were *not* influential during the Great Recession.

Overall, most state policymakers and education insiders agreed that teachers unions were influential—either by keeping TWPs off the agenda in their state or by influencing how these policies were crafted in the

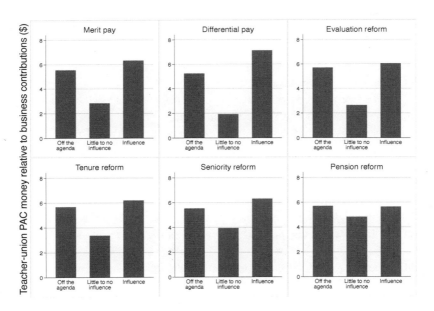

FIGURE 6.10 Teachers unions that donate more relative to business interests deemed more influential in state education-reform policymaking during the Great Recession

Notes: Figures show the breakdown in responses from nearly two hundred state education officials and education-policy insiders asked about the "extent to which teacher unions/teacher associations impacted policy outcomes for each issue during the latest legislative session," relative to the amount of campaign contributions that teachers unions gave to candidates for state office (relative to contributions from business groups) in a respondent's state.

Source: Data on teacher-union political giving relative to business groups is from Terry M. Moe, *Special Interest: Teachers Unions and America's Public Schools* (Washington, DC: Brookings Institution Press, 2011): 293–94.

legislative process. For example, respondents who said that teachers unions either (1) blocked merit-pay proposals from the agenda or (2) influenced those proposals in the legislative process in their state, came from states where (on average) the unions raised $400 of revenue per teacher and contributed six times more to state politics than business groups.

In contrast, where statehouse insiders reported that teachers unions were not influential, the unions almost always commanded significantly fewer resources in state politics. In sum, the policymakers and education insiders who had a front-row seat to the surge in reform policymaking that occurred during the Obama RttT era reported that teachers unions remained influential in shaping their state's school-reform agenda. Even in this period of political setback, then, by all accounts, teachers unions remained an important and influential actor in state education politics.

While some may object that the perception of policy influence is a less reliable measure than "first face of power" policy adoptions, this criticism is often not borne out. Take the salient issue of teacher-evaluation reform. In 2009, the nonpartisan National Council on Teacher Quality (NCTQ) reported that just fifteen states required teacher evaluations to include objective measures of student learning. By 2015, NCTQ reported that forty-three states had enacted such laws. On the surface this shift seems like a massive policy victory for education reformers and clear evidence that teachers unions had little to no influence in teacher evaluation policymaking. So why opt for a measure of policymakers' reports on influence over this more concrete measure of policy adoption? As it turns out, many of these teacher-evaluation laws—the majority in fact—did *nothing* to change the evaluation process for teachers in a meaningful way. For example, most of these laws did little to ensure that teachers whose students failed to improve from one year to the next received low evaluation ratings. In other words, simply looking at whether states made a change to their evaluation laws would tell us little about less-visible aspects of influence during the legislative sausage-making process—the aspects that would matter when it came to changing practices.

Still, those who prefer looking at specific policy-reform adoptions as the best way to assess union influence can be assured by the findings of two broader studies on the subject, including one of my own. During the pre-RttT era, Patrick Flavin and I demonstrated that union-opposed reforms on a variety of issues, not simply TWPs, were far less likely to pass in states where the teachers unions contribute more to state political causes.[66] Likewise, Leslie Finger has shown that in the post-RttT era, the adoption of

TWPs is constrained by both the first and second face of power.[67] Using an event-history framework, she too found that union resources matter. States where teachers unions have more resources are also states that have been less likely to adopt TWP reforms.

Conclusion

What gives organized teacher interests an edge in state education politics? The same thing that gives groups like the NRA an effective veto power over gun control. Teachers unions and their members strategically prioritize state elections. Teachers are more easily mobilized and willing to prioritize their occupational interests in these elections. Put simply, teachers are the consummate issue public in American education. Despite decades of bipartisan support for reforming many of the rules that govern the teaching profession (e.g., TWPs), most state officials most of the time have remained cautious about challenging teachers unions on these controversial occupational issues. Forty years after the onset of the performance-based era of American education, the status quo in teacher pay and evaluation remains largely intact today. Teachers unions have lost some battles along the way. Yet in a federal political system with multiple veto points, losses at the state level are rarely the last word. In the chapter that follows, we will see how organized teacher interests have a valuable political firewall in American education: lowly contested local-school-board elections.

CHAPTER SEVEN

Teachers Unions in Local Politics

The flaw in the pluralist heaven is that the heavenly chorus sings with a strong upper-class accent.[1] — E. E. Schattschneider, 1960

In recent years, political scientists have found considerable empirical support for Schattschneider's oft-cited claim. Wealthy elites tend to drown out the voices of ordinary Americans in national politics.[2] In contrast, politics in the nation's local school districts are often portrayed as far more democratic and egalitarian. According to one leading study, America's "ten thousand little democracies" are beacons of policy responsiveness juxtaposed against our national sea of political inequality. Not only are school boards responsive to the public, but they are mostly immune from the influence of teachers unions who, these authors conclude, do little to diminish the degree to which boards represent the public's interest.[3]

This perspective goes well beyond a single study. As Terry Moe once bemoaned, the scholarly literature tends to characterize school-board politics as pluralist affairs with "numerous groups competing for power."[4] Accordingly, a diverse cast of characters—from homeowners to parents, business interests, and educators—are all equally active and important stakeholders. In turn, board decision-making is shaped by good old-fashioned political competition.

Occasionally, scholars will highlight inequities. Yet the focus is usually on disparities in racial and ethnic representation,[5] the power of business,[6] or the influence of homeowners.[7] Some even claim that the power of business has grown stronger in recent years. An alliance of school-choice advocates and corporate philanthropists are, according to critics, using their newfound power to privatize public schools.[8] Even scholars who do not advance these particular claims still see a shift in the balance of power in local school politics, with reform groups gaining a greater foothold over unions and other establishment interests.[9]

Contrary to these assessments, this chapter marshals an array of evidence to show that school-board politics are neither pluralist nor dominated by a new breed of school reformers. Instead, consistent with previous chapters, I find that local school politics are dominated by organized teacher interests. Drawing on a variety of evidence, both nationally and within specific states, I find that teacher influence is both widespread and rooted in the advantage that teachers wield in electoral politics—an advantage that I have shown governments helped foster and maintain today.

Though I am hardly the first to suggest that teachers unions are active in school-board elections, our current understanding of the size, scope, and breadth of their influence remains limited. This chapter aims to fill in the bigger picture by answering three important questions:

(1) How well are teacher-union interests represented on school boards?
(2) Relative to other stakeholders, how active are teachers and their unions in local school politics?
(3) What are the effects of organized teacher political activism on school-board policymaking?

While there are surely exceptions from district to district, overall I find that public school teachers are (1) the single most active, (2) best represented, and (3) most influential constituency group in local education politics. In sum, the findings that emerge from this chapter point to a far different sort of heavenly chorus. Rather than Schattschneider's upper-class accent, in school-board politics, the chorus is overwhelmingly conducted by teacher-union interest groups, with rank-and-file educators carrying the tune.

Organized Teacher Interests in Local School Politics

Teachers unions attempt to shape the composition of school boards in two basic ways. First, they endorse candidates (of any stripe) that that they believe will be responsive to their members' interests. Second, they recruit sympathetic current and former educators to serve on school boards. A handful of studies have looked at both these dynamics.

The most influential set of studies were carried out by Terry Moe early in the first decade of the 2000s.[10] Drawing on a survey of some five hundred candidates in over 250 California school districts, Moe found that teachers unions were enormously successful at getting their favored candidates (76 percent of them) elected to office. He also found that union support was as powerful a factor as incumbency in predicting whether a candidate won.

Moe's studies offered two other valuable insights. First, he showed that occupational self-interest is at the heart of the unions' mobilization efforts. Teachers who lived outside the district where they taught were not especially likely to vote. But teachers who lived where they worked turned out anywhere from two to seven times more than other citizens. In other words, the ability of unions to mobilize teachers to elect sympathetic school-board members is driven by the rational self-interest of school employees—the chance for them to help elect their employer. Importantly, Moe then showed that union electioneering creates the conditions for more union-friendly boards. Winning candidates who were endorsed by the union held more pro-union attitudes than unendorsed candidates who lost. A few years later, Strunk and Grissom found even more direct evidence that union electioneering begets more union-friendly board policymaking. Returning to California, these authors showed that school boards that were composed of (1) more educators and (2) more union-endorsed members adopted more union-friendly contracts.[11] Taken together, these studies suggest that when unions are able to mold the composition of school boards in their favor, they are well-positioned to influence local education policy.

Of course, a lot has happened in education politics since these studies were carried out. The political environment facing teachers unions in the aftermath of the Great Recession has been characterized by greater austerity and significant labor retrenchment. Teachers unions have also faced greater competition from new education-reform advocacy groups. And, as discussed throughout the book, in 2018 unions were dealt a major financial blow with the Supreme Court's *Janus* decision. Some scholars have begun to speculate that these changes have collectively narrowed the power of teachers unions in school-board elections.[12]

Teachers Unions Remain Influential in School-Board Elections

As part of a separate research project, over a period of several years, I collected data on over four thousand union endorsements of school-board candidates in two states—California and Florida. Importantly, these data

TABLE 7.1 **Electoral outcomes for union-endorsed school-board candidates, by state**

Type of candidate	California (1995–2020)	Florida (2010–2020)
Endorsed (all)		
Won	71%	63%
Lost	29%	37%
Number of candidates	(4,075)	(361)
Unendorsed (all)		
Won	27%	32%
Lost	73%	68%
Number of candidates	(4,948)	(419)
Endorsed incumbents		
Won	87%	84%
Lost	13%	16%
Number of candidates	(1,586)	(117)
Unendorsed incumbents		
Won	52%	64%
Lost	48%	36%
Number of candidates	(1,186)	(89)
Endorsed challengers		
Won	61%	53%
Lost	39%	47%
Number of candidates	(2,489)	(244)
Unendorsed challengers		
Won	18%	23%
Lost	82%	77%
Number of candidates	(3,762)	(330)

Source: Information on union endorsements is from the author's original database. Election data for California comes from the California Elections Data Archive (CEDA). In Florida, election outcomes are made available by the Florida School Boards Association (FSBA).

include elections held before *and* after the Great Recession and *Janus*. The California data included contests held between 1995 and 2020 while the Florida data included elections from 2010 to 2020.

Table 7.1 displays the electoral outcomes for all the endorsed and un-endorsed candidates in my data set, separated by incumbency status and by state. The most striking feature of the table is how remarkably similar it looks to the one presented by Moe in his study from the first few years of the 2000s. Remember, Moe found that union-backed school-board candidates in California won 76 percent of the time, with challengers and incumbents winning 62 percent and 92 percent of their races respectively. In my own much-larger sample of over 2,300 California elections, shown here

in table 7.1, those numbers are 71 percent, 61 percent, and 87 percent—
nearly identical rates of union electioneering success.

On the other hand, California is known as a state where teachers unions
are especially strong, and we need to be careful about making a general
statement about union power based on their electioneering success there
alone. Florida provides an attractive comparison. It is also a large and
racially diverse state, but its labor laws have historically been less favorable to teachers unions. But as table 7.1 shows, even in Florida, where
we have good reasons to anticipate that unions won't make nearly as
strong a showing, they did surprisingly well: 63 percent of Florida candidates who received union support prevailed. Although Florida's teachers unions operate at a comparative disadvantage, they are remarkably
successful—overcoming the headwinds of both on-cycle elections and a
more-conservative electorate.

The results presented in table 7.1, however, are just a starting point. To
examine whether union influence in school-board elections has narrowed
in recent years, we need to assess their electioneering success over time.
Figure 7.1 presents some basic evidence on this score, showing how union-
backed candidates in California and Florida have fared over the past two
decades. The figure reveals a number of interesting patterns. First, contrary to the narrative of decline, union-endorsed candidates continue to
win office at impressive rates. Across twenty-five separate election cycles
in California, in not a single year do union-endorsed candidates win fewer
than 60 percent of their races. In Florida, union-backed candidates exceed
the 60 percent win threshold in all but two election cycles (narrowly missing with 56 percent and 59 percent win rates).

These descriptive data only scratch the surface of what this larger project revealed about the full extent of teacher-union power in school-board
elections today.[13] But two sets of findings from the study's more technical
analyses are most relevant here.

First, even after controlling for a variety of candidate- and election-
specific factors (e.g., incumbency, competitiveness), I found zero evidence
of a decline in union influence in school-board elections. To the contrary,
I estimate that the electoral benefit of receiving teacher-union support is
equivalent to the benefit of being the incumbent. What's more, in board
elections held during the Trump and *Janus* era (2016–2020), I found that
union endorsements were a *stronger* predictor of candidate victory than
was incumbency. Altogether, candidates who receive a union endorsement in a competitive school-board race continue to win about 70 percent
of the time.

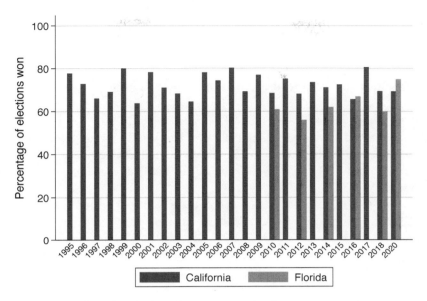

FIGURE 7.1 Teacher-union electioneering success over time, by state

Notes: Figure displays the percentage of competitive school-board elections won by union-endorsed candidates in each year, separately by state.

Source: Information on union endorsements is from the author's original database. Election data for California comes from the California Elections Data Archive (CEDA), available at https://csus-dspace.calstate.edu/handle/10211.3 /210187. In Florida, election outcomes are made available by the Florida School Boards Association (FSBA); see https://fsba.org/elections/.

Since interest groups are strategic, my study also probed whether teachers unions simply support candidates who are already more likely to win. However, I determined that union support exerts a strong independent effect on school-board election outcomes, increasing a candidate's likelihood of victory irrespective of candidate quality. By following the same candidates over time (and employing candidate fixed effects), I compared how candidates performed in races where they received union support relative to ones where they were not endorsed. This analysis revealed that union support matters: gaining an endorsement enabled losers to become winners and losing union support regularly cost incumbents their reelection. In other words, union-endorsed candidates are not more likely to win school-board elections simply because they are stronger candidates ex ante, but rather because union support confers an advantage that makes endorsed candidates more formidable on Election Day.

The bottom line is this: in strong and weaker union states alike, teachers unions continue to do exceedingly well in getting their endorsed candidates

elected, and they have done well even after Republican-led labor retrenchment efforts and *Janus*.

Teachers Are Well Represented on School Boards

Scholars of American education have also had very little to say about
school-board members' occupational backgrounds. For example, few studies have asked whether school employees can influence education policy
"from the inside," by helping elect more union-allied teacher members to
boards.[14]

The fact that so little attention has been paid to whether boards are
disproportionately composed of education employees is puzzling. In low-
turnout, nonpartisan elections, there are good reasons to think that a
politician's occupation will take on added salience. In his study of representation in the US Congress, for example, Barry Burden found that
members' personal attributes often influenced their in-office decision-
making.[15] School boards are clearly less partisan than Congress, so board
members may well lean even more on their own personal backgrounds
and experiences.

Public employees also have much stronger incentives (compared to the
marginal voter) to care about the single-purpose governments that hold
power and authority over their livelihoods.[16] Unsurprisingly, when school
employees have the opportunity to help elect their own employers, they
participate more reliably in school-board elections than their fellow citizens do.[17]

Outside of education, research has shown that interest groups can
secure more policy influence inside of government when they can help
install public officials who share their occupational interests. Anzia and
Moe, for example, find that employee representation on state pension
boards is associated with more union-friendly pension policy.[18] In a similar vein, Eric Hansen and colleagues found that state legislatures that are
composed of more former insurance professionals regulate the industry
more favorably.[19] Finally, Patricia Kirkland has shown that mayors with
backgrounds as business executives reduce redistributive spending and
boost investment in infrastructure.[20] These same insights may apply to
educators serving on school boards. In a clever study that leveraged the
order in which school-board candidates' names appeared on the ballot,
economists Ying Shi and John Singleton found that districts that elected

TABLE 7.2 **Educator representation on school boards (2001–2018)**

Study authors	Board sample	Sample size	Response rate	Survey year	Percentage of educators among respondents
Hartney and Hayes	California	372	31%	2018	25%
Ford and Ihrke	National	5,002	18%	2016	20%*
Hartney	National	460	21%	2015	32%
Hartney and Flavin	California	325	26%	2015	36%
Hartney and Wegrzyn	Indiana	410	26%	2013	23%
Hartney and Dunn-Pirio	Virginia	259	30%	2012	30%
Strunk	California	829	23%	2010	20%*
Hess and Meeks	National	900	24%	2009	27%
Nylander	National	1,926	28%	2009	25%
Grissom	California	677	61%	2006	17%*
Hess	National	827	41%	2001	13%*
Pooled results		11,987	30%		22%**

Notes: *Indicates that estimate is downward-biased due to survey using "retiree" as a stand-alone occupation.
**Denotes the weighted average (based on sample size).

one additional teacher board member increased teachers' salaries and authorized fewer charter schools.[21]

To investigate these dynamics further, I turned to several surveys of school-board members that I conducted between 2012 and 2018, along with a handful of surveys shared by other scholars. In total, I examined the responses of nearly twelve thousand board members across eleven surveys. Table 7.2 shows, across each survey, the percentage of school-board members who reported that they were current or former educators. The results are striking. If attorneys dominate Congress, then rank-and-file teachers punch far above their weight on the nation's school boards. Using a simple weighted average from all eleven surveys, I find that nearly a quarter (22 percent) of all school-board members are current or former educators.[22]

Of course, board members who responded to these surveys may be different than members who did not. If teacher board members were more likely to respond, these estimates may be inflated. To deal with this concern, I asked board members in two of my own surveys to report how many of their colleagues were current or former (retired) K–12 teachers. Using this approach, I estimate that the average California school board is made up of a full quarter of teachers. In fact, about one in ten boards in California were educator-majority boards. In my national sample, I estimate that 21 percent of board seats are held by teachers. The fact that we see such similar results from one survey to the next provides greater assurance that these estimates represent the true extent of teacher representation on boards. Teachers, it appears, hold anywhere from one-fifth to one-quarter of all US school-board seats.

Since, according to the Bureau of Labor Statistics (BLS), fewer than 6 percent of Americans work in elementary and secondary education, teachers are approximately 400 percent overrepresented on school boards relative to their share of the population.

Do these exceptionally high rates of descriptive representation enhance the power of teachers unions in education politics? There are certainly reasons to think so. Surveys of the mass public show that teachers and non-teachers hold considerably different views about education reform, especially on issues related to teacher policy.[23] Moreover, Shi and Singleton note that teacher board members are more likely to have been endorsed by the local teachers union. In theory, teachers unions should find it easier to advance their members' interests if teacher board members are more sympathetic to teachers unions' policy objectives.

To explore this possibility, I examined a national survey of nine hundred school-board members carried out by the National School Boards Association (NSBA) in 2009.[24] Board members were asked about their own personal characteristics (including their occupation) and their attitudes toward several education-reform proposals that were salient at the time of the survey.

Descriptively, teacher and non-teacher board members hold strikingly different attitudes about education policy. For example, while just 22 percent of teacher board members supported performance pay, nearly half of non-teacher board members (44 percent) thought "linking teacher pay to student performance" was important for boosting student achievement. Whereas 44 percent of teacher board members believed that across-the-board teacher pay raises are either "very important" or "extremely important," just 25 percent of non-teacher board members agreed. On collective bargaining, 42 percent of non-teachers said it was a barrier to their district undertaking needed reforms. In contrast, fewer than 30 percent of educator board members saw collective bargaining as problematic.

To explore these relationships more rigorously, I estimate two models predicting board members' support for two different types of education-reform policies. Specifically, I created both an index of union-favored education reforms and one of union-opposed reforms. The index of union-favored reforms included support for lowering class sizes and raising teacher pay across the board. Union-opposed reforms included support

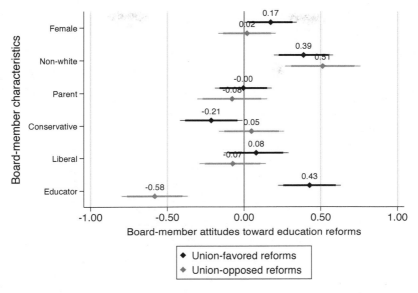

FIGURE 7.2 Predicting school-board members' support for different education reforms

Notes: Figure displays the regression coefficients (with 95 percent confidence intervals) where the dependent variables are board-member support for two types of education reform. Standard errors are clustered by board members' school districts.

for teacher performance pay, charter schools, and alternative certification programs like Teach for America (TFA).

I then (separately) regress board members' support for each reform index on an indicator for whether a board member is a current or former teacher along with several other demographic characteristics of each board member. Figure 7.2 displays the results.

Controlling for a host of other factors—including a board member's political ideology—I find that a board member's background as a K–12 educator stands apart; it is the *strongest* predictor of their preferred vision of education reform. Being a current or former educator reduces a board member's support for union-opposed reforms by half a standard deviation. Teacher board members are also more likely to support union-favored initiatives like reducing class size and adopting across-the-board pay raises. Specifically, being a current or former educator is associated with an increase of more than one third of a standard deviation in support for these union-favored policies. Notably, all the other demographic characteristics—ones that scholars have shown shape the behavior of more conventional politicians—are far weaker predictors of school-board

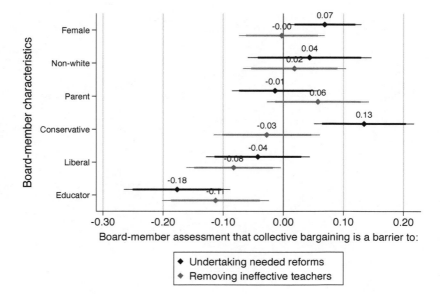

FIGURE 7.3 Predicting school-board members' beliefs that collective bargaining is a barrier

Notes: Figure displays the regression coefficients (with 95 percent confidence intervals) where the dependent variables are two questions asking board members whether collective bargaining is a barrier to their district (1) undertaking needed reforms and (2) removing ineffective teachers. Standard errors are clustered by board members' school districts.

members' policy views. The only other factor that has an independent and powerful effect on board members' attitudes are whether that board member is a racial minority. Nonwhite school-board members were more supportive of both the union-favored and union-opposed policy reforms than were white board members.

I next examined board members' attitudes about collective bargaining. Respondents were first asked whether bargaining poses a barrier to their district enacting needed education reforms. Second, I evaluate how board members respond when asked whether bargaining acts as a barrier to removing ineffective teachers in their district. The models here are the same as before, with one small difference. In these two regressions, I include state fixed effects to account for the fact that states have different collective-bargaining regimes and board members' answers are likely to be sensitive to these differences.

Figure 7.3 displays the results of these two regressions. Even after accounting for a board member's political ideology, current and former educators are much less likely to see collective bargaining in a negative light.

Specifically, teacher board members were 11 percent less likely to say that bargaining created a barrier to removing ineffective teachers in their district, and 18 percent less likely to say that bargaining made it more difficult to enact needed reforms.

Taken together, the results of these four analyses point in a uniform direction. Teacher representation on school boards matters a great deal. By electing more teachers to boards, unions are more likely to find themselves negotiating with a school board that is composed of members who are more sympathetic to their policy agenda. With nearly a quarter of the nation's ninety thousand school-board seats held by educators, this descriptive-substantive representation boost is both a consequential and overlooked factor that shapes the balance of power in local school politics.

Teachers Unions Are the Most Active Group in Local School Politics

Teachers unions are clearly capable of electioneering the composition of school boards more in their favor. However, interest groups cannot rely solely on showing up on Election Day to maintain their influence. Instead, groups need to remain active and engaged in between elections. Interest groups that can organize and regularly mobilize their supporters to contact and lobby their elected officials are less likely to be taken for granted. *Consistent* activism helps remind elected officials that an interest group represents an important constituency—one that will show up at the next election and judge their record as incumbents accordingly.

It is important therefore to consider how consistently active organized teacher interests are in local school politics. In particular, we need to know how active teacher groups are *relative* to their potential competition: other education stakeholders. Remember, if school-board politics is characterized by pluralism (as much of the literature contends), then a variety of different groups should be active and organized in local school politics.

To assess how teachers unions stack up against their competition, I returned to six of the surveys presented earlier in the chapter. The six surveys I revisited all asked school-board members a similar set of questions about the level of political activity undertaken by different groups in their district. For example, in my own surveys of school-board members in California, Indiana, Virginia, and nationally, I asked board members the following question: *From attending board meetings to participating in school*

TABLE 7.3 **School-board member ratings of different stakeholders' levels of political activism in local school politics**

Study authors	Survey year	Board sample	Teachers unions	Parent groups	Business community
Hartney and Hayes	2018	California	1st	2nd	3rd
Hartney	2015	National	1st	2nd	3rd
Hartney and Wegrzyn	2013	Indiana	1st	2nd	3rd
Hartney and Dunn-Pirio	2012	Virginia	1st (tie)	1st (tie)	3rd
Hess	2002	National	1st	2nd	3rd
Moe	2001	California	1st	2nd	3rd

Source: Author's analysis of the school-board member surveys reported in table 7.2

elections, many different groups are involved in local education politics. Generally speaking, how politically active are each of the following groups in your school district? Board members were then shown a list of different groups—including business groups, parent groups, teachers unions/associations, civil rights organizations, and religious groups—after which they were asked to rate each group's level of activism.

The results are displayed in table 7.3. To keep things as simple as possible, I report only the top-line ranking of the three most active groups that board members identified in each survey. Across all six surveys, I find that school-board members consistently rated teachers unions as the most active group in local school politics. Irrespective of the year, question asked, and geography of the sample (e.g., national vs. state, RTW vs. CB state), the results point in a consistent and uniform direction: board members overwhelmingly classify teachers as the most politically active group in their district. More importantly, there is no evidence of union decline in the aftermath of the Great Recession. Board members reported that teacher groups were just as active in 2015 and 2018 as they did when Moe and Hess asked them to evaluate the political activity of various stakeholders in their districts in the early aughts.

Notably, only one other group comes close to demonstrating the same level of political activism recorded by teachers: parents. They manage to "tie" teacher groups in Virginia. However, these patterns may say more about the strength of organized teacher interests than they do about the prowess of parents in the commonwealth. As I discuss more in a detailed case study later in the chapter, teachers in Virginia have long been regarded as politically weak and ineffectual, owing to the fact that the commonwealth banned collective bargaining in the late 1970s. Thus, the fact that school-board members in Virginia report that teacher groups hold their own against parents in this comparatively weaker union state, is, in and of itself, a noteworthy accomplishment.

Teachers Participate More in Local Politics than Other Stakeholders

The evidence so far is consistent. Teachers are well represented on school boards and their unions hold a sharp participation advantage (relative to other groups) in local school politics. But what about the behavior of individual teachers? Are they also more active than other citizens who have vested interests in the local public schools (e.g., parents, homeowners)? This question is theoretically important and politically relevant because teachers unions should be in a stronger position to influence policy if they can mobilize educators to participate in local politics.

For evidence on this question, I turn to data from the 2017 Current Population Survey (CPS) Volunteering and Civic Life Supplement.[25] The CPS is useful here in several respects.

First, it asks very detailed questions about respondents' political and civic engagement. I focus on six different survey items. The first two pertain specifically to local politics. Respondents were asked whether they had (1) "voted in their last local elections, such as for mayor or school board" and (2) whether they had "attended a public meeting, such as a zoning or school board meeting, to discuss a local issue." The next pair of questions were about political participation more generally. The first item asked respondents whether, in the past year, "they had contacted or visited a public official—at any level of government—to express their opinion." The second item asked whether they had made a donation in excess of $25 to "a political organization, party, or campaign" during that same time period. The final pair of questions asked about nonpolitical forms of civic engagement. First, respondents were asked a repeated series of questions about the types of organizations they had volunteered for over the past year. I used respondents' answers to classify whether they had volunteered for any type of nonpolitical organization. Finally, I looked specifically at whether respondents said they volunteered for a "social or community service organization."

The second major advantage of the CPS is that it includes detailed industry and occupational classifications for each respondent. This information is useful in two key respects. First, it allows me to compare the

TABLE 7.4 **Participation in local politics by various education stakeholders**

	Local politics		General politics		Nonpolitical civic engagement	
	Vote in last local election	Attend local political meeting	Contribute money to a candidate/ cause	Contact an elected official	Volunteer (any group)	Volunteer (service group)
Teachers (public)	82%	41%	16%	29%	73%	30%
Parents	58%	17%	12%	17%	77%	31%
Homeowners	74%	21%	20%	24%	69%	40%
Teachers (private)	77%	20%	8%	22%	80%	25%

Notes: Each entry shows the percentage of each stakeholder group reporting they engaged in each activity. Because teachers are highly educated, only respondents with (at least) a four-year college degree are included. Sample sizes vary depending on the survey item but include approximately 680 public school teachers; 900 parents; 14,000 homeowners; and 300 private school teachers. Parent and homeowner categories exclude teacher-parents and teacher-homeowners.
Source: Author's analysis of the 2017 Current Population Survey Volunteering and Civic Life Supplement. See United States Bureau of the Census, United States Department of Labor, Bureau of Labor Statistics, and Corporation for National and Community Service, *Current Population Survey, September 2017: Volunteering and Civic Life Supplement (ICPSR 37303)* (Ann Arbor, MI: Inter-University Consortium for Political and Social Research, 2019), https://doi.org/10.3886/ICPSR37303.v2

political participation of teachers to other groups of citizens who are usually regarded as active and influential in local school politics: parents and homeowners. I also compare *public* school teachers to their *private* school counterparts. The comparison is revealing because it enables us to see whether public school teachers are uniquely motivated to participate more in local politics because they are employed by local governments and far more likely to be unionized.

Finally, and most importantly, I restrict my analysis to CPS respondents who have at least a four-year college degree. This restriction is important because teachers, on average, have higher levels of education than non-teachers, so this adjustment in the sample ensures more apples-to-apples comparisons between teachers and non-teacher homeowners and parents.

Table 7.4 shows the results, focusing on the mean participation rates of each group separately by type of activity.

The first two columns show how involved respondents in each group were in local politics. As expected, I find that public school teachers are especially engaged in local politics. Since the sample only includes highly educated respondents, we might expect homeowners and parents to hold their own. They do not. Whereas 41 percent of public school teachers said that they attended a local political meeting, a mere 17 percent of parents and 21 percent of homeowners indicated they had done so. Turning to voting, over 80 percent of public school teachers reported turning out for their last local election. Yet fewer than 60 percent of parents said they turned out to vote. In other words, public school teachers enjoy a 20-plus-percentage-point turnout advantage over parents in local elections. And while homeowners and private school teachers reported more favorable turnout rates, they still trailed public school teachers.[26]

The public school teacher participation advantage narrows when we turn from local to general political participation. Whereas public school teachers are somewhat more likely than other groups to contact public officials, they are no more likely (and in one case less likely) to make contributions in excess of $25 to candidates or political causes. That said, public school teachers are still highly engaged—for example, they are twice as likely to make a political donation than are private school teachers.

The final two columns display respondents' reported participation in nonpolitical forms of civic life. These results are important for what they do not show. There is no evidence that public school teachers are more likely to get involved with nonpolitical organizations or causes; nor are public school teachers any more likely to volunteer for community-service organizations. For the most part they are just as involved as—no more and no less than—parents, homeowners, and private school educators. In short, we can conclude that teachers are not more engaged in local politics because they are more civically minded as a general matter. The more plausible explanation, consistent with Terry Moe's analysis of patterns of teacher voting in school-board elections, is that teachers increase their levels of political engagement when their occupational interests are on the line. Overall, the CPS data indicate that public school teachers are active in all forms of politics, but they are especially active in local politics. And they are more active in local politics than other stakeholders who also have a vested interest in the public schools.

The Bigger Picture

Political inequality reigns in local school politics. But it is not the sort of inequality that critics of corporate philanthropy, charter-advocacy groups, and the business sector point to when they raise concerns about democracy in education politics. Instead, the analysis up to this point has revealed that teachers unions hold several distinct advantages in local education politics. In brief, my findings underscore how the dominance

of organized teacher interests challenges pluralist characterizations of
school-board politics.

—First, union-endorsed school-board candidates win the overwhelming majority of contested school-board elections. Even after *Janus*, they win 70 percent
of the time.

—Second, teachers are overrepresented on school boards. Consistent with prior
research that shows teachers and non-teachers hold different views about education policy, the large fraction of teachers who serve on school boards bring
more teacher-union-friendly views to their board work. Indeed, a school-board
member's teaching background is the most significant predictor of how they
approach policymaking.

—Third, the majority of school-board members say teachers unions are the
most politically active group in district politics. More than any other group,
teachers unions are the most active stakeholder in local school elections. Indeed, the only other group that ever comes close to matching the intensity of
teachers unions are parent groups.

—Fourth, public school teachers participate far more in local politics than other
similarly educated non-teacher citizens. Public school teachers vote more consistently in local school-board elections and more often attend board meetings
than college-educated parents, homeowners, and private school teachers.

In sum, the bigger-picture landscape of interest-group competition in school-
board politics is—well—that there isn't much competition. Organized
teacher interests are the most consistently active group, and they are often unopposed. These findings suggest that politically active teachers are
well positioned to influence the direction of local education policy. But
that expectation must be tested and demonstrated, not merely asserted.
Consequently, in the remainder of the chapter, I undertake three separate
studies that explicitly test for the effects of local teacher political activism
on school-board policymaking.

The Effects of Teacher Political Activism on Local School Policy

Quantifying the effects of teacher political activism on school-board policymaking is a daunting challenge. With well over thirteen thousand school

districts, there are tradeoffs involved in choosing which districts to analyze. Also, unlike members of Congress or state legislatures, school boards rarely vote on the same bills, making cross-district comparisons difficult. Finally, researchers cannot randomly assign different levels of teacher political activism to districts. Therefore, creative approaches, including triangulating from different studies, will be needed to evaluate the connection between teacher political activism and policy influence.

To deal with these many complications, I pursue three separate analyses. My first study focuses on school districts in Washington State. It examines how teacher participation in school-board elections and teacher PAC giving enhance their unions' ability to negotiate higher teacher salaries. The fact that nearly all districts in Washington bargain collectively makes this single-state study useful. It shows how variation in teacher political activism provides a complementary source of power for teachers to influence policy alongside what happens at the bargaining table.

My second study draws on a survey experiment embedded in two of the school-board surveys introduced earlier in the chapter (Indiana and the 2015 national sample). The experiment provides evidence that, in school districts where unions are politically active and boards are composed of more educator members, school-board members are more responsive to teachers than to parents.

In a third study, I examine the relationship between teacher political activism and union efforts to protect teachers' continuing contracts (tenure) in Virginia. Evidence that organized teacher interests can be influential in Virginia—a state where teacher bargaining was illegal up until 2021—shows that teachers are far from helpless in the absence of strong labor laws.

Without further elaboration, I present each study in turn.

Teacher Political Activism and Teacher Pay in Washington

Evaluating whether teacher political activism influences school-board policymaking requires two types of data. First, I need measures of teacher participation in local school politics. Then, I need a district-level policy (outcome variable) that teachers care about. Fortunately, both types of data can be found in Washington state.

I measure teacher political participation in two different ways. First, I estimate teacher turnout in Washington school-board elections. More specifically, I estimate the *turnout advantage* that teachers hold over non-teachers in these elections. Since Washington holds its school-board elections in November of odd years, I focus on turnout in the November 2011 election. This election was an otherwise unremarkable one with little else on the ballot beyond a handful of statewide initiatives that were neither education-related nor controversial. This point is important because it means that turnout measures voter interest and activism in *local* school politics, untainted by unrelated national or state issues.

To estimate teachers' turnout advantage, I began with a directory of school employees provided by the state's Department of Education. I then matched each teacher to the state's voter file, a separate database that includes each registered voter's turnout history. Using each teacher's full name, date of birth, and place of employment, I located 51,211 teachers in the voter file, for a successful match rate of just under 90 percent.[27]

I next identified the school district of residence for every registered voter. After identifying each registered voter's school district and whether they voted, I aggregated turnout to the district level, separately for teachers and non-teachers. After subtracting non-teacher turnout from teacher turnout in each district, I am left with a measure of the *teacher-turnout advantage* for 293 of Washington's 295 school districts.[28] This measure takes a positive value in districts where teachers voted in school-board elections at higher rates than non-teachers.[29] There is significant variation in the turnout advantage that teachers hold, ranging from a low of -3.4 in Omak School District to a high of 29.2 in Wapato School District (mean = 14.1, SD = 6). By way of comparison, teachers in two well-known districts, Seattle and Spokane, held turnout advantages of 17.5 and 17.0, respectively.

Next, I incorporate a second measure of teacher political participation, one introduced earlier in chapter 3: the percentage of teachers in each district who contributed to the Washington Education Association's political action committee (WEA-PAC). Since this money can be and is often spent in local politics, including in school-board races, it provides a nice complement to the turnout-advantage measure. In all the analyses that follow, I include both these measures of teacher political activism.

For my policy outcome of interest, I examine differences in teacher pay across districts. Salaries are one of the few comparable policy outcomes on which teachers and their unions have uniform preferences. Whereas teachers have strong incentives to prefer higher salaries, non-teachers likely hold more ambivalent views about teacher pay, especially since salary increases are funded by taxes. In short, if local education policy is influenced by who holds power in local school politics, the generosity of teacher pay provides an excellent outcome to test whether teachers can use politics to move district policy in their preferred direction.

Unfortunately, a naive regression analysis explaining variation in average teacher salaries across districts would tell us very little. Historically, the state government has set baseline teacher salaries in Washington. However, there is one component of teacher pay in Washington—known as Time, Responsibility, Incentive (TRI) pay—that has historically been funded directly by local school districts.[30] TRI pay captures the independent efforts made by local school boards to enhance the baseline teacher salaries set by the state. Not surprisingly, TRI pay varies significantly across districts. In 2013, average TRI pay ranged from $0 (in several districts) to a high of $21,056 in the Everett school district in Snohomish County (part of the Seattle-Tacoma-Bellevue metropolitan region).

I model variation in TRI pay in 2013 as a function of each district's teacher-turnout advantage *and* the share of each district's teachers contributing to WEA-PAC in 2011. Several relevant control variables are also included in the model. Specifically, I include a measure of district size (enrollment in thousands) and wealth (median family income), since larger and wealthier districts tend to offer more TRI pay.[31] I also use the comparable wage index (CWI) to control for local labor-market conditions, which accounts for the fact that districts in regions with a higher cost of living may need to offer higher salaries.[32] I likewise include a district-level measure of unemployment to account for local labor-market conditions more generally.

To account for the fact that variation in TRI pay is prone to be related to voters' tastes and preferences for higher/lower teacher salaries, I include the percent of the vote share earned by President Obama in 2012 in each school district's parent county. My expectation is that more liberal (Democratic) districts will offer more generous TRI pay. Additionally, I include a measure of the percent of nonwhite students in each district since the willingness of voters to spend more on their local schools may be influenced by the racial composition of those schools. Finally, to ensure fair comparisons across school districts on my measure of turnout advantage, I make two minor restrictions to the sample. First, I confine my analyses to non-rural districts, which serve the vast majority of students.[33] Second, I eliminate a single district that did not have any board seats up for election in 2011.

Table 7.5 presents the results of four separate regression models. The model in column 1 shows the results of regressing TRI pay on my two measures of teacher political activism. In this first model, the coefficient on the teacher-turnout advantage variable is both positive and statistically

TABLE 7.5 **Relationship between teacher pay and teacher political activism in Washington State**

	Teacher pay (dollars)		Superintendent pay (dollars)	
	Baseline pay (1)	Pay growth (2)	Baseline pay (3)	Pay growth (4)
Teacher-turnout advantage	123.51***	51.25**	-179.30	-287.38
(percent)	(42.231)	(22.674)	(198.996)	(177.744)
Teacher-union PAC	73.18***	17.79*	87.92	19.73
contribution rate	(17.319)	(9.299)	(81.080)	(72.113)
District size	179.79***	6.80	257.03	-89.34
	(34.981)	(18.781)	(163.632)	(145.697)
District wealth	0.00	-0.01	0.01	-0.07
	(0.016)	(0.009)	(0.077)	(0.072)
Obama vote share	74.80**	33.80*	-162.74	54.37
	(32.261)	(17.321)	(150.428)	(139.390)
Comparable-wage index	83.75***	4.95	325.11**	171.11
	(26.561)	(14.261)	(124.829)	(112.720)
Unemployment rate	-150.72	-205.66**	535.85	-740.67
	(175.312)	(94.125)	(821.110)	(729.764)
Percent nonwhite	0.16	-1.11	51.29	63.76
	(16.187)	(8.691)	(62.645)	(55.959)
Teacher experience	-447.04**	-255.65**		
	(211.021)	(113.298)		
Teacher education	48.84	46.79*		
	(45.999)	(24.697)		
Constant	-2,297.40	-473.36	-3,313.53	583.60
	(4,734.999)	(2,542.225)	(8,495.093)	(7,666.995)
Observations	141	141	139	137
R-squared	0.61	0.23	0.15	0.06

Notes: Cell entries are OLS regression coefficients, with standard errors reported in parentheses. *p<0.1, **p<0.05, ***p<0.01.

significant (p<0.01), indicating that school boards pay teachers more when teachers more reliably outvoted non-teachers in the prior school-board election. Each additional percentage point by which teachers outvoted non-teachers is associated with $123 extra dollars of TRI pay. This effect size is large. Unions that successfully mobilized a modest 5 percent turn-out advantage negotiated an additional $615 of TRI pay per teacher. This amount represents 9 percent of the average TRI stipend paid by the full sample of school districts in my analysis.

My second measure of teacher political activism, teacher PAC giving, is also a strong predictor of higher TRI pay. Each additional 1 percent of teachers who donate to WEA-PAC is associated with an additional $73 of TRI pay. Moving from a school district where the percentage of teachers contributing to WEA-PAC is one standard deviation below the sample mean (5 percent) to a district where contributions are one standard deviation above it (33 percent) is associated with over $2,000 in additional TRI pay per teacher. The control variables behave mostly as expected. District size and labor-market conditions (cost of living) explain much of the variation in TRI pay across districts. Unsurprisingly, more-liberal districts offer more-generous TRI pay. Every additional 1 percent of vote share earned by President Obama in 2012 is associated with a little over $70 in additional TRI pay per teacher.

One concern with the model in column 1 is the fact that baseline rates of TRI pay may have (historically) always been higher in districts where teachers are more politically active. To better isolate the relationship between pay and teacher activism, column 2 focuses on the *growth* (change) in TRI pay that districts paid between 2011 and 2013. Using growth in TRI pay as the outcome (dependent) variable, I continue to find a positive relationship between teacher pay and political activism. A 1 percent turnout advantage is associated with a $51 increase in TRI pay disbursed between 2011 and 2013. Similarly, each additional 1 percent of teachers who donate to WEA-PAC is associated with an $18 increase in the amount of TRI pay disbursed between 2011 and 2013. In sum, regardless of how TRI pay is measured, I find that higher rates of teacher activism in local school politics enable teachers unions to exert greater influence in school-board policymaking.[34]

How certain can we be that districts are paying teachers higher wages *because* they are more active in local politics? I carry out one final test designed to strengthen our confidence that teacher activism is, in fact, the cause of greater union influence in salary negotiations. If school boards are agreeing to more generous TRI pay because they are responding to the political activity of teachers, we should *not* observe those same school boards paying higher salaries to other, non-teacher employees in the district. Specifically, we should not expect to see higher administrator salaries in districts where teachers are more politically active. In other words, if I were to find that higher rates of teacher political activism were also associated with more generous superintendent pay, then it is likely that the relationship I have uncovered between teacher activism and higher TRI pay is caused by some other unobserved factor that influences districts' expenditures more generally. However, if the turnout advantage posted by teachers in school-board elections and teacher PAC giving has no similar effect on the generosity of superintendent salaries, this finding would be additional evidence in support of my argument that teacher activism has a strong independent effect on school-board policymaking.

To that end, columns 3 and 4 replicate the models presented in columns 1 and 2, but instead change the dependent variable to superintendent, rather than teacher, pay. These analyses reveal that teacher political activism has no similar effect on the generosity of superintendents' salaries (the coefficient on teacher-turnout advantage is actually negative, though not statistically different from zero). Likewise, there is no statistically significant relationship between superintendent pay and the share of each district's teachers who contribute to WEA-PAC. The model in column 3 focuses on baseline TRI pay for superintendents. In contrast, column 4 focuses on changes in TRI pay. Across the board, these null results provide additional confidence that the effect of local teacher political activism on teacher pay is not spurious. Instead, these results are consistent with my larger theory that organized teacher interests can and do influence school-board policymaking through their clout in local school politics.

Teacher Political Activism and School-Board Responsiveness

While the Washington analysis reveals a strong association between teacher political activism and policy influence, teacher turnout and PAC giving are clearly not exogenous. It could well be that teachers participate more in districts where boards are more likely to be responsive to their interests. To strengthen the case that teacher political activism translates into policy influence, we need to do more. Ideally, we would randomly assign different levels of teacher political activism to different school districts, step back, and observe how their board members respond. However, since this is not possible, I approximate such a scenario using a survey experiment embedded in two original surveys of school-board members (N=870).[35]

The experiment tests whether school-board members are more responsive to teachers' policy preferences when board members are primed about the intensity of those preferences. In the experiment, I randomly assigned school-board members to one of three conditions (one baseline, two treatments). Board members assigned to the baseline condition were asked:

> In some school districts, information about a teacher's impact on their students' test scores is made available to parents and the general public. What do you think about this idea? Would you be inclined to favor or oppose such a policy in your district?

These board members did not receive any additional information. In contrast, board members assigned to one of the two treatment conditions were given additional information about the views of either (1) their parent constituents or (2) their teacher constituents. Specifically, board members in one of the treatment conditions were informed that, according to a recent public opinion poll conducted by Harvard University researchers, a majority of the *parents/teachers* in their state *favored/opposed* the policy proposal. Because the version of the question that each board member received was chosen at random, any differences in board members' willingness to support or oppose the reform can be attributed directly to the treatment: pressure from either parent or teacher constituents.[36] The exact language of the experimental conditions as seen by school-board members responding to the survey item is shown below.

Baseline condition (N=295)
In some school districts, information about a teacher's impact on their students' test scores is made available to parents and the general public. What do you think about this idea? Would you be inclined to favor or oppose such a policy in your district?

Parent treatment (N=275)
In some school districts, information about a teacher's impact on their students' test scores is made available to parents and the general public. *According to a recent survey conducted by Harvard University researchers, 70 percent of parents nationally, including a majority of parents in [R's state shown] SUPPORT such a policy.* What do you think about this idea? Would you be inclined to favor or oppose such a policy in your district?

Teacher treatment (N=300)
In some school districts, information about a teacher's impact on their students' test scores is made available to parents and the general public. *According to a recent survey conducted by Harvard University researchers, 70 percent of teachers nationally, including a majority of teachers in [R's state shown] OPPOSE such a policy.* What do you think about this idea? Would you be inclined to favor or oppose such a policy in your district?

Although the information in the treatments is only an approximation of the actual opinions of board members' constituents, because parents and teachers are, in reality, so strongly divided on this issue, the differences in constituent opinion are likely to persist when moving from the state to the district level (as if we had a true measure of district opinion). In fact, teachers are the only subgroup in the population that opposed making test-score data available to parents and the public. In contrast, 76 percent of whites, 74 percent of African Americans, 83 percent of Latinos, 79 percent of Republicans and 77 percent of Democrats supported the proposal.

The specific treatments were chosen to appeal directly to the different political incentives faced by school-board members. As discussed earlier in the chapter, parents are the only constituency group who school-board members said routinely come close to matching teachers in the intensity of their activism. Consequently, my experiment is designed to provide the toughest possible test of my claim that teachers unions are unrivaled in their influence in local education politics. If any other group should be able to win the support of school-board members, it would be politically active parents. Finally, the treatments have the added benefit of being factually true: no deception is used in this experiment.[37]

I chose to assess the willingness of school-board members to support test-score transparency for several reasons. Note, I did *not* select this policy because it has been shown to improve student performance. My focus on this issue should not be interpreted as a test for whether board members are reform minded. There are good arguments on both sides of these data-transparency debates, but the normative desirability of the policy itself is not relevant to the purpose of the experiment. Instead, I asked about test-score transparency because the issue is uniquely well suited to testing how board members will respond to their two most active constituencies— parents and teachers—when they disagree on the direction of school policy.

First, the debate over value-added test-score transparency was (at that time) sufficiently novel to make the treatment information (constituency opinion) plausibly "useful" to board members interested in relying on their constituents' opinions. It is also worth emphasizing that the experiment presents board members with more than a hypothetical scenario. At the time the experiments were administered, two of the nation's largest school districts—Los Angeles Unified (LAUSD) and New York City— had garnered national attention for releasing this type of test-score data to the public. These debates had also played out in Virginia as some parents battled the Virginia Education Association (VEA) under the state's freedom of information law to access value-added test-score data. In each of these real-world examples, efforts to make test-score data public were met with stiff opposition from teachers and their unions.[38]

Since the experiment is designed to test whether school boards are more responsive to teachers or parents, the fact that many board members would have *already* known that teachers opposed transparency makes my experiment a conservative test, biased against finding that boards prioritize teacher interests. In other words, because teacher groups loudly rallied against test score transparency, board members are theoretically more likely to know (prior to the experiment) where teachers stand. In contrast, board members who received information indicating that parents strongly support transparency should find that information more "useful" on account of its novelty.[39]

What did the experiment reveal? First, and perhaps most surprisingly, a narrow majority (55 percent) of school-board members in the baseline condition—those who were not given any information about their constituents' opinions—indicated they favored transparency. That is, absent any political pressure from constituents, a narrow majority of board members viewed the proposal favorably. However, in the real world, the absence of any advocacy for or against such a controversial proposal is inconceivable. Were a school-board member to float this sort of reform proposal, we would readily expect that the local teachers union (most assuredly) and parents (potentially) would make their views heard at the next board meeting.

The point is that in a real-world setting, the proposal would have to survive the political process, including competition between parent and teacher constituents. Board members would then need to decide whether to support or reject the proposal. While we cannot directly observe how such a scenario would play out in each one of the nation's thirteen thousand–plus school districts, the experiment can give us some insight into how board members respond after learning where these two constituency groups stand. As figure 7.4 shows, board members responded quite differently to the proposal depending on whether they had been informed about the policy preferences of parents or teachers. Board members in the parent treatment were no more likely to support reform, even after they learned that the vast majority of parents supported it. In contrast, board members who were randomly informed that teachers opposed the proposal showed considerably less support for it. Specifically, support dropped a full 10 percentage points (to just 45 percent) when board members learned that the majority of teachers were strongly opposed (a statistically significant difference, $p<0.05$).[40]

Why were school-board members more responsive to teachers than to parents? One plausible reason—consistent with the argument of this

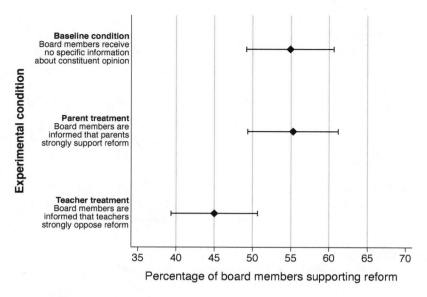

FIGURE 7.4 School board member responsiveness to teacher and parent groups

Notes: Figure displays the mean level of board-member support for the test-score transparency reform proposal in each of the three experimental conditions.

Source: Author's original surveys.

book—is that board members have strong incentives to line up behind the policy preferences of the most politically active and organized groups in their district. If that is correct, we should expect the main treatment effect—that board members are more inclined to respond to teacher opinion—to grow stronger in districts where teachers engage more reliably in political activity.

To examine this possibility, figure 7.5 reports the results of the experiment separately by the level of political activism that board members said teacher groups bring to bear in their district. For example, school districts where board members said that the local teachers union/association is "very active" or "active" in school-board politics were classified as *politically active* districts. In contrast, districts where board members said organized teacher interests are "inactive" or "not very active" were classified as *not politically active* districts. As the figure shows, board members are more responsive to teachers in districts where their unions are politically active. Specifically, the willingness of board members to support transparency drops 15 percentage points in districts where unions are politically active (compared to the average treatment effect of 10 percentage points for the entire sample of districts). What's more, these effects completely disappear in districts where school-board members report that the local teachers union is not politically active (a minority of districts).[41]

In figure 7.6, I assess how different configurations of teacher and parent political activism influence board-member responsiveness. Starting with the top row of figure 7.6, I present the treatment effects for board members who characterized their districts as ones where teachers were active but parents were inactive. As we might expect, in the absence of any political competition between parents and teachers, board members who received the treatment item emphasizing teacher opposition to reform break even harder in the direction preferred by teachers. Support for transparency drops 20 percentage points for board members who serve in these districts. The middle row of figure 7.6 shows what happens when parent and teacher groups are both politically active. When parents and

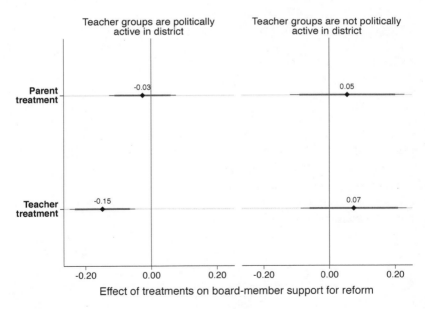

FIGURE 7.5 School board member responsiveness by a district's level of teacher political activism

Notes: Figure displays the regression coefficients on the treatment conditions separately for districts where board members characterized teachers unions as more or less active in district politics.

Source: Author's original surveys.

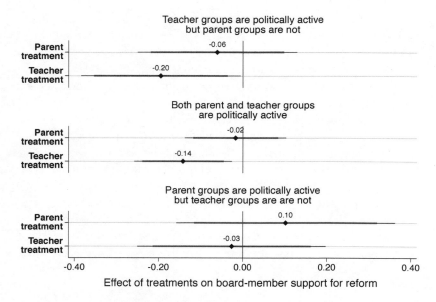

FIGURE 7.6 School board member responsiveness by a district's level of teacher and parent activism

Notes: Figure displays the regression coefficients on the treatment conditions separately for districts where board members characterized teachers unions/parent groups as more or less active in district politics.

Source: Author's original surveys.

teachers both participate consistently, board members are still inclined to respond more to teachers, but less so. Under this competitive scenario, the teacher treatment drops board-member support for transparency by 14 percentage points. Finally, in the rare handful of districts where parents are politically active but unions are not active, the teacher treatment has no effect on board members' attitudes. However, even in this unlikely scenario, board members are not responsive to parents.

Perhaps board-member responsiveness to teachers is also enhanced by the outsized representation that educators achieve on school boards. Recall from earlier in the chapter that nearly a quarter of school-board members are themselves current or former educators.[42] To the extent that this descriptive representation translates into greater substantive representation for teacher interests, then we might expect educator board members to be more sensitive to teachers' opinions. We can examine this possibility by disaggregating the results of the experiment by board-member occupation. These results, shown in figure 7.7, confirm the expectation that teacher board members will be more responsive to teacher interests. When educator board members received the teacher treatment, their support for test-score transparency dropped by 18 percentage points (relative to the baseline condition). Notably, however, I found no similar dynamic among board members who were parents of school-aged children. That is, parent board members who were informed that parents strongly supported test score transparency were no more likely to support transparency than parent board members in the baseline condition.

The finding that many school-board members will abandon a policy proposal popular with parents simply by virtue of being informed of teachers' opposition to it has significant implications for our understanding of democratic accountability in local school politics. Unlike many survey experiments where questions about external validity raise doubts about applications to the real world, the experiment here largely mimics the real-world dynamics of politics in the typical American school district. Teachers are, after all, far more active than other organized groups in most districts, including parents. In other words, school-board members are already

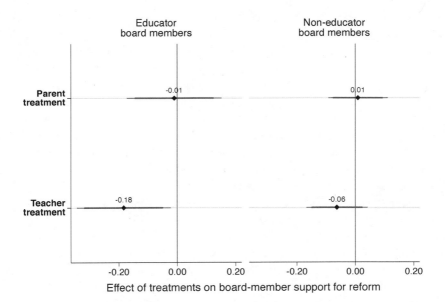

FIGURE 7.7 Educator board members are more responsive to teacher groups

Notes: Figure displays the regression coefficients on the treatment conditions separately for teacher and non-teacher board members.

Source: Author's original surveys.

more likely to find themselves on the receiving end of teacher political advocacy. The results also mimic the political reality that unfolded in American education during the COVID-19 pandemic. After schools closed in the spring of 2020, school boards faced tremendous pressure from their constituents to get schools back up and running safely in the fall. Much like the dynamics in this experiment, teachers and parents often locked horns on the reopening issue: many parents complained that reopening was happening too slowly, while teachers and their unions often pressed for a more cautious approach out of concern for their members' health and safety. As I explain at the conclusion of this chapter, one of the reasons that teachers tended to prevail in these debates was because of their superior political clout in local school politics.

Teacher Political Activism in a Right-to-Work State

So far, I have shown that teachers are active and influential in local school politics. But does that activism and influence apply in districts located throughout the United States? Teachers are, after all, usually regarded as politically weak in conservative "right-to-work" (RTW) states. Yet, as I have argued, after collective bargaining spread to a majority of states, organized teacher interests in all fifty states grew stronger on account of their affiliation with the NEA. Though teachers in states without CB laws operate at a disadvantage, they can still draw on the support of the NEA's federated interest-group network, mobilizing teachers in politics even when they are shut out of the bargaining table. As the red-state teacher strikes showed in 2018, collective bargaining is no requirement for teacher activists to grab state and local officials' attention.

If I am correct, the strongest test of my claim would be to show that it is true in an RTW state without teacher bargaining. Therefore, in my final study, I examine organized teacher political activism in Virginia, a state where, until 2021, teacher bargaining had been prohibited since 1977. Specifically, I analyze how Virginia's NEA affiliate—the Virginia Education Association (VEA)—coordinated a political effort to protect continuing contracts (tenure) at a time when the political currents on this issue were running strongly against teachers unions nationwide.

The story begins in 2012. That year, Virginia's Republican governor, Bob McDonnell, was as well positioned as any state executive to win legislative approval of his signature education-reform package. Virginia's teachers had good reason to be worried when McDonnell proposed to eliminate their continuing contracts, the commonwealth's equivalent of tenure.[43] In a warning shot, McDonnell told teachers, "You perform well, you keep your job. You don't perform well for an extended period of time, you don't get a guarantee."[44]

The challenges for the VEA were manifold. Republicans held a governing trifecta, enabling them to advance McDonnell's agenda without Democratic support. Public opinion on the issue was not favorable for teachers. Polls showed that a majority of Virginians favored the elimination of continuing contracts.[45] Governors in much stronger union states had already capitalized on the political climate of the Great Recession to weaken tenure protections. Armed with a Republican majority, a nationwide trend moving against teachers unions, and the public on his side, McDonnell should have been positioned for an easy victory on tenure repeal. That his proposal was ultimately defeated testifies to the impressive strength of organized teacher interests in education politics, even where we least expect them to be powerful.

As McDonnell and his allies worked to build legislative support for his reform proposal, the VEA responded with a two-front counterattack. First, the VEA lobbied its supporters in the statehouse, leaning on legislators who had personal connections to educators and those who hailed from districts where VEA members were especially active and engaged. Second, it mobilized a massive grassroots lobbying campaign targeting the state's 132 school boards. Working through its local associations, the VEA asked boards to adopt resolutions declaring their opposition to the governor's proposal and their intention to support continuing contracts. The VEA carefully monitored the status of board support for its resolution, publicly praising boards who agreed to defend and preserve continuing contracts. Altogether, the VEA succeeded in convincing twenty-one local school boards—from districts that represented 40 percent of the state's public school students—to adopt its pro-tenure resolution.

Due to the VEA's dogged efforts, the governor's proposal to eliminate continuing contracts died in the Virginia senate in 2012. Although the bill had passed in the general assembly (55–43), ultimately, three Republican senators defected to kill the tenure-repeal measure for good. Importantly, two of the three Republican defectors had close personal connections to VEA members. "'I'm married to a teacher, for cryin' out loud. Blood runs thicker than water,' [Senator John] Watkins [one of the GOP defectors] said after the floor session."[46]

After McDonnell's tenure proposal was defeated, in early 2013 he signed a compromise piece of legislation known as the "Educator Fairness Act" into law. Interestingly, the new law earned the support of the VEA. However, the compromise measure was a far cry from the governor's original proposal. Instead of eliminating continuing contracts outright, the new law gave local school boards the option of increasing the length of teacher probationary periods from three to five years. In other words, continuing contracts would remain in place but, *at the discretion of local school boards*, obtaining one could take two additional years.

Compared to McDonnell's initial bill, this was a clear victory for Virginia teachers. It meant that the VEA now had 132 veto points where its members could resist attempts to lengthen teachers' probationary periods. Advocates for tenure reform faced a far tougher task. They would need to win 132 separate victories to meaningfully alter the state's tenure policy. And these political battles would take place in local school districts where, as we saw earlier in the chapter, teachers are especially active and organized. Then-VEA president Meg Gruber summed it up well when she told teachers that the "Educator Fairness Act" was a good winning compromise. "It was through our sustained efforts that we preserved Continuing Contract and made it untenable for the Governor to again propose term contracts," she said.[47]

Was Gruber correct? To determine whether more politically active teachers were, in fact, able to dilute the impact of the Educator Fairness Act, I hand-collected information on each Virginia school district's continuing contract policy in 2018 (five years after the compromise legislation had been adopted). Districts that sided with the VEA and elected *not* to change their continuing-contract policy were assigned a score of 1, while districts that lengthened their probationary period from three to five years were coded 0.

To measure teachers' political strength across districts, I use data from an original survey of Virginia school-board members that I carried out in 2012.[48] The survey (N=259 board members serving in 105 separate districts) included two separate measures of teachers' political strength. First, the survey included a battery of questions assessing how politically active different groups were in the respondent's district. Specifically, each board member was asked:

From attending board meetings to participating in school elections, many different groups are involved in local education politics. Generally speaking, how politically active are each of the following groups in your school district: (1) Teachers' association (local NEA or AFT-affiliate) (2) parent groups (3) business groups (4) civil rights groups (5) religious groups.[49]

Even in Virginia, where teachers have historically been characterized as weak, board members rated them as highly active in local politics. On average, across all 105 school districts represented in the survey, board members rated teachers as the single most active group in 25 percent of districts. Including ties, teachers were rated the most active group in 61 percent of districts. Parents were the only other group that held their own with teachers. Parents were the single most active group (even more active than teachers) in 18 percent of districts. They tied for the most active group in 57 percent of districts.

Since individual school-board members may have different baseline perceptions of what constitutes "high" versus "low" levels of activism, and because I am interested in the *relative* level of teachers' political activism in each district, my first measure of teacher-union strength is operationalized as the average level of political activism (1–4) that board members assigned to teacher group relative to their rankings of the other, non-teacher groups in their district. This measure is created by subtracting the average activism-rating boards assigned to non-teacher groups from the average rating of teacher groups. Higher values indicate that teacher groups are more politically active compared to other groups.[50]

My second measure of teacher political activism focuses on the percentage of school-board members in each district that reported receiving the endorsement of the local teachers union/association. This measure ranges from 0 to 100 percent and it helps capture the strength of teachers in local politics by assessing the degree to which local school officials were elected with or without the support of organized teacher interests.

I also include several relevant control variables, all measured at the school district level. These variables include: the share of low-income and racial-minority students; President Obama's vote share in 2012; the percentage of students in each district who were proficient in math; and an indicator for whether a district is in a rural locale. I also include a measure of teacher vacancies since the difficulty that districts have in attracting and retaining teachers may reduce their incentive to lengthen teachers' probationary periods. Finally, because a nontrivial number of school boards in Virginia are appointed rather than elected, I include an indicator for whether a district's board is elected.

TABLE 7.6 **Local union strength and school-board support for teacher tenure in Virginia**

	(1)	(2)	(3)
Union strength	0.349*	-1.032	1.254**
	(0.181)	(0.701)	(0.493)
Elected board	0.049	-0.451	—
	(0.477)	(0.490)	
Union strength * Elected board		1.571**	
		(0.731)	
Teacher vacancies	0.043	0.025	-0.200
	(0.116)	(0.111)	(0.186)
Student poverty	-2.782**	-3.194**	-3.627**
	(1.251)	(1.304)	(1.542)
Rural district	-0.034	-0.164	-0.137
	(0.334)	(0.327)	(0.381)
Obama vote share	3.944***	4.252***	4.323***
	(1.331)	(1.397)	(1.446)
Math proficiency	0.024	0.027*	0.024
	(0.015)	(0.016)	(0.017)
Constant	-2.947*	-2.674	-2.797
	(1.544)	(1.690)	(1.774)
Pseudo R^2	0.20	0.25	0.28
Observations	105	105	88

Notes: Cell entries are probit regression coefficients, with standard errors in parentheses. Virginia school districts are the unit of analysis. The dependent variable is a binary indicator denoting that a district declined to raise tenure requirements (1= yes, 0=no). The measure of union strength in the models reported in columns 1 and 2 is based on school board members' evaluations of teacher activism in their districts. The measure of union strength in column 3 is based on the share of board members endorsed by the local teachers union. *$p<0.1$, **$p<0.05$, ***$p<0.01$.

I estimate three separate regression models, the results of which are shown in table 7.6. In each model the dependent variable is equal to 1 when a district *sided with the VEA* and declined to lengthen teachers' probationary periods.

The baseline model is presented in column 1. Consistent with my expectations, I find that in districts where teachers were rated more politically active than other groups, school boards more often declined to make tenure harder to achieve. Likewise, more-liberal districts (those that voted for President Obama) were more likely to maintain the shorter three-year probationary period for teachers. However, including this control does not dampen the effect of teacher political activism. This finding is important because it shows that, even after accounting for the electorate's political preferences, organized teacher interests exert an independent influence on the tone and direction of school policy.

If school boards are more responsive to organized teacher interests because teachers are more politically active in local politics, this relationship should be even stronger in districts where board members are elected.

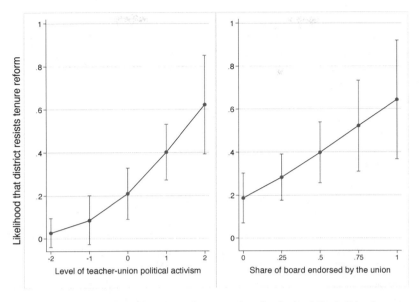

FIGURE 7.8 Marginal effects of teacher-union strength on local school districts' implementation of teacher tenure reform

Notes: Figure displays the marginal effects (with 95 percent confidence) of local teacher-union strength in each Virginia school district on the likelihood that a school board declined to use the Educator Fairness Act to raise teacher tenure requirements in their district.

The model presented in column 2 confirms this expectation. In this model, I interact teacher political activism with an indicator for whether a district elects its school-board members. The coefficient on this interaction term is both positive and statistically significant, indicating that teacher political activism is a stronger predictor of a district's tenure policy in districts where boards are elected rather than appointed.

Finally, in column 3, I replace my measure of union political activism, swapping it out for an alternative measure of union political strength: the percentage of school-board members who were endorsed by their district's teachers union. I find that this alternative measure of teacher-union strength is also a powerful predictor of how districts chose to implement the Educator Fairness Act. Districts where more board members were elected with the union endorsement were far more likely to retain a shorter probationary period for teachers.

Figure 7.8 graphs the marginal effects of these results. The left side of the figure shows the relationship between the average level of political activism that boards assigned to teachers and the likelihood that the district stood pat and did not change its tenure policy. With all of the control variables in the model set at their mean value, an increase in the relative level of teacher political activism from one standard deviation below the mean to one above it is associated with a 14-percentage-point increase in the probability that a board adopted a pro-tenure stance. The right-hand side of the figure shows the marginal effects of electing more union-endorsed school-board members. With all control variables set at their mean value, moving from a district where 25 percent of the school board received the teachers unions' endorsement to a district where 75 percent of the board did is associated with a 23-percentage-point increase in the probability that a board stuck with the three-year probationary period as preferred by the VEA.

Our examination of the politics of teacher tenure in Virginia has taken us in several different directions. The story began during the Great Recession in a period of Republican dominance. In that challenging climate, teachers turned to grassroots lobbying and ultimately their clout in local school politics to defend their job protections. But the story doesn't end there. Instead, the final act is another reminder about the importance of perspective—of understanding how organized teacher interests are well positioned to remain influential in school politics over the long run. In 2018, 70 percent of Virginia students attended school in a district that had declined to use the Educator Fairness Act to raise teacher tenure requirements. Two years later, after Democrats had won a governing trifecta of their own, they passed a law returning the state to a three-year probationary policy for all teachers. What's more, after a fifty-year ban on teacher bargaining, this new Democratic majority accomplished the unimaginable. They authorized teacher bargaining. By 2021, a new era of teacher influence was dawning in Old Dominion.

Why Local School Politics Matter

The findings in this chapter point in an unambiguous direction: teachers unions have no comparable rival in local education politics and their influence matters a great deal for the tone and direction of school-board policymaking. Union-endorsed candidates win the majority of competitive school-board elections, teachers have the most descriptive representation on school boards, and across a variety of different indicators, teachers participate more reliably in local school politics than other education stakeholders. Three distinctly different empirical case studies (Washington, Indiana, and Virginia) provided evidence that the grassroots advantage that organized teacher interests wield in local school politics provides them with significant influence at the local level.

Taken together, these results indicate that organized teacher interests need to be at the center of research on American education, especially in work that attempts to understand the dynamics of political power and influence in local school districts.

Unfortunately, researchers have, on the whole, paid little attention to organized teacher interests in local school politics. This lack of attention is not altogether surprising. It is challenging to study local elections. Measuring the influence of interest groups in these backwater environments is even more difficult. As Sarah Anzia explains, "research on local politics in the United States tends to ignore interest groups, and research on interest groups tends to ignore local government."[51]

This oversight is a mistake. For one thing, the demise of local control in American education has been greatly exaggerated. One need look no further than the COVID-19 pandemic to see that localism remains a powerful and enduring force in the United States. Even as mounting scientific evidence showed that schools could be reopened safely, two US presidents and numerous governors found they had little practical power to reopen schools when local school boards struggled to obtain cooperation from teachers unions. While more-centralized education systems in other parts of the world reopened far more quickly, the inability of school boards to ink reopening agreements with their teachers unions played no small role in keeping half of all students out of school for a full year.[52] Bradley Marianno explains well why we underestimate teacher-union influence when we pay insufficient attention to union activity in local school politics:

> There are far more education interest groups and competing education policy ideas at the state level, making it much more difficult for a single organization to garner a dominant voice among policymakers. When these [school reopening] decisions are brought down into local school board meetings, there remain only a few organizations that are organized enough to exert influence. The teachers' unions are the largest elephant in the room.[53]

Even when federal and state authorities do assert themselves, *local* officials are the ones who must implement education policy on the ground.[54] Implementation is itself a political process rife with contestation. School-board members routinely confront outside political pressure from interest groups—often the local teachers union—that oppose reform proposals that threaten to undo existing education policies that benefit their members. Focusing too much on federal and state policymaking causes us to risk missing all the influential local politicking that goes on during this crucial implementation stage of policymaking.

Consider the claim that teachers unions lost significant clout in education in recent years. Proponents of this view often point to various education-reform debates—on charter schools and teacher pay and evaluation reform—that teachers unions "lost" during the Bush-Obama years. However, when one looks beneath the surface, the most controversial elements of those reforms stalled out when local officials encountered strong resistance from teachers in the trenches. Even after states adopted tougher teacher evaluation laws, for example, most school districts simply went through the motions—giving favorable evaluations to most teachers and removing few low performers from the classroom. Likewise, when states passed laws encouraging districts to replace union-favored salary schedules with performance-based pay systems, districts tended to demur in the face of educator resistance.[55]

In sum, localism provides many opportunities for active and organized interest groups like teachers unions to shape education policy from the ground up. The power of organized teacher interests, therefore, still very much hinges on the degree of influence that they can exert in local school-board politics. It is these arenas that determine whether the officials who are so instrumental in implementation will be sympathetic to teachers' concerns or resistant to them. The fact that I have shown that teachers remain an influential force in local school politics today—even after labor retrenchment and the loss of agency fees—would appear to narrow the recent claim that their power has been seriously eroded in American education.

Chapter Appendix

2012 Virginia School Board Member Survey (VSBMS)

The VSBMS was an online survey of Virginia school-board members administered between October 26, 2012 and November 8, 2012. The project was approved as exempt by the Institutional Review Board (IRB) at the University of Notre Dame on October 15, 2012. The target sample was Virginia's entire population of school-board members. In total, 850 board members were invited to participate. Completed responses were received from 259 board members for a response rate of 30 percent. Respondents hailed from 105 of the commonwealth's 132 unique school districts. At the time of the survey, these 105 districts combined to educate more than 85 percent of Virginia's public school students. Responding and non-responding districts shared similar demographic characteristics. The only significant difference between responding and non-responding districts was district size (enrollment). Responding board members hailed from districts that had (on average) 10,000 students compared to 7,400 students for non-responding districts. This disparity was most likely due to the fact that it was somewhat easier to find email contact information for board members in larger districts (compared to smaller rural ones).

2013 Indiana School Board Member Survey (ISBMS)

The ISBMS was an online survey of Indiana school-board members administered between April 11, 2013 and May 8, 2013. The project was approved as exempt by the IRB at the University of Notre Dame on April 10, 2013. The target sample was the entire population of Indiana school-board members. In total, 1,600 board members were invited to participate. Completed responses were received from 410 board members for a response rate of 26 percent. Respondents hailed from 195 of the state's 289 unique school districts. At the time of the survey, these 195 districts combined to educate 80 percent of all Indiana public school students. Responding and non-responding districts shared very similar demographic characteristics. For example, the average graduation rate was exactly 89 percent in responding and non-responding districts; teacher-union density was 77 percent in responding districts compared to 81 percent in non-responding districts. The percentage of students eligible for free lunch was 46 percent for responding districts and 44 percent for nonresponding ones. As in the VSBMS survey, the only significant difference between responding and non-responding districts was in district size (enrollment). It was more difficult to reach board members in the smallest districts, limiting my ability to generalize findings to small rural districts in Indiana.

2015 National School Board Member Survey (NSBMS)

The NSBMS was a survey of school-board members administered online between April 27, 2015 and May 13, 2015. The project was approved as exempt by the Human Subjects Review Committee at Lake Forest College on April 23, 2015. The target sample included all school-board members who, as of 2015, were serving on boards in one of 418 K–12 public school districts that had previously been surveyed by the National School Boards Association in 2009. This resampling strategy was intentionally done to build a repeated cross section of survey responses from board members serving in the same districts a few years apart. In total, 2,210 board members were invited to participate. This effort yielded completed responses from 460 board members representing 219 unique districts for a response rate of 21 percent.

CHAPTER EIGHT

Teacher-Union Power and Student Achievement

The fact is that, in some instances, we have used our power to block uncomfortable changes to protect the narrow interest of our members, and not to advance the interests of students and schools.[1]—NEA President Bob Chase (1997)

The previous two chapters revealed that organized teacher interests influence education policy through their political power in subnational politics. An obvious question that arises, then, is whether the unions' power to influence policy affects student academic achievement. Remarkably, fifty years after unions became a fixture in American education, researchers continue to vigorously debate this question. Here I venture into that highly contentious debate with the aim of making three contributions.

First, I reassess the existing literature. This exercise is enlightening because it reveals that older scholarship, which was constrained by the data and methodological techniques of the time, gave rise to a misleading view that union strength promotes higher rates of student achievement. I show that more-sophisticated studies, especially those that identify the long-term effects of union power, paint a different picture. That picture is one in which union power is not always benign. Rather it sometimes limits education policymakers' ability to improve student outcomes.

Second, I review the two most common perspectives that guide most efforts to understand the relationship between unions and student achievement: democratic voice and rent seeking. Building on the rent-seeking model, I adopt a framework that emphasizes necessary and sufficient conditions: while strong unions are not necessary for low achievement to persist, the need for teachers unions to defend their members' interests can sometimes come into conflict with policymakers' efforts to improve student learning. No less an authority than former NEA president Bob Chase conceded that his union spent the first two decades of the education reform movement defending teachers' occupational interests, sometimes at the expense of student learning needs.

Finally, I present an original state-level analysis examining the relationship between union power and student achievement. My own study improves on existing work in three ways. First, it draws on new measures of student achievement that are more comparable across states. Second, it incorporates measures of union strength that are richer and more conceptually appropriate. And third, it uses recent changes in states' teacher labor laws to estimate the effect of union retrenchment on student achievement. Overall, I find no evidence that Great Recession labor retrenchment decreased student achievement. To the contrary, I find some suggestive evidence that student performance modestly improved in states that adopted these laws compared to states that did not.

The Conventional Wisdom

Sometimes early wisdom becomes received wisdom. Consider the debate over school spending. Early intuitions were driven by what seemed obvious; surely there was a connection between education spending and student achievement. Yet in the aftermath of the famous Coleman Report in 1966, scholars coalesced around a belief that money didn't matter.[2] Recently, however, a new wave of studies has shown that more money can make a difference.[3]

The lesson here is simple. Often it's wise to revisit the conventional wisdom and scrutinize the evidence to see if that wisdom still holds. When policymakers consider whether more should be spent on schools, context is crucial. Money that isn't spent well is unlikely to move the needle. Funds that are wisely targeted—perhaps in response to decades of underfunding—may make a world of difference.[4]

When it comes to assessing the impact of teachers unions on student achievement, the research literature is plagued with similar issues. A popular but misleading narrative has emerged that says union power cannot be a cause of low student achievement in the United States. This claim is frequently repeated among journalists writing for respected national media outlets. For example, Nicholas Kristof once opined in the pages of the *New York Times* that "Republicans sometimes suggest that our biggest educational problem is teachers' unions themselves. That's absurd. States with strong teachers' unions in the North like Massachusetts have better schools than states in the South with weak unions."[5]

Union leaders frequently appeal to the same reasoning. In a 2010 appearance on ABC's *This Week*, AFT president Randi Weingarten sought to discredit any potential linkage between unions and lower student achievement by arguing that "the states that actually have lots of teachers in teacher unions tend to be the states that have done the best in terms of academic success . . . And the states that don't tend to be the worst."[6] Former United Federation of Teachers (UFT) vice president Leo Casey similarly concludes that "the weight of the literature clearly falls on the side of a positive relationship between teacher unionism and the quality of schooling [even if it is far from definitive]."[7]

It is understandable that journalists and advocates engage in this type of analysis. But such thinking has also made its way into the scholarly community. For example, Richard Kahlenberg, a senior fellow at the Century Foundation, claims that "if collective bargaining were really a terrible practice for education, we should see stellar results where it does not occur: in the American South and in the charter school arena, for example." He then asks: "Why, then, aren't the seven states that forbid collective bargaining for teachers . . . at the top of the educational heap?"[8] In 2011, education historian Diane Ravitch told NPR's audience, "They're [teachers unions] not the problem. The state with the highest scores on the national test—that state is Massachusetts—which is 100 percent union. The nation with the highest scores in the world is Finland, which is 100 percent union."[9] Finally, sociologist Robert Carini summarized the relationship between unions and student achievement in a 2008 review article by claiming, "[Teacher] bargaining exhibits small, but positive, effects for most students. The most comprehensive review [of the literature] turned up only 17 well-cited studies . . . Studies that reported favorable effects outnumbered those that reported negative effects by more than a 2 to 1 ratio." Carini went on to conclude: "Unions do not hamper what is ostensibly the most important charter of public schools—student learning—and [they] provide material benefits and collegial support for millions of teachers and staff."[10]

Reassessing the Evidence on Unions and Student Achievement

Unfortunately, there are several problems with the reasoning and evidence that undergirds this collection of highly repeated claims that unions promote higher rates of student academic achievement, or, at the very least, can do nothing to cause lower achievement. First, the straight comparison between northern and southern states does not control for any other factors that might influence these outcomes. Second, and more importantly, the summary of the evidence that is relied upon to make these claims is outdated, both temporally and methodologically.

Contrast two reviews of the literature early in the first decade of the 2000s—the aforementioned Carini paper and one by Charles Taylor Kerchner—with very recent summaries by Katharine Strunk and Joshua Cowen in 2015 and 2020.[11] Kerchner and Carini's reviews engaged in a straightforward "study counting" exercise, weighting each piece of scholarship equally before concluding that unionization has at best a positive and at worst no negative impact on achievement. But as Cowen and Strunk explain, in recent years, "the research literature has moved from largely focusing on observational studies to more advanced attempts to provide robust causal inference."[12] In other words, simply counting up studies and reporting the cumulative direction of their findings can obscure more than it illuminates. The earliest studies did not account for the fact that unionization is endogenous to student achievement. Moreover, it tended to rely on "simple indicators of union status," failing to incorporate broader measures of union strength (e.g., political power)—measures that I have shown influence education policymaking.

Does it matter that these earlier studies that showed a positive correlation between unions and student achievement relied disproportionately on inferior data and research designs? Cowen and Strunk believe so. According to their 2020 review, not only does more-recent scholarship point in the opposite direction, but so too do the more rigorously designed studies that are better suited to making causal claims:

> The most recent evidence tends to suggests that at best unions appear to have no corresponding positive effects on student achievement—and in fact in many instances negative impacts are shown in some of the most rigorous research available, especially for at-risk students—we conclude that at the time of this writing [2020] an evidence-based appraisal of union impacts supports the notion that union priorities (especially those won at the bargaining table) do not necessarily align with academic success in the classroom.[13]

To bring additional evidence to this debate, I built an original database of all the existing empirical studies examining the relationship between student achievement outcomes and teacher-union strength (see table A8.1 in the chapter appendix). This database combines all the studies cited in the afore-mentioned literature reviews along with a handful of additional papers authored since the publication of the most recent Strunk and Cowen review.

If we naively categorize all of these studies (N=44) by whether they found a negative, mixed, or positive relationship between union strength and student achievement, the results are as follows: 34 percent positive (N=15); 23 percent mixed (N=10); and 43 percent negative (N=19). Simply counting studies, however, is a flawed approach. It tells us nothing about the quality of the studies, nor about the strength of the research designs employed. As Cowen and Strunk note, early work failed to deal with endogeneity issues, relying on cross-sectional analyses that could not account for student outcomes prior to and after unions gained power.

With that criticism in mind, I reevaluated the studies in table A8.1, focusing only on the studies that used within-unit fixed effects research designs or those that could make stronger causal claims (N=23). The results of that exercise echo the takeaway from Cowen and Strunk, providing more justification for the rent-seeking hypothesis. In 52 percent of these more rigorously designed studies, the authors uncovered a negative relationship between union strength and student achievement. Mixed results were found in 26 percent of these papers, while just 22 percent found a positive relationship between unions and achievement.

Another major limitation of the existing literature is the problem of measurement. There are three basic measurement issues that raise important concerns. First, teacher unionization happened in the 1960s and 1970s, long before researchers had reliable access to good cross-state and cross-district measures of student academic achievement outcomes. This particular issue is problematic because it makes it difficult for researchers to examine within-state or within-district changes in student outcomes before and after teachers unions gained power. Two notable exceptions are an influential early paper by Stanford economist Caroline Hoxby and a 2019 study by Michael Lovenheim and Alexander Willén of Cornell University.[14] Both studies were able to credibly identify the causal impact of unionization—which in both cases proved negative—on the high school dropout rate (Hoxby) and later life earnings (Lovenheim and Willén). Until recently these sorts of pre-post research designs were not possible to carry out, since teacher labor law stood in equilibrium from 1980 onward. Since experiments cannot be run on unionization, these sorts of research designs are arguably the strongest way to try and isolate the effects of unionization on achievement.

A second major shortcoming is the inadequacy of measures of teacher-union strength. Specifically, union power is almost always operationalized as a simple indicator that exhibits little to no variation over time. For example, the presence of an RTW law, a mandatory bargaining law, or the fraction of teachers who are union members are all measures of union strength that, for most districts, were mostly set in stone by 1980. What these measures tell us decades later is unclear. They do little to shed light on the variation in union political power and policies in teacher collective bargaining agreements (CBAs) today.[15] Fortunately, in recent years a handful of scholars have begun to examine teacher-union strength in the content of CBAs, highlighting ways in which some CBAs are restrictive toward school management. The vast majority of these CBA-restrictiveness studies have found that restricting the autonomy of school leaders is associated with negative impacts on student achievement, especially for disadvantaged students.[16] Still, more needs to be done to broaden the measures of union strength that are used. Among other things, scholars should do more to incorporate alternative measures of union power such as union political resources—an approach adopted by only one study to date.[17]

Third, the ways in which scholars measure education outcomes remains highly problematic. Many early state-level studies used ACT or SAT scores, a practice that raises obvious problems pertaining to who takes college entrance exams.[18] More problematic still, since unionization and many observed and unobserved state differences in demographics and poverty are correlated, test-score outcomes that are unadjusted for demographic differences in test-takers tell us very little about the impact of unions on differences in states' education performance. Nearly all the state-level studies that have examined union strength and education outcomes have *not* sufficiently corrected for these biases.

Why Would Unions Impact Student Achievement?

So far, I have focused on the technical challenges to estimating the effects of unions on student achievement. The more fundamental issue, however, is identifying the appropriate theoretical perspective for thinking about how unions are likely to impact policymakers' efforts to raise student achievement.

Early research focused more narrowly on the fiscal costs of unionization on schools. Beyond that, theorizing about the linkage between unions and student achievement was extremely limited. Some hypothesized that unions served to standardize the organization of schooling. Standardization was thought to benefit average pupils but undermine efforts to teach low- and high-achieving ones.[19] The lack of theory building is attributable to a few factors. First, labor economists, who were the ones developing this new literature, imported their field's knowledge about the role of unions in private-sector employment. Unfortunately, little effort was made to understand the political aspects of teacher unionization that are most salient in public-sector bureaucracies, including the political incentives that elected officials confront when managing a government workforce. Additionally, the education-reform movement was still in its infancy at the time that theories about union effects on student achievement were being developed. Systematic efforts to reform the policies and practices of American schooling to boost academic achievement were not yet the focus of policymakers or researchers.

Only after the school-reform movement began in earnest would scholars begin to think more comprehensively about the relationship between teacher and student interests.[20] As chapter 6 noted, the excellence movement spurred new competition between school-reform groups and teacher-union interests. They clashed over accountability, school choice, and teacher quality reforms. In response, new perspectives about the potential relationship between union power and student achievement emerged. One such perspective was articulated by Terry Moe, who in the first decade of the 2000s began to argue that teachers unions "shape the schools from the bottom up, through collective bargaining activities that are so broad in scope that virtually every aspect of the schools is somehow affected . . . and from the top down, through political activities that give them unrivaled influence over the laws and regulations imposed on public education by government."[21]

Today, there is wide agreement that collective bargaining and political advocacy are the twin pillars that enable teachers unions to influence education policy. The UFT's Leo Casey, for example, argues that bargaining and political advocacy are two of the most important tools that teachers unions wield in their effort to influence schooling policies and practices. Likewise, economist Dan Goldhaber emphasizes the underappreciated role that union political advocacy plays in empowering teachers unions to influence education policymaking. "Teachers unions," Goldhaber explains, "may have [even] more direct long-term effects [on student achievement] through their political power to influence school reform efforts."[22]

Since both union critics and supporters agree that any linkage between unions and student achievement is likely to be channeled through collective bargaining and political advocacy, what remains to be adjudicated is whether unions are more likely to use these levers of influence to benefit students, benefit themselves, or benefit both. It is here where union supporters and critics part company. Union supporters argue that collective bargaining and union political advocacy enable teachers to bring their democratic voice and educational expertise to bear on education. In contrast, union critics advance what political economists call a "rent-seeking" perspective, in which unions myopically seek occupational benefits, which in turn can promote suboptimal schooling policies and practices. Below, I briefly review these two perspectives before subjecting them to my own critical analysis.

The Democratic-Voice Perspective

Teacher-union advocates contend that student and teacher interests are not only compatible, they are linked such that more of one typically yields more of the other. As former UFT vice president Leo Casey once put it, "the common good of educators that teachers unions pursue is largely congruent . . . with the educational interests of the students whom they teach. The working conditions of teachers are, in significant measure, the learning conditions of students, and so improvements in the work lives of teachers generally translate into improvements in the education of students."[23] The AFT's Randi Weingarten has echoed the sentiment. Most recently, she did so when talking about the teacher strikes that erupted across the United States during late 2018. Weingarten argued that the strikes made it clear to America "that teachers want what students need."[24]

Importantly, advocates of the democratic-voice perspective recognize that the interests of teachers and their unions don't always—and, by definition, don't have to—coincide with those of students. However, most of the time and on the big issues, they argue, the convergence of teacher and student interests is strong. Among the most frequently cited examples of this overlap are things like overall education spending and smaller class sizes (both of which unions back, and which their supporters contend directly promote the good of students), as well as salary and pension policies that promote the retention of accomplished teachers and thus indirectly advance the interests of students.

In the absence of strong organized teacher interests, union supporters are quick to point out, it is far from clear that policymakers would be free to pursue the unfettered interests of students. For example, politicians may underinvest in education and prefer to reduce taxes.[25] In fact, alongside parents, teachers and their unions may be some of the most reliable advocates for students in an educational landscape that is also shaped by businesses, the nonparent general public, and other organized interests. As Richard Kahlenberg, a senior fellow at the Century Foundation, argues, "Certainly the interests of teachers in ensuring adequate educational investment are far stronger than they are for most voters, who don't have children in the school system and may be more concerned about holding down taxes than investing in the education of other people's kids."[26] In this sense, teachers unions are seen as providing democratic voice to a group that would otherwise be excluded from politics.

The Rent-Seeking Perspective

Union critics couldn't see things more differently.[27] "Asking if teachers unions are a positive force in education is a bit like asking if the Tobacco Institute is a positive force in health policy or if the sugar lobby is helpful in assessing the merits of corn syrup," education scholar and Heritage Foundation senior research fellow Jay Greene explains. He elaborates:

> The problem is not that teachers unions are hostile to the interests of students and their families, but that teachers unions, like any organized interest group, are specifically designed to promote the interests of their own members and not to safeguard the interests of nonmembers. To the extent that teachers benefit from more generous pay and benefits, less-demanding work conditions, and higher job security, the unions will pursue those goals, even if achieving them comes at the expense of students. That is what interest groups do.[28]

In a similar vein, Terry Moe argues that teachers unions "represent the job-related interests of their *members*, and these interests are simply *not the same* as the interests of children. Some things are obvious," Moe reasons. "It is not good for children that ineffective teachers cannot be removed from the classroom. It is not good for children that teachers cannot be assigned to the schools and classrooms where they are needed most. It is not good for children that excellent young teachers get laid off before mediocre colleagues with more seniority. Yet these are features of ... schooling that the unions fight for, in their own interests."[29]

Teacher and Student Interests

Together, these two theoretical perspectives—democratic voice and rent-seeking—raise a fundamental question about whether teacher and student interests are congruent. I evaluate this question in two ways—one empirical and one theoretical.

Empirically, I draw on a survey experiment that I embedded in the Wisconsin Teacher Recall Survey introduced previously in chapter 6. My experiment was designed to determine whether teachers themselves view teacher and student interests as qualitatively different from one another. To carry out this experiment, I divided and then randomly assigned my Wisconsin teacher respondents into one of two separate groups. Each group was asked to evaluate and rank the advocacy efforts of an identical list of Wisconsin political or policy-advocacy organizations. These organizations included the states' two largest teachers unions, the Wisconsin Education Association Council (WEAC) and the Wisconsin Federation of Teachers (WFT); the Wisconsin Parent Teacher Association; the Wisconsin School Boards Association (WSBA); and the Wisconsin Republican and Democratic parties respectively. However, one group of teachers was asked to evaluate the advocacy efforts of these groups on behalf of *teachers*, while the other group was asked to evaluate the advocacy efforts of these same groups on behalf of *students*. The text of the actual question respondents received appeared as follows:

Teachers are often busy focusing on the needs of their students and don't always have time to keep a close eye on the decisions of elected officials that impact our schools. In your experience, which of the following groups act as the most reliable advocate for *teacher interests / student interests* in Wisconsin? Rank each group from 1st to 6th where (1) represents the most reliable advocate for *teachers / students* and (6) represents the least reliable advocate.

Wisconsin Education Association Council (WEAC)
Wisconsin Federation of Teachers (WFT)
Wisconsin Parent Teacher Association
Wisconsin School Boards Association (WSBA)
Wisconsin State Democratic Party
Wisconsin State Republican Party

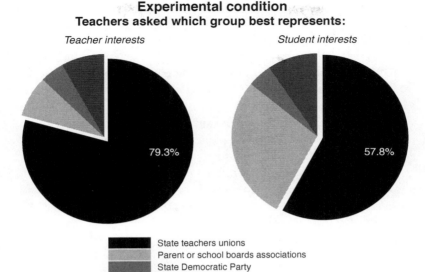

Experimental condition
Teachers asked which group best represents:

Teacher interests   *Student interests*

79.3%   57.8%

State teachers unions
Parent or school boards associations
State Democratic Party
State Republican Party

FIGURE 8.1 Teachers acknowledge that teachers unions represent teachers more than students

Notes: Figure shows the distribution of responses from teachers when asked which group is the most reliable advocate for teacher interests/student interests in their state.

Source: Author's 2012 survey of Wisconsin teachers. This analysis: N=3,481.

How did teachers in each group respond? Figure 8.1 displays the percentage of teachers who ranked one of Wisconsin's two teachers unions (either WEAC or the WFT) the single most reliable advocate depending on the version of the question they received. As the graphs indicate, the subtle shift from asking teachers who best represents teachers' interests (left side of figure) to asking who best represents students' interests (right side) resulted in a 22-percentage-point decrease in the number of teachers rating their unions first. Indeed, teachers who were asked which group best represents the interests of students were three times more likely to identify the state PTA or state school boards association.

In other words, while teachers may be prone to rhetorically substituting teacher and student interests in everyday conversations about education policy, a subtle priming change in the context of a survey experiment enables them to more accurately match political advocacy organizations with the stakeholders those organizations exist to represent. For teachers, the organizations that best serve them are clearly and appropriately their unions. However, teachers also recognize that other advocacy organizations may better serve *student* interests. These results are telling. These teachers were being surveyed in the throes of a controversial recall election in which their unions were on the front lines defending their vision of public education in Wisconsin. If ever there were a time when teachers would cling to their unions and identify them as pursuing what was in the best interest of all education stakeholders, it would have been in Wisconsin in 2012. And yet even during this unique moment of union solidarity, teachers were candidly quick to recognize that teacher and student interests are not, in fact, one and the same.

As striking as the results of this framing experiment are, we should not conclude that teachers see a serious conflict between their unions' pursuit of teacher interests and what is good for kids. In fact, Terry Moe has shown that just the opposite is true. When surveyed, most teachers say that they do not see any significant tension between their unions' push for restrictive CBAs—to give just one example—and student learning needs. In other words, while teachers may agree that their unions are designed to be teacher (rather than student) advocacy organizations, they tend not to see a conflict between their interests as employees and student learning needs.

What really matters, then, is how aligned the interests of students and teachers are with one another. My own perspective on this question is outlined schematically in figure 8.2. The figure shows three stylized Venn diagrams that provide a visual representation of the continuum that exists between the pure rent-seeking and the pure democratic-voice perspectives. The near-perfect overlapping circles shown in the upper-left-hand quadrant of the figure represent the idealized version of the democratic-voice perspective, best articulated by the sentiments expressed by Randi Weingarten and Leo Casey when they state that "teachers want what students need." On the other end of the spectrum, the pure rent-seeking view is shown in the upper-right-hand quadrant of the figure. Here, teacher interests reliably diverge from student interests as teachers unions lobby for education policies that benefit school employees but are uniformly suboptimal for students.

My argument is that neither of these first two illustrations paints an accurate picture of the relationship between student and teacher interests. Instead, I argue that these interests overlap in a way that is best characterized as *contingent and mixed*. The relationship between student and teacher interests is mixed because teachers unions do sometimes advo-

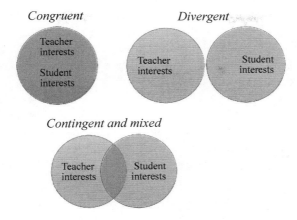

FIGURE 8.2 Possible relationships between teacher and student interests

cate for policies that benefit student learning needs. Yet as I discuss below, there are also numerous instances where teachers unions defend policies that are not ideal for students because those same policies are beneficial to teachers as employees. The relationship between teacher and student interests is contingent because the convergence of teacher and student interests is largely coincidental. Teachers unions and student advocacy organizations are literally designed to represent different stakeholders. This fact does not mean that unions' advocacy efforts never result in policies that benefit non-teacher stakeholders, including students. It does mean, however, that such outcomes are largely coincidental. They are neither a reliable nor predictable consequence of teachers unions advocating for their members' interests.

To show how the relationship between teacher and student interests are contingent and mixed, let's return to the arguments referenced earlier by Randi Weingarten and Leo Casey. Both union leaders argued that increases in (1) education-funding inputs and (2) school employees—increases that together can be used to support smaller class sizes—help promote student learning needs and teachers' working conditions alike. For example, Casey observes that "to the extent that the common good of teachers is realized, therefore, it directly (such as in the case of lower class size) or indirectly (such as in salary and pension policies that promote the retention of accomplished teachers) improves the quality of education for students."[30]

But this argument subtly conflates coincidental interests with mutual shared interests. Moreover, it overlooks the possibility that, in other instances, policies that are beneficial for school employees are not so beneficial for students. Table 8.1 provides some relevant examples, showing how teacher and student interests should be characterized as contingent and mixed. Consider the policy debate over class size (item A, discussed in row 1 of the table). When Casey highlights how unions fight to reduce class sizes, there is rigorous research supporting the union's position that small classes can benefit students. Here, on first blush, what is good for teachers appears to be good for students too. Parents and students tend to favor small classes. Teachers find them more appealing too. And research has shown that students often make stronger academic progress when they are taught in smaller classes.

Probing more deeply, however, shows that even in debates over class size, the relationship between student and teacher interests will be contingent and mixed. Yes, research indicates that lower class sizes boost student learning, but this finding tends to apply narrowly to students in lower grades (K–3) and only when policymakers spend significant sums of money to substantially lower class sizes. In other words, if policymakers set out to establish class-size policies with only one objective in mind—doing what class-size research shows is best for kids—they would surgically steer education dollars into lowering class sizes in the early grades. Policymakers might even opt for larger class sizes for older students so that they could redirect these less efficient expenditures to some other needs. If teacher and student interests were perfectly congruent, teachers unions would adopt the very same position, lobbying for reduced class sizes *only* in cases where the research shows that it matters for students.[31] Yet the historical record shows that this is not how unions have approached class-size debates. In California and Florida, for example, they advocated for across-the-board reductions that, in the end, cost both states millions of dollars without leading to significant student achievement gains.[32]

To be clear, this is *not* a criticism of the position that teachers unions have staked out on class-size policy. As teacher advocacy organizations, their job is to lobby for policies that benefit school employees. And teachers have entirely legitimate reasons to prefer smaller classes, irrespective of whether the costs needed to maintain those smaller classes provide the best return on investment for student learning. As political scientist Lorraine McDonnell explains:

TABLE 8.1 **Evidence of research-based tensions between teacher and student interests**

Issue	Teacher interests	Student interests	Relevant research
A. Class size reduction Debate over whether class sizes should be lowered across the board, including universal caps.	• Unions support lowering class sizes across the board (see the 2019 *NEA Handbook*, resolution B-12). • As employees, teachers benefit from having fewer students to teach. Unions benefit too. Lower class sizes require more hiring—which leads to more members and more union revenue.	• Students can benefit from targeted class-size reductions. • No ostensible harm to students; however, universal class-size reductions are costly and may not be the most efficient or effective way to help students.	Research shows that large reductions in class sizes in the early grades (K–3) boost student learning. Beyond that, there is little systematic evidence that money spent on class-size reductions improves student learning.[1]
B. Single-salary schedules Current approach used to pay most teachers in the United States. Salary schedules link compensation to experience and degree credentials.	• Unions strongly favor the single-salary schedule (see the 2019 *NEA Handbook*, resolution F-9). • Senior and lower-performing teachers benefit by earning more under rigid schedules. However, younger and higher-performing teachers earn less under rigid schedules.	• Students' sole interest is in having highly effective teachers. • Higher salaries should make teaching more attractive, making teacher and student interests congruent. However, failing to differentiate pay makes it harder to attract talent and deploy it where it is needed most.	Research shows that union-induced wage frictions can explain much of the decline in teacher academic aptitude between 1950 and the present.[2] Research shows that performance pay has a small but positive effect on student achievement;[3] it also appeals more to higher-quality teachers.[4]
C. Tenure Current policy of granting teachers job security after a short probationary period.	• Unions strongly support and defend tenure for teachers (see the 2019 *NEA Handbook*, resolution F-18). • Tenure benefits teachers' occupational interests in having greater job security.	• Students' sole interest is in having highly effective teachers. • Job security is a form of compensation that could make teaching a more attractive profession. However, there is little evidence that more highly effective employees prefer job security as a form of compensation.	Recent research shows that Florida's policy of eliminating tenure had a positive impact on student performance.[5] Some research estimates that removing and replacing the lowest-performing tenth of teachers could, in the long run, boost GDP by 1.6 percent, or roughly the amount we now spend on total annual teacher compensation.[6]

(continues)

TABLE 8.1 *(continued)*

Issue	Teacher interests	Student interests	Relevant research
D. Paying teachers for advanced degrees Near-universal practice of paying a premium to teachers for earning master's degrees.	• Unions support additional pay for earning advanced degrees (see the 2019 *NEA Handbook*, resolution F-9). • Teachers who earned advanced degrees have a vested interest in keeping the salary premium, irrespective of whether it is an effective human-resources policy for attracting and retaining highly effective teachers.	• Students' sole interest is in having highly effective teachers. • Since advanced degrees are not a proxy for teacher effectiveness, these costs represent a lost opportunity to allocate money in ways that improve students' access to better-quality teachers.	Teachers who earn advanced degrees are not, as a rule, more effective at raising their students' achievement.[7]
E. Seniority provisions Policies that make teacher seniority determinative or important factors in pay and human-resources considerations (e.g., layoffs, transfers).	• Unions support using seniority and experience in pay and layoff-and-transfer policy (see the 2019 *NEA Handbook*, resolution F-19). • Senior teachers and veteran teachers who came into the system when seniority policies were in place have a vested interest in seeing such systems maintained, as they benefit those teachers professionally.	• Students' sole interest is in having highly effective teachers. • Since years of experience are not a reliable proxy for teacher effectiveness, pay and human-resources policies that strictly and narrowly reward teachers based on their years of service impose an unnecessary cost on policymakers by making it more costly and difficult to adopt workforce policies that strictly prioritize students' learning needs.	If seniority were a reliable way to measure teacher effectiveness, policies that make teacher experience a key factor in human-resources decisions would benefit students. However, research indicates that additional experience beyond the first few years of a teacher's career is a less consistent predictor of their effectiveness. Research also indicates that strict seniority policies in CBAs can be harmful to students.[8]

| F: Defined-benefit pensions
Existing policy of providing retirement benefits through a defined-benefit plan (commonly called a pension). | • Unions strongly oppose eliminating defined-benefit pensions (see the 2019 *NEA Handbook*, resolution F-62).
• Veteran teachers strongly benefit from defined-benefit pension plans. Teachers who are less mobile do too. Unions have strongly resisted efforts to replace defined-benefit pension plans with defined-contribution ones. For younger, more mobile teachers, defined-benefit plans may not be especially generous. | • Students' sole interest is in having highly effective teachers.
• To the extent that pensions subsume a large portion of compensation, it is ideal for students if that compensation is shown to induce higher-quality teachers to enter and stay in the profession. Research suggests any such inducement is not significant and that pensions can be a drag on the efficient allocation of compensation dollars.[9] | Research shows that when given a choice, teachers who choose DC plans with mobile benefits are, on average, moderately more effective as measured by value-added test scores.[10] |

Notes: 1 Matthew M. Chingos, "The Impact of a Universal Class-Size Reduction Policy: Evidence from Florida's Statewide Mandate," *Economics of Education Review* 31, no. 5 (2012): 543–62; Matthew M. Chingos, "Class Size and Student Outcomes: Research and Policy Implications," *Journal of Policy Analysis and Management* 32, no. 2 (Spring 2013): 411–38.

2 Caroline Hoxby and Andrew Leigh, "Pulled Away or Pushed Out? Explaining the Decline of Teacher Aptitude in the United States," *American Economic Review* 94, no. 2 (2004): 236–40.

3 Lam D. Pham, Tuan D. Nguyen, and Matthew G. Springer, "Teacher Merit Pay: A Meta-Analysis," *American Educational Research Journal* 58, no. 3 (February 2020): 527–66.

4 Eric A. Hanushek, Marc Piopiunik, and Simon Wiederhold, "The Value of Smarter Teachers: International Evidence on Teacher Cognitive Skills and Student Performance," *Journal of Human Resources* 54, no. 4 (2019): 857–99; Michael Jones and Michael T. Hartney, "Show Who the Money? Teacher Sorting Patterns and Performance Pay across US School Districts," *Public Administration Review* 77, no. 6 (2017): 919–31.

5 Celeste Carruthers, David Figlio, and Tim Sass, *Did Tenure Reform in Florida Affect Student Test Scores?*, Evidence Speaks Reports 2, no. 52 (May 2018): 52.

6 Eric A. Hanushek, "Teacher Deselection," in *Creating a New Teaching Profession*, eds. Dan Goldhaber and Jane Hannaway (Washington, DC: Urban Institute Press, 2009): 165–80, at 172–73; National Council on Teacher Quality, *Restructuring Teacher Pay to Reward Excellence*, report, Washington, DC, December 2010: 3, https://files.eric.ed.gov/fulltext/ED521227.pdf.

7 National Council on Teacher Quality, *Restructuring Teacher Pay to Reward Excellence*, report, Washington, DC, December 2010: 3, https://files.eric.ed.gov/fulltext/ED521227.pdf.

8 Matthew M. Chingos and Paul E. Peterson, "It's Easier to Pick a Good Teacher than to Train One: Familiar and New Results on the Correlates of Teacher Effectiveness," *Economics of Education Review* 30, no. 3 (2011): 449–65; Donald Boyd, Hamilton Lankford, Susanna Loeb, and James Wyckoff, "Teacher Layoffs: An Empirical Illustration of Seniority versus Measures of Effectiveness," *Education Finance and Policy* 6, no. 3 (2011): 439–54; Matthew A. Kraft, "Teacher Layoffs, Teacher Quality, and Student Achievement: Evidence from a Discretionary Layoff Policy," *Education Finance and Policy* 10, no. 4 (2015): 467–507.

9 Ben Backes, Dan Goldhaber, Cyrus Grout, Cory Koedel, Shawn Ni, Michael Podgursky, P. Brett Xiang, and Zeyu Xu, "Benefit or Burden? On the Intergenerational Inequity of Teacher Pension Plans," *Educational Researcher* 45, no. 6 (August 2016): 367–77.

10 Matthew M. Chingos and Martin R. West, "Which Teachers Choose a Defined Contribution Pension Plan? Evidence from the Florida Retirement System," *Education Finance and Policy* 10, no. 2 (Spring 2015): 193–222; Dan Goldhaber and Cyrus Grout, "Which Plan to Choose? The Determinants of Pension System Choice for Public School Teachers," *Journal of Pension Economics & Finance* 15, no. 1 (January 2016): 30–54.

To suggest that organized teachers, because of the kinds of demands they are making and by their superior numbers and resources, may be excluding other groups affected by public education from the policy process is not to argue against teachers organizing to achieve better working conditions. Nor is it to say that teachers should not participate in educational decision-making. Rather, what we have tried to indicate is that in making evaluations about educational policies, organized teachers are not solely guided by the professional criterion of student learning effectiveness . . . They also have self-interests that may, at times, come into conflict with the public interest as it relates to education.[33]

Continuing with table 8.1, items B–F highlight five different teacher policy issues where studies have shown that what students need—to excel academically—can conflict with what teachers understandably desire as employees. Collectively, these examples serve to illustrate how unions must sometimes pursue policies that benefit teachers professionally, but are, in some or all cases, suboptimal policies for students' learning needs.

Column 2 carefully explains how, for each policy issue at hand, the status quo policies benefit teachers' interests as employees. Column 3 does the same thing for students, noting that when it comes to any teacher workforce policy, students' sole interest is in having policies that increase their access to highly effective teachers. Consider item D in row 4, which provides a simple example to illustrate the logic of my argument. This item relates to the divergent interests that teachers and students have in the current practice of automatically paying teachers more for having earned an advanced degree (most typically a master's degree).

Teachers, unions, and other establishment education interests (e.g., colleges of education) have a vested material interest in the current practice of paying teachers more for earning advanced degrees. For veteran educators who were once told that the only way to earn a raise was by earning an advanced degree, eliminating the master's-degree premium would be grossly unfair. Unfortunately, research shows that students do not, as a general rule, benefit from being taught by teachers who have an advanced degree.[34] According to one recent meta-analysis of this scholarly literature, "out of 102 statistical tests examined, approximately 90 percent showed that advanced degrees had either no impact at all or, in some cases, a negative impact on student achievement."[35] While there are some important exceptions to this general rule,[36] the immense resources that are currently devoted to paying teachers a premium for earning a master's degree are not creating much of a learning return for students. Were school districts to redirect those current investments away from paying for advanced degrees and toward, say, offering higher starting teacher salaries or paying teachers more to teach in hard-to-staff schools, then student and teacher interests would be working more in concert with one another.[37]

Too often, however, that is not what happens. No one is personally at fault when the student and teacher interests diverge. This problem occurs naturally when education employees and students both have separate material interests at stake. However, once state and school-district governments make policy commitments to their teachers—from seniority benefits (item E, row 5) to defined-benefit pension guarantees (item F, row 6) to tenure protections (item C, row 3)—if new research suddenly comes along and shows that such policies are no longer uniformly beneficial for students, this clash of interests will occur. By definition, these dynamics will tend to narrow and constrain the menu of reforms that are available for those policymakers who wish to focus singularly on raising student achievement.

The Bigger Picture

Union advocates and critics will never agree about the precise degree to which teacher and student interests overlap. However, the schematic concept illustrated in figure 8.2 suggests something obvious about the relationship between union power and policymakers' efforts to improve student achievement. Where teacher and student interests diverge, policymakers will, by definition, find it more challenging to enact and sustain reforms to address student learning needs. Admittedly, that is a controversial claim. I would note, however, that union leaders themselves have, on occasion, recognized these same tensions. Several years before NEA president Bob Chase delivered his famous "new unionism" speech, NEA legal counsel Robert Chanin commented on the inherent tension between teachers unions and school reform:

> The essential question is, can an education reform movement that is premised on a sharing of common interests, mutual trust, and consensus building find happiness in a system of labor relations that is inherently adversarial in nature? The principle of seniority is the cornerstone of American labor relations, in

both the public and private sectors. Seniority provides an objective standard by which employment decisions can be made, as opposed to unilateral and often arbitrary employer action . . . But how can we deny that seniority . . . reduces what some consider to be "managerial flexibility" in the operation of school systems?

I am not so naïve or Pollyannaish as to rule out the possibility that these two tracks—collective bargaining and education reform—may on occasion cross. As the education reform movement progresses, proposals may be developed that are . . . objectionable to NEA only because they do not adequately protect the collective bargaining rights of employees. Accommodation may prove impossible, and NEA may be forced . . . to make a choice it would rather not have to make—to perhaps establish priorities between its commitment to education reform and its commitment to collective bargaining . . . Should this become necessary, for me, the choice is relatively clear . . . I firmly believe that if we back away from exclusive recognition, seniority, grievance arbitration, and the other protections that current collective bargaining structure gives us, we will most assuredly, and rather promptly—find ourselves subject to the same authoritarian structure and in the same subservient status that we were prior to the advent of collective bargaining.

I am fully aware of the need to improve the quality of education in order to save public education, and the need for NEA to be deeply involved in that effort in order for NEA to remain relevant, but I do not believe that education reform should be achieved at the expense of employee rights . . . Education employees have achieved, through collective bargaining, important and well-deserved rights. We cannot allow these rights to be taken away in the name of education reform, and we must resist any attempt to weaken collective bargaining.[38]

To be clear, teachers unions cannot (and should not) be blamed for everything that ails American education.[39] However, if one accepts that teacher and student interests sometimes diverge, then union power can be a sufficient impediment to raising student achievement. In other words, my argument is fairly narrow and modest: union power can sometimes be sufficient, even if it is not necessary, to constrain policymakers' efforts to raise student performance.

Note two additional things about this argument. First, it does not imply that all reform proposals that teachers unions oppose will "work" to improve student learning. Second, union power is not a necessary condition for states to fail to make much progress. Instead, my argument is that the ability of policymakers and administrators to turn around low-performing schools entails difficult and not-well-understood work. There is no guaranteed template for success. So, any external force—be it powerful union opposition or something else—that constrains the boundaries of school reform by taking certain ideas "off the table" is inconsistent with any standard notion of best organizational practices. Few turnaround experts would advise a struggling organization to eliminate potential turnaround solutions from consideration simply because they clash uncomfortably with the interests of one subset of that organization's stakeholders. And as long as such clashes happen (e.g., those shown in table 8.1), there are reasons to anticipate that they may limit the ability of policymakers to enact and sustain needed reforms.

A New Study

We now turn from the theoretical to the empirical. In what follows, I undertake a new study that—while hardly definitive—improves on most prior state-level studies estimating the impact of union power on student achievement. My analysis addresses three specific weaknesses in existing state-level work. First, I pay close attention to issues of timing and the long-term effects of union power on achievement. Second, my estimates rely on more-comparable measures of student achievement and more-comprehensive measures of union strength. Third, I leverage changes in union power within states over time to estimate the causal effect of labor retrenchment (reduced union power) on student achievement.

Assume that unions influence student achievement through their political power to shape the tone and direction of school-reform efforts.[40] Estimating the effects of union power on student achievement would, by definition, need to account for the timing and sequence of both these phenomena. For example, analysts would want to assess the relationship between union power and student achievement during a time period in which policymakers were actively working to enact performance-based school reforms. Studying unionization and student outcomes before the reform movement, for example, would tell us nothing about whether union political power blunts policymakers' reform efforts to boost achievement.

Unfortunately, most of the state-level work on teacher-union effects was carried out long before the excellence movement began. Even fewer such studies have been carried out in the post–No Child Left Behind era. For example, one frequently cited state-level study—Kleiner and Petree's analysis of union strength and states' SAT/ACT scores—was conducted between 1972 and 1982, long before policymakers got serious about choice, accountability, and teacher quality reforms.[41] What effect would one expect union power to have on policymakers who had not yet themselves decided dramatic reforms were needed?

State-level studies suffer from a second timing-related deficiency. Most work that has correlated union strength and rates of student achievement across the states has failed to consider the effects of union power on student learning gains over the long run. In fact, this literature has rarely focused on *changes* in long-term student-achievement outcomes. These are major shortcomings if we want to rigorously test the hypothesis that union political power impacts student achievement by constraining the ability of policymakers to enact meaningful reforms. What we need to do is to carefully track the progress that states have made over time, not simply where states started out. These latter baseline performance levels are mostly a reflection of longstanding demographic differences in states' student and family population characteristics.

Unlike prior cross-sectional studies that naively correlate union strength and student achievement across states, I analyze the relationship between union strength and changes in states' performance on the National Assessment of Educational Progress (NAEP). In my own analyses, I adopt two important correctives to the literature.

First, I measure variation in union strength—my key explanatory variable—using a richer set of indicators that more fully capture the multi-dimensionality of teacher-union power. Specifically, I use two measures of union interest-group power across the states: the Fordham Institute's comprehensive ranking of teacher-union power across states, as well as the total dues revenue (per teacher) generated by each NEA state affiliate between 1980 and 2017. In contrast to prior studies that focus narrowly on membership rates or the presence of a bargaining law enacted half a century ago, my approach puts union politics and resources at the center of the analysis. For example, the Fordham measure includes indicators that account for teachers unions' campaign contributions in state politics, the fraction of Democratic Party convention delegates in each state that are teacher-union members, and more general resource measures, including dues revenue and the strength of states' teacher labor laws. In sum, this broader measurement approach recognizes that teachers unions—like all interest groups—rely on a variety of strategies to maximize their influence in education politics and policymaking.[42]

Second, when measuring student achievement, I address the fact that states vary in all sorts of different ways that most likely correlate with union strength (e.g., demographically, socio-economically). Specifically, I use "adjusted" NAEP scores to measure student performance across states. These adjusted scores—first released in 2015 by the Urban Institute's Matthew Chingos—use restricted-use NAEP micro-data to construct aggregate NAEP scores that are fully comparable across states.[43] As Chingos explains, adjusted NAEP scores enable researchers to "compare the average performance of students in each state compared to demographically similar students around the country." Put simply, the adjusted scores make it possible for us to compare student performance in Mississippi and Massachusetts directly, without including any additional controls to account for differences in test takers.

Although cross-sectional comparisons remain imperfect, these two innovations—a better measure of union political power and demographically adjusted, comparable measures of student performance—represent an improvement over existing state-level studies. Finally, I focus on the test-score *gains* that students made over time in each state on the adjusted NAEP.[44] Specifically, my outcome variable of interest is measured as the gain in adjusted NAEP performance that states made between two points of time, rather than a simple level of NAEP performance at any given time.

I examine two specific periods of long-term NAEP performance gains. Since adjusted NAEP scores are available beginning for mathematics in 1996 and most recently in 2019, the first outcome examined is the achievement gains that states made during this twenty-three-year time period. I also examine a second period of adjusted NAEP gains between 1998 and 2019, since the earliest available adjusted reading scores are those from 1998.[45] Because I am interested in modeling gains in NAEP performance between two different points of time, I include the baseline adjusted NAEP score on the right-hand side of my regression models to account for the fact that making gains is more difficult for states that start out with higher scores on the NAEP exam.[46] However, because adjusted NAEP scores already incorporate differences in test takers' individual demographic characteristics, it is unnecessary to include state-level demographic control variables in the main analyses.[47] Indeed, that is the entire rationale of using the adjusted scores.[48]

The results of eight separate regression analyses examining the relationship between union strength and long-term changes on states' adjusted NAEP scores are presented in tables A8.2 and A8.3 in the chapter appendix. Irrespective of the particular measure of teacher-union strength that is used, I find evidence that states with stronger unions made lower adjusted NAEP gains. Specifically, across five of the eight models, states with stronger teachers unions—those where NEA affiliates generated more union revenue per teacher and those ranked stronger on the Fordham union-strength index—made smaller adjusted NAEP gains between the 1990s and late 2010s.

Importantly, there is one measure of union strength that does *not* correlate with reduced NAEP gains across states. As a robustness check, I included a placebo measure of union political strength in my analysis: the amount of *federal* NEA-PAC contributions generated (per member) by each state NEA affiliate. As discussed earlier in the book, these federal PAC funds capture the general level of activism among teacher-union members in politics, but they have little to no practical way of impacting state education politics and policymaking because these federal PAC dollars are geared toward federal elections. In short, the null results of this placebo test indicate that it is not the case that more generally politically active teachers are associated with weaker student achievement. Rather, we see that states' adjusted NAEP gains are associated with only one specific kind of teacher-union power: the power that unions bring to bear in *state* politics. This finding is important because it is precisely what we would expect to happen if Goldhaber's hypothesis—that "[teachers] unions may have more direct long-term effects through their political power to influence school reform efforts"—is true.

The relationship between union power and lower adjusted NAEP gains is not only statistically significant but also substantively meaningful. Moving from a state where union revenue per teacher is one standard deviation below the mean to one where it is one standard deviation above is associated with four fewer points gained on the fourth grade NAEP mathematics exam between 1996 and 2019. Similarly, moving from a state in the bottom ten of Fordham's union-power ranking to one in the top ten was associated with five fewer points gained on the fourth-grade mathematics exam. Substantively, four points represents an effect size of more than half a standard deviation. This relationship between union strength measured as union dues revenue per teacher and adjusted NAEP gains on fourth-grade mathematics between 1996 and 2019 is shown visually in figure 8.3.

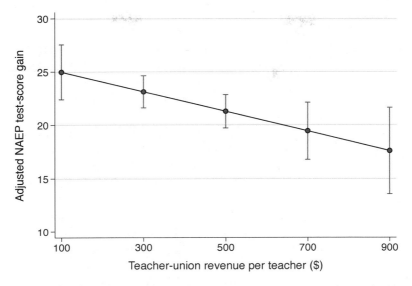

FIGURE 8.3 Relationship between states' adjusted NAEP test-score gains and teacher-union resources

Notes: Figure shows the marginal effects of union power (measured as union revenue per teacher for each NEA state affiliate) on the gains states made in fourth-grade mathematics between 1996 and 2019. NAEP scores are adjusted scores that are appropriate for making over-time comparisons. See Matthew Chingos, *Breaking the Curve: Promises and Pitfalls of Using NAEP Data to Assess the State Role in Student Achievement* (Washington, DC: Urban Institute, 2015), http://www.urban.org/research/publication/breaking-curve-promises-and-pitfalls-using-naep-data-assessstate-role-student-achievement/view/full_report. The data itself is available at https://apps.urban.org/features/naep/.

All together, these results provide an important corrective to what has been a longstanding tendency in popular (and even some scholarly) discourse to emphasize the positive correlation between union membership rates and higher raw test scores (e.g., SAT/ACT or NAEP) across states. However, my own cross-sectional analyses are not without limitations. Though they improve on prior work, these estimates are still not well identified because they are not able to control for unobserved differences across states that are correlated with union strength in a state.

To account for unobserved differences between states, we need to move beyond simple cross-sectional analyses to isolate the within-state effects of union strength on achievement. To that end, I leverage the fact that the Great Recession prompted state lawmakers in a handful of states to disrupt longstanding patterns in teacher-union strength by weakening the legal landscape in which they bargain collectively. These changes—the first significant ones that states made to their teacher labor laws since the 1980s and 1990s—enable us to see how, if at all, student achievement changes *after* union power is curtailed. Specifically, I focus on five states that adopted union retrenchment laws in 2011 that weakened teachers unions by narrowing collective bargaining rights: Idaho, Indiana, Michigan, Tennessee, and Wisconsin. These five states become the "treated" states in my analysis, taking a value of 1 for student cohorts that were educated within their borders after 2011 and a 0 for those educated before.

Since this particular analysis aims to uncover the effects of sudden changes in union strength within states over time, a unique feature of the NAEP testing program makes unadjusted NAEP scores more useful than adjusted ones. Specifically, I am able to create *cohort-gain scores* on the NAEP exam to test whether changes in union strength impact the test-score gains made by specific cohorts of students before and after labor retrenchment occurred in their states. This difference-in-difference approach is made possible because the NAEP has been administered to representative samples of fourth- and eighth-grade students in all fifty states on a biennial basis since 2003. A popular approach to examining test-score gains on the NAEP, therefore, has been to link cohorts of students across time. In other words, I can compare eighth-grade student performance in a state during a given year with the performance registered by the state's fourth-graders four years earlier. Although the specific students selected to take the NAEP test in a state change each year, this approach helps control for any unobserved commonalities that impact specific cohorts of students in a state over the specific time period when they are in school.[49]

Specifically, I am able to examine the achievement gains registered by seven separate cohorts of eighth-grade students who took the NAEP between 2007 and 2019. For example, the earliest cohort of eighth-grade students are those whose performance gains in 2007 can be calculated with reference to that cohort's performance as fourth-graders four years earlier in 2003. The key independent variable is a binary indicator for whether a state in a given year had curtailed union power by implementing a labor-retrenchment law during the year a cohort was educated. This "retrenchment" treatment variable is equal to 1 if the state had fully implemented such a law during each cohort's fourth-to-eighth-grade learning years. All of these models incorporate state and year fixed effects to ensure that the effect of my main explanatory variable of interest—the adoption of a law reducing union strength—is estimated in a way that also accounts for any unobserved differences across states that are constant over time (e.g., poverty, education, culture).

The results of this analysis are presented in table A8.4 in the chapter appendix. The first two models estimate the impact of a reduction in union power within a state on the NAEP gains made by eighth graders in mathematics (column 1) and reading (column 2) for all fifty states. In columns 3 and 4, I narrow the sample to the thirty-four states that began the period of this analysis with a mandatory teacher collective bargaining law. This is my preferred set of estimates, since the "treatment" states that weakened union power arguably started out most similar to states that also had strong teacher CB laws.

Since the treatment variable for union retrenchment is binary (1= reductions in union power, 0= no changes), interpretation is straightforward. In both math and reading, student cohorts educated in states that had rolled back union power made higher relative gains than students in states that left union power untouched. The impact of union retrenchment ranges from 2.4 to 3.6 more points gained on the NAEP between fourth and eighth grade. These differences represent an effect size of about three-quarters of a standard deviation.[50]

How confident can we be that these test-score gains were related to states' policies reducing union power? The inclusion of state fixed effects certainly helps guard against the possibility that the relationship is driven by unobserved differences across states. Still, if states that were more likely to reduce union power in 2011 were changing in some other way at that particular time compared to states that did not curtail union power, we might be misattributing these achievement gains to union retrenchment laws. To guard against that possibility, I take advantage of the fact that the state of Ohio enacted a union retrenchment law in 2011 — only to have it overturned in a statewide referendum before it could be implemented. Ohio can thus serve as a "placebo" test since it shared a similar political environment to the states that enacted union retrenchment during the Great Recession. As the results in table A8.4 show, however, Ohio did not share a similar trajectory on NAEP gains to actual treatment states. In fact, it experienced a combination of decreases and increases in achievement. In other words, there is no consistent relationship like we observe in the true retrenchment states, which uniformly saw achievement gains after union power was curtailed. Finally, it is worth noting that these findings are robust to the inclusion of controls for time-varying changes, such as the level of private-sector union power in a state and the overall policy liberalism in a state (nonspecific to union retrenchment). In sum, the five states that reduced teacher-union strength made larger NAEP cohort gains after the implementation of retrenchment compared to non-retrenchment states, even after accounting for baseline performance, state fixed effects, and changing characteristics related to political culture and private-sector union power.

Taken together, these results seem to indicate two things. First, states that enacted labor-retrenchment laws increased the pace of learning gains between fourth and eighth grade in the years after those laws went into effect. Second, irrespective of gains, comparable student populations performed no worse and, in the case of reading, better by the time they reached eighth grade after their state had weakened its teacher labor law. At the very least, these results indicate that the string of labor-retrenchment laws that were adopted in 2011 had no significant negative impact on student performance in the aggregate. Eight full years after retrenchment laws went into effect, eighth-grade students—whose schooling had occurred entirely under weaker labor laws—fared no worse and, on the whole, mostly better than their peers in the previous decade, when their state had stronger teacher labor laws. This finding is important because, if policymakers were able to realize costs savings of any kind in the aftermath of labor-law reforms, those cost savings came without any significant negative returns to student achievement. What remains to be seen is whether policymakers will actually take advantage of the flexibility these legal changes have given them, especially at the school-district level, in the years ahead.[51]

Putting It All Together

The findings presented here should be taken seriously but not definitively. They should be taken seriously because there are several reasons that these findings may well underestimate the effects of union power on slowing states' efforts to increase student performance.

For one thing, the treatment variable in the over-time analysis is imperfectly measured. Many school districts in the treated states that adopted labor-law reforms could not make immediate practical use of their new-found managerial autonomy until a few years later when collective bargaining agreements expired, rendering my treatment variable in the analysis biased toward finding no effects for retrenchment.

Additionally, the analysis omits Washington, DC, which researchers have shown experienced a boost in NAEP performance even after accounting for gentrification, on account of the reforms Michelle Rhee and her successors enacted—including reforms that weakened the power of the Washington Teachers Union.[52] Finally, the long-run effects of union strength on student achievement—the kind that economists Michael Lovenheim and Alexander Willén document in their important 2019 study—cannot be factored into an analysis that is confined to looking at the effects of retrenchment within the first decade of its implementation. Studying the long-run effects of unionization—particularly union political power—is near impossible due to the fact that the period in which the unions' state affiliates gained political power happened long before comparable cross-state test scores and other measures of academic progress were administered and collected.

That said, some caution should be taken in interpreting the findings of these analyses. Although my results should put to rest the oft-repeated claims that positive correlations between state union density and raw NAEP scores mean unions reliably boost (or at least can't be said to hinder) student performance, my own study is imperfect. It will hardly be the last word on the subject. As Terry Moe cautioned readers of his book *Special Interest*: "teachers unions are [not] solely responsible for the nation's education problems . . . but they are at the heart of the problems, and the unions themselves and the various roles they play in collective bargaining and politics need to be much better studied and understood."[53]

Whatever one's normative position regarding unions in American education, recent changes in long-entrenched labor laws (including new pro-labor laws that I discuss in the next chapter) mean that researchers will have more fertile ground to study union effects in the years ahead. With access to better measures of student outcomes—including both cognitive and noncognitive measures—more sophisticated and nuanced studies are sure to be added to the field in the coming years. Even if the normative divide and controversy surrounding these issues is unlikely to thaw, more high-quality research will be a positive outcome. As Michael Lovenheim acknowledged of his recent study showing that the long-run effects of unionization negatively impacted the lifetime earnings of men: "There's no sugar-coating it. That's absolutely the case . . . But I don't think the policy recommendation is necessarily, 'Let's outlaw collective bargaining.' There's more evidence being introduced on these questions, and so I think whenever we do policy, we want to take into account the body of evidence. We should never make policy based on one study."[54]

Although scholars have studied the relationship between unionization and student achievement for decades, the conclusions drawn from this body of work have often been mischaracterized. After outlining the extraordinary empirical challenges confronting researchers who study these thorny issues, I reevaluated four decades of prior work. That reassessment revealed that more-recent and more–rigorously designed studies provide qualified support for the rent-seeking hypothesis—that union power can promote suboptimal schooling policies which, in turn, can make it more difficult to raise student achievement.

After issuing these correctives, I then proposed a new way of thinking about the influence of union power on student achievement that is anchored in necessary and sufficient conditions. While states can fail to make progress for all sorts of reasons having nothing to do with union power, such power can be more than sufficient in its own right to stymie progress, especially in contexts where policymakers are committed to reform but find themselves facing stiff opposition from vested interests. My argument was supported in two principal ways. First, experimental evidence revealed that teachers themselves recognize that their interests as education employees are qualitatively different than those of students. Teachers acknowledge that the purpose of their unions is to advocate for their interests as education employees, not primarily to advance student interests. At the very least, teachers appear to recognize that union and student interests are not one and the same.

I then showed that the degree to which teacher and student interests mesh is highly contingent and mixed. Often, tensions between student and teacher interests produce zero-sum scenarios where one party stands to lose. Across a variety of issues—ranging from salary schedules to seniority provisions—unions must sometimes subvert student interests in order to faithfully advocate for the members they represent. Teachers have completely legitimate reasons to value many existing education policies that run counter to student interests. There is nothing evil about a clash between student and teacher interests; in fact, it is an inherent and unavoidable aspect of relying on democratic political institutions to define the boundaries of education policy. That said, these dynamics need to be acknowledged and understood. We cannot gloss over the fact that, at best, such tensions greatly complicate policymakers' efforts to advance policies that are singularly concerned with promoting student learning needs.

Since little effort has been made to understand the long-term consequences of union political power on the performance of state education systems, I concluded the chapter by embarking on one of the very first empirical tests of Goldhaber's hypothesis that "[teachers] unions may have more direct long-term effects through their political power to influence school reform efforts." To formally test that expectation, I examined the relationship between union political power in the 1980s and 1990s and states' demographically adjusted student performance on the NAEP in subsequent decades. Overall, I found consistent evidence that, all else equal, states made less progress on the NAEP when organized teacher interests wielded greater resources in state politics. In contrast to previous studies that rely on naive correlations between union density and average ACT/SAT scores, my own study shows that the theoretically appropriate way to measure union power—state union affiliates' political resources— strongly predicts weaker achievement gains on demographically adjusted NAEP scores. Finally, I leveraged changes in the strength of teacher bargaining laws that arose exogenously during the Great Recession shock to conduct an analysis that had previously been impossible. After decades of equilibrium in labor law, I estimate that states that gained additional autonomy from union power made more progress than peer states that made no changes to labor law during this era.

For many readers, these arguments and findings will seem wide of the mark. Even though he readily concedes that "teacher and student interests are not perfectly aligned," union advocate Richard Kahlenberg wonders, "who are the selfless adults who better represent the interests of kids? The hedge fund managers who support charter schools and also want their income taxed at lower rates than regular earned income, thereby squeezing education budgets?" Kahlenberg explains that he'd prefer to place his faith ". . . in the democratically elected representatives of educators who work with kids day in and day out."[55] Others argue that teachers unions play a key role in counterbalancing the power of big business in American politics. Columbia University political scientist Alex Hertel-Fernandez, for example, worries that laws that undermine the power of public-sector unions only enhance the power of corporations at the expense of ordinary workers.[56] In the absence of strong private-sector unions, Kahlenberg and Hertel-Fernandez see the teachers unions as indispensable, a bulwark against the expansion of corporate power and the rightward shift in US policymaking. Of course, this view is not without thoughtful criticism too. CUNY political scientist Dan DiSalvo, for one, is skeptical that public-sector unions behave like private-sector unions to advance sociotropic, rather than narrow self-interested, concerns.[57]

This larger debate about the broader role of labor unions in American politics is beyond the reach and focus of my work here. However, these arguments, in my estimation, sidestep the narrow issue at hand: the role of teachers unions in constraining the menu of school reforms that education policymakers are given license to experiment with to try and raise and improve student performance. It can both be true that the teachers unions play an important role in propping up what is left of the labor movement in the United States, while at the same time remaining a force that is unapologetic and relentless in pursuing teachers' occupational interests in schools in such a way as to constrain policy reform in the education arena.

The results of this chapter seem to suggest that when a narrow vested interest becomes too dominant, the ability of policymakers to enact reforms to drive improvement is reduced. In a recent podcast interview with *Education Next*, political scientist Robert Maranto—no cheerleader for the unions—cautions reformers that weakening unions is no panacea for improving student performance. Yet even in cautioning us to avoid putting too much blame on the unions, he concedes that union power can be sufficient to snuff out reform. "The way I would frame it," Maranto explains, "is by going back to James Madison. Any faction, if it gains too much power, is going to seek monopoly rents. So I think that where unions have too much power, they have tended to behave in ways that are not good for students. But conversely, where administrators and school boards have too much power, sometimes they have behaved in ways that are not necessarily good for children. So I think you need a mix."[58]

Consistent with Maranto, I have argued that teachers unions are neither the only nor a necessary ingredient to slow education progress. But when and where the unions have gained outsized power and influence, their intransigence may be sufficient to mute student performance gains across the American states. The key question that remains is how much of a force the unions will be in the decades ahead. Will the reductions in teacher bargaining power that I focused on in this chapter spread more rapidly to other states in years to come? In the aftermath of the Supreme Court's *Janus* decision, have we entered an era of teacher-union decline? It is to these issues that I turn in the next chapter.

Chapter Appendix

TABLE A8.1 **Summary of union effects research literature 1983–present**

Year	Student outcomes measured at:	Union strength measured at:	Author(s)	Impact on student outcomes?	Causal research design?
1984	District level	District measure	Eberts and Stone	Mixed	No
1986	District level	District measure	Eberts and Stone	Mixed	No
1987	Student level	District measure	Eberts and Stone	Mixed	No
1987	State level	State measure	Kurth	Negative	No
1988	State level	State measure	Kleiner and Petree	Mixed	Yes
1988	State level	State measure	Nelson and Gould	Positive	No
1991	Student level	State measure	Register and Grimes	Positive	No
1993	State level	State measure	Peltzman	Negative	No
1994	Student level	District measure	Zigarelli	Positive	No
1995	Student level	District measure	Argys and Rees	Mixed	No
1996	District level	District measure	Hoxby	Negative	Yes
1996	State level	State measure	Nelson and Rosen	Positive	No
1996	State level	State measure	Peltzman	Negative	Yes
1997	Student level	District measure	Milkman	Positive	No
2000	State level	State measure	Steelman, Powell, and Carini	Positive	No
2008	Student level	District measure	Carini	Positive	No
2009	District level	District measure	Lovenheim	Mixed	Yes
2009	District level (CA)	CBA restrictiveness measure	Moe	Negative	No
2010	District level (CA)	District measure	Rose and Sonstelie	Negative	No
2011	State level	State measure	Lindy	Mixed	Yes
2011	District level (CA)	CBA restrictiveness measure	Strunk	Negative	No
2011	District level (CA)	CBA restrictiveness measure	Strunk and McEachin	Negative	No
2013	District level	State measure	Lott and Kenney	Negative	No
2015	District level (CA charters)	District measure	Hart and Sojourner	Mixed	Yes
2015	Student level	District measure	Vachon and Ma	Positive	No
2018	District level (WI)	District measure	Baron	Positive	Yes
2018	District level (CA)	CBA restrictiveness measure	Marianno and Strunk	Negative	Yes
2019	District level (MI)	District measure	Anderson, Cowen, and Strunk	Negative	Yes
2019	District level	District measure	Han and Maloney	Positive	No
2019	State level	State measure	Lovenheim and Willén	Negative	Yes

(*continues*)

Year	Student outcomes measured at:	Union strength measured at:	Author(s)	Impact on student outcomes?	Causal research design?
2019	District level (WI)	District measure	Roth	Negative	Yes
2020	State level	State measure	Brunner, Hyman, and Ju	Positive	Yes
2020	District level (OH)	CBA restrictiveness measure	Cook, Lavertu, and Miller	Negative	Yes
2020	State level	State measure	Dabbs	Negative	Yes
2020	District level	District measure	Han	Positive	Yes
2020	District level	District measure	Han and Keefe	Positive	No
2020	State level	State measure	Ju	Mixed	Yes
2021	District level (WI)	District measure	Baron	Negative	Yes
2021	District level (WI)	District measure	Biasi	Negative	Yes
2021	District level (CA)	District measure	Marianno	Mixed	Yes
2021	District level (CA)	CBA restrictiveness measure	Marianno, Bruno, and Strunk	Negative	Yes
2021	District level (CA charters)	School level (charters)	Matsudaira and Patterson	Positive	Yes
2021	District level (CA)	School board elections	Shi and Singleton	Negative	Yes
2021	State level	State measure (RTW laws)	Lyon	Positive	Yes

TABLE A8.2 **Teacher-union strength (revenue) and adjusted NAEP score gains**

	Math gain		Reading gain	
	Grade 4 (1)	Grade 8 (2)	Grade 4 (3)	Grade 8 (4)
Baseline NAEP test scores	-0.624***	-0.568***	-0.861***	-0.653***
	(0.119)	(0.140)	(0.120)	(0.150)
Union-revenue strength	-0.009**	-0.007	-0.008*	-0.004
	(0.004)	(0.005)	(0.004)	(0.004)
Union-strength placebo	0.244	-0.745	0.867	0.367
	(0.787)	(1.157)	(0.855)	(1.000)
Constant	161.910***	170.936***	194.602***	176.105***
	(26.357)	(37.330)	(25.867)	(39.098)
R^2	0.45	0.50	0.63	0.45
Observations	42	42	39	36

Notes: Cell entries are OLS regression coefficients, with standard errors reported in parentheses. *$p<0.1$, **$p<0.05$, ***$p<0.01$.

TABLE A8.3 **Teacher-union strength (Fordham ranking) and adjusted NAEP score gains**

	Math gain		Reading gain	
	Grade 4 (1)	Grade 8 (2)	Grade 4 (3)	Grade 8 (4)
Baseline NAEP test scores	-0.651***	-0.590***	-0.830***	-0.648***
	(0.131)	(0.129)	(0.120)	(0.145)
Union strength (Fordham)	-0.159***	-0.146***	-0.135***	-0.069
	(0.049)	(0.047)	(0.048)	(0.045)
Union-strength placebo	0.238	-0.564	1.022	0.482
	(0.707)	(1.016)	(0.773)	(0.943)
Constant	160.033***	170.044***	181.211***	171.560***
	(28.813)	(34.444)	(25.850)	(38.287)
R^2	0.50	0.54	0.66	0.48
Observations	42	42	39	36

Notes: Cell entries are OLS regression coefficients, with standard errors reported in parentheses. *$p<0.1$, **$p<0.05$, ***$p<0.01$.

TABLE A8.4 **The effect of teacher-union retrenchment laws on unadjusted NAEP cohort gains**

	All states		Bargaining states only	
	Math (1)	Reading (2)	Math (3)	Reading (4)
Baseline test scores	-0.620***	-0.732***	-0.649***	-0.739***
	(0.089)	(0.072)	(0.103)	(0.094)
Retrenchment law	2.477***	2.502***	3.509***	3.679***
	(0.788)	(0.507)	(0.850)	(0.692)
Placebo law (Ohio)	0.797*	-0.791**	1.324***	-0.116
	(0.405)	(0.310)	(0.464)	(0.355)
Log per-pupil spending	1.020	-1.895	4.223	0.761
	(3.296)	(3.210)	(3.556)	(3.533)
State policy liberalism	-0.012	0.713	0.942	1.856
	(1.191)	(1.038)	(1.402)	(1.205)
Private-union density	-0.324	-0.179	-0.129	-0.053
	(0.205)	(0.170)	(0.267)	(0.193)
State fixed effects	Yes	Yes	Yes	Yes
Year fixed effects	Yes	Yes	Yes	Yes
R^2	0.81	0.81	0.81	0.81
Observations	350	350	238	238

Notes: Cell entries are OLS regression coefficients, with standard errors clustered by state reported in parentheses. *$p<0.1$, **$p<0.05$, ***$p<0.01$.

TABLE A8.5 **The effect of teacher-union retrenchment laws on adjusted NAEP performance**

	All states		Bargaining states only	
	Math (1)	Reading (2)	Math (3)	Reading (4)
Retrenchment law	1.194	1.767*	2.391	3.015**
	(1.390)	(0.889)	(1.484)	(1.148)
Placebo law (Ohio)	0.744	-0.534	1.479**	0.229
	(0.476)	(0.398)	(0.592)	(0.558)
Log per-pupil spending	-3.290	-5.753**	-1.200	-3.860
	(3.039)	(2.801)	(3.779)	(3.838)
State policy liberalism	1.449	2.251***	2.387**	3.284***
	(0.942)	(0.778)	(1.141)	(1.004)
Private-union density	-0.275	-0.045	-0.133	0.030
	(0.187)	(0.145)	(0.250)	(0.186)
State fixed effects	Yes	Yes	Yes	Yes
Year fixed effects	Yes	Yes	Yes	Yes
R²	0.91	0.88	0.91	0.89
Observations	450	450	306	306

Notes: Cell entries are OLS regression coefficients, with standard errors clustered by state reported in parentheses.
*p<0.1, **p<0.05, ***p<0.01.

CHAPTER NINE

The Resilience of Teachers Unions

In 2009, the stock market hit bottom. The broader American economy was on the brink of collapse, and consumer confidence tumbled to an all-time low. A few years later, however, President Barack Obama cruised to reelection. US equities, which had shed half their value during the Great Recession, roared back to life. By 2016, Wall Street was enjoying an unprecedented bull run while Main Street cheered record low unemployment and modest wage growth.

US economic volatility during the Great Recession mimics the rollercoaster ride the nation's teachers unions have been on this past decade. Just as it would have been foolish to predict the demise of the American economy in 2009, it would be equally foolish to suggest today that teachers unions are on a path to extinction. To the contrary, organized teacher interests have shown tremendous resilience during these politically challenging times. To understand how they have maintained strength and why they are poised to remain influential, we must dissect both what has happened and what has not happened to them in the intervening years from *A Nation at Risk* to the *Janus* defeat in 2018.

Let's start by examining what has actually happened.

Teachers Unions under Attack

There is no denying that teachers unions have faced real challenges since the excellence movement began in the 1980s. And the unions' difficulties grew more severe during the Great Recession. The most visible threat has been the effort to roll back states' teacher bargaining laws. The very labor laws that helped give rise to the unions' political power in the 1970s were significantly weakened in a handful of states. Shortly thereafter, the

US Supreme Court eliminated unions' access to agency fees, a policy that I showed helped increase teacher-union membership and dues revenue. These losses are both real and significant. But, at the same time, they need to be assessed relative to the overall trajectory of teacher labor law.

From 1960 to 1990, public-sector labor law was in full-on expansionary mode. By the end of the 1980s, most states' teacher bargaining laws had stabilized in a pro-union direction. As chapter 5 showed, unions leveraged these victories to expand their political power throughout the country. After three decades of teacher labor law moving in a pro-union direction (1960–1990), followed by two decades of equilibrium (1990–2010), this very recent period of retrenchment represents a relative blip in the grander scheme of things. Retrenchment began in 2011 with Act 10 in Wisconsin and culminated in the 2018 *Janus* decision. Both events were major setbacks for teachers unions. Yet when the smoke cleared, only a handful of states had formally eliminated teacher bargaining rights. One state, Virginia, granted them. And *Janus* applied to teachers in just twenty states that had previously allowed their unions to charge agency fees.

What's more, retrenchment has spawned a powerful counter-mobilization by teachers unions and their allies in state government. During the earlier expansionary era of labor-law development—a clear period of union ascendance—the unions faced limited political opposition. For example, many Republican state lawmakers voted to give teachers bargaining rights.[1] In contrast, today's period of labor retrenchment cannot be characterized as a one-sided battle that has resulted in a unilateral victory for anti-union forces. As I discuss later in the chapter, Democrats in state government are working hard to find ways to blunt the impact of *Janus*, just as Republicans fight to preserve the victories they notched during the recession. Even in Wisconsin, where the unions suffered their greatest defeat, there is no guarantee that Act 10 will remain in place for good. It has survived so far. But the unions finally ousted Scott Walker in 2018, replacing him with a union ally in former state superintendent of public education, Tony Evers. Governor Evers has promised to try and restore some of the powers that teachers and other public employees lost under Walker.

Partisan Polarization and Labor Retrenchment

More than anything, it *is* partisan political dynamics that best explain the unions' recent struggles. During the expansionary era of labor-law development, partisan polarization was not as acute as it is today. The political coalitions that supported strong teacher labor laws in the 1960s and 1970s were more bipartisan. States' elected officials (on both the right and the left) once tended to accept the fact that, once their state had chosen a system of public-sector labor relations, it would remain in place irrespective of temporary political shifts in the control of state government. For example, by 1980, conservative states that had never adopted strong labor laws—mainly in the South and West—stood pat. Similarly, liberal states that had adopted strong bargaining laws maintained their pro-union equilibrium, even when Republicans took over a branch of state government from time to time.

However, by the late aughts, this state of affairs changed. A surge in single-party state governing combined with increased partisan polarization eroded the existing equilibrium. Alabama is a strong case in point. For decades, the Alabama Education Association (AEA) ruled the roost in Montgomery. In the 1990s, the AEA's executive director, Paul Hubbert, was nearly elected governor. The state even passed a law banning lobbyists from making gestures in the capitol building gallery after it was rumored that education bills lived or died with Hubbert's thumbs-up or thumbs-down motions from the balcony.[2] As discussed in chapter 6, the AEA's power was partly a function of its formidable political war chest, which existed because of a favorable dues-checkoff law that Democrats adopted to help the AEA in 1983.

However, in 2010, Republicans captured the entire state government for the first time in 136 years. The Alabama GOP quickly set to work to weaken its longtime nemesis in the AEA. Republicans banned payroll deduction of teacher-union dues, walking back the 1983 law that had been so instrumental to the AEA's power. Suddenly, the AEA went from having one of the strongest dues-checkoff laws in the country to one that prohibited even basic dues collection. For decades, teachers had been the single biggest contributor in Alabama state politics. But without an easy way to collect PAC donations, the AEA was forced to scale back its political advocacy. As then-AEA president Sheila Remington explained to a local reporter: "We're out of the [PAC giving] business . . . we're out of giving people money to run campaigns. As far as people calling and asking us for campaign contributions, I don't see us getting involved with that anymore."[3]

Similar partisan retrenchment dynamics unfolded in other states. Indiana teachers unions, for example, lost agency fees in 1995. They later saw

their collective bargaining rights scaled back under Republican governor
Mitch Daniels in 2011. Both times, the retrenchment occurred after Republicans had won governing trifectas. GOP lawmakers had straightforward incentives to punish Indiana teachers unions, since the unions long
comprised the largest source of campaign support for the state's Democratic Party.[4]

What is the broader lesson here? The simple fact is that the close alliance between teachers unions and the Democratic Party was unprob-
lematic so long as Democrats kept control of power or enough moderate
Republicans resisted breaking up the long-existing equilibrium in teacher
labor law. But, when those political conditions evaporated, as they did in
both Alabama and Indiana in the 2010s, teachers unions found themselves
helpless.

I do not wish to downplay these defeats. They are real and meaningful losses for teachers unions. They represent the costs that these unions
have incurred for having largely confined their support to the Democratic
Party. That approach had few downsides when teachers unions could be
assured that one branch of state government would remain in Democratic
hands. However, the rise of the Tea Party and the surge in Republican-
controlled state governments in 2010 changed that calculus, making episodes of retrenchment that previously seemed unthinkable a more regular political occurrence.

Public Attitudes about American Education

A second factor that put teachers unions on the defensive was the growing *bipartisan* consensus that America's K–12 education system was failing and that reform was sorely needed. Since the onset of the excellence
movement in the 1980s, but especially by late in the first decade of the
2000s, a popular narrative had taken hold that teachers unions were a
major obstacle to reforming America's "failing" schools.[5] News coverage
helped solidify this mindset. In the early 1980s, a cover story in *Time* read:
"Help! Teacher Can't Teach."[6] In 2014, the magazine featured a second
cover story on education. This time, "Rotten Apples: It's Nearly Impossible to Fire a Bad Teacher" was sprawled across *Time*'s iconic cover on news-
stands across the country.[7]

By late in the first decade of the 2000s, school reform had hit the political mainstream. Establishment media outlets including the *Washington*

Post, the *New York Times*, *Newsweek,* and the *Economist* blamed some of the failures of American education on union intransigence.[8] Davis Guggenheim's documentary film *Waiting for Superman* fed the same narrative: that teachers unions stood in the way of common-sense reforms. Business icons like Steve Jobs made statements criticizing the unions for their unwillingness to overhaul teacher workforce policies that some saw as obsolete.[9] Maggie Gyllenhaal, Viola Davis, and Uzo Aduba all starred in feature films that portrayed teachers unions as self-interested and unwilling to support parental-choice reforms to improve educational opportunity for underserved kids. Irrespective of the truth behind any of these specific claims, the message was powerful because it came at a time when more Americans were saying that public education wasn't performing up to snuff.

Two specific changes in public opinion about the nation's schools stood out. First, ordinary Americans had begun to lose confidence in the quality of the nation's public schools. As the dashed line in figure 9.1 shows, the percentage of the public holding a "great deal" or "quite a lot" of confidence in the nation's public schools declined from a high of 60 percent just prior to *A Nation at Risk* to below 40 percent by the 1990s and then below 30 percent by the 2010s. At the same time, more Americans ranked education a top problem (see the solid black line in figure 9.1). Put simply, education reform, which became more salient after the 1983 report, put teachers unions in the political hot seat. "The schools," Robert Chanin explained at a union meeting in 2000, "had largely been ignored by the general public, but they were [now] all of a sudden under close scrutiny and were found to be wanting."[10]

Altogether, then, since *A Nation at Risk* the political climate has been less hospitable to teachers unions. The changing partisan politics that accompanied polarization, especially the spread of Republican governing trifectas in the states, gave union opponents the opportunity to weaken some of the favorable labor policies that had been enacted in prior decades. Additionally, the Great Recession offered a unique moment for anti-union reformers to make the case that it was time to curtail laws that in their view had given the unions too much power—power that they argued was the genesis of the unions' ability to preserve outdated teacher workforce policies, such as defined-benefit pensions, that reformers characterized as unsustainable.[11] An increasingly conservative Supreme Court only exacerbated some of these challenges. Culminating with the *Janus* decision, the Court's narrow conservative majority began to show more

FIGURE 9.1 Confidence in public schools and the salience of education reform (1973–2019)

Notes: Author's analysis of two different historical series of Gallup data. Data on confidence in public schools comes from the organization's historical-trend series "Confidence in Institutions," https://news.gallup.com/poll/1597 /Confidence-Institutions.aspx. Gallup data on the public's perception of the most important problem facing the country was previously compiled by Heffington et al. (2019). See Colton Heffington, Brandon Beomseob Park, and Laron K. Williams, "The 'Most Important Problem' Dataset (MIPD): a New Dataset on American Issue Importance," *Conflict Management and Peace Science* 36, no. 3 (2019): 312–35. Data itself available at http://faculty.missouri.edu /williamslaro/mipdata.html.

skepticism about the legality of some public-sector labor policies that had strengthened teachers unions since the 1970s.[12] While these losses should not be minimized, when we dive deeper into the specifics of retrenchment—and consider not only what has happened but also what has *not* happened—the picture that emerges is far different. That picture, as we shall see, is one of union resilience in the face of threat—resilience that, after the pandemic and the 2020 elections, has begun to evolve into a story of teacher-union revitalization.

The Resilience of Teachers Unions

As painful as recent labor-law rollbacks and Republican takeovers of state governments have been for the unions, there are several reasons why we should not expect them to easily relinquish their power or influence.

History teaches us better. Teachers unions have, on more than one occasion, recognized their own political vulnerability, only to respond effectively by doubling down and fighting back against their adversaries.

In the early 1980s, at the dawn of the excellence movement, then-NEA president Mary Hatwood Futrell sensed that the zeitgeist in American education was turning against her union. Futrell worried that the NEA's tendency to reflexively oppose reforms would marginalize the union and lead to its undoing. She implored her colleagues to "acknowledge serious problems in public education" . . . and use *A Nation at Risk* "as an opportunity to build political support for improving the current public school system."[13] Ultimately, however, her advice was dismissed. The majority of Futrell's colleagues on the NEA's executive committee—including future NEA president Bob Chase—rejected her suggestions. Instead, the union responded to calls for reform by "defending the record of the public schools" and focusing "its efforts on protecting school employees and winning increased resources from the existing system." In other words, the NEA responded to the excellence movement like an ostrich, claiming that "the whole premise that America's public schools were failing was false."[14]

Ironically, in 1996, when Chase took over as NEA president, he found himself returning to the reform-oriented approach for which Futrell had advocated decades earlier. With the NEA facing continued attacks on its public image, Chase commissioned an in-house report entitled *An Institution at Risk* to assess where the NEA's political strategy had gone wrong. Chase even confessed in a public statement at the National Press Club that his opposition to Futrell had been "the biggest mistake of [his] career." Yet when the rubber met the road, Chase's speech amounted to very little in the way of meaningful policy change inside the union. The NEA's affiliates vigorously pushed back on Chase's reform vision of a "new unionism." Ultimately, the concept was marginalized by future NEA leaders.[15] In hindsight, Chase probably overestimated the consequences of losing the public-relations battle. The NEA was never really an institution at risk. In practice, the strategy of hunkering down and resisting reforms that teachers found unacceptable proved to be a reasonably effective strategy over the long run.

It is easy to be a prisoner of the moment when one sees new governors like a Scott Walker or a Chris Christie take office and quickly go about trying to dismantle teachers unions. Yet, in reality, governors from as far back as the 1980s and 1990s—politicians like John Engler (MI), Tom Ridge (PA), Tommy Thompson (WI), Jeb Bush (FL), and Lamar Alexander

(TN)—have targeted teachers unions.[16] Engler and Thompson curtailed some aspects of collective bargaining. Bush and Alexander enacted choice and accountability reforms. Bush even got Florida to enact a law (later repealed) that reduced the incentive for teachers to join the union.[17] The bottom line is that political opposition from anti-union politicians is nothing new under the sun. But, over the long run, these defeats are usually temporary setbacks. That is because—as I have shown throughout the book—the unions' political power is rooted in much deeper fundamentals that cannot be easily undone by any one opponent or legislative defeat. Unlike a hostile elected official who must eventually leave office, teachers unions are permanently embedded in the operational fabric of American school governance. Their influence clearly ebbs and flows, but the foundational role they play in education policymaking is, by the very design of America's education system, structured to endure.

The unions' public-relations problems—whatever they are—are also exaggerated. That some newspapers and business leaders increased their criticism of teachers unions for steadfastly opposing various media- and corporate-favored school reforms did little to change the actual power dynamics in education. The NRA is seldom spared media criticism when it regularly opposes modest gun-control legislation. Such criticism has hardly weakened that interest group's influence over the Republican Party or the overall direction of gun policy in the United States. Teachers unions are no different. They took plenty of criticism from the media for their role in prolonging school closures during the COVID-19 pandemic. Yet that criticism did nothing to reduce their wide-ranging influence over the sluggish pace of school reopenings.

The American electorate is also far less worried about the state of American education than are political elites. Earlier I presented some evidence that, in the aftermath of *A Nation at Risk*, public confidence in America's schools declined. It is tempting to see this as a major problem for teachers unions. But public support for a radical overhaul of America's schools is much less robust than this single data point would suggest. Yes, the public tend to give the *nation's* schools (as a whole) low marks, but most voters—and especially most public-school parents—give top marks to their local schools. As figure 9.2 shows, since 1980 there has not been a single year in which fewer than 60 percent of parents graded their eldest child's public school B or better. Middle- and upper-class voters who have the most clout—the ones most likely to donate and agitate—are also the least likely to have personal stakes in pushing for reform, since they also

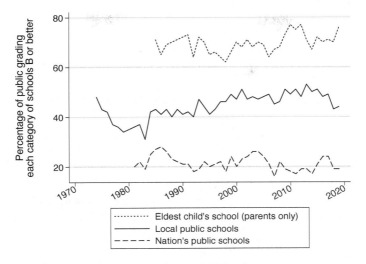

FIGURE 9.2 Most Americans give their local schools high ratings

Source: Author's analysis of several waves of Gallup/PDK's annual Poll of the Public's Attitudes Toward the Public Schools, https://pdkpoll.org.

tend to be the most satisfied with their public schools. In sum, the lack of any serious demand-side pressure for reform minimizes the salience of the unions' public-relations problems. The best testament to this lack of urgency among most voters is the fact that education is almost always on the periphery of national political debates. *A Nation at Risk* and NCLB changed that to some extent. However, as figure 9.1 showed earlier, even at its height of salience, only one in ten Americans said that education was the nation's leading problem.

If anything, teachers unions can begin to take comfort in the fact that their image has been on the mend since the Great Recession, perhaps a product of now being seen as political "underdogs."[18] Stagnating teacher salaries, combined with the publicity of statewide teacher strikes, have helped teachers unions win back the public (at least before the pandemic). In 2013, Harvard's *Education Next* survey found that just 32 percent of Americans felt that teachers unions had a positive impact on America's schools. However, by 2019, 43 percent of the public said the unions played a mostly positive role. After previous *Time* magazine covers had depicted teachers as untested and underqualified, the headline had now changed. In the aftermath of the 2018 summer of red-state teacher strikes, *Time* put a schoolteacher on its cover once again. The cover message read quite differently this time: "I have a master's degree, 16 years of experience, work two extra jobs and donate blood plasma to pay the bills. I'm a teacher in America!"[19] Suffice it to say, the teachers unions' image was not permanently tarnished during the darkest days of the recession. The dynamics of education politics can and often do evolve in ways that make it easier for teachers unions to position themselves more favorably with the electorate.

Teacher Labor Law Remains Union-Friendly Even after *Janus*

Janus in particular is unlikely to eradicate union influence in education for several reasons. First, and most importantly, the majority of America's public school teachers (62 percent) still work in one of the thirty-three states where the law requires school districts to recognize and engage in collective bargaining with the exclusive-representative teachers union.[20] Unlike other education stakeholders, teachers unions will continue to have a formal seat at the policymaking table. This advantage is significant for them—both from an organizational standpoint and in the policymaking process. Most recently, that advantage has best been illustrated by the influential role that unions played in the school-reopening debates surrounding the COVID-19 pandemic.

Even as mounting scientific evidence began to show that schools could be reopened safely,[21] two US presidents and countless governors struggled to reopen them, in part because of significant union resistance in the trenches. In this instance, having a seat at the table meant that school districts were often required to reach formal agreements with teachers unions before they could reopen. In contrast, private schools and public schools that were not legally required to engage in teacher bargaining mostly kept their doors open. All told, the inability of local school-district governments to secure reopening agreements with their teachers unions prolonged closures and kept upwards of half of all US students out of school for an entire year.[22]

Regardless of how one feels about the highly contentious debate about reopening schools amid the pandemic, the political preferences of teachers were clearly better represented during these policy debates than the voices of parents and other education stakeholders. The reason for this imbalance is obvious: in many parts of the country, the law literally required that teachers unions be made a formal partner in decision-making. Bringing teachers unions on board was thus a prerequisite for many districts to reopen their schools.

Second, even after *Janus*, many of the subsidizing benefits in teacher labor law remain in place.[23] For example, the key Association-rights provisions that chapter 3 showed help unions more easily organize and recruit teachers into politics are left untouched. So too are many of the security provisions that were the focus of chapter 5. American labor law retains exclusive bargaining as its key operating principle. Courts still allow teachers unions to redistribute resources between affiliates through the principle of affiliated representation. *Janus* also does nothing to prohibit them from collecting dues and PAC money with the assistance of their school-district employer's payroll office. While some states enacted bans on such activity, on balance, teacher labor law remains a helpful organizing tool for unions' political advocacy efforts.

Third, teachers unions today are starting from a position of strength. They simply need to *retain* their members and money, not build their organizations anew like they did in the 1960s and 1970s. There is some evidence to suggest that labor law has asymmetric effects on teacher organizing, depending on whether new laws are being enacted or old ones are being weakened. In chapter 5, for example, I showed that when states first made agency fees available to teachers unions that these provisions strengthened them financially. Pennsylvania is a case in point. It enacted its mandatory CB law for teachers in 1970, but it did not amend that law to allow teachers unions to charge agency fees until 1988. After the revision, membership in the Pennsylvania State Education Association (PSEA) rose significantly (along with revenue).

In contrast, in the handful of cases where states eliminated agency fees, the outcome did not prove to be a death knell for their teachers unions. Three states eliminated such fees prior to *Janus*: Indiana in 1995, Wisconsin in 2011, and Michigan in 2012. On average, the loss of these fees resulted in modest union-membership declines. Admittedly, teachers unions in Wisconsin lost half their members. But Wisconsin does not really provide a compelling example of what losing agency fees portends for teachers unions after *Janus*. Recall that Act 10 did far more to diminish teacher-union power than simply eliminating agency fees.[24] Indiana provides a far more plausible case for how *Janus* is likely to impact teacher-union membership in most states. When Hoosier state lawmakers eliminated agency fees in 1995, the Indiana State Teachers Association saw no significant drop in membership. It only experienced modest membership losses many years later, after the law had been fully implemented and older teachers began to retire. In sum, since the unions are starting from a position of strength, some membership losses will happen, but we are unlikely to see a true hemorrhaging.

Fourth, interest groups rarely tend to lose power if they remain an important constituency of a major political party. Even though President Obama and teachers unions squabbled over his education-reform agenda, both teachers unions and the Democratic Party spent the second half of the 2010s strongly united against Donald Trump and Betsy DeVos's Republican Party. One important consequence of this repaired relationship is that teachers unions have been able to minimize their losses by working with their Democratic allies in state governments to pass new laws blunting the impact of *Janus* and promoting teacher organizing.

These post-*Janus* legal changes target three of the specific subsidies that I emphasized in the first half of the book. The first such subsidy is providing unions with access to teacher employees. Newly passed laws in New York, California, Maryland, Massachusetts, and Washington, for example, require that teachers unions be given access to newly hired teachers so that they can more easily recruit teachers to join and pay union dues. These laws stipulate that union leaders be given specific opportunities to visit schools for the purpose of pitching membership and/or require that school districts furnish unions with all employees' personal contact information. In New Jersey, for example, the NJEA's (union) president Marie Blisten lauded NJEA-endorsed Democratic governor Phil Murphy for signing the state's "Workplace Democracy Enhancement Act," calling it a "real win for working people in New Jersey," one that "shows that New Jersey respects the value of [public sector] unions and the right of employees to join together and advocate for the values that matter to them."[25] Among other things, the act mandates that unions have access to employees at orientation meetings or by ensuring union release time. It even requires that school districts, within ten days of hiring, turn over contact information— including teachers' home or cell-phone numbers—to the union.

Part of the unions' post-*Janus* counter-mobilization strategy has been to make sure that their political opponents—often conservative think tanks funded by groups like the American Legislative Exchange Council (ALEC)—are not given access to employee contact information that the unions can obtain for themselves. Several states have moved to prevent these nonunion groups from getting access to teachers so that they can remind them that the *Janus* ruling allows teachers to stop paying union dues. Relatedly, California, New Jersey, and Washington have all passed laws that prohibit school districts from notifying teachers that unions can no longer charge fees to nonmembers. These laws are key to the unions' counter-mobilization movement because they mute the efforts of anti-union groups seeking to run grassroots campaigns aimed at getting teachers to quit their unions.

Longtime California education-reform activist and union critic Larry Sand explains that the unions' efforts to ensure California lawmakers eased their post-*Janus* burden came long before the court's ruling. "When *Janus* was looming, legislators enacted [a new] law which stipulates that a public employer must give the union the 'name, job title, department, work location, work, home, and personal cellular telephone numbers, personal email addresses on file with the employer, and home address of any newly hired employee within 30 days of the date of hire. . . .' and requires them to attend a mandatory union 'orientation' meeting, during which the captive audience is harangued about the joys of union membership."[26]

The second plank of the unions' counter-mobilization plan is to lobby for rules and regulations that make it more onerous for members to quit. The best example of this is the state of Washington, which recently amended the rules for dues deductions from a teacher's paycheck. The new rules make it incredibly easy for a teacher to authorize a deduction to the union (teachers can use email, phone, or written correspondence to do that), but harder to quit paying dues (only a formal letter to the union suffices for that). Sometimes the unions themselves have devised strategies to discourage workers from quitting by specifying a very brief period each year when workers can opt out of paying dues.

The third element of the unions' counter-mobilization agenda has been to develop new ways to incentivize membership in the absence of agency fees. For example, to make teacher-union membership more attractive, states can allow unions to provide members-only benefits, even if those benefits were previously ones that went to all employees as part of the collective bargaining agreement that covered all workers. New York's largest teachers union, for example, no longer provides a variety of healthcare and life-insurance benefits to teachers who refuse to join and pay full union dues. Massachusetts responded to the *Janus* decision by enacting a new law that allows unions to charge nonmembers for representation in grievance or arbitration proceedings. These sorts of rules encourage teachers to remain in the union and also provide teachers unions with new, selective incentives to highlight during recruitment pitches.

The common thread running through all this new regulation is to help buoy teachers unions' organizing and membership-retention efforts. For its part, the NEA has been encouraging state and local affiliates to lobby for and secure access to these new organizing tools. In two recent promotional publications, the nation's largest teachers union has instructed the leaders of its affiliates to focus on securing all of the following: (1) a place for the union on the agenda at new-employee orientations, (2) access to member information and communications platforms, (3) release time for union business, and (4) dues deduction.

Ironically then, although this counter-mobilization was born in weakness (the *Janus* decision) its practical effect has been to leave teachers unions in some states more heavily subsidized than they were before *Janus*. For example, the Association-rights provisions that chapter 3 showed make it easier for unions to recruit teachers to participate in politics are now being adopted directly at the state level. Previously, unions mostly had to win these sorts of concessions one school district at a time. Now, many of the aforementioned legal responses to *Janus* simply make it a requirement in state law that all districts give access, release time, and communication platforms. This change represents a net increase in the reach of these beneficial provisions for the unions, despite the fact that they arose in response to the loss of agency fees.

What the Great Recession really did, more than anything, was to blow the lid off the naive and untenable notion that public-sector labor laws are neutral institutional arrangements that merely exist to promote stable relationships between governments and their employees. Public-sector labor law is now seen for what it truly is: an important political institution that can either enhance or dilute the political advocacy efforts of unions in electoral politics.[27] Of course, teachers unions have long known this, but the issue very much remained on the periphery of American politics until the Great Recession provided anti-union Republicans with a unique window of opportunity. Now that the issue is out in the open, Democrats in state government are not being shy about their efforts to counteract the Supreme Court's *Janus* ruling by pushing for new laws that can help revitalize teachers unions.

For example, in 2020, Virginia lawmakers passed a bill giving teachers collective bargaining rights for the first time in fifty years.[28] The bill was adopted along a party-line vote and marks the first time a southern state has moved in a pro-union direction since Tennessee enacted its public bargaining statute in 1978.[29] Similarly, in 2021, Illinois lawmakers expanded teachers' bargaining rights in the nation's third-largest school district (Chicago).[30] Elsewhere, union supporters have been looking for new policy innovations that would allow state governments to make agency fees legal again by having the state directly pay the cost. This movement is best exemplified by a series of recent law-review articles written by former Sotomayor Supreme Court clerk Aaron Tang.[31] As noted in chapter 4, Justice Sotomayor herself advanced the notion that under American public-sector labor law, exclusive-representative unions are already quasi-state entities. Tang and others who advance this new state-subsidization legal theory are now building a legal case to have public-employees unions funded directly by state governments, sidestepping the problem of forcing nonunion teachers to contribute to exclusive-bargaining regimes.

Power versus Ideas

I am sure that the power of vested interests is vastly exaggerated compared with the gradual encroachment of ideas.[32] — John Maynard Keynes (1936)

With all due respect to Keynes, one of the claims I have made in this book is that he's wrong. In the case of public education, or any arena of public policy, the power of vested interests will almost certainly trump the influence of even broadly popular reform ideas. If ideas matter at all in the shaping of public policy—and as an academic I certainly hope that they do—they matter far less than organized political power, particularly when that power is wielded by vested interests that have been subsidized by the state itself.

To that end, my findings foreshadow that teachers unions will remain a resilient force in both American education and American politics for years to come. It would take an unprecedented and unanticipated force—a "black swan" event—to upset the basic equilibrium of union power in American education. Teacher-union supporters will no doubt be pleased to hear this, after having spent the better part of the prior decade on the political defensive. Conversely, union critics would be unwise to gloat about a decade of modest victories. They would be foolish to declare that the unions are on their way to extinction simply because the *Janus* ruling went their way. The reality is that a fundamental revolution in the structure of education politics is unlikely to occur anytime soon.

For one thing, the traditional levers of American democracy are simply too weak to upset the foundation of union power that chapters 2–5 showed governments entrenched when they designed American labor law to the unions' advantage in the 1960s and 1970s. Moreover, battles over education reform are waged within democratic institutions that are even less responsive to the public than the American political system as a whole. Off-cycle school-board elections and fragmented education governance, for example, minimize the likelihood that a bloc of "education voters" will be able to organize into a consistent political force that challenges union power. As discussed in chapter 7, even after *Janus* union-endorsed candidates still win about 70 percent of contested school-board elections.

The decades since *A Nation at Risk* also showed that an idea "whose time has come" or a popular political reformer were both insufficient in and of themselves to disrupt the structural advantages that teachers unions have in education politics. For example, in the 1990s, statistician William Sanders's discovery of value-added measures of teacher effectiveness seemed like it might eventually revolutionize teacher workforce policies around the country.[33] Yet twenty-five years later, most states still cling to teacher pay and evaluation policies used in the 1960s. Even the states that undertook teacher-evaluation reforms in the 2010s are now retreating from them, implementing them so weakly that few teachers are held accountable for student learning. Similarly, Barack Obama was heralded as a game-changer for the politics of education reform. He showed that a Democrat could break with the unions and lead a bipartisan reform coalition. Yet for all his popularity within the Democratic Party, Obama was not able to convince teachers unions to embrace his agenda, and his top education lieutenant, Arne Duncan, was shunned for pursuing reforms the unions opposed. Although Obama was able to leverage some unusual fiscal conditions during his tenure to encourage states to undertake reform, by the time the waivers and grant money dried up, Democratic lawmakers no longer had strong incentives to stay the course. Instead, they moved to repair their relationship with teachers unions and partner with them to fight back against a decade of Tea Party attacks and the Trump-DeVos education agenda.

If *ideas* mattered most in education politics, William Sanders or Barack Obama would be seated alongside Horace Mann and John Dewey somewhere on the Mount Rushmore of American education. But if I am correct that *power* matters most, then it will be the lesser-known labor lawyer Robert Chanin who will claim a place among education's most influential. Chanin, who served as the NEA's head legal counsel for over forty years, played a critical role in helping develop teacher bargaining laws during the 1960s and 1970s.[34] As even staunch union critic Myron Lieberman conceded, "Chanin has had a larger impact on public education over the past thirty years than any other individual, in or out of government." In his retirement address in 2009, Chanin spoke candidly to his union about the growing opposition they faced in American education and what they should do about it:

> Why are these conservative and right-wing bastards picking on NEA and its affiliates? I will tell you why. It is the price we pay for success. NEA and its affiliates have been singled out because they are the most effective unions in the United States. ...The objective [of these attacks] is to limit the effectiveness of NEA and its affiliates by restricting our ability to participate in the political process, cutting off our sources of revenue, and diverting our energies from advancing our affirmative agenda to defending ourselves. At first glance, some of you may find these attacks troubling, but you would be wrong. *They are, in fact, really a good thing.*[35]

A good thing? How could a razor-sharp lawyer like Chanin take the recent era of labor retrenchment as a good thing at the very same time that union leaders were publicly declaring Armageddon? Chanin explained:

> When I first came to NEA in the early 1960s, it had few enemies and was almost never criticized, attacked, or even mentioned in the media. This was because no one really gave a damn about what NEA did or what NEA said. It was the proverbial sleeping giant, a conservative, apolitical, do-nothing organization. But then NEA began to change. It embraced collective bargaining. It supported teacher strikes. It established a political action committee . . . What NEA said and did began to matter. And the more we said and did, the more we pissed people off. And in turn, the more enemies we made. So the bad news, or depending on your point of view, the good news, is that NEA and its affiliates will continue to be attacked . . . as long as we continue to be effective advocates . . .[36]

But what would make the NEA effective in this new era of performance-based reform, in which teachers unions found themselves on the defensive? Did Chanin think that his union needed to mount a vigorous public-relations campaign to defeat the reform movement's ideas? Would he try and convince teachers that they needed to tell a more compelling story—to contrast their vision with that of their opponents in the reform movement? Hardly.

> And that brings me to my final—and most important—point, which is why, at least in my opinion, NEA and its affiliates are such effective advocates. Despite what some of us would like to believe, it is not because of our creative ideas.

It is not because of the merit of our positions. It is not because we care about children. And it is not because we have a vision of a 'great public school for every child.' NEA and its affiliates are effective advocates because we have power. And we have power because there are more than 3.2 million people who are willing to pay us hundreds of millions of dollars in dues each year because they believe that we are the unions that can most effectively represent them, the unions that can protect their rights and advance their interests as education employees.[37]

This book has provided an array of evidence demonstrating that Chanin is correct. So long as the fundamentals of labor law enable the teachers unions to remain better organized and better resourced than their political adversaries, the unions' power will prevail over even the most popular reform ideas. Is there anything that could change this basic equilibrium, eradicating the status quo of union power? Reformers may take solace in what some believe will happen once new technologies disrupt traditional schooling and learning practices. For example, as Terry Moe and John Chubb argue in *Liberating Learning*, technology is poised to eventually alter the delivery of education in even unforeseen ways—changes that may unravel the monopoly that organized labor has had in supplying the conventional forms of human capital that governments have long relied upon to provide schooling.[38] Likewise, exceedingly rare windows for a change in the balance of power sometimes come about from a confluence of unanticipated, if not otherwise horrible cataclysmic events, such as what happened with Hurricane Katrina and the rebirth of the New Orleans Public School System after the storm eliminated union power.[39]

However, in the absence of these sorts of highly unusual external forces, the internal forces of stability will almost certainly continue to prevail. Those powerful internal forces of stability aren't simply confined to American education. The politics of other domestic policy arenas, from health care to climate change to gun policy, point in a similar direction. In all these arenas, meaningful reform requires that policy entrepreneurs do something quite unlikely: overcome the power of entrenched interests. Yet, as we have seen throughout this book, when private interests are subsidized by elected officials inside of government—as has been the case for teachers unions throughout postwar American politics—those interests are primed to remain secure in their power and influence for decades to come.

CHAPTER TEN

The Scorecard

Unions versus Reformers

Who is the greatest athlete of all time? Most lists put Michael Jordan on top, with boxer Muhammad Ali, football icon Jim Brown, and track star Jesse Owens trailing just behind. One athlete you won't see mentioned is Spanish tennis star Rafael Nadal. In fact, as good as Nadal is, he isn't even the best tennis player of his era. That distinction belongs to his rival, Roger Federer. With *one* exception.

On clay courts, Rafael Nadal is almost unbeatable. Even Federer is no match for the Spaniard when the two meet head to head on the red dirt. Nadal boasts a 90 percent winning clip against tennis's all-time great on clay. What explains his advantage? Nadal's superior physical conditioning is a more valuable asset on clay because the game slows down and produces longer rallies that reward a player's endurance. Nadal's athleticism, especially his ability to slide in the dirt, make it harder for his opponents to get the ball past him. In other words, Nadal's *defensive* capabilities are maximized on clay.[1]

Just as Nadal isn't the world's greatest athlete, teachers unions aren't the most powerful organized interest in American politics. Big business is far better represented than either labor or public-interest groups in Washington.[2] And, after *Citizens United*, right-leaning PACs have spread their tentacles into every nook and cranny of government.[3] Even the narrower claim that teachers unions dominate education politics can provoke pushback. Teachers' modest salaries lead some to see only modest union influence. For example, in reviewing Terry Moe's book *Special Interest*, political scientist Paul Frymer grumbled that "one side is portrayed as self-interested, powerful, and disruptive of student needs. The other side is portrayed as wanting only what is good for our children. The good and simultaneously weak side includes some politicians, administrators, and business leaders. The bad and powerful side—teachers and their unions— make an average salary of just under $54,000 a year."[4]

Frymer is right, but for the wrong reason. Teachers unions can't negotiate six-figure salaries for each one of the nation's three million teachers. But that's not where their real power lies. Despite Samuel Gompers' claim that unionism is about getting "more," teachers unions are influential because they ensure *less*—fewer of the reforms that their members steadfastly oppose. None of this is to say that teachers unions can't win victories at the bargaining table, but the problem with gauging their influence by looking at average teacher salaries is what political scientist Sarah Anzia calls "looking for influence in all the wrong places."[5]

Just as Nadal dominates on clay, teachers unions are heavyweights in *subnational* politics, the surface on which the most important battles over education policy are won and lost. Just as clay boosts Nadal's defensive capabilities, the structure of American education governance—multiple veto points, federalism, localism, low-turnout elections—makes teachers unions, as David Tyack put it, "the [interest] group with the greatest power to veto or sabotage [reform] proposals."[6]

The political battles during the late aughts over using students' test scores to evaluate teachers provides a compelling case in point. In 2008, the United Federation of Teachers (UFT) was trying to prevent New York City's then-superintendent, Joel Klein, from using test scores as a factor in teacher tenure decisions. When it appeared the UFT might lose this battle to Klein, the union went directly to Albany and got legislators to adopt a budget-bill amendment prohibiting such scores from being used in tenure decisions.[7] A few years later, teachers unions used the exact opposite strategy. After President Obama's Race to the Top (RttT) program induced New York to begin using students' progress on state tests in teacher evaluations, the union lobbied for local school districts to retain discretion over the process.[8] The strategy worked: few districts ended up giving teachers low ratings and, after President Obama left office, the unions convinced the legislature to "gut" the testing component of the law: "Local school districts and teachers' unions in New York will now . . . be allowed to decide together how educators should be evaluated, with some oversight from [the state], and no requirement that standardized tests must play a role" the *New York Times* explained.[9]

Teachers unions are highly effective in these sorts of situations because political authority is fragmented, multiplying the number of veto

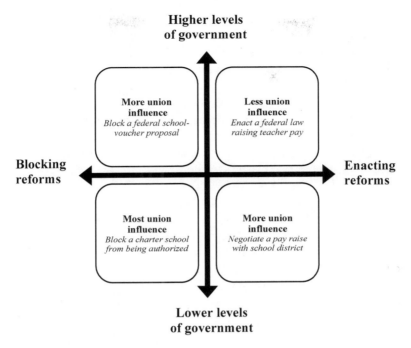

Higher levels of government

Blocking reforms

More union influence
Block a federal school-voucher proposal

Less union influence
Enact a federal law raising teacher pay

Most union influence
Block a charter school from being authorized

More union influence
Negotiate a pay raise with school district

Enacting reforms

Lower levels of government

FIGURE 10.1 Predicting teacher-union influence based on the nature of the issue and the level of government involved

points for them to ward off threatening reforms. Moreover, in venues like an education-committee hearing in a state legislature or a school-board meeting, teachers unions are usually the most organized and powerful stakeholder in the room. The narrower and less visible the policy issue (e.g., technical regulatory matters like tenure and evaluation) the less likely unions will face competition from groups that are equally well organized, resourced, informed, and committed to the issue at hand. To block change, unions only need to convince one decision-maker to side with them. By contrast, their reform opponents must run the table, winning at every point along the way. Figure 10.1 illustrates these dynamics, pinpointing where we should expect teachers to prevail in education politics. As the horizontal axis shows, unions engage in two types of advocacy: they lobby in favor of their preferred policies and they attempt to block reforms they oppose. Their advocacy efforts occur at all levels of government (vertical axis). But their level of influence in education politics will hinge on where contestation occurs along these two separate dimensions.

The lower-left quadrant of the figure shows that when teachers unions are on defense in state and local government where there is typically less competition and more veto points, they stand to be highly influential. For example, if unions in a large urban school district with a significant number of charter schools desire to cap or slow charter growth, the union has myriad options. It can lobby the local school board directly, file a lawsuit in state court, threaten a strike campaign, or make charters an issue during contract negotiations. If the local board refuses to back down, the union can go to the state capitol and lobby for statewide restrictions on charters. While victory is never guaranteed, unions will tend to exercise the most influence under these favorable conditions.

But teachers unions are not all-powerful. As with other interest groups, their influence will be more pedestrian when they are the group seeking to enact new reforms, especially if those reforms are costly and require broad tax hikes. It is hardly surprising, for example, that Vice President Kamala Harris's campaign proposal to raise teacher salaries by massively increasing federal education spending faded into obscurity after the election.[10] It is always more difficult for interest groups—no matter how powerful they are—to convince federal lawmakers to raise taxes to benefit one narrow constituency (see the upper-right quadrant of figure 10.1). Instead, teachers will be better positioned to negotiate pay increases through collective bargaining with their local district, an arena where they face less competition and their unions tend to be the top interest group in board politics (lower-right quadrant of the figure).[11]

The Status Quo Bias in American Education

> Our schools look remarkably like they did in 1983. The way we hire, use, pay, deploy, and evaluate teachers . . . the way we organize schools and classrooms [has scarcely changed]. We have gone through several spins of the standards cycle. We have school choice nothing like what one could have imagined in the early 1980s. There are entrepreneurial ventures in the charter school space and the teacher space that were literally unimaginable in the early 1980s. These are all incremental steps forward. But, in the scheme of things, if we were on our own 20-yard line in 1983, I'd say we're on the 25- or 26-yard line 30 years later.[12]—Frederick Hess (2013)

One theme that I have emphasized throughout this book is the significant degree to which education policymaking is biased against reform and in favor of maintaining the status quo. While this insight applies to all of American politics,[13] it has special relevance to education policy because of the messy structure of school governance in the United States. As discussed in chapter 6, America's K–12 education system is characterized by fragmentation and localism.[14] This fragmentation means that opponents of reform have access to numerous veto points—*at multiple levels of government*—where they can seek to block, dismantle, or dilute reform.[15] Implementation is also an important stage in the policymaking process where reform opponents can apply political pressure to slow change.[16] Even when reformers manage to get their preferred policies enacted into law, they can still expect to encounter resistance during implementation. Relative to the teachers unions, the education-reform movement is disadvantaged because it is school employees who are the street-level bureaucrats tasked with implementing education policy on the ground.[17] Many of these same employees also share a vested interest in resisting the reforms that threaten their occupational interests.[18]

The fact that it is easier to block than it is to enact and sustain reform is well established. But one implication of this insight is easily overlooked. Despite the many advantages that they hold in education politics, teachers unions will find it more difficult to realize their own policy goals than they will to block their opponents' reform agendas. This difficulty is especially evident when unions advocate for policies that (1) require higher taxes or (2) take funding away from other public programs. Since local governments are fiscally constrained,[19] teachers will often have to press state and federal authorities for more revenue. However, these higher levels of government engender more political competition, including pushback from taxpayer advocacy groups and conservative politicians who are reluctant to raise taxes.

For decades then, teachers unions (since the 1960s) and the modern education-reform movement (since the 1980s) have each been trying to push education policy in their preferred direction. For their part, unions have lobbied for policies that expand education programs and benefit their members (e.g., higher pay, smaller classes, more support staff) while at the same time resisting proposals championed by reformers in the excellence movement (e.g., school choice, TWP reforms). One irony is that both sides come away frustrated with the limited progress they are able to achieve in advancing their own agendas. Teachers unions have been disappointed with stagnant teacher salaries, for example, while education-reform groups are frustrated that their efforts to enact choice and accountability reforms rarely scale up in any meaningful or lasting way.

Consider the fate of several major education policies that teachers unions (table 10.1) and the excellence movement (table 10.2) have each advocated for over the years. The first column of each table lists a specific goal or policy objective that has been central to each group's agenda. Column 2 assesses whether the objective was met or not. The final column provides some key examples that substantiate my overall assessment of victory or defeat. The purpose of this exercise is straightforward. It allows us to assess the reform movement's most enduring policy "victories" while considering how effective unions have been at blocking the reformers' objectives. We can also see whether and when teachers have been successful at achieving their own policy goals. In other words, this stylized policy history sheds light on the nature of teacher-union influence in education politics in two separate arenas: reforming and blocking.

When Teachers Unions Go on the Offensive

Let's begin by looking at some of the objectives that teachers unions have pursued since they first burst onto the political scene. The NEA had three major policy goals throughout the 1970s (rows 1–3 of table 10.1).[20] First, they wanted a cabinet-level federal department of education. Second, they lobbied for a federal collective bargaining law that would apply to teachers in all fifty states. Finally, the NEA wanted the federal government to take more responsibility for funding K–12 education. Specifically, they wanted Uncle Sam to fund one-third of all school spending. Consistent with my claim that we should expect union influence to be maximized in (1) subnational politics and (2) blocking reform, the NEA only managed to secure one of its key federal-policy priorities. President Jimmy Carter rewarded the NEA for supporting him in the 1976 election by creating a federal department of education.[21] Although the NEA succeeded in holding Carter to his promise, its two other objectives—a larger federal role in education funding and a federal bargaining law—were soundly defeated. Consequently, teachers unions today have no federal collective bargaining rights and Washington contributes (on average) just one out of every ten dollars of total K–12 education spending.

These defeats are not surprising. They would have required winning consensus from a broad set of actors in national politics. One of the proposals (a federal bargaining law) would have tested basic tenets of American federalism and constitutional law at that time,[22] while the other

TABLE 10.1 **Teachers unions' policy agenda (1970–present)**

Teachers unions' policy objectives	Outcome for unions	Relevant examples/evidence
(1) Establish a federal department of education.	*Won*	• President Jimmy Carter delivered on his campaign promise to the NEA to establish a federal (cabinet-level) department of education (DOE). • Subsequent GOP-led efforts to eliminate the DOE have failed.
(2) Enact a federal (nationwide) public-sector collective bargaining law.	*Lost*	• In the 1970s, Congress considered several bills that would have established a federal bargaining law. However, none of these efforts succeeded. • Today, all teacher bargaining is done under state labor laws.
(3) Get the federal government to provide a third of all K–12 education funding.	*Lost*	• The federal government's share of K–12 education funding has rarely exceeded 10 percent and has (on average) constituted just 9 percent of total school spending since 1970.
(4) Expand the sources of education revenue to increase K–12 education spending.	*Mixed success*	• Since 1970, state governments' share of K–12 education funding rose to 47 percent. In the two decades prior to teacher bargaining (prior to 1970), states contributed about 40 percent. • In the 1970s, teachers unions supported lawsuits challenging states' education-funding systems. Several state supreme courts ruled against systems that relied too heavily on property taxes. These judgements mandated that state officials redesign their school-funding systems to both increase spending and to make spending more equitable.
(5) Raise teacher pay for all teachers across the board.	*Mixed success*	• Since the Great Recession, average teacher salaries have failed to rebound. In some states, salaries have even declined (after adjusting for inflation). • Through a series of statewide teacher strikes in 2018, teachers unions managed to win some modest pay increases from state officials. • Economists continue to debate vigorously whether teachers are undercompensated. What is clear is that teachers unions have been less successful at keeping average teacher salaries rising than they have been at (1) increasing hiring and (2) ensuring that teacher benefits remain strong (e.g., pensions and retiree healthcare).
(6) Establish a publicly funded and comprehensive universal early-childhood education program (ECE).	*Mixed success*	• Since the 1970s, teachers unions have fought for federal legislation that would fully fund universal ECE programs. • The federal government still does not provide publicly funded universal ECE. However, many states do. In other words, the US relies on a piecemeal approach to providing ECE. • In 2013, President Obama's "Preschool for All" legislation was blocked in Congress.
(7) Reduce class sizes.	*Mostly successful*	• The NEA has consistently lobbied for federal funding and mandates in support of class-size reduction (CSR) policies. • Many state governments have enacted aggressive CSR policies. • From 1970 to 2016, the student-teacher ratio declined from 22.3 to 16.

(a one-third federal-funding commitment) would have required raising taxes or redirecting funds away from other programs, each with their own political constituencies. The bar was simply too high and the political competition too steep for teachers to achieve all their federal-policy goals in the first decade after they became active in national politics.

However, teachers unions would go on to experience more success in subnational politics. Table 10.1 lists four additional goals teachers unions have consistently lobbied for over the years: increased education spending (row 4), higher teacher salaries (row 5), early childhood education programs (row 6), and smaller class sizes (row 7).

Despite not being able to obtain large new funding commitments from Washington, the unions have had some notable successes in pushing state governments to ramp up their spending. For example, after the US Supreme Court refused to strike down state education-funding regimes that relied heavily on property taxes,[23] in the 1970s and 1980s teachers benefitted from state-level lawsuits challenging the equity of states' funding systems.[24] Several state supreme courts ruled in their favor, striking down funding regimes that relied too much on property taxes. These victories were typically major ones for teachers unions because they forced state governments, which are less fiscally constrained than local ones, to provide more revenue for education.[25] In the two decades prior to teacher bargaining (before 1970), the state share of education funding stood at about 40 percent. Since 1970, state commitments have surpassed local ones, with states accounting for just under 50 percent of all K–12 education spending.

Most of those expenditures are on teacher compensation (row 5), an issue that has become one of the most-heated debates in all of education. Due to the zero-sum nature of the issue (higher pay for some teachers can mean lower pay for others), it has provoked a large debate in the scholarly literature about whether teachers are underpaid.[26] Setting aside the important nuances of that debate, there are a few points that are not in serious dispute. First, average teacher pay has been (at best) stagnant since the Great Recession. In fact, after accounting for inflation, in many states, average salaries are lower today than they were before the economic downturn.[27] However, it is also true that a large share of teacher compensation is provided in non-salary benefits. These benefits include defined-benefit pension plans and retiree healthcare—forms of compensation that are much less common in the private sector. Writing in *Forbes*, Frederick Hess notes that "according to calculations from a former Obama administration official, as a percentage of total [teacher] compensation, teacher retirement benefits cost twice as much as those for other workers." Hess then concludes that "bringing the cost of teacher retirement into line with other workers could account for about one-third of a 15-percent salary increase [for teachers]."[28]

According to the NEA's Research Division, after adjusting for inflation, per-pupil education spending in the United States has grown by nearly 16 percent since 2011–12.[29] So why exactly have teacher salaries lagged? One reason is that school districts have hired a substantial number of new employees over the past several decades, even as student enrollment has declined. So while policymakers have talked relentlessly about teacher *quality*, what they actually invested in was teacher *quantity*.[30] According to the National Center for Education Statistics (NCES), the number of students per teacher declined from 22.3 in 1970 to just 16 in 2016.[31] Part of this hiring spree reflects a response to regulatory changes in special education that require districts to add instructional staff to support students with disabilities.[32] But some of it is also due to the fact that both parents and teachers favor smaller classes, and unions have not been shy about lobbying for states to enact class-size reduction laws.[33] Unfortunately, there tends to be a tradeoff between paying teachers more and hiring additional school employees.

None of this is to say that teachers unions can't call upon their strength in subnational politics to persuade lawmakers to increase teacher salaries. My analysis in chapter 7, for example, showed that Washington school districts provide more generous pay when teachers are more active in local school politics. Washington provides an especially revealing example of how teachers unions can achieve their objectives when they are strategically active in *both* state and local politics. By coordinating complementary state and local advocacy campaigns, Washington's largest teachers union, the WEA, has been more effective than unions in other states in raising teacher salaries.[34]

At the state level, the WEA recently spent millions of dollars funding a lawsuit that resulted in the Washington State Supreme Court striking down the state's school-finance system. The problem was inequity: poor districts struggled to raise revenue whereas wealthy ones passed large property-tax levies. For decades this system led to huge disparities in spending (and teacher salaries) across the state. In 2018, the legislature finally satisfied the court's order that it shoulder a much larger share of K–12 education funding. But this victory came at a cost. The compromise brokered by the legislature was a "levy-swap." State taxes would go up, but local property taxes would go down as districts were told to reduce their reliance on local levy funds. This swap put the WEA in a bind. While the union supported the huge increase in state education funding, it wanted the best of both worlds: to retain the ability to negotiate pay bumps with school boards through local levy funds *and* the assurance that the state would spend more overall to ensure equity.

To achieve these two objectives, the WEA implemented a two-pronged strategy. First, it encouraged its local affiliates to pressure school boards to use the new state-funding windfall to provide teachers with large, permanent salary increases. Many WEA locals either threatened to go on strike or did in the first year after the new state funds were available.[35] One former Washington school-board member who was critical of the WEA argued that "elected school boards were intimidated or were comprised of union-supporters and gave in to WEA's extraordinary wage demands. WEA even posted a war map, crowing about raises ranging from 12 percent to 34 percent."[36]

In subsequent years, the WEA and its allies have lobbied the legislature to relax the levy-swap deal that set limits on how much local districts could raise in levy funds.[37] While the union's position is certainly understandable given its objective to raise revenue and salaries, even some of its Democratic allies have voiced concerns that returning to the old levy-reliant system will bring the state back to where it started: in court, facing another equity-finance lawsuit.[38] Irrespective of one's ideal school-finance system, the important lesson from Washington's school-finance battles is that teachers unions can win spending and salary increases when they engage in coordinated and strategic political advocacy at both the state and local levels.

Altogether then, teachers unions have been able to achieve some of their policy goals. Education spending has continued to tick upward in the United States and the share of support from state governments has steadily risen since the onset of teacher bargaining. Districts have also hired a large number of additional school employees and average pupil/teacher ratios have significantly declined since the 1970s. Still, teachers unions have tended to fall short of meeting all their objectives, especially the costliest ones. For example, despite funding several early-childhood programs (e.g., Head Start), the federal government has never agreed to pay for a comprehensive universal early-childhood education program (another union priority shown in row 6 of table 10.1). And, as previously discussed, average teacher salaries have remained flat in most states since the Great Recession. Instead, consistent with insights from the literature on the politics of public policymaking, organized teacher interests have been more successful in protecting less-visible forms of compensation (e.g., pensions and benefits). It is far easier for elected officials to make commitments to these less-visible forms of compensation that are typically in the "electoral blind spot" of voters.[39] It also helps when elected officials won't have to worry about paying for these commitments up front, but can instead "kick the can down the road" as often happens with pensions and retiree healthcare benefits.[40]

When Teachers Unions Play Defense

If teachers unions are moderately successful when they are on the political offensive, they are significantly stronger when playing defense. In table 10.2, I list the specific policy objectives pursued by the education-reform movement. Overall, very few of these union-opposed reforms have taken broad hold in American education since *A Nation at Risk*.

One idea that drew significant interest from school reformers at the outset of the excellence movement was teacher competency testing (row 1). It began as a popular and bipartisan proposal championed by a new breed of self-described "education governors." Bill Clinton, for example, had enjoyed strong support from teachers in Arkansas. But he broke rank and sided with business leaders in his state to support the periodic testing of teachers. Shortly after Clinton floated his proposal, teacher opposition and union-backed lawsuits prompted state policymakers to abruptly abandon the idea. By the time President George H. W. Bush took office in 1989, no state was engaged in teacher-competency testing. Despite broad support from the public and politicians in both parties, the idea was stopped dead in its tracks.[41] This is not to say that teacher testing would have improved teacher effectiveness. There are many reasons to think that it would not.[42] But this example reveals how a popular early reform idea at the onset of the excellence movement was quickly defeated when teachers unions rose up to oppose it.

As discussed in chapter 6, the excellence movement's effort to reform the traditional teacher salary schedule suffered a similar fate (row 2). Today, no more than 10 percent of school districts pay teachers based on their on-the-job performance, fewer than 15 percent pay a premium for

TABLE 10.2 **The education-reform movement's policy agenda (1983–present)**

Reform movement's policy objectives	Outcome for reformers	Relevant examples/evidence
(1) Teacher testing	*Lost*	• Bill Clinton's teacher-testing proposal defeated in Arkansas. • Subsequent efforts to adopt similar teacher-testing policies became a third rail in education politics, and these proposals were scrapped.
(2) Teacher pay reform	*Lost*	• Very few examples of sustained teacher-pay reforms. • One promising example where union and reform groups collaborated on teacher-pay reform (Denver) was dismantled in the late 2010s as teacher support for the program waned and the union went on strike. • Today, few school districts meaningfully differentiate teacher pay.
(3) Private-school choice (e.g., vouchers, tax credits)	*Limited success*	• A tiny fraction (1 percent) of all K–12 students are enrolled in private-school choice programs. • Private choice programs have been mostly defeated at the ballot box (e.g., AZ, CA, CO, OR, UT, WA). • Private choice advocates have not been able to build the same large bipartisan coalition that their public-school choice (charter) counterparts built in the 1990s and the first decade of the 2000s.
(4) Public-school choice (e.g., charter schools)	*Mixed success*	• Fewer than 10 percent of all K–12 students attend a charter school. • During the Trump presidency, the once-bipartisan coalition that had supported charters fragmented along partisan lines. • Some of the states and school districts with the most demand for charter schooling have begun to restrict growth (e.g., Los Angeles, CA).
(5) Standards, assessment, and accountability (e.g., NCLB)	*Lost*	• No Child Left Behind (NCLB) was replaced by the Every Student Succeeds Act (ESSA) in 2015. • ESSA eliminates punitive NCLB-style accountability and devolves more decision-making to states (where unions are more influential). • Anti-testing movement gains steam in the 2010s. Teachers unions and even some parent groups succeed in pushing back on high-stakes testing.
(6) Teacher workforce policy reforms (e.g., tenure and evaluation reforms)	*Lost*	• Many states enact teacher evaluation reforms during the Great Recession. • Political resistance contributes to these evaluation reforms being watered down. Consequently, few low-performing teachers are identified by these weakly implemented evaluation systems. • After ESSA is enacted, many states repeal or weaken the evaluation reforms they adopted during the Great Recession.
(7) Rollback of teacher collective bargaining laws	*Limited success*	• Several anti-union governors elected in 2010 succeed in curtailing teachers' bargaining rights. • *Janus* bans agency fees. • Most of the anti-union governors elected in 2010 are defeated or term-limited by 2018. One state (Virginia) that replaced its anti-union governor with a pro-union one authorizes teacher bargaining in 2020. • Mandatory teacher bargaining remains in place in most states (33). • After *Janus*, several states enact laws to dilute the effect of the court's decision and strengthen teacher organizing.

TABLE 10.2 (*continued*)

Reform movement's policy objectives	Outcome for reformers	Relevant examples/evidence
(8) Washington, DC: governance/Rhee reforms	*Won*	• Mayor Adrian Fenty loses reelection in 2008 and his Chancellor, Michelle Rhee, is forced to step down in the aftermath of that election. • Most of Rhee's reforms, including the district's new teacher evaluation program (IMPACT) are retained and remain in place as of 2021. • DC continues to remain a charter friendly city with nearly half of the city's public school students enrolled in a charter school.
(9) New Orleans, LA: state take-over; creation of Recovery School District and new choice-based system	*Won*	• The new "choice-based" school system that the state put in place after Katrina remains fully in place as of 2021. • Research by Tulane University economist Douglas Harris has since revealed that New Orleans' post-Katrina reforms helped boost student test scores, graduation rates, and college attendance.

teachers in shortage fields, and fewer than 10 percent pay more for teaching in hard-to-staff schools.[43] Despite broad public support for moving away from the single-salary schedule, teachers unions have been highly effective at blocking or diluting efforts to scrap the traditional salary schedule and meaningfully differentiate teacher pay.[44] Although both the NEA and the AFT have signaled some openness to pay reform in recent years, both organizations continue to assert that any changes must occur at the bargaining table and not be mandated in state policy.

One particular pay-reform effort merits special attention. In 2005, the Denver Classroom Teacher Association (DCTA) agreed to support what was then characterized as a model for how to redesign pay to promote more effective teaching. The ProComp plan (short for "professional compensation") was heralded nationally as an example of union-reformer collaboration. Denver voters were so impressed they agreed to a tax hike, so long as pay increases were linked to performance-based criteria and not simply the automatic pay bumps provided under the old system. ProComp earned wide praise for de-emphasizing the traditional approach of paying teachers based on longevity and credentials, and instead rewarding teachers for their willingness to take on the toughest assignments. Union leaders pointed to ProComp as an example of how reformers and unions could design a system that served both students' interests and teachers' concerns. It was supposed to be a proof point that former NEA president Bob Chase's "new unionism" could work, even on the controversial issue of teacher pay.

But in 2019 it all came apart. Denver teachers went on strike over their dissatisfaction with ProComp. When the dust had settled, core elements of the reform were scaled back, and the district agreed to reorient pay around the salary schedule. Teachers walked away with a 15 percent salary increase and the ability to use professional-development courses to move up on the salary schedule.[45] In contrast to the collaboration touted by union leaders when ProComp was first enacted, the reform became a warning to other districts thinking about following suit. As then-NEA president Lily Eskelsen García said after joining Denver teachers on their picket line, "There is not one school district in the country that is going to look at Denver and think, 'Oh, I think I'll try that [reform].'"[46]

I next consider the reform movement's effort to expand school choice in American education (rows 3 and 4). Private-school choice programs—school vouchers and tuition tax credits—were first proposed by libertarian economist Milton Friedman and then later (unsuccessfully) championed by the Reagan administration in the 1980s. Choice advocates have won some important legal battles in the intervening years. In 2002, for example, the US Supreme Court ruled that an Ohio voucher program was constitutional.[47] More recently, in 2020, the high court struck down a Montana law that had excluded private religious schools from participating in an education tax-credit program.[48] While some Republican-leaning states have taken advantage of these favorable court decisions to enact private-school choice programs, on the whole, these programs have failed to scale up. According to one of the nation's leading choice advocacy organizations, in 2020, just 1 percent of all K–12 students attended school with the assistance of a private-school choice program.[49]

While they have largely been able to keep private choice programs from scaling up, teachers unions have had to contend with a rise in the popularity of charter schools (row 4). Charters are public schools that do not have to observe the same regulations as district schools and are also far less likely to be unionized. Since Minnesota adopted the nation's first charter law in the early 1990s, charters have grown to serve a large share of students in certain states and districts. President Obama was a strong proponent of these schools. Obama's RttT grant program incentivized states to strengthen their charter laws and he helped to ensure that the charter movement remained bipartisan. Despite these clear successes, it would be hard to characterize charter schooling as a straightforward victory for education reformers. As of 2020, fewer than one in ten students in the United States attended a charter school. Growth has often been slowed because unions have successfully lobbied for laws that (1) restrict the type of entities that can authorize new charters and (2) put a cap on the total number of charters that may be granted. These legal constraints mean that charter supply can fail to keep up with enrollment demand, requiring lotteries in which only a select number of students can earn a spot in oversubscribed charters.

Finally, the politics of school choice—once celebrated for its bipartisanship—began to come undone in the late 2010s, undermining broad support for the charter movement. In 2019, despite having one of the largest charter-school markets in the country, the Los Angeles Unified School Board placed a moratorium on new charters. Democratic gubernatorial candidates also began to come out against charters.[50] With President Obama no longer leading the Democratic Party, many prominent Democrats, including then-candidate Joe Biden, began to sour on charters too. On the primary campaign trail in South Carolina, Biden stated, "I am not a charter-school fan because it takes away the options available and money for public schools."[51]

The reform movement's push for standards, assessment, and accountability reached its zenith in 2002 with the adoption of the federal No Child Left Behind (NCLB) law (row 5). NCLB required all students to demonstrate proficiency on state assessments, or else districts and schools would face punitive sanctions. On the one hand, NCLB was a loss for unions and a win for reformers. It put a spotlight on student achievement and new pressure on schools to improve in a way that no previous federal law had ever done. But NCLB proved to be a short-term loss for teachers unions. Ultimately, the law's poor construction, including its reliance on student proficiency rather than student improvement (growth) led to its undoing. What began as a popular idea (accountability) quickly fell out of favor when many schools were labeled failures merely because a single group of students performed poorly on a single test. In any event, NCLB cannot be considered a big victory for the reform movement (or a loss for unions) for one simple reason: the law was abandoned in 2015 when a bipartisan majority in Congress replaced it with the Every Student Succeeds Act (ESSA). There is little doubt that ESSA *is* a political victory for teachers unions. The new law devolves authority back to the states—an arena where, as we saw in chapter 6, the unions are especially active and politically influential.

As noted in chapter 1, the push for greater teacher accountability gained political momentum much later on, during the Obama years, when RttT and the opportunity to receive a federal waiver from NCLB gave reformers rare leverage to induce states to reform their teacher workforce policies (TWPs). It is true that many states enacted significant changes to their teacher tenure and evaluation laws (see row 6 of table 10.2). In fact, outside of the union retrenchment laws adopted during the Great Recession, TWP reforms provide the strongest support for the claim that teachers unions were significantly weakened during the Obama years.

As detailed in chapter 6, the National Council on Teacher Quality (NCTQ) reported that many states responded to the Obama administration's push for teacher accountability by enacting tougher teacher-evaluation laws. When the recession began in December 2007, for example, just sixteen US states required objective measures of student learning to be included in a teacher's evaluation. But, by 2013, more than forty states had enacted new laws that ostensibly required that a teacher's evaluation be linked, in part, to the progress of their students. Similarly, in late 2007, only five states required student learning to be the main criteria in teacher evaluations. By 2015, nearly half of states required that teachers be evaluated primarily based on student learning outcomes. Finally, prior to the Great Recession, there wasn't a single US state that required a teacher's classroom effectiveness to be a factor in deciding whether to grant that teacher tenure. Remarkably, by 2015, nearly twenty states had enacted policies that said a teacher's effectiveness should be considered when making tenure decisions.

On paper, these sorts of teacher-accountability reforms appear to be serious losses for teachers unions (and significant victories for the reform movement). However, when one carefully examines how these laws were written and implemented, the picture looks quite a bit different. Education economists Matthew Kraft and Allison Gilmour, for example, investigated how these tougher teacher-evaluation laws were actually implemented at the local level.[52] They found that the vast majority of these new evaluation laws were either constructed or implemented so weakly that few teachers ever received an unsatisfactory evaluation score. The median percentage of teachers who earned an ineffective rating in the twenty-four states that these researchers examined was fewer than 4 percent. Why did the unions' concern that hard-nosed teacher-evaluation systems would punish educators not come to fruition? Kraft and Gilmour note that giving low evaluations is difficult for principals and administrators on a personal level. It is also no doubt difficult on a political level too.

Political pushback came from several directions. For one thing, many of the states that handed out the largest number of low evaluation scores were immediately met with union-backed lawsuits. New Mexico, the state that had handed out the largest share of low teacher-evaluation scores, had its evaluation system enjoined by state courts. The enjoinment lasted long enough that, when a Democratic candidate who pledged to undo the Republican administration's teacher-evaluation law won in 2018, the system was ditched entirely. Similar episodes played out in other states. According to the *Washington Post*, "union officials say they expect to see more lawsuits in the future, especially over evaluations that use complex and controversial algorithms—called 'value-added models'—to figure out how much of a student's learning can be attributed to their teacher."[53] AFT President Randi Weingarten, whose union supported the New Mexico lawsuit, explained: "There will be more challenges because things are not being seen as credible and fair. What we've gotten to is this routinized, mechanized displacement of human judgment, and that's what I think you're seeing—that is the underlying issue that is the root of this agita about evaluations."[54] Union critic and education economist Eric Hanushek countered Weingarten by arguing that "teacher unions don't want any evaluation. That's what they're angling for."[55]

Irrespective of one's views about the optimal teacher-evaluation system, the important point is that teachers unions were eventually successfully in turning the tide on the punitive evaluation systems that arose in the 2010s. The simple fact is that most of these evaluation systems never identified large fractions of teachers as low-performing. Those systems that did were taken to court and halted. Finally, many states eventually repealed these evaluation reforms after the federal funding incentives to adopt them were no longer in place.[56]

On the whole then, teachers unions have been highly effective at blocking the reform movement's largest policy goals from scaling up widely in American education. However, there are two notable exceptions to this general pattern—exceptions where the reform movement has managed to enact and sustain reforms over teachers unions' objections. The final two rows (8, 9) of table 10.2 highlight two significant reform victories that, so far, have proven too stable for teachers unions to roll back or dilute. First, the teacher-accountability reforms enacted under Michelle Rhee in Washington, DC between 2006 and 2008 have largely been retained, even though teachers unions ultimately succeeded in ousting both Rhee and the mayor who appointed her (Adrian Fenty) from office.[57] Second, the choice-based charter school system that governs schools in New Orleans has managed to remain in place for nearly a decade after it first came into place. Washington, DC and New Orleans were significant defeats for teachers unions. And supporters of these reforms can certainly point to both cases as evidence that sometimes reformers can win meaningful policy victories that endure.

However, when looked at in another way, these examples actually help substantiate my overall claim that teachers unions are resilient and poised to remain dominant actors in American education. The unions' two largest defeats since the onset of the 1983 reform movement were ones that (1) required an unprecedented natural disaster in Hurricane Katrina and (2) stemmed from a radical governance change that gave a mayor-superintendent unprecedented powers—for two years only—to overhaul a widely criticized school district's human-resource policies. In the latter case, the face of the DC reform movement (Rhee) was sacrificed after unions helped defeat the mayor that appointed her. The lesson here is that a significant amount of political capital, aided by entirely unforeseen events that severed the institutional foundation of teacher-union power, was needed to advance reforms in just two of the nation's thirteen thousand–plus school districts. In short, this recipe for reform is not generalizable. As both Terry Moe and Douglas Harris have separately conceded about New Orleans' unique school-reform experience, this example is something that simply cannot be replicated across the country.

Democracy and Our Schools

Elsewhere, I have characterized teachers unions as American education's "quintessential Rorschach test."[58] Where their critics see intransigent interest groups opposed to common-sense education reforms, their defenders see unions as essential champions of broader social-welfare policies that benefit the common good.

My purpose in writing this book was never to bridge this divide. Instead, I have sought to document the causes and consequences of organized teacher political power in the postwar United States—a story about policy feedback, interest groups, and the dynamics of power in American education.

However, my findings do raise some important normative questions for both teachers unions and their critics in the education-reform movement. The fact is, neither side is likely to win a total and complete victory over the other. And America's schools are not likely to make dramatic improvements without both teachers and education reformers being involved. To acknowledge this truism is not to be Pollyannaish about the likelihood of meaningful and lasting union-reform collaboration. To the contrary, I have argued that power and vested interests will continue to override ideas and altruism in education politics and policymaking. However, this reality does not mean that unions and reformers have nothing to learn from one another.

The fact is both groups tend to overlook important aspects of democracy in education. While each side believes that its own political advocacy efforts promote democracy, objectively speaking, they do so in a narrow sense. Unions unapologetically defend the means (the democratic voice of school employees) while reformers focus on the democratic ends (pushing public education to be more responsive to families and students). But this current state of gridlock means that both sides fall short in some important respects.

Reformers are eager to dismantle institutions and structures that prevent too many kids from getting a great education. This eagerness has led them, for example, to attack established policies and procedures surrounding teacher tenure, pay, and evaluation. It also has meant that they tend to define public education much more broadly than do teachers unions and other establishment interests. If a choice-based system or "portfolio model" expands the number of high-quality learning options available to families, then education reformers rarely care whether those schools are traditional neighborhood schools or whether authority is vested in a for-profit or nonprofit institution, or a mayor versus an elected school board.[59]

There is nothing wrong with these impulses per se, but in their zeal to dismantle existing institutions and procedures, reformers often gloss over the fact that their ideas are likely to fail if the majority of education employees feel shut out of the process. It's no accident, for example, that the last two major top-down federal education reforms (e.g., NCLB, RttT) left reformers significantly underwhelmed and disappointed. They saw firsthand what happens when reform ideas, once put into practice, fail to gain support from the educators required to implement them and whose lives are so affected by them.[60]

Part of the problem is that reformers too often assume they will prevail if large majorities of the public agree with their vision of reform. But the wave of teacher strikes over the past decade illustrate that reformers cannot rest their case on polling support for their ideas. Strikes and protests reveal what happens when educators disagree with policymakers' reform ideas. Reformers will struggle to implement their ideas when educators resist them. This fact suggests that reformers have but two options. They can either give in to teachers' demands or they can try and recruit educators who support their agenda. Neither of these options is simple. As special-education teacher Brandon Wolford told a reporter during West Virginia's teacher walkout in 2018, "What do [teachers] have to lose by going on strike, even if those strikes are technically against the law? [Teachers] basically just say, what are you going to do? You [the school district] have got over 700 vacancies. To heck with the law. We are out. *Replace us if you can.*"[61]

But there is another side to this coin. While reformers tend to overlook the problems that arise from ignoring the voices of educators, teachers unions often appear oblivious or even unconcerned about what the public wants from its schools. They seem to forget that the other side of democracy is *responsiveness*. Political scientist V.O. Key said it best: "Unless mass views have some place in the shaping of policy, all the talk about democracy is nonsense." As Frederick Hess has observed:

> Talented educators regularly gripe to me about dumb accountability systems, teacher evaluation schemes, and such. They gripe about politicians who aren't willing to spend enough on schools, to listen to them, or to ask their advice. They exclaim that policymakers ought to mind their own business and let educators run the schools. I get it. It's an understandable premise . . . But I tell these folks they need to step back and look at this with fresh eyes. See how it looks to the policymakers. After all, *public schools spend public dollars and hire public employees to serve the public's children.* For better or worse, they're going to be governed by public officials. Those officials are going to set the policies that shape what educators can and can't do, how money is to be spent, how performance will be judged, who can be hired, and much else.[62]

The irony here is that teachers unions rarely acknowledge the tension between their support for the procedural side of democracy (i.e., traditional district-run schools governed by an elected board) and their resistance to the substantive side of it (i.e., opposing reforms that public majorities support).[63] The response might be to shrug and say that parents and the general public are wrong about the merits of reform and that teachers know better. But when families and students exit traditional public schools for charters and other choice programs, part of the reason surely has some-

thing to do with all the ways in which the existing system (and its defenders) are not responsive to their needs or interests. For public education
to be truly democratic, it also means that the voices of non-teachers (the
majority of the public) must count for something too.

It seems fitting to conclude a book about interest groups by contem-
plating what the architect of American democracy, James Madison, would
have thought about teachers unions in the United States today. By cur-
tailing their powers in Wisconsin, for example, was Scott Walker making
the mistake of curing the mischiefs of faction by removing its causes and
undermining liberty? Or was he merely controlling its effects by level-
ing the playing field for all education stakeholders? However one comes
down on this final question, I hope all readers have come away persuaded
that the policies governments enact have significant and often enduring
implications for interest-group competition, the politics of education, and
the balance of power in American democracy more generally.

Acknowledgments

A book this long in the making truly does take a village.
Getting the final manuscript across the finish line would not have been possible without the support of a few key individuals. First and foremost, I am indebted to Terry Moe for believing in both me and the project when many others did not. I simply cannot thank him enough for his sage advice and steady support throughout the publication process. I am also indebted to several other important mentors: Dave Campbell, David Nickerson, and Christina Wolbrecht. Individually and collectively they provided valuable feedback in the project's early going that made the book far better these many years later. David Nickerson, in particular, was helpful in pushing me to think carefully about causality while insisting that I never apologize for asking big questions that are sometimes beyond the reach of an experiment.

The project also benefitted from the feedback of a number of other colleagues, including Sarah Anzia, Dave Bridge, Emmerich Davies, Dan DiSalvo, Brittany Dunn-Pirio, Chuck Fagan, Leslie Finger, Pat Flavin, Sam Hayes, Lauren Honig, Vlad Kogan, Anne Marie Green, Renu Mukherjee, Taylor Nardone, Carl Palmer, Sarah Reckhow, Claudia Rodriguez, Arnie Shober, David Wakelyn, and Paul Wilford. I am grateful to Chuck Myers at the University of Chicago Press for pushing me to make the book more accessible. Chuck also chose two fantastic reviewers whose feedback helped sharpen my arguments and simplify my presentation.

Writing a book that covers seventy years of political development in American education required building numerous original data sets. That simply would not have been possible without the help of some truly fantastic research assistants. Many thanks to Grace Christenson, Reilly Conroy, Matt Davis, Jaehun Lee, Sofi Marino, Adam Martin, Chelsea McDonald, Pari Michalopoulos, Madeleine O'Shea, Mike Skeen, and Tea Thaning. Of course, without the help of library staff at Boston College and the Special Collections Research Center at the George Washington University, I would not have had access to such rich historical data in the first place. Anne Kenny at BC and Vakil Smallen at GWU, in particular, went above and beyond. Shirley Gee also provided steady administrative support and was a source of encouragement throughout. I would also like to thank the National Academy of Education/Spencer Foundation and the Hoover Institution for providing generous financial support to make this research possible.

Parts of chapter 3 were previously published in Patrick Flavin and Michael T. Hartney, "When Government Subsidizes Its Own: Collective Bargaining Laws as Agents of Political Mobilization," *American Journal of Political Science* 59, no. 4 (2015): 896–911, © 2015 Midwest Political Science Association. These parts of the chapter are reprinted with the permission of Wiley-Blackwell. Parts of chapter 9 were previously published in Daniel DiSalvo and Michael T. Hartney, "Teachers Unions in the Post-*Janus* World," *Education Next* 20, no. 4 (July 2020): 46–55, © 2020 Education Next Institute, Inc. These parts of the chapter are reprinted with the permission of Education Next Institute, Inc.

Finally, I am grateful to my family and friends for sacrificing so much quality time with me during the years that it took to complete the book. My parents, Michael Sr. and Sheryl, have been enormously supportive. I now look forward to seeing more of them and of my entire support network, including Todd Adkins, Henry Crosby, James Kuhn, Evan Mason, and Taylor Smith. A special thanks to Esther Kim for being such an accepting partner and for showing genuine interest in my work. Her support was only exceeded by that of Megan Lee who, by spoiling me with so many delicious Korean meals, freed up a lot of extra time for me to write.

Notes

Preface

1. Robert Pear, "Education Chief Calls Union 'Terrorist,' Then Recants," *New York Times*, February 24, 2004.

2. Caitlin Emma, "NEA Leader's Task: Win Back Public," *Politico*, July 6, 2014.

3. See, e.g., Steven Brill, "The Teachers' Unions' Last Stand," *New York Times Magazine* 5, no. 17 (May 17, 2010); Debra Viadero, "Is the End Near for Teachers' Unions?," *Education Week*, May 7, 2009; Garrett Keizer, "Labor's Last Stand," *Harper's Magazine*, September 2018; Madeline Will, "Are Teachers' Unions on the Brink of Demise?," *Education Week*, February 13, 2018.

4. See, e.g., Michelle Croft, Gretchen Guffy, and Dan Vitale, *The Shrinking Use of Growth: Teacher Evaluation Legislation since ESSA*, ACT Research & Policy issue brief, July 2018, https://www.act.org/content/dam/act/unsecured/documents /teacher-evaluation-legislation-since-essa.pdf; Matt Barnum, "No Thanks, Obama: 9 States No Longer Require Test Scores Be Used to Judge Teachers," *Chalkbeat*, October 8, 2019, https://www.chalkbeat.org/2019/10/8/21108964/no-thanks-obama -9-states-no-longer-require-test-scores-be-used-to-judge-teachers.

5. See, e.g., Madeline Will, "'A Game Changer': Virginia Teachers Close to Getting Collective Bargaining Rights," *Education Week*, March 10, 2020, https://www .edweek.org/teaching-learning/a-game-changer-virginia-teachers-close-to-getting -collective-bargaining-rights/2020/03; Ballotpedia staff, "Virginia to Allow Public-Sector Collective Bargaining Starting on May 1st," *Ballotpedia News*(blog), April 30, 2021, https://news.ballotpedia.org/2021/04/30/union-station-public-sector-collective -bargaining-legal-in-virginia-as-of-may-1/.

6. Kalyn Belsha, "Teachers Unions Will Have Newfound Influence in a Biden Administration," *Chalkbeat*, November 17, 2020, https://www.chalkbeat.org/2020/11 /17/21571346/teachers-unions-influence-biden-administration.

7. Mike Antonucci, "Has Teachers Union Pressure on CDC Turned the Government's Best Scientific Guidelines into a Bargaining Chip?," *The74*, May 5, 2021,

https://www.the74million.org/article/antonucci-has-teachers-union-pressure-on
-cdc-turned-the-governments-best-scientific-guidelines-into-a-bargaining-chip/.

8. See, e.g., Michael T. Hartney and Leslie K. Finger, "Politics, Markets, and Pandemics: Public Education's Response to Covid-19," *Perspectives on Politics* (2021): 1–17, https://doi.org/10.1017/S1537592721000955; Bradley D. Marianno, Annie Hemphill, Ana Paula S. Loures-Elias, Libna Garcia, and Deanna Cooper, "Power in a Pandemic: Teachers' Unions and Their Responses to School Reopening" (working paper, 2021), https://drive.google.com/file/d/1Ay3fTUch_eTu3fTD cuWhU5kRNBdP9R-0/view; Corey DeAngelis and Christos Makridis, "Are School Reopening Decisions Related to Union Influence?," *Social Science Quarterly* (March 25, 2021), https://doi.org/10.1111/ssqu.12955; Douglas N. Harris, Engy Ziedan, and Susan Hassig, *The Effects of School Reopenings on COVID-19 Hospitalizations*, technical report, National Center for Research on Education Access and Choice, January 24, 2021, https://www.reachcentered.org/publications/the -effects-of-school-reopenings-on-covid-19-hospitalizations; Matt Grossmann, Sarah Reckhow, Katharine Strunk, and Meg Turner, "All States Close but Red Districts Reopen: The Politics of In-Person Schooling during the COVID-19 Pandemic," EdWorkingPaper: 21–355, Annenberg Institute, Brown University, 2021, https:// doi.org/10.26300/cb1f-hq66.

9. See Michael T. Hartney and Patrick Flavin, "From the Schoolhouse to the Statehouse: Teacher Union Political Activism and State Education Reform Policy," *State Politics and Policy Quarterly* 11, no. 3 (2011): 251–68.

10. On the multiple and contested purposes of public education, see David F. Labaree, "Public Goods, Private Goods: The American Struggle over Educational Goals," *American Educational Research Journal* 34, no. 1 (1997): 39–81.

11. On the public and democratic purposes of K–12 American education, see, e.g., Frederick M. Hess, *The Same Thing Over and Over: How School Reformers Get Stuck in Yesterday's Ideas* (Cambridge, MA: Harvard University Press, 2010); E. D. Hirsch Jr., *The Making of Americans: Democracy and Our Schools* (New Haven, CT: Yale University Press, 2010).

12. For example, Harvard University's *Education Next* poll has asked a representative sample of Americans the following question every year since 2013: "Do you think teachers unions have a generally positive effect on schools, or do you think they have a generally negative effect?" Averaging across the seven-year time series, roughly 35 percent of Americans said that the unions have a positive effect compared to 38 percent who said the unions have a negative effect. See https:// www.educationnext.org/ednext-poll/ for all *Education Next* poll data.

Chapter 1

1. See, e.g., Terry M. Moe, *Special Interest: Teachers Unions and America's Public Schools* (Washington, DC: Brookings Institution, 2011); Terry M. Moe and

Susanne Wiborg, "Introduction," in *The Comparative Politics of Education*, ed. Terry M. Moe and Susanne Wiborg (Cambridge: Cambridge University Press, 2017): 1–23. Theda Skocpol once described America's teachers unions as a "stalwart in state and local as well as national Democratic Party politics." See Theda Skocpol, *Diminished Democracy: From Membership to Management in American Civic Life* (Norman: University of Oklahoma Press, 2003): 157.

2. Merriam-Webster's defines *subsidy* as "a grant by a government to a private person or company to assist an enterprise deemed advantageous to the public" (*Merriam-Webster*, s.v. "subsidy," accessed September 6, 2021, https://www .merriam-webster.com/dictionary/subsidy). This definition nicely captures the sentiment here, but with a twist. The target of the subsidies that I examine are not individual citizens (as with, e.g., a child tax credit) or corporations (as with, e.g., a subsidy to an energy company), but instead, newly emerging teacher-union interest groups, striving to find their political footing and gain influence in American education.

3. See, e.g., Kathleen Bawn, Martin Cohen, David Karol, Seth Masket, Hans Noel, and John Zaller, "A Theory of Political Parties: Groups, Policy Demands and Nominations in American Politics," *Perspectives on Politics* 10, no. 3 (September 2012): 571–97; Jacob S. Hacker and Paul Pierson, *Winner-Take-All Politics: How Washington Made the Rich Richer—and Turned Its Back on the Middle Class* (New York: Simon & Schuster, 2010); Jacob S. Hacker and Paul Pierson, "After the 'Master Theory': Downs, Schattschneider, and the Rebirth of Policy-Focused Analysis," *Perspectives on Politics* 12, no. 3 (2014): 643–62; Terry M. Moe, "Vested Interests and Political Institutions," *Political Science Quarterly* 130, no. 2 (2015): 277–318.

4. As Sarah Anzia explains, "research on local politics has tended to ignore interest groups, and research on interest groups has tended to ignore local government . . ." See Sarah F. Anzia, *Local Interests: Interest Groups and Public Policy in U.S. City Government* (Chicago: University of Chicago Press, 2022).

5. See, e.g., Richard Colvin, "Straddling the Democratic Divide," *Education Next* 9, no. 2 (2009): 10–17; William G. Howell, "President Obama's Race to the Top," *Education Next* 15, no. 4 (2015): 58–67; Patrick McGuinn, "From No Child Left Behind to the Every Student Succeeds Act: Federalism and the Education Legacy of the Obama Administration," *Publius: The Journal of Federalism* 46, no. 3 (2016): 392–415.

6. See, e.g., Steven Greenhouse, "Strained States Turning to Laws to Curb Unions," *New York Times*, January 3, 2011; Bradley D. Marianno, "Teachers' Unions on the Defensive?: How Recent Collective Bargaining Laws Reformed the Rights of Teachers," *Journal of School Choice* 9, no. 4 (2015): 551–77.

7. See, e.g., Madeline Will, "Post 'Janus,' Nation's Largest Teachers' Union Sees Signs of Membership Decline," *Education Week*, October 25, 2018; Mike Antonucci, "Union Report: NEA's New 'Community Allies' Membership Could Mean Million-Dollar Shot in the Arm to Union's Political Action Committee," *The74*, July 31, 2019.

8. Erik Kain, "How Republican Trifectas Across the Country Could Change American Politics," *Forbes*, September 15, 2011, https://www.forbes.com/sites/erik kain/2011/09/15/of-trifectas-and-the-electoral-college/.

9. For a detailed journalistic account of the battle between Walker and certain public-sector unions in Wisconsin, see Jason Stein and Patrick Marley, *More than They Bargained for: Scott Walker, Unions, and the Fight for Wisconsin* (Madison: University of Wisconsin Press, 2013).

10. See Sophie Quinton, "Lawmakers in Blue States Try to Protect Organized Labor," *Stateline*, August 1, 2018, https://www.pewtrusts.org/en/research-and-anal ysis/blogs/stateline/2018/08/01/lawmakers-in-blue-states-try-to-protect-organized -labor.

11. See, e.g., Madeline Will, "'A Game Changer': Virginia Teachers Close to Getting Collective Bargaining Rights," *Education Week*, March 10, 2020, https:// www.edweek.org/teaching-learning/a-game-changer-virginia-teachers-close-to -getting-collective-bargaining-rights/2020/03; Ballotpedia staff, "Virginia to Allow Public-Sector Collective Bargaining Starting on May 1st," *Ballotpedia News* (blog), April 30, 2021, https://news.ballotpedia.org/2021/04/30/union-station-public-sector -collective-bargaining-legal-in-virginia-as-of-may-1/.

12. US Department of Education, "Public School Expenditures," in *The Condi-tion of Education 2019*, NCES 2019–144, Institute of Education Sciences/National Center for Education Statistics, 2019, https://nces.ed.gov/pubs2019/2019144.pdf.

13. National Association of State Budget Officers (NASBO), *2019 State Ex-penditure Report: Fiscal Years 2017–2019* (Washington, DC: National Union of State Budget Officers, 2019): 3, https://higherlogicdownload.s3.amazonaws.com /NASBO/9d2d2db1-c943-4f1b-b750-0fca152d64c2/UploadedImages/SER%20Ar chive/2019_State_Expenditure_Report-S.pdf.

14. See, e.g., Dan Goldhaber, "In Schools, Teacher Quality Matters Most: Today's Research Reinforces Coleman's Findings," *Education Next* 16, no. 2 (2016): 56–63.

15. According to one summary of this research literature, "having five years of good teachers in a row (1.0 standard deviation above average, or at the 85th qual-ity percentile) could overcome the average seventh-grade mathematics achieve-ment gap between lower income kids (those on the free or reduced-price lunch program) and those from higher-income families." See Eric A. Hanushek and Ste-ven G. Rivkin, "How to Improve the Supply of High-Quality Teachers," *Brookings Papers on Education Policy*, no. 7 (2004): 7–44, at 21, https://www.jstor.org/stable /20067265.

16. See, e.g., Eric A. Hanushek and Steven G. Rivkin, "The Distribution of Teacher Quality and Implications for Policy," *Annual Review of Economics* 4, no. 1 (2012): 131–57.

17. As Goldhaber and colleagues note, "The small group of studies that examine one set of CBA provisions—seniority-based transfer and vacancy protections— and their association with teacher distribution suggests the transfer protections in

teacher CBAs contribute to inequities in the distribution of teachers across schools by influencing patterns in teacher transfers that occur within-district." See Dan Goldhaber, Katharine O. Strunk, Nate Brown, Andrea Chambers, Natsumi Naito, and Malcolm Wolff, *Teacher Staffing Challenges in California: Exploring the Factors That Influence Teacher Staffing and Distribution*, Getting Down to Facts II Technical Report, September 2018, https://files.eric.ed.gov/fulltext/ED594738.pdf.

18. Jill Anderson, "After 'Vergara': HGSE Experts Weigh In," Harvard Graduate School of Education website, June 27, 2014, https://www.gse.harvard.edu/news/14/06/after-vergara-hgse-experts-weigh.

19. See, e.g., Steven Greenhouse, "Strained States Turning to Laws to Curb Unions"; Associated Press, "States Weakening Teacher-Tenure Protections," January 25, 2012, https://www.governing.com/archive/ap-states-weakening-teacher-tenure-protections.html.

20. Tabitha Grossman, *Building a High-Quality Education Workforce: A Governor's Guide to Human Capital Development*, NGA Center for Best Practices, 2009, https://files.eric.ed.gov/fulltext/ED507631.pdf.

21. Trip Gabriel and Sam Dillon, "GOP Governors Take Aim at Teacher Tenure," *New York Times*, January 31, 2011.

22. Randi Weingarten, "When Reform Touches Teachers" (public event, Thomas B. Fordham Institute, Washington, DC, August 23, 2011).

23. Paul E. Peterson, Michael Henderson, and Martin R. West, *Teachers versus the Public: What Americans Think about Schools and How to Fix Them* (Washington, DC: Brookings Institution Press, 2014).

24. On the general importance of street-level bureaucrats in policy implementation, see Michael Lipsky, *Street-Level Bureaucracy: Dilemmas of the Individual in Public Services, 30th Anniversary Expanded Edition* (New York: Russell Sage Foundation, 1980).

25. See Jennifer L. Hochschild and Nathan Scovronick, *The American Dream and the Public Schools* (New York: Oxford University Press, 2003).

26. See, e.g., Amy Gutmann, *Democratic Education* (Princeton, NJ: Princeton University Press, 1987); David E. Campbell, *Why We Vote: How Schools and Communities Shape Our Civic Life*, vol. 87 (Princeton, NJ: Princeton University Press, 2006); Meira Levinson, *No Citizen Left Behind*, vol. 13 (Cambridge, MA: Harvard University Press, 2012).

27. See, e.g., Robert Balfanz and Nettie E. Legters, *Locating the Dropout Crisis: Which High Schools Produce the Nation's Dropouts? Where Are They Located? Who Attends Them?* (Baltimore, MD: Center for Social Organization of Schools, Johns Hopkins University, 2004); Eric A. Hanushek, Paul E. Peterson, Laura M. Talpey, and Ludger Woessmann, "The Achievement Gap Fails to Close," *Education Next* 19, no. 3 (2019).

28. See, e.g., Jay Greene and Josh McGee, "When the Best Is Mediocre," *Education Next* 12, no. 1 (2012): 34–40; Eric A. Hanushek, Paul E. Peterson, and Ludger

Woessmann, "U.S. Students from Educated Families Lag in International Tests," *Education Next* 14, no. 4 (Fall 2014): 9–18.

29. Grossman, *Building a High-Quality Education Workforce*, 5.

30. See, e.g., Moe, *Special Interest*; Moe, "Vested Interests and Political Institutions."

31. Although neither develops a broad theory of teacher-union power, the work of two other scholars is also relevant. In *Black Mayors and School Politics*, Wilbur Rich documents the influence of what he calls the "public school cartel" in urban education politics: "a coalition of professional school administrators, school activists and union leaders who maintain control of school policy to promote the interests of its members." Rich's case studies show how the cartel is both "incredibly skillful at staying in power" and highly capable of vetoing school reforms that run counter to its members' interests. See Wilbur C. Rich, *Black Mayors and School Politics: The Failure of Reform in Detroit, Gary, and Newark* (New York: Garland Publishing, 1996). In a different vein, Sarah Anzia's work on election timing has shown how low-turnout, off-cycle school-board elections enhance the political power and influence of teachers unions in local school politics. See Sarah F. Anzia, "Election Timing and the Electoral Influence of Interest Groups," *Journal of Politics* 73, no. 2 (2011): 412–27.

32. Moe, *Special Interest*, 8.

33. This priority isn't a matter of selfishness, but simply the reality of democratic politics. Just as public-school systems are subject to democratic forces, teachers unions face pressure to be responsive to their members. For example, even if a majority of voters wanted to see tenure reformed, teachers unions would face pressure to resist if their members felt that the proposed reforms weakened their job protections. In short, when teachers unions fail to defend their members' interests, union leaders may lose the support of their rank and file. See Moe, *Special Interest*.

34. Moe, "Vested Interests and Political Institutions," 287.

35. Moe, "Vested Interests and Political Institutions," 291.

36. Jeffrey R. Henig, Richard C. Hula, Marion Orr, and Desiree S. Pedescleaux, *The Color of School Reform: Race, Politics, and the Challenge of Urban Education* (Princeton, NJ: Princeton University Press, 2001): 152.

37. McDonnell writes that "to suggest that organized teachers, because of the kinds of demands they are making and by their superior numbers and resources, may be excluding other groups affected by public education from the policy process is not to argue against teachers organizing to achieve better working conditions ... Rather, what we have tried to indicate is that in making evaluations about educational policies, organized teachers are not solely guided by the professional criterion of student learning effectiveness ... They also have self-interests that may, at times, come into conflict with the public interest as it relates to education." See Lorraine Mary McDonnell, *The Control of Political Change within An Interest Group: The Case of the National Education Association* (PhD diss., Stanford University, 1975): 304.

38. David B. Tyack, *The One Best System: A History of American Urban Education*, vol. 95 (Cambridge, MA: Harvard University Press, 1974): 289.

39. See Moriah Balingit, "Billionaire Bill Gates Announces a $1.7 Billion Investment in U.S. Schools," *Washington Post*, October 19, 2017, emphasis added.

40. See Howard Blume, "Broad Foundation Suspends $1-Million Prize for Urban School Districts," *Los Angeles Times*, February 9, 2015.

41. See, e.g., Christina A. Samuels, "Education Donors Shift Priorities, Survey Suggests," *Education Week*, February 27, 2019; Steven Lawrence and Melinda Fine, *Trends in Education Philanthropy: Benchmarking 2018–19*, Grantmakers for Education report, 2019, https://files.eric.ed.gov/fulltext/ED595154.pdf.

42. See Nat Malkus and R. J. Martin, "When It Comes to Merit Pay, Newark's Teacher Contract Is Out With the New and in With the Old," *The74*, September 8, 2019. For a broader account of the Zuckerberg-Newark school reform initiative, see Dale Russakoff, *The Prize: Who's in Charge of America's Schools?* (New York: Houghton Mifflin Harcourt, 2015).

43. Moe, "Vested Interests and Political Institutions," 285.

44. NJ Rev Stat § 18A:31-2 (2013).

45. Daniel DiSalvo, *Government against Itself: Public Union Power and Its Consequences* (New York: Oxford University Press, 2015): 124.

46. Robert Chanin, "Remarks to the RA" (Speech, 88th Annual Representative Assembly Meeting of the National Education Association, San Diego, CA, July 6, 2009).

47. Tom Verducci, "Totally Juiced: Confessions of a Former MVP," *Sports Illustrated*, June 3, 2002.

48. See, e.g., Jack L. Walker, *Mobilizing Interest Groups in America: Patrons, Professions, and Social Movements* (Ann Arbor: University of Michigan Press, 1991); David C. King and Jack L. Walker, "The Provision of Benefits by Interest Groups in the United States," *Journal of Politics* 54, no. 2 (1992): 394–426.

49. See Andrea Campbell, "Policy Makes Mass Politics," *Annual Review of Political Science* 15 (June 2012): 333–51.

50. See, e.g., Sidney Verba, Kay Lehman Schlozman, and Henry Brady, *Voice and Equality: Civic Voluntarism in American Politics* (Cambridge, MA: Harvard University Press, 1995); Steven J. Rosenstone and John Mark Hansen, *Mobilization, Participation, and Democracy in America* (New York: Macmillan, 1993).

51. See Aaron Epstein, "How Pentagon Boosted NRA," *Philadelphia Inquirer*, May 14, 1979.

52. See Sarah F. Anzia and Terry M. Moe, "Do Politicians Use Policy To Make Politics? The Case of Public-Sector Labor Laws," *American Political Science Review* 110, no. 4 (2016): 763–77.

53. See Governor's Committee on Public Employee Relations, *Final Report*, US Department of Justice/National Institute of Justice, March 31, 1966: 29, https://www.ojp.gov/pdffiles1/Digitization/78885NCJRS.pdf.

54. See Martin West, "Bargaining with Authority: The Political Origins of Public Sector Bargaining" (paper presented at the 2008 Policy History Conference, St. Louis, MO, May 29–June 1, 2008).

55. Teachers unions were wise to pursue exclusive representation. The benefits of obtaining exclusive recognition far outweigh the costs. The best evidence in support of this claim is the simple fact that, even after the US Supreme Court banned agency fees in 2018, few unions suggested switching to a system of "members-only" collective bargaining. To the contrary, teachers have a long history of supporting exclusive recognition. For example, in the late 1960s, while testifying before the US Advisory Commission on Intergovernmental Relations, then-NEA Executive Director Sam Lambert argued that "the majority organization should have the exclusive right to negotiate on behalf of all employees in the negotiating unit." See US Advisory Commission on Intergovernmental Relations, *Labor-Management Policies for State and Local Government*, report A–35, Washington, DC, September 1969: 137, https://library.unt.edu/gpo/acir/Reports/policy/a-35.pdf.

56. See Richard C. Kearney and Patrice M. Mareschal, *Labor Relations in the Public Sector* (New York: Taylor & Francis, 2014).

57. See Perry Education Association v. Perry Local Educators' Association, 460 U.S. 37 (1983).

58. E. E. Schattschneider, *Politics, Pressure, and the Tariff* (New York: Prentice-Hall, 1935).

Chapter 2

1. See, e.g., David W. Nickerson, "Quality Is Job One: Professional and Volunteer Voter Mobilization Calls," *American Journal of Political Science* 51, no. 2 (2007): 269–82.

2. Details on the Wisconsin Teacher Recall Survey can be found in the chapter appendix.

3. Edward B. Fiske, "National Teachers' Group Asserts Its Power at the Polls," *New York Times*, October 28, 1980.

4. See NEA Research Division, "Status of the American Public School Teacher," *NEA Research Bulletin* 35, no. 1 (February 1957): 5– 63. The NEA distributed this survey in March of 1956 to a stratified random sample of K–12 public school teachers. Responses were returned in April and May (before the 1956 November elections). State and local school directories were the sampling frame. 12,098 invitations were sent and 5,602 teachers responded for a response rate of 45 percent. The final data were weighted to be representative of the nation's teacher workforce in 1956.

5. See John Rosales, "5 Things We Learned from Election 2018," *NEA Today*, November 13, 2018, https://www.nea.org/advocating-for-change/new-from-nea/5-things-we-learned-election-2018.

6. See Terry M. Moe, "Teacher Unions and School Board Elections," in *Besieged: School Boards and the Future of Education Politics*, ed. William G. Howell (Washington, DC: Brookings Institution Press, 2005): 254–87; Michael T. Hartney, "Teachers Unions and School Board Elections: A Reassessment," *Interest Groups & Advocacy* (forthcoming).

7. I do not make direct comparisons here between teachers and non-teachers in the ANES because there are too few teacher respondents in these waves of the survey to generate reliable estimates. However, for transparency's sake, I can report that I uncover similar participation gaps in the ANES. That is, non-teachers report higher rates of participation on the nonvoting items in the ANES than do the (tiny) sample of teachers in the ANES during the 1950s.

8. See Thomas Toch, *In the Name of Excellence: The Struggle to Reform the Nation's Schools, Why It's Failing, and What Should Be Done* (New York: Oxford University Press, 1991).

9. See Beth Bazar, *State Legislators' Occupations: A Decade of Change* (Denver, CO: National Conference of State Legislatures, 1987); *Educators Serving in State Legislatures* (Washington, DC: National Council of State Education Associations, 1975).

10. See, e.g., Ronald J. Hrebenar and Clive S. Thomas, eds., *Interest Group Politics in the Southern States* (Tuscaloosa: University of Alabama Press, 1992); Ronald J. Hrebenar and Clive S. Thomas, eds., *Interest Group Politics in the American West* (Salt Lake City: University of Utah Press, 1987); Ronald J. Hrebenar and Clive S. Thomas, eds., *Interest Group Politics in the Midwestern States* (Ames: Iowa State University Press, 1993); Ronald J. Hrebenar and Clive S. Thomas, eds., *Interest Group Politics in the Northeastern States* (University Park: Pennsylvania State University Press, 1993).

11. See Frederick M. Wirt and Leslie Christovich, "Administrators' Perceptions of Policy Influence: Conflict Management Styles and Roles," *Educational Administration Quarterly* 25, no. 1 (1989): 5–35.

12. See Frederick M. Wirt and Michael W. Kirst, *The Political Dynamics of American Education* (Berkeley, CA: McCutchan 1997): 156.

13. See, e.g., Frederick M. Hess, *School Boards at the Dawn of the 21st Century: Conditions and Challenges of District Governance*, National School Boards Association, 2002, https://files.eric.ed.gov/fulltext/ED469432.pdf.

14. See Sidney Verba, Kay Lehman Schlozman, and Henry Brady, *Voice and Equality: Civic Voluntarism in American Politics* (Cambridge, MA: Harvard University Press, 1995).

15. For research showing that public employees participate more reliably in politics than their private sector counterparts, see Ronald N. Johnson and Gary D. Libecap, "Public Sector Employee Voter Participation and Salaries," *Public Choice* 68, no. 1–3 (1991): 137–50.

16. See Cynthia Menzel, "A Fond Farewell to CTA's Top (Dog)Gett," *California Educator*, July 2013: 20.

17. See National Education Association, *Addresses and Proceedings of the 114th Annual Meeting Held at San Francisco, California, June 30–July 6, 1970*, vol. 108 (Washington, DC: NEA, 1970): 14.

18. See Verba, Schlozman, and Brady, *Voice and Equality*, 133. On the importance of organizational recruitment for political participation, see also, e.g., Steven J. Rosenstone and John Mark Hansen, *Mobilization, Participation, and Democracy in America* (New York: Macmillan, 1993).

19. See Constance Shotts, *The Origin and Development of the National Education Association Political Action Committee, 1969–1976* (PhD diss., Indiana University, 1977): 1–2, ProQuest document ID 302804645.

20. See Terry M. Moe, *Special Interest: Teachers Unions and America's Public Schools* (Washington, DC: Brookings Institution Press, 2011): 38.

21. See, e.g., Clyde W. Summers, "Exclusive Representation: A Comparative Inquiry Into a Unique American Principle," *Comparative Labor Law and Policy Journal* 20, no. 1 (1998): 47–70.

22. See Karen Crummy, "Colorado Teachers Unions under Fire for Taxpayer Subsidies from School Districts," *Denver Post*, December 17, 2011, denverpost .com/2011/12/17/colorado-teachers-unions-under-fire-for-taxpayer-subsidies-from -school-districts/.

23. Crummy.

24. Crummy.

25. See Michael Edwards and Mark Walsh, *More Than a Lawyer: Robert Chanin, the National Education Association, and the Fight for Public Education, Employee Rights, and Social Justice* (Washington, DC: National Education Association, 2010): 72.

26. See Robert Chanin and Donald Wollett, *The Law and Practice of Teacher Negotiations* (Washington, DC: Bureau of National Affairs, 1970) section 3: 69–70.

27. The majority reasoned that "to permit one side of a debatable public question to have a monopoly in expressing its views to the government is the antithesis of constitutional guarantees." See City of Madison v. Wisconsin Employment Relations Commission, 429 U.S. 167 (1976).

28. See, e.g., Deborah Schmedemann, "Of Meetings and Mailboxes: The First Amendment and Exclusive Representation in Public Sector Labor Relations," *Virginia Law Review* 72, no. 1 (February 1986): 91–138.

29. See Abood v. Detroit Board of Education, 431 U.S. 209 (1977).

30. See Minnesota Board for Community Colleges v. Knight, 465 U.S. 271 (1984).

31. Prior to *Perry*, the majority of federal court decisions had authorized school districts to provide Association rights to the teachers union that had won exclusive recognition. See, e.g., Connecticut State Federation of Teachers v. Board of Education Members, 538 F.2d 471 (2d Cir. 1976); Memphis American Federation of Teachers, Local 2032 v. Board of Education, 534 F.2d 699 (6th Cir. 1976).

32. Perry Education Association v. Perry Local Educators' Association, 460 U.S. 37 (1983), emphasis added.

33. See Sarah F. Anzia, "The Backlash Against School Choice and Accountability Policies: The Organizations and Their Politics," *Urban Affairs Review* 56, no. 3 (2020): 987.

34. See, e.g., Richard L. Hall and Alan V. Deardorff, "Lobbying as Legislative Subsidy," *American Political Science Review* 100, no. 1 (2006): 69–84.

35. See, e.g., Martin R. West, Michael Henderson, and Paul E. Peterson, "The Education Iron Triangle," in *Forum*, vol. 10, no. 1 (2012); Sarah F. Anzia and Terry M. Moe, "Interest Groups on the Inside: The Governance of Public Pension Funds," *Perspectives on Politics* 17, no. 4 (2019): 1059–78.

36. Perry Education Association v. Perry Local Educators' Association, 460 U.S. 37, 1983.

37. See, e.g., Patrick McGuinn, "Fight Club: Are Advocacy Organizations Changing the Politics of Education?," *Education Next* 12, no. 3 (2012): 25–31; Paul Manna and Susan Moffitt, *New Education Advocacy Organizations in the US States* (New York: Wallace Foundation, 2014); Andrew P. Kelly, *Turning Lightning into Electricity: Organizing Parents for Education Reform*, American Enterprise Institute, December 2014, https://www.aei.org/wp-content/uploads/2014/12/Kelly_Turning-Lightning-Into-Electricity.pdf.

38. See, e.g., Anthony J. Nownes and Grant Neeley, "Public Interest Group Entrepreneurship and Theories of Group Mobilization," *Political Research Quarterly* 49, no. 1 (1996): 119–46.

39. For a historical overview of the struggles that parents have faced in trying to obtain more power and influence in American education, see William W. Cutler, *Parents and Schools* (Chicago: University of Chicago Press, 2015).

40. See, e.g., McGuinn, "Fight Club"; Patrick McGuinn, "Mobilizing Mom and Dad: Engaging Parents behind Systemic School Reform," in Patrick McGuinn and Andrew P. Kelly, *Parent Power: Grass-Roots Activism and K–12 Education Reform* (American Enterprise Institute working paper, July 31, 2012), https://www.aei.org/wp-content/uploads/2012/07/-parent-power-grassroots-activism-and-k12-education-reform_134233335113.pdf?x91208; Kelly, *Turning Lightning into Electricity*.

41. See, e.g., Frederick M. Hess and Daniel K. Lautzenheiser, "Putting the Punch in Parent Power," in American Enterprise Institute for Public Policy Research, *Education Outlook no. 5* (August 2012), https://files.eric.ed.gov/fulltext/ED535402.pdf; Andrew P. Kelly, "Parent Voice, School Choice, and the New Politics of Education Reform," in Patrick McGuinn and Andrew P. Kelly, *Parent Power*; McGuinn, "Mobilizing Mom and Dad"; Kelly, *Turning Lightning into Electricity*.

42. See Sean Cavanagh, "'Parent Unions' Join Policy Debates," *Education Week*, March 7, 2012.

43. See, e.g., "Year-Old Parents' Union Takes Off the Gloves," *Philadelphia Evening Bulletin*, January 13, 1974; Babette E. Edwards, "Why a Harlem Parents

Union?," in *Parents, Teachers, and Children: Prospects for Choice in American Education.*, ed. James S. Coleman (San Francisco, CA: Institute for Contemporary Studies, 1977); Don Davies and Ross Zerchykov, "Parents as an Interest Group," *Education and Urban Society* 13, no. 2 (1981): 173–92; Gladys Craven Fernandez, *Parents' Influence on School Policy and Practice: A Narrative on the Philadelphia Parents Union for Public Schools* (PhD diss., Temple University, 1984), ProQuest document ID 303335258.

44. The Philadelphia Parents Union, for example, was founded in response to a series of teacher-union strikes that shut down the city's school system in the early 1970s. See Gladys (Happy) Craven Fernandez, "Empowering Parents," *Urban Review* 11, no. 2 (1979): 89–96. More recently, in 2020, California parents founded "OpenSchoolsCA" as a response to their frustration with the state's slow approach to reopening public schools during the COVID-19 pandemic. One of the group's founders, Megan Bacigalupi, explained the motivation for the group's genesis this way: "Parent voices and student interests should never again be ignored or deprioritized as they have been during this year. Parents and kids must have *a seat at the table*." See Howard Blume, "Parents Frustrated by Pandemic Education Launch Activist Group to Raise Their Voices," *Los Angeles Times*, June 2, 2021.

45. On the hidden costs of subsidies in CBAs, see Myron Lieberman, *Understanding the Teacher Union Contract: A Citizen's Handbook*, vol. 1 (New Brunswick, NJ: Transaction Publishers, 2000).

46. CBA data for the 2000s comes from the National Council on Teacher Quality's TR3 Database, which contains teacher-union contracts and employee handbooks for over 140 of the nation's largest school districts.

Chapter 3

1. By "idiosyncratic," I do *not* mean that adopting and non-adopting states were perfectly alike. Instead, I simply mean to say that the specific year of adoption often varied for reasons that were somewhat idiosyncratic and unpredictable. For example, in some union-friendly states, lawmakers held off on adopting a CB law until they could enact one that was sufficiently "prolabor." Likewise, because many Republican state legislators often faced pressure from their public-employee constituents to support CB laws, several of these laws were adopted by state governments that were either entirely (or partly) Republican-led, meaning law adoptions were not a simple and straightforward response to conventional partisan dynamics. See, e.g., Sarah F. Anzia and Terry M. Moe, "Do Politicians Use Policy To Make Politics? The Case of Public-Sector Labor Laws," *American Political Science Review* 110, no. 4 (2016): 763–77.

2. See Robert G. Valletta and Richard B. Freeman, "Appendix B: The NBER Public Sector Collective Bargaining Law Data Set," in *When Public Sector Workers*

Unionize, ed. Richard B. Freeman and Casey Ichniowski (Chicago: National Bureau of Economic Research and University of Chicago Press, 1988). This data set was later extended by Kim Rueben to 1996, and then to 2020 by the author.

3. Teachers are identified using that survey year's specific occupation code from 1956 to 1982, and by using the seventy-one-category occupation code (VCF0154a) in the ANES cumulative file from 1984 to 2004 (the final year for which these detailed occupation codes are publicly available). Unfortunately, the ANES occupation codes do not indicate whether a teacher is employed by a public school or a private school (whose teachers would not be subject to a state's mandatory-bargaining law). This means that private school teachers (who between 1955 and 2004 comprised, on average, 13.8 percent of the US teaching workforce) are lumped in with public school teachers in my analysis. This grouping has the practical effect of (mis)assigning the "treatment" (a mandatory CB law) to a small but unknown portion of private school teachers in the analysis, a fact which would ultimately bias my results toward zero (i.e., make it more difficult for me to demonstrate a significant link between mandatory CB laws and higher rates of teacher political participation).

4. See, e.g., Jan E. Leighley, "Attitudes, Opportunities and Incentives: A Field Essay on Political Participation," *Political Research Quarterly* 48, no. 1 (March 1, 1995): 181–209; Sidney Verba, Kay Lehman Schlozman, and Henry Brady, *Voice and Equality: Civic Voluntarism in American Politics* (Cambridge, MA: Harvard University Press, 1995).

5. Because figure 3.1 displays the difference in political participation before and after a state implemented a mandatory collective-bargaining law, only states that changed their laws during a given indicated time period were included in the figure.

6. Controlling for whether a teacher is a union member (or not) is especially important because it allows me to evaluate whether CB laws had an independent effect on teacher participation above and beyond the fact that (1) CB laws increased the propensity of teachers to join a union and (2) union members are generally more likely to participate in politics than nonmembers. See, e.g., Herbert B. Asher, Eric S. Heberlig, Randall B. Ripley, and Karen Snyder, *American Labor Unions in the Electoral Arena: People, Passions, and Power* (Lanham, MD: Rowman and Littlefield, 2001); Patrick Flavin and Benjamin Radcliff, "Labor Union Membership and Voting Across Nations," *Electoral Studies* 30, no. 4 (2011): 633–41; Jan E. Leighley and Jonathan Nagler, "Unions, Voter Turnout, and Class Bias in the U.S. Electorate, 1964–2004," *Journal of Politics* 69, no. 2 (2007): 430–41; John Thomas Delaney, Marick F. Masters, and Susan Schwochau, "Unionism and Voter Turnout," *Journal of Labor Research* 9, no. 3 (September 1, 1988): 221–36. However, my results are substantively similar if I exclude this measure of union membership from the analysis.

7. Similarly, I include year dummies to account for the fact that citizens' participation rates are likely to be higher or lower in certain years (e.g., presidential

versus off-year elections). I also include a measure of the mean level of political participation reported by non-teachers in each teacher-respondent's state-year. This variable is meant to control for any idiosyncratic events that might have led to higher- or lower-than-average political participation for individuals residing in a particular state during a particular election year or a changing political culture across states. In all cases, standard errors are clustered by state-year to account for the fact that respondents nested within the same state-year are not statistically independent from one another. See Kevin Arceneaux and David W. Nickerson, "Modeling Certainty with Clustered Data: A Comparison of Methods," *Political Analysis* 17, no. 2 (2009): 177–90.

8. See table A3.1 in the appendix for the full results from these estimations.

9. Note: the sample sizes are smaller in these models because the adoption of these mobilization and recruitment questions occurred later and in different periods of the ANES.

10. See, e.g., Verba, Schlozman, and Brady, *Voice and Equality*; Steven J. Rosenstone and John Mark Hansen, *Mobilization, Participation, and Democracy in America* (New York: Macmillan, 1993).

11. This result is consistent with the expectations of a traditional mediation analysis. See Reuben M. Baron and David A. Kenny, "The Moderator–Mediator Variable Distinction in Social Psychological Research: Conceptual, Strategic, and Statistical Considerations," *Journal of Personality and Social Psychology* 51, no. 6 (1986): 1173.

12. Specifically, I use Hicks and Tingley's medeff mediation package in Stata to calculate how much of a teacher's propensity to participate more in politics in CB districts is explained by higher rates of union recruitment in CB districts. This analysis confirms that the effects of CB on teacher participation is strongly mediated through additional union recruitment requests in CB districts. Specifically, 76 percent of the CB effect on participation is channeled through the higher rates of union recruitment that CB enables, not the existence of CB on its own. See Raymond Hicks and Dustin Tingley, "Causal Mediation Analysis," *Stata Journal* 11, no. 4 (2011): 605–19.

13. Coding was relatively straightforward since the vast majority of CBAs included a specific section outlining "Association rights" that the district guaranteed the local teachers union. However, in all cases a full examination of each contract was performed.

14. The PCA validates my theoretical argument that these nine separate measures represent a single latent dimension of union subsidization within a CBA. Specifically, the individual items load nicely onto one dimension with a single eigenvalue over 1, with the first factor explaining just under half of the variance for the nine separate items. These nine items also have a Cronbach's alpha scale reliability coefficient of .84, meaning that the individual subsidies are closely related and demonstrate a high degree of internal consistency. The items with the highest loadings are (in order): access to school buildings, access to a union bulletin board, access to the district mail system/mailboxes, and union release time.

15. See Dan Goldhaber, Lesley Lavery, Roddy Theobald, Dylan D'Entremont, and Yangru Fang, "Teacher Collective Bargaining: Assessing the Internal Validity of Partial Independence Item Response Measures of Contract Restrictiveness," *SAGE Open* 3, no. 2 (April 1, 2013): 1–16, https://doi.org/10.1177/2158244013489694.

16. For more details on the PIIR method for coding CBAs, see Katharine O. Strunk and Sean F. Reardon, "Measuring the Strength of Teachers' Unions: An Empirical Application of the Partial Independence Item Response Approach," *Journal of Educational and Behavioral Statistics* 35, no. 6 (2010): 629–70.

17. E. E. Schattschneider, *The Semisovereign People: A Realist's View of Democracy in America* (New York: Holt, Rinehart and Winston, 1960).

18. Rosenstone and Hansen, *Mobilization, Participation, and Democracy in America*, 36.

19. See Andrea L. Campbell, *How Policies Make Citizens: Senior Political Activism and the American Welfare State* (Princeton, NJ: Princeton University Press, 2003).

20. See, e.g., Kristin A. Goss, Carolyn Barnes, and Deondra Rose, "Bringing Organizations Back In: Multilevel Feedback Effects on Individual Civic Inclusion," *Policy Studies Journal* 47, no. 2 (May 2019): 451–70; Delphia Shanks and Mallory E. SoRelle, "The Paradox of Policy Advocacy: Philanthropic Foundations, Public Interest Groups, and Second-Order Policy Feedback Effects," *Interest Groups & Advocacy* 10 (May 2021), 137–57.

21. See National Education Association, *Eight Essentials to a Strong Union Contract without Fair-Share Fees*, Center for Advocacy internal report, 2018; National Education Association, *Advancing Advocacy in a Changing Environment*, NEA internal report, 2017, https://ctago.org/wp-content/uploads/2017/07/Advancing-Advocacy-in-a-Changing-Environment.pdf.

22. See Mark Walsh, "Justices Decline Challenge to Exclusive Public-Employee Union Representation," *Education Week*, April 29, 2019.

23. Uradnik's attorneys have indicated they plan to go back to the lower courts, establish a factual record, and hope the US Supreme Court will hear the case on the merits. However, as of May 2021, the high court had still *not* granted certiorari to any plaintiff seeking to challenge the constitutionality of exclusive representation in public-sector collective bargaining.

24. Additional statistics accompanying the instrumental variables estimates suggest that the instrument performs well. For example, the F statistic in the IV estimation exceeds 1000.

Chapter 4

1. Oral arguments in Friedrichs v. California Teachers Association, 578 U.S. ___ (2016).

2. See, e.g., Lorraine Mary McDonnell, *The Control of Political Change Within An Interest Group: The Case of the National Education Association* (PhD diss.,

Stanford University, 1975), ProQuest document ID 302782553; Allan M. West, *The National Education Association: The Power Base for Education* (New York: Free Press, 1980); Charlene Haar, Myron Lieberman, and Leo Troy, *The NEA and AFT: Teacher Unions in Power and Politics* (Rockport, MA: Pro Active Publications, 1994); Theda Skocpol, *Diminished Democracy: From Membership to Management in American Civic Life* (Norman: University of Oklahoma Press, 2003); Terry M. Moe, *Special Interest: Teachers Unions and America's Public Schools* (Washington, DC: Brookings Institution, 2011).

3. See Robert W. Merry, "Teacher Group's Clout on Carter's Behalf Is New Brand of Special Interest Politics," *Wall Street Journal*, August 13, 1980. Florida governor Bob Graham made similar remarks in an address to teacher delegates at the NEA's 1980 Representative Assembly. Graham noted: "No presidential candidate who wants to win in November ignores the National Education Association anymore." National Education Association, *Proceedings of the 59th Representative Assembly Held at Los Angeles, California, July 3–July 6, 1980*, vol. 118 (Washington, DC: NEA, 1980): 32.

4. See Stephen Chapman, *New Republic* 183, no. 15 (October 11, 1980): 9–11.

5. See Myron Lieberman, *The Teacher Unions: How They Sabotage Educational Reform and Why* (San Francisco. CA: Encounter Books, 2000): 288–91.

6. See Julie Johnson, "Michigan Teacher to Head Education Union," *New York Times*, July 4, 1989, sec. 1.

7. See Sarah F. Anzia, "The Backlash Against School Choice and Accountability Policies: The Organizations and Their Politics," *Urban Affairs Review* 56, no. 3 (2020): 987.

8. See, e.g., John E. Chubb and Terry M. Moe, *Politics, Markets, and America's Schools* (Washington, DC: Brookings Institution Press, 1990); Moe, *Special Interest*.

9. See, e.g., Robert D. Putnam, *Bowling Alone: The Collapse and Revival of American Community* (New York: Simon and Schuster, 2001); Skocpol, *Diminished Democracy*. Skocpol characterized the NEA's ascendance as a "countertrend" to professionally managed groups supplanting large membership associations as the dominant interests in American politics.

10. See Robert Chanin, "Remarks to the RA," (Speech, 88th Annual Representative Assembly Meeting of the National Education Association, San Diego, CA, July 6, 2009).

11. See, e.g., Mancur Olson, *The Logic of Collective Action* (Cambridge, MA: Harvard University Press, 1965).

12. See James Q. Wilson, *Political Organizations* (Princeton, NJ: Princeton University Press, 1995): 225.

13. According to former NEA executive director Don Cameron, "NEA's transition from professional association to union came rapidly in the mid 1960s—almost overnight . . . During a single decade from 1965 to 1975, the blink of an eye by NEA standards, teacher members converted NEA from a tea-and-crumpets

organization to one that endorsed collective bargaining and embraced unionism for its members." See Don Cameron, *The Inside Story of the Teacher Revolution in America* (Lanham, MD: Rowman & Littlefield, 2005): 41, 77.

14. See, e.g., Marshall O. Donley, "The American Schoolteacher: From Obedient Servant to Militant Professional," *Phi Delta Kappan* 58, no. 1 (1976): 112–17.

15. See, e.g., Wayne J. Urban, *Gender, Race, and the National Education Association: Professionalism and Its Limitations* (New York: Routledge, 2000).

16. See Moe, *Special Interest*, 63.

17. Other scholars have emphasized the importance of public-sector labor laws in promoting teacher unionization. See, e.g., Gregory M. Saltzman, "Bargaining Laws as a Cause and Consequence of the Growth of Teacher Unionism," *ILR Review* 38, no. 3 (1985): 335–51; Gregory M. Saltzman, "Public Sector Bargaining Laws Really Matter: Evidence from Ohio and Illinois," in *When Public Sector Workers Unionize*, ed. Richard B. Freeman and Casey Ichniowski (Chicago: National Bureau of Economic Research and University of Chicago Press, 1988): 41–80. But, with the exception of Moe, this work tends to focus narrowly on how labor laws increased the share of unionized teachers. In contrast, my emphasis is on showing how and why specific provisions in these new labor laws made it easier for teachers unions to create and maintain strong and financially secure interest-group advocacy organizations.

18. This obligation is known as a labor union's "duty of fair representation," and harkens back to the landmark 1944 US Supreme Court case of *Steele v. Louisville & N.R.R.* In *Steele*, the court was confronted with a union—the Brotherhood of Locomotive Firemen and Enginemen—that had won the exclusive right to represent employees working on railroad lines in the southeast. The union tried to exclude African American workers from its collective bargaining agreement with the railroad company. However, the court intervened. In establishing the duty of fair representation, the justices unanimously held that unions have a duty to represent all workers in a bargaining unit. See Steele v. Louisville & Nashville Railway Co., 323 U.S. 192 (1944).

19. On the role of agency fees in promoting union security in the public sector, see Jay W. Waks, "Impact of the Agency Shop on Labor Relations in the Public Sector," *Cornell Law Review* 55, no. 4 (April 1970): 547–93; Joyce M. Najita, "The Mandatory Agency Shop in Hawaii's Public Sector," *Industrial and Labor Relations Review* 27, no. 3 (April 1, 1974): 432–45.

20. Data on agency-fee and dues-checkoff policies reported by the NEA. See National Education Association, *NEA Collective Bargaining Laws Manual State Summaries*, NEA internal report, 2017.

21. Data on maintenance of membership in Pennsylvania taken from the Commonwealth Foundation. See Commonwealth Foundation, "School District Labor Contracts: Surprising Provisions," policy memo, August 17, 2016, www.commonwealth foundation.org/issues/detail/school-district-labor-contracts-surprising-provisions.

22. For a rare exception, see Myron Lieberman, *Understanding the Teacher Union Contract: A Citizen's Handbook* (New Brunswick, NJ: Transaction Publishers, 2000).

23. The precedent that Justice Sotomayor was referring to in this exchange was the Supreme Court's 1983 *Perry* decision. That case is discussed in detail in chapter 2. See Perry Education Association v. Perry Local Educators' Association, 460 U.S. 37 (1983); oral argument transcript available at https://www.supremecourt.gov/oral_ar guments/argument_transcripts/2015/14-915_e2p3.pdf, 12–13, emphasis added.

24. See, e.g., Jack L. Walker, *Mobilizing Interest Groups in America: Patrons, Professions, and Social Movements* (Ann Arbor: University of Michigan Press, 1991); Anthony J. Nownes and Allan J. Cigler, "Public Interest Groups and the Road to Survival," *Polity* 27, no. 3 (1995): 379–404; Theodore Lowi, *The End of Liberalism: The Second Republic of the United States* (New York: W. W. Norton, 1979); Michael Lipsky and Steven Rathgeb Smith, *Nonprofits for Hire: The Welfare State in the Age of Contracting* (Cambridge, MA: Harvard University Press, 1993); Andrew S. McFarland, "Interest Groups and Theories of Power in America," *British Journal of Political Science* 17, no. 2 (1987): 129–47; Anthony J. Nownes, "Local and State Interest Group Organizations," in *The Oxford Handbook of State and Local Government*, ed. Donald P. Haider-Markel (Oxford: Oxford University Press, 2014).

25. See John Mark Hansen, "The Political Economy of Group Membership," *American Political Science Review* 79, no. 1 (1985): 94.

26. Aaron Epstein, "How Pentagon Boosted NRA," *Philadelphia Inquirer*, May 14, 1979.

27. Aaron Epstein, "How Pentagon Boosted NRA."

28. For labor unions, the one exception is hard-money campaign contributions to candidates running for federal political office. Federal campaign-finance law does not allow unions to use their general treasury funds (e.g., dues dollars) to make these hard-money donations.

Chapter 5

1. National Education Association, *Proceedings of the 74th Representative Assembly Held at Minneapolis, Minnesota, July 3–July 6, 1995*, vol. 133 (Washington, DC: NEA, 1995): 10, emphasis added.

2. For detailed histories of the NEA's organizational transformation, see Allan M. West, *The National Education Association: The Power Base for Education* (New York: Free Press, 1980); Lorraine Mary McDonnell, *The Control of Political Change Within An Interest Group: The Case of the National Education Association* (PhD diss., Stanford University, 1975), ProQuest document ID 302782553; Lorraine M. McDonnell, "The Internal Politics of the NEA," *Phi Delta Kappan* 58, no. 2

(1976): 185–201; Wayne J. Urban, *Gender, Race, and the National Education Association: Professionalism and Its Limitations* (New York: Routledge, 2000).

3. For example, at its 1962 annual meeting in Denver, Colorado, the NEA's leadership acquiesced to the growing demands of teachers by supporting "professional negotiations" (its version of collective bargaining). It also passed a resolution endorsing "sanctions" (boycotts) of school systems that refused to improve teachers' working conditions (the NEA's answer to the AFT's approval of strikes). Former union organizer Myron Lieberman explains how this rivalry with the AFT changed the NEA's posture toward unionism. "Without question, the organizational rivalry between the NEA and AFT has been an important stimulus to teacher militancy. At all levels, the two organizations and their state and local affiliates have come under much more pressure to achieve [teacher] benefits than would be the case if there were only one organization . . . Any failure to press vigorously for teacher objectives becomes a threat to organizational survival." See Myron Lieberman, "Implications of the Coming NEA-AFT Merger," *Phi Delta Kappan* 50, no. 3 (November 1968): 139.

4. Until 1969, the NEA had been classified as a 501(c)(3) charitable organization. The Internal Revenue Service (IRS) moved it to a 501(c)(6) "business league" in 1969 before formally designating it as a labor union in 1978. For more details, see Charles W. Baird, "The NEA and Its Federal Charter," *Government Union Review* 17, no. 3 (1996): 1–45; West, *The National Education Association: The Power Base for Education.*

5. See, e.g., Urban, *Gender, Race, and the National Education Association*; McDonnell, *The Control of Political Change Within An Interest Group.*

6. See Mancur Olson, *The Logic of Collective Action* (Cambridge, MA: Harvard University Press, 1965).

7. Robert D. Putnam, *Bowling Alone: The Collapse and Revival of American Community* (New York: Simon and Schuster, 2001). ABA and AMA membership numbers are updated from Putnam's data. NEA membership figures are taken from the organization's *NEA Handbook* series.

8. Throughout the chapter, I define states as having a strong teacher labor law if they *both* (1) mandate that school districts engage in collective bargaining with the exclusive-representative teachers union and (2) do not have a right-to-work law (RTW). RTW laws weaken mandatory CB laws because they do not allow for strong union-security provisions (e.g., agency fees).

9. Consequently, the NEA struggled to grow. After launching a major initiative to enroll one million members by 1957, it fell five hundred thousand members short of that goal, even losing members in one year after it had implemented a dues increase.

10. See National Education Association of the United States, *NEA Handbook for Local, State, and National Associations (1958)* (Washington, DC: National Education Association, 1958): 297.

11. Technically, the mandate was applied to the state associations themselves. When the NEA mandated that all state affiliates "unify" by 1972 (i.e., require their own state association members to join the NEA), a state affiliate's failure to do so would result in the NEA formally disaffiliating it. This happened to the Missouri State Teachers Association (MSTA), the only state association that refused the NEA's requirement to unify. Immediately after disaffiliating the MSTA, the NEA started its own state organization in Missouri, the Missouri-NEA (MNEA).

12. See Judith Axler Turner, "Nation's Teachers Gear Up For Major Role in 1972 Campaigns," *National Journal*, December 18, 1971: 2491, emphasis added.

13. See, e.g., National Education Association, "A Vast Cadre of Human Resources," *NEA Today*, January 2001.

14. For a good overview of the role that UniServ plays in supporting state and local NEA affiliates today, see Mike Antonucci, "Never Heard of UniServ? It Holds the National Education Association Together—and Could Tear It Apart," *The74*, March 13, 2018, https://www.the74million.org/article/antonucci-never-heard-of-uniserv -it-holds-the-national-education-association-together-and-could-tear-it-apart/.

15. See Urban, *Gender, Race, and the National Education Association*; West, *The National Education Association: The Power Base for Education*.

16. Turner, "Nation's Teachers Gear Up For Major Role in 1972 Campaigns," 2494.

17. See, e.g., Carl F. Ameringer, *The Health Care Revolution: From Medical Monopoly to Market Competition* (Berkeley: University of California Press, 2008).

18. See Frank D. Campion, *The AMA and U.S. Health Policy since 1940* (Chicago: Chicago Review Press, 1984).

19. National Education Association, *Facts about Unification*, internal report (Washington, DC: NEA, 1969).

20. Specifically, I use a Cox proportional-hazards model to estimate the likelihood that a state affiliate voted for unification in a given year between 1944 and 1976 (the year all fifty affiliates finally had to unify or else face expulsion). My results are fully robust to different hazard-model specifications, including the use of a proportional-hazards model with a piecewise exponential baseline where the hazard changes from year to year.

21. In the early days of public-sector bargaining, few states explicitly addressed agency fees in statute. That does not mean that union-security provisions were not used by teachers unions. To the contrary, statutory silence often meant that, in practice, unless a state had an RTW law prohibiting them, they could negotiate security provisions to incentivize teachers to join and remain members. See, e.g., US Advisory Commission on Intergovernmental Relations, *Labor-Management Policies for State and Local Government*, report A–35, Washington, DC, September 1969, https://library.unt.edu/gpo/acir/Reports/policy/a-35.pdf.

22. See Terry M. Moe, *Special Interest: Teachers Unions and America's Public Schools* (Washington, DC: Brookings Institution Press, 2011).

23. Information on the number of K–12 public school teachers in each state/year were hand-entered from two sources: (1) the NEA Research Division's estimates of school statistics, as found in their annual *Rankings and Estimates* reports, available for download at https://www.nea.org/research-publications and (2) the US Census Bureau's *Statistical Abstracts of the United States*, available for download at https://www.census.gov/library/publications/time-series/statistical_abstracts.html.

24. Data on citizens' ideological liberalism across the American states comes from Devin Caughey and Christopher Warshaw, "The Dynamics of State Policy Liberalism, 1936–2014," *American Journal of Political Science* 60, no. 4 (2016): 899–913.

25. Similarly, year fixed effects are included to account for the fact that certain years may have been better or worse for union organizing than others.

26. The results of the full regression models are displayed in table A5.2 in the chapter's appendix.

27. In 2019, the ABA adopted "Resolution 2019," lowering membership dues, especially for early-career attorneys, in an effort to improve membership recruitment and slow decline. See Lee Rawles, "New Membership Model Will Mean Lower Dues," *ABA Journal*, August 6, 2018.

28. See, e.g., Susan Crawford and Peggy Levitt, "Social Change and Civic Engagement: The Case of the PTA," in *Civic Engagement in American Democracy*, ed. Theda Skocpol and Morris P. Fiorina (Brookings Institution Press, 1999): 249–96; Kelly D. Patterson and Matthew Singer, "The National Rifle Association in the Face of the Clinton Challenge," in *Interest Group Politics*, 6th ed., ed. Allan J. Cigler and Burdett A. Loomis (Washington, DC: CQ Press, 2002): 55–77; Christine L. Day, *AARP: America's Largest Interest Group and Its Impact* (Santa Barbara, CA: ABC-CLIO, 2017).

29. One of the ballot initiatives proposed to extend—from two to five years—the time it took for a K–12 public school teacher to earn tenure. For an overview of the CTA's role in this California special election, see Joetta L. Sack, "California Teachers Rally Against Ballot Measures," *Education Week*, October 25, 2005.

30. See, e.g., Mike Antonucci, "California Teachers Association's Proposed Dues Increase Would Raise More Than $54 Million to Fight Governor Schwarzenegger," *Education Intelligence Agency* (blog), March 17, 2005, http://www.eia online.com/archives/20050317.htm.

31. This estimate is based on data collected by Myron Lieberman in the mid-1990s. He found that the NEA claimed 63 percent of its expenditures were "chargeable" (i.e., spent on collective bargaining and other representational activities). See Myron Lieberman, *Agency Fees: How Fair Are "Fair Share" Fees? EPI Series on Teacher Unions* (Washington, DC: Education Policy Institute, 1999).

32. See NEA Research Division, NEA Member Poll (Washington, DC: National Education Association, 1967).

33. Full-time employee members would pay 0.28 percent of the average teacher salary in the United States (in addition to whatever amount their state and local NEA affiliates charged in dues).

34. See, e.g., Jay W. Waks, "Impact of the Agency Shop on Labor Relations in the Public Sector," *Cornell Law Review* 55, no. 4 (1970); Patricia N. Blair, "Union Security Agreements in Public Employment," *Cornell Law Review* 60, no. 2 (1975): 183–230.

35. See National Education Association, *Addresses and Proceedings of the 116th Annual Meeting Held at Dallas, Texas, July 3–July 6, 1978*, vol. 116 (Washington, DC: NEA, 1978): 131–35.

36. Since state affiliates—just like the NEA after 1979—often use a ratio rate, I converted the dollar amount each affiliate charged into a percentage of the average teacher salary in an affiliate's state. This conversion is important because it removes differences in dues rates that are merely a reflection of higher teacher salaries in a state. Since higher salaries could also be a result of stronger labor laws, measuring each state affiliate's dues rate as a percentage of salary allows me to better isolate the impact of agency fees on affiliates' dues rates.

37. Specifically, I once again include state fixed effects in the analysis to isolate the impact of permitting agency fees on union dues rates while accounting for unobservable differences across states that are constant over time that may also influence the rate of dues charged by unions in a given state (e.g., history, culture, union strength).

38. For a detailed account of the creation and early maintenance of NEA-PAC, see Constance Shotts, *The Origin and Development of the National Education Association Political Action Committee, 1969–1976* (PhD diss., Indiana University, 1977), ProQuest document ID 302804645.

39. See National Education Association, *Addresses and Proceedings of the 111th Annual Meeting Held at Portland, Oregon, June 30-July 6, 1973*, vol. 111 (Washington, DC: NEA, 1973).

40. See, e.g., Richard H. Thaler and Cass R. Sunstein, *Nudge: Improving Decisions about Health, Wealth, and Happiness* (New Haven, CT: Yale University Press, 2008). In the next chapter, I bring some empirical evidence to bear on this topic, examining how the reverse checkoff helped the NEA's state affiliates raise more PAC revenue.

41. Federal Election Commission, *Labor-Related Political Committees Receipts and Expenditures*, FEC Disclosure Series report, Washington, DC, January 1978.

42. Federal Election Commission v. National Education Association et al., 457 F. Supp. 1102 (D.D.C. 1978).

43. On the controversy surrounding the NEA's property-tax exemption in the 1970s and 1980s, see, e.g., Lawrence Feinberg, "Teachers' Unions Take Their Rivalry to the Taxman," *Washington Post*, August 12, 1979; Jack Eisen, "D.C. Urged to Study Tax Exemption Cuts," *Washington Post*, March 9, 1979; Jack Eisen, "Hill Presses City To Revoke NEA's Tax Exemption," *Washington Post*, August 30, 1980.

44. See Baird, "The NEA and Its Federal Charter."

45. See Jeff Archer, "NEA Agrees To Abandon Property-Tax Break," *Education Week*, October 1, 1997.

46. See National Education Association, *Addresses and Proceedings of the 107th Annual Meeting Held at Philadelphia, Pennsylvania, June 30–July 5, 1969*, vol. 107 (Washington, DC: NEA, 1969): 28.

47. See Susan Crawford and Peggy Levitt, "Social Change and Civic Engagement: The Case of the PTA."

48. National Education Association, *Addresses and Proceedings of the 114th Annual Meeting Held at Miami Beach, Florida, June 27-July 1, 1976*, vol. 114 (Washington, DC: NEA, 1976).

49. For a discussion of the potential advantages and disadvantages that decentralized labor law poses to America's labor unions, see Alexis N. Walker, *Divided Unions: The Wagner Act, Federalism, and Organized Labor* (Philadelphia: University of Pennsylvania Press, 2019); Daniel DiSalvo, "Review of Divided Unions: The Wagner Act, Federalism, and Organized Labor," *Publius: The Journal of Federalism* 50, no. 4 (n.d.): e11.

50. In 1992, New Mexico became the 34th and final state to enact a mandatory teacher CB law.

51. The NEA had long tried get Congress to enact a federal public-employee bargaining law, but those efforts fizzled after the Supreme Court's decision in *National League of Cities v. Usery*, 426 U.S. 833 (1976). On the NEA's effort to secure a federal bargaining law, see the statement of Dr. Samuel Lambert, executive director, National Education Association, Washington, DC, in US Advisory Commission on Intergovernmental Relations, *Labor-Management Policies for State and Local Government*.

52. See Bess Keller, "NEA Members, Budget Up; Workers Down," *Education Week*, December 12, 2006.

53. For example, Skocpol and colleagues have argued that federated structures allow the national branch of a federated interest-group organization to support its local affiliates: when "a local club or lodge ran into trouble . . . supralocal leaders could make a real difference, especially in the larger, well-established federations. They might ask neighboring chapters to support faltering units . . . During economic downturns, national or state officials might forgive shares of local dues; when meeting houses burned down, they orchestrated appeals for aid." See Theda Skocpol, Marshall Ganz, and Ziad Munson, "A Nation of Organizers: The Institutional Origins of Civic Voluntarism in the United States," *American Political Science Review* 94, no. 3 (2000): 527–46, at 537.

54. See Leslie K. Finger and Michael T. Hartney, "Financial Solidarity: The Future of Unions in the Post-Janus Era," *Perspectives on Politics* 19, no. 1 (2021): 19–35.

55. Lehnert v. Ferris Faculty Association, 500 U.S. 507 (1991).

56. See, e.g., Locke v. Karass, 555 U.S. 207 (2009).

57. Don Cameron, *The Inside Story of the Teacher Revolution in America* (Lanham, MD: Rowman & Littlefield, 2005).

58. George Archibald, "Union Will Target Swing States in '04," *Washington Times*, June 30, 2003.

Chapter 6

1. Quotation is from James Howard Mason Jr.'s 1973 unpublished doctoral dissertation on the AEA. See James Howard Mason Jr., *The Alabama Education Association and Its Influence on Legislative Decisions Regarding Education in the State of Alabama, 1965–1972* (PhD diss., Auburn University, 1973), ProQuest document ID 302664871.

2. Quotation is reported in Marshall O. Donley Jr, *The Future of Teacher Power in America*. (Bloomington, IN: Phi Delta Kappa Educational Foundation, 1977).

3. See, e.g., Richard L. Hall and Alan V. Deardorff, "Lobbying as Legislative Subsidy," *American Political Science Review* 100, no. 1 (2006): 69–84; Stephen Ansolabehere, John M. de Figueiredo, and James M. Snyder, "Why Is There so Little Money in U.S. Politics?," *Journal of Economic Perspectives* 17, no. 1 (2003): 105–30.

4. See, e.g., J. Baxter Oliphant and John Gramlich, "Supporters of Stricter Gun Laws Are Less Likely to Contact Elected Officials," Pew Research Center, October 12, 2017, https://www.pewresearch.org/fact-tank/2017/10/12/supporters-of-stricter-gun-laws-are-less-likely-to-contact-elected-officials/.

5. Bloomberg spent over $2.5 million in 2019 on Virginia state legislative races compared to just $800,000 from the NRA. Bloomberg also paid $10 million to run a national ad during the 2020 Super Bowl promoting his gun control agenda. See Gregory S. Schneider, "Money Flowing to Virginia Legislative Races from Both Sides of Gun Control Issue," *Washington Post*, September 5, 2019.

6. See, e.g., Kristin A. Goss, *Disarmed: The Missing Movement for Gun Control in America* (Princeton, NJ: Princeton University Press, 2010).

7. Terry M. Moe and Susanne Wiborg, "Introduction," in *The Comparative Politics of Education*, ed. Terry M. Moe and Susanne Wiborg (Cambridge: Cambridge University Press, 2017): 1–23.

8. See, e.g., David B. Tyack, *The One Best System: A History of American Urban Education*, vol. 95 (Cambridge, MA: Harvard University Press, 1974); Michael W. Kirst, "Turning Points: A History of American School Governance," in *Who's in Charge Here?: The Tangled Web of School Governance and Policy*, ed. Noel Epstein (Washington, DC: Brookings Institution Press, 2004): 14–41.

9. See, e.g., Frederick M. Wirt and Michael W. Kirst, *The Political Dynamics of American Education* (Berkeley, CA: McCutchan, 1997); Noel Epstein, ed., *Who's in Charge Here?: The Tangled Web of School Governance and Policy*.

10. See, e.g., Sarah F. Anzia, "Election Timing and the Electoral Influence of Interest Groups," *Journal of Politics* 73, no. 2 (2011): 412–27; Sarah F. Anzia, *Timing and Turnout: How Off-Cycle Elections Favor Organized Groups* (Chicago: University of Chicago Press, 2013).

11. See, e.g., Claudia Goldin, "The Human Capital Century and American Leadership: Virtues of the Past" (National Bureau of Economic Research Working Paper no. 8239, April 2001), https://www.nber.org/papers/w8239.

12. For more details on the rise of the excellence movement and the broader causes and consequences of the performance-based era in American education, see Thomas Toch, *In the Name of Excellence: The Struggle to Reform the Nation's Schools, Why It's Failing, and What Should Be Done* (New York: Oxford University Press, 1991); Jal Mehta, *The Allure of Order: High Hopes, Dashed Expectations, and the Troubled Quest to Remake American Schooling* (Oxford: Oxford University Press, 2013).

13. See, e.g., Paul Manna, *School's In: Federalism and the National Education Agenda* (Washington, DC: Georgetown University Press, 2006); Patrick J. McGuinn, *No Child Left Behind and the Transformation of Federal Education Policy, 1965–2005* (Lawrence: University Press of Kansas, 2006).

14. See, e.g., Michael T. Hartney and Christina Wolbrecht, "Ideas About Interests: Explaining the Changing Partisan Politics of Education," *Perspectives on Politics* 12, no. 3 (2014): 1–28.

15. See Manna, *School's In: Federalism and the National Education Agenda*.

16. See Toch, *In the Name of Excellence*, 1991.

17. See, e.g., Terry M. Moe, "Teacher Unions and School Board Elections," in *Besieged: School Boards and the Future of Education Politics*, ed. William G. Howell (Washington, DC: Brookings Institution Press, 2005): 254–87; Terry M. Moe, "Political Control and the Power of the Agent," *Journal of Law, Economics, and Organization* 22, no. 1 (2006): 1–29; Anzia, "Election Timing and the Electoral Influence of Interest Groups."

18. Anzia, "Looking for Influence in All the Wrong Places: How Studying Subnational Policy Can Revive Research on Interest Groups," *Journal of Politics* 81, no. 1 (2019): 343–51.

19. See Malcolm E. Jewell and Penny M. Miller, *The Kentucky Legislature: Two Decades of Change* (Lexington: University Press of Kentucky, 2015).

20. See Paul Braun, Ryland Barton, Joe Hernandez, Ben Paviour, Mallory Noe-Payne, and Acacia Squires, "Why These 5 States Hold Odd-Year Elections, Bucking The Trend," *NPR*, November 4, 2019, https://www.npr.org/2019/11/04/767959274/why-these-5-states-hold-odd-year-elections-bucking-the-trend.

21. See Terry M. Moe, "Political Control and the Power of the Agent," 1–29.

22. See, e.g., Citizens United v. Federal Election Commission, 558 U.S. 310 (2010).

23. See, e.g., Anne E. Baker, "Are Federal PACs Obsolete?," *Interest Groups & Advocacy* 7, no. 2 (2018): 105–25.

24. "WEA WEA-PAC Site," Camas Educational Association (website), accessed September 14, 2021, https://www.weteachcamas.org/WEA-PAC/.

25. See Matthew Futterman and James M. O'Neill, "Despite Setbacks, Teachers Union Remains a Political Force," *Philadelphia Inquirer*, November 14, 1996.

26. Eugenia F. Toma, Indrias Berhane, and Corinna Curl, "Political Action Committees at the State Level: Contributions to Education," *Public Choice* 126, no. 3–4 (2006): 465–84.

27. See Terry M. Moe, *Special Interest: Teachers Unions and America's Public Schools* (Washington, DC: Brookings Institution, 2011): 293–94.

28. These authors found that unions accounted for 99 percent of the contributions from 2000 to 2003 and 92 percent between 2014 and 2017. See Leslie K. Finger and Sarah Reckhow, "Policy Feedback and the Polarization of Interest Groups," *State Politics and Policy Quarterly* (November 2021), 1–26.

29. See Indiana State Teachers Association, *Advancing the Cause of Education: A History of the Indiana State Teachers Association, 1854–2004* (West Lafayette, IN: Purdue University Press, 2004).

30. This is a key insight in the 2009 bestseller *Nudge* by economists Richard Thaler and Cass Sunstein. These authors explain that individuals' decisions are often shaped by the "choice architecture" embedded in institutions—institutions which are never fully neutral in their design. See Richard H. Thaler and Cass R. Sunstein, *Nudge: Improving Decisions about Health, Wealth, and Happiness* (New Haven, CT: Yale University Press, 2008).

31. Federal Election Commission v. National Education Association et al., 457 F. Supp. 1102 (1978).

32. While a handful of conservative activists sought to ban this practice by pushing a reform they called "paycheck protection," only a few states adopted these measures and the movement mostly petered out by the end of the 1990s. See, e.g., Andy Furillo, "'Paycheck Protection' Measures Have Little Impact in 4 of 5 States," *Knoxville News-Sentinel*, June 25, 2005.

33. See Phillip Rawls, "State Employees Group Banks on Bucks for Clout," *Associated Press*, May 28, 1989.

34. See Indiana State Teachers Association, *Advancing the Cause of Education.*

35. For example, NEA members in states with a reverse checkoff gave $1.30 to NEA-PAC compared to $1.21 per member in opt-in states. This difference is not statistically significant.

36. See, e.g., Chris Baylor, "Teachers' Unions May Not Raise Pay—but They Do Bolster the Democratic Party," *Washington Post*, May 18, 2018.

37. See, e.g., Karen M. Kaufmann, John R. Petrocik, and Daron R. Shaw, *Unconventional Wisdom: Facts and Myths about American Voters* (New York: Oxford University Press, 2008); Michael S. Lewis-Beck, William G. Jacoby, Helmut Norpoth, and Herbert F. Weisberg, *The American Voter Revisited* (Ann Arbor: University of Michigan Press, 2008).

38. See, e.g., Hartney and Wolbrecht, "Ideas About Interests: Explaining the Changing Partisan Politics of Education."

39. Yannick Dufresne and Catherine Ouellet, "Public Issues or Issue Publics? The Distribution of Genuine Political Attitudes," *Behavioural Public Policy* 5, no. 3 (2018): 279–300, at 286.

40. Details on the Wisconsin Teacher Recall Survey can be found in the appendix for chapter 2.

41. To ensure that the version of the question teachers received was, in fact, randomly assigned, I carried out an analysis testing for balance in teachers' demographic characteristics in each group. The results of these tests confirmed that there was strong balance across experimental conditions and that the randomization process was successful.

42. See, e.g., Taylor E. Dark, *The Unions and the Democrats: An Enduring Alliance* (Ithaca, NY: Cornell University Press, 1999); Hartney and Wolbrecht, "Ideas About Interests: Explaining the Changing Partisan Politics of Education"; Matt Grossmann and David A. Hopkins, *Asymmetric Politics: Ideological Republicans and Group Interest Democrats* (New York: Oxford University Press, 2016).

43. On the concept of electoral capture, see Paul Frymer, *Uneasy Alliances: Race and Party Competition in America* (Princeton, NJ: Princeton University Press, 2010).

44. For example, in 2017, the New Jersey Education Association (NJEA) supported a pro-Trump Republican against then-Senate president Steve Sweeney. Sweeney, a Democrat, had angered the union by working with former governor Chris Christie to enact pension reforms that reduced teachers' benefits. Similarly, in Georgia, Democratic governor Roy Barnes lost his reelection bid in 2002 after the state's largest teachers association withheld its endorsement on account of his support for union-opposed school reforms. Only until Barnes went on what many in the media described as an "apology tour" and mended fences with Georgia's teachers was he able to regain his position in 2010. For more details, see Moe, *Special Interest*, 309.

45. Frederick M. Hess, "Our Achievement-Gap Mania," *National Affairs* (Fall 2011), https://www.nationalaffairs.com/publications/detail/our-achievement-gap -mania.

46. See, e.g., William G. Howell and Asya Magazinnik, "Presidential Prescriptions for State Policy: Obama's Race to the Top Initiative," *Journal of Policy Analysis and Management* 36, no. 3 (2017): 502–31; William G. Howell and Asya Magazinnik, "Financial Incentives in Vertical Diffusion: The Variable Effects of Obama's Race to the Top Initiative on State Policy Making," *State Politics & Policy Quarterly* 20, no. 2 (December 2019): 185–212.

47. See, e.g., Liana Loewus, "Are States Changing Course on Teacher Evaluation?," *Education Week*, November 28, 2017; Michelle Croft, Gretchen Guffy, and Dan Vitale, *The Shrinking Use of Growth: Teacher Evaluation Legislation since ESSA*, ACT Research and Policy issue brief, July 2018, https://www.act.org/con tent/dam/act/unsecured/documents/teacher-evaluation-legislation-since-essa .pdf; Matt Barnum, "No Thanks, Obama: 9 States No Longer Require Test Scores Be Used to Judge Teachers," *Chalkbeat*, October 8, 2019, https://www.chalkbeat .org/2019/10/8/21108964/no-thanks-obama-9-states-no-longer-require-test-scores -be-used-to-judge-teachers.

48. See, e.g., Kate Walsh, Nithya Joseph, Samuel Lubell, and Kelli Lakis, *Running in Place: How New Teacher Evaluations Fail to Live Up to Promises*, National Council on Teacher Quality report, January 2017, https://www.nctq.org/publications /Running-in-Place:-How-New-Teacher-Evaluations-Fail-to-Live-Up-to-Promises.

49. See, e.g., Kevin Mahnken, "Inside the Perfect Political Storm: From California to New Jersey, Why More Democrats Are Calling to End Charter School Growth," *The74*, June 17, 2019, https://www.the74million.org/article/inside-the-perfect-polit ical-storm-from-california-to-new-jersey-why-more-democrats-are-calling-to -end-charter-school-growth/; Frederick M. Hess, "Bernie, Bloomberg, Booker, and the New Politics of Education," *Education Next*, January 24, 2020, https://www .educationnext.org/bernie-bloomberg-booker-and-new-politics-education/.

50. See, e.g., Moe, *Special Interest*, 275–341.

51. James Q. Wilson, *Political Organizations* (New York: Basic Books, 1973).

52. See, e.g., Sarah Reckhow, *Follow the Money: How Foundation Dollars Change Public School Politics* (New York: Oxford University Press, 2013); Megan E. Tompkins-Stange, *Policy Patrons: Philanthropy, Education Reform, and the Politics of Influence* (Cambridge, MA: Harvard Education Press, 2020).

53. See, e.g., Steven G. Rivkin, Eric A. Hanushek, and John F. Kain, "Teachers, Schools, and Academic Achievement," *Econometrica* 73, no. 2 (2005): 417–58; Raj Chetty, John N. Friedman, and Jonah E. Rockoff, "The Long-Term Impacts of Teachers: Teacher Value-Added and Student Outcomes in Adulthood" (National Bureau of Economic Research Working Paper no. 17699, December 2011), http:// www.equality-of-opportunity.org/assets/documents/teachers_wp.pdf; Raj Chetty, John N. Friedman, and Jonah E. Rockoff, "Measuring the Impacts of Teachers II: Teacher Value-Added and Student Outcomes in Adulthood," *American Economic Review* 104, no. 9 (2014): 2633–79.

54. Gallup Organization, Gallup Poll # 1958-0607: Elections/Political Parties, Question 3, USGALLUP.58-607.Q003, Gallup Organization (Cornell University, Ithaca, NY: Roper Center for Public Opinion Research, 1958), accessed November 23, 2019.

55. See Gallup/PDK's annual Poll of the Public's Attitudes toward the Public Schools for 1970, 1984, 1991, 2010, https://pdkpoll.org/.

56. Thomas Toch, *In the Name of Excellence*.

57. For data on teachers' attitudes toward pay and pay-reform issues, see Paul E. Peterson, Michael Henderson, and Martin R. West, *Teachers versus the Public: What Americans Think about Schools and How to Fix Them* (Washington, DC: Brookings Institution Press, 2014). For evidence that teachers are more risk-averse than other workers, see Daniel H. Bowen, Stuart Buck, Cary Deck, Jonathan N. Mills, and James V. Shuls, "Risky Business: An Analysis of Teacher Risk Preferences," *Education Economics* 23, no. 4 (2015): 470–80.

58. National Education Association of the United States, *NEA Handbook* (Washington, DC: National Education Association, 2019).

59. See, e.g., Caroline Hoxby and Andrew Leigh, "Pulled Away or Pushed Out? Explaining the Decline of Teacher Aptitude in the United States," *American Economic Review* 94, no. 2 (2004): 236–40.

60. Toch, *In the Name of Excellence*, 175.

61. See, e.g., Thad Kousser and Justin H. Phillips, *The Power of American Governors: Winning on Budgets and Losing on Policy* (New York: Cambridge University Press, 2012); Daniel Coffey, "Measuring Gubernatorial Ideology: A Content Analysis of State of the State Speeches," *State Politics & Policy Quarterly* 5, no. 1 (2005): 88–103.

62. For details about the survey, see Amber M. Winkler, Janie Scull, and Dara Zeehandelaar, *How Strong Are US Teacher Unions? A State-by-State Comparison*, Thomas B. Fordham Institute report, October 2012, https://files.eric.ed.gov/full text/ED537563.pdf.

63. The list included the following entities: (1) business roundtable or chamber of commerce, (2) civil-rights groups, (3) education-reform advocacy organizations, (4) parent coalitions, (5) state association of school administrators, (6) state association of school principals, (7) state charter-school association, (8) state school board or board of regents, (9) state school-boards association, (10) teachers union/ teachers association, and (11) textbook companies. Respondents were also invited to select "other" and provide an open-ended response.

64. See, e.g., Peter Bachrach and Morton S. Baratz, "The Two Faces of Power," *American Political Science Review* 55 (1962): 947–52.

65. See Terry M. Moe, *The Politics of Institutional Reform: Katrina, Education, and the Second Face of Power* (New York: Cambridge University Press, 2019).

66. See Michael Hartney and Patrick Flavin, "From the Schoolhouse to the Statehouse: Teacher Union Political Activism and State Education Reform Policy," *State Politics and Policy Quarterly* 11, no. 3 (2011): 251–68.

67. See Leslie K. Finger, "Vested Interests and the Diffusion of Education Reform Across the States," *Policy Studies Journal* 46, no. 2 (2018): 378–401; Leslie K. Finger, "Interest Group Influence and the Two Faces of Power," *American Politics Research* 47, no. 4 (July 2018): 852–86.

Chapter 7

1. E. E. Schattschneider, *The Semisovereign People: A Realist's View of Democracy in America* (New York: Holt, Rinehart and Winston, 1960).

2. See, e.g., Kay Lehman Schlozman, Sidney Verba, and Henry E. Brady, *The Unheavenly Chorus: Unequal Political Voice and the Broken Promise of American Democracy* (Princeton, NJ: Princeton University Press, 2012); Martin Gilens, *Affluence & Influence: Economic Inequality and Political Power in America* (Princeton, NJ: Princeton University Press, 2012).

3. See Michael B. Berkman and Eric Plutzer, *Ten Thousand Democracies: Politics and Public Opinion in America's School Districts* (Washington, DC: Georgetown University Press, 2005).

4. Terry M. Moe, "Teacher Unions and School Board Elections," in *Besieged: School Boards and the Future of Education Politics*, ed. William G. Howell (Washington, DC: Brookings Institution Press, 2005): 254–87, at 258.

5. See, e.g., Kenneth J. Meier, Joseph Stewart, and Robert E. England, *Race, Class, and Education: The Politics of Second-Generation Discrimination* (Madison: University of Wisconsin Press, 1990); Kenneth J. Meier and Amanda Rutherford, *The Politics of African-American Education: Representation, Partisanship, and Educational Equity* (New York: Cambridge University Press, 2016).

6. See, e.g., Frederick M. Wirt and Michael W. Kirst, *The Political Dynamics of American Education* (Berkeley, CA: McCutchan, 1997).

7. See, e.g., William A. Fischel, *The Homevoter Hypothesis* (Cambridge, MA: Harvard University Press, 2009).

8. See, e.g., Diane Ravitch, *Reign of Error: The Hoax of the Privatization Movement and the Danger to America's Public Schools* (New York: Knopf, 2013); Leo Casey, "Is There A 'Corporate Education Reform' Movement?," *Shanker Blog*, Albert Shanker Institute, April 10, 2013, https://www.shankerinstitute.org/blog/there-corporate-education-reform-movement; Barbara Ferman and Nicholas Palazzolo, "The Fight for America's Schools: Grassroots Organizing in Education," in *The Fight for America's Schools: Grassroots Organizing in Education*, ed. Barbara Ferman (Cambridge, MA: Harvard Education Press, 2017): 17–32; Jack Schneider and Jennifer Berkshire, *A Wolf at the Schoolhouse Door: The Dismantling of Public Education and the Future of School* (New York: New Press, 2020).

9. See, for example, Sarah Reckhow, *Follow the Money: How Foundation Dollars Change Public School Politics* (Oxford: Oxford University Press, 2013); Sarah Reckhow, Jeffrey R. Henig, Rebecca Jacobsen, and Jamie Alter Litt, "'Outsiders with Deep Pockets': The Nationalization of Local School Board Elections," *Urban Affairs Review* 53, no. 5 (2017): 412–27; Jeffrey R. Henig, Rebecca Jacobsen, and Sarah Reckhow, *Outside Money in School Board Elections: The Nationalization of Education Politics.* (Cambridge, MA: Harvard Education Press, 2019).

10. See Terry M. Moe, "Teacher Unions and School Board Elections," 254–87; Terry M. Moe, "Political Control and the Power of the Agent," *Journal of Law, Economics, and Organization* 22, no. 1 (2006): 1–29.

11. Katharine O. Strunk and Jason A. Grissom, "Do Strong Unions Shape District Policies? Collective Bargaining, Teacher Contract Restrictiveness, and the Political Power of Teachers' Unions," *Educational Evaluation and Policy Analysis* 32, no. 3 (2010): 389–406.

12. For example, in a study of school-board elections in five large school districts, Sarah Reckhow and her colleagues found that networks of wealthy donors enabled reform candidates to match or exceed the funds raised by union-backed

ones. While these authors were careful to acknowledge that these competitive dynamics are probably not representative of "the broad universe of districts with elected boards," they nevertheless see more pluralist dynamics at work in school-board elections today. "Teacher unions," they explain, "have often been portrayed as the eight-hundred-pound gorilla in local school politics—and our evidence already shows that this image is overblown—but the *Janus* decision [in 2018] throws up new barriers for unions' political efforts." See Henig, Jacobsen, and Reckhow, *Outside Money in School Board Elections*, 15, 186.

13. For more details, see Michael T. Hartney, "Teachers Unions and School Board Elections: A Reassessment," *Interest Groups & Advocacy* (forthcoming).

14. For the one exception, see Ying Shi and John D. Singleton, "School Boards and Education Production: Evidence from Randomized Ballot Order," *American Economic Journal: Economic Policy* (forthcoming).

15. Barry C. Burden, *Personal Roots of Representation* (Princeton, NJ: Princeton University Press, 2007).

16. See, e.g., Christopher R. Berry, *Imperfect Union: Representation and Taxation in Multilevel Governments* (New York: Cambridge University Press, 2009).

17. Moe, "Political Control and the Power of the Agent."

18. Sarah F. Anzia and Terry M. Moe, "Interest Groups on the Inside: The Governance of Public Pension Funds," *Perspectives on Politics* 17, no. 4 (2019): 1059–78.

19. Eric R. Hansen, Nicholas Carnes, and Virginia Gray, "What Happens When Insurers Make Insurance Laws? State Legislative Agendas and the Occupational Makeup of Government," *State Politics & Policy Quarterly* 19, no. 2 (2019): 155–79.

20. Patricia A. Kirkland, "Business Owners and Executives as Politicians: The Effect on Public Policy," *Journal of Politics* (forthcoming), published ahead of print, August 25, 2021, https://doi.org/10.1086/715067.

21. Shi and Singleton, "School Boards and Education Production."

22. Admittedly, "educator" is an overly inclusive category that may include nonteaching personnel. Fortunately, in several of the surveys, respondents were invited to clarify whether they were, in fact, a current or former K–12 teacher. In the three surveys that incorporated this additional follow-up opportunity, approximately 80 percent of board members who had selected "education" as their occupation said they were a current or former K–12 teacher.

23. See, e.g., Paul E. Peterson, Michael Henderson, and Martin R. West,, *Teachers versus the Public: What Americans Think about Their Schools and How to Fix Them* (Washington, DC: Brookings Institution Press, 2014).

24. For more details about this survey, see Frederick M. Hess and Olivia Meeks, *Governance in the Accountability Era*, report published by the National School Boards Association, Thomas B. Fordham Institute, and Iowa School Boards Foundation, 2010.

25. See United States Bureau of the Census, United States Department of Labor, Bureau of Labor Statistics, and Corporation for National and Community

Service, *Current Population Survey, September 2017: Volunteering and Civic Life Supplement (ICPSR 37303)* (Ann Arbor, MI: Inter-University Consortium for Political and Social Research, 2019), https://doi.org/10.3886/ICPSR37303.v2.

26. As one might expect, the teacher advantage grows even larger when all respondents (including those without a four-year degree) are included in the non-teacher parent and homeowner samples.

27. The majority of the 5,719 unmatched teachers (10 percent of teachers statewide) are most likely not registered to vote. Since the statewide non-registration rate in Washington was 24 percent at that time, a 10 percent non-registration rate among teachers (whom we would expect to register and vote at higher rates than the general public) seems quite plausible. Still, any inaccuracies in the matching process should bias my results toward zero since registered teachers whom I am not able to locate in the voter file would tend to reduce my estimate of teacher turnout.

28. I am missing data for two school districts that are literally "one-room" schoolhouses: Palisades and Star school districts.

29. Unfortunately, my turnout measure is based on the percentage of registered teachers and non-teachers who vote (rather than a measure of turnout among all eligible voters). There is simply no way to identify where the unmatched/missing 5,719 teachers reside. In other words, I only know the number of teachers who teach in each school district and not the number of teachers who live in each district. Since teachers can live and work in different districts, I cannot create comparable turnout measures beyond turnout among registered voters. However, as a robustness check, I use a measure of teacher turnout where the denominator is the number of teachers who are employed by each school district, rather than the actual number who live in each district. All of my results hold when using this alternative (albeit flawed) turnout measure.

30. The acronym stands for "additional time, responsibilities, and incentives" pay. Despite this nomenclature, TRI pay is *not* incentive- or merit-based. Rather, it provided a way for school districts to use local levy funds to raise teachers' salaries across the board. As the *Seattle Times'* Neal Morton explained in a 2017 story on the history of teacher pay in Washington: "Over the years . . . TRI has grown into a way to boost pay for teachers—fueled by districts wanting to offer more attractive salaries, and by the state which gave districts that power, and avoided having to fund teacher raises out of its own coffers." See Neal Morton, "Extra Pay for Teachers Varies Widely—and Is Key to Answering McCleary Ruling," *Seattle Times*, February 8, 2017.

31. According to an internal study commissioned by the state legislature, variation in TRI pay is mostly explained by the size, wealth, geography, and local labor-market conditions in a school district. See Annie Pennucci, *How Much TRI Pay Can All Basic Education Teachers Earn? Preliminary Survey Data*, Technical Advisory Committee to the Joint Task Force on Basic Education Finance, Washington

State Institute for Public Policy, July 21, 2008, http://www.schoolcontracts.info/Re
sources/TRIforTAC.pdf.

32. See, e.g., Lori L. Taylor and William J. Fowler Jr., *A Comparable Wage Approach to Geographic Cost Adjustment*, National Center for Education Statistics Research and Development report NCES-2006–321, May 2006, https://files.eric.ed.gov/fulltext/ED491640.pdf.

33. Washington defines rural school districts as those with fewer than one thousand students. Because there are often fewer than ten teachers in these districts, a single error in the matching process can lead to significant discrepancies (inaccuracies) in estimating teacher turnout. In other words, my turnout measure for teachers is more reliable in medium- and larger-sized districts.

34. It is also worth noting that when I include measures of teacher and nonteacher turnout separately (rather than as a single turnout advantage measure) I find similar results. Namely, the variable on teacher turnout is positive and statistically significant and the coefficient on non-teacher turnout is negative and significant.

35. The experiment was first conducted on a sample of Indiana school-board members carried out in 2013 (N=410). In 2015, I ran the same experiment on a national sample of board members (N=460). The response rates were 21 percent and 26 percent respectively. The chapter appendix contains more information about each survey.

36. To ensure that the version of the question school-board members received was, in fact, randomly assigned, I carried out an analysis in each survey testing for balance between the treatment and control groups on a variety of individual- (e.g., gender, race, and partisanship) and district-level characteristics (e.g., size, poverty). The results of these tests confirmed that there was strong balance across experimental conditions that the randomization process was successful.

37. Specifically, I drew on question 27b in the 2012 *Education Next* poll, https://www.educationnext.org/wp-content/uploads/2020/07/EN_PEPG_Survey_2012_Tables1.pdf.

38. See, e.g., Jason Felch, Jason Song, and Doug Smith, "Who's Teaching LA's Kids? A Times Analysis, Using Data Largely Ignored by LAUSD, Looks at Which Educators Help Students Learn, and Which Hold Them Back," *Los Angeles Times*, August 14, 2010.

39. Some research indicates that elected officials become more responsive to their constituents when they are better informed about their constituents' opinions. See, e.g., Daniel M. Butler and David W. Nickerson, "Can Learning Constituency Opinion Affect How Legislators Vote? Results from a Field Experiment," *Quarterly Journal of Political Science* 6, no. 1 (2011): 55–83.

40. The results are robust to a more fully specified regression model that includes a dummy variable controlling for the specific sample (Indiana or the national survey).

41. Only 25% of board members characterized teachers unions as inactive or not too active in local school politics.

42. Roughly 27% of board members in my responsiveness experiment were current or former educators (N=225).

43. The VEA argued that continuing contracts were not analogous to tenure. The *Washington Post*, on the other hand, characterized them as "akin to tenure." I use both terms interchangeably in this chapter. No one disputes that continuing contracts provide teachers with more job security. All teachers in Virginia begin their career on a three-year "probationary period" before they are eligible to receive a continuing contract. Those who earn continuing contracts after their probationary period "are evaluated every three years and, under state code, can be dismissed for 'incompetency, immorality, noncompliance with school laws' and other transgressions." According to one federal survey, Virginia school districts dismissed (on average) just 1.3 percent of teachers during the 2007–08 school year. See Emma Brown, "Virginia Lawmakers Debate Teacher Tenure," *Washington Post*, February 12, 2012.

44. Editorial Board, "The Governor's Education Plan for Virginia," *Washington Post*, January 15, 2012.

45. See, e.g., Farrah Stone Graham, *Commonwealth Education Poll 2011–2012*, VCU Commonwealth Education Poll, Commonwealth Education Policy Institute at Virginia Commonwealth University, January 11, 2012, https://cepi.vcu.edu/me dia/cepi/pdfs/2011-12poll.pdf.

46. Senators Watkins and Norment both "took a walk," opting to abstain and thereby handing the Democrats a 20–18 victory to preserve tenure. Watkins' wife was a retired educator. Norment, the Republican Senate majority leader at the time, had a daughter who was a Virginia public school teacher. See CBS/Associated Press, "Virginia Senate Opts To Leave Teacher Contracts Unchanged," *CBS Washington Local News*, February 14, 2012, https://washington.cbslocal.com/2012/02/14 /virginia-senate-opts-to-leave-teacher-contracts-unchanged/.

47. Statement by Virginia Education Association President Meg Gruber, "Due Process Preserved," January 17, 2013, https://www.veadailyreports.com/2013/01 /due-process-preserved.html.

48. The survey was administered online between October 26, 2012 and November 8, 2012. The response rate was 30 percent. The chapter appendix contains more information about the survey.

49. Response categories were: (1) Very active; (2) Somewhat active; (3) Not too active; (4) Not at all active.

50. The measure ranges from -2.75 in Bath County to 2.25 in Charlotte County (mean = 0.40, SD = 0.83).

51. See Sarah F. Anzia, *Local Interests: Interest Groups and Public Policy in U.S. City Government* (Chicago: University of Chicago Press, 2022).

52. Five separate studies have shown that the decisions made by local school boards about when and how to reopen schools during the pandemic were heavily

influenced by the strength of a local district's union. See Michael T. Hartney and Leslie K. Finger, "Politics, Markets, and Pandemics: Public Education's Response to COVID-19," *Perspectives on Politics* (2021): 1–17, https://doi.org/10.1017/S153 7592721000955; Bradley D. Marianno, Annie Hemphill, Ana Paula S. Loures-Elias, Libna Garcia, and Deanna Cooper, "Power in a Pandemic: Teachers' Unions and Their Responses to School Reopening" (working paper, 2021), https://drive .google.com/file/d/1Ay3fTUch_eTu3fTDcuWhU5kRNBdP9R-0/view; Matt Grossmann, Sarah Reckhow, Katharine Strunk, and Meg Turner, "All States Close but Red Districts Reopen: The Politics of In-Person Schooling during the COVID-19 Pandemic," EdWorkingPaper: 21–355, Annenberg Institute, Brown University, 2021, https://doi.org/10.26300/cb1f-hq66; Corey DeAngelis and Christos Makridis, "Are School Reopening Decisions Related to Union Influence?," *Social Science Quarterly* (March 25, 2021), https://doi.org/10.1111/ssqu.12955; Douglas N. Harris, Engy Ziedan, and Susan Hassig, *The Effects of School Reopenings on COVID-19 Hospitalizations*, technical report, National Center for Research on Education Access and Choice, January 24, 2021, https://www.reachcentered.org/publications /the-effects-of-school-reopenings-on-covid-19-hospitalizations.

53. Bradley D. Marianno, "Teachers' Unions: Scapegoats or Bad-Faith Actors in COVID-19 School Reopening Decisions?," *Brown Center Chalkboard* (blog), Brookings Institution, March 25, 2021, https://www.brookings.edu/blog/brown-center -chalkboard/2021/03/25/teachers-unions-scapegoats-or-bad-faith-actors-in -covid-19-school-reopening-decisions/.

54. See, e.g., Paul Manna, *Collision Course: Federal Education Policy Meets State and Local Realities* (Washington, DC: CQ Press, 2011).

55. I discuss these dynamics more extensively in the book's final chapter. See, e.g., Stuart Buck and Jay P. Greene, "Blocked, Diluted, and Co-Opted," *Education Next* 11, no. 2 (2011): 26–32.

Chapter 8

1. Robert Chase, "The New NEA: Reinventing the Teachers Unions for a New Era" (address to the National Press Club, Washington, DC, February 5, 1997), http:// www.eiaonline.com/ChaseNewUnionism1997.pdf.

2. See, e.g., James S. Coleman, "Equality of Educational Opportunity," *Integrated Education* 6, no. 5 (1968): 19–28; Eric Hanushek, "The Failure of Input-Based Schooling Policies" (National Bureau of Economic Research Working Paper no. 9040, July 2002), https://www.nber.org/system/files/working_papers/w9040/w9040 .pdf; Eric A. Hanushek, "Throwing Money at Schools," *Journal of Policy Analysis and Management* 1, no. 1 (Autumn 1981): 19–41.

3. See C. Kirabo Jackson, Rucker C. Johnson, and Claudia Persico, "The Effects of School Spending on Educational and Economic Outcomes: Evidence

from School Finance Reforms," *Quarterly Journal of Economics* 131, no. 1 (2016): 157–218.

4. For an exchange between prominent scholars who have produced research that reaches different conclusions in this debate, see C. Kirabo Jackson, Rucker C. Johnson, and Claudia Persico, "Money Does Matter After All," *Education Next* (blog), July 17, 2015, https://www.educationnext.org/money-matter/; Eric A. Hanushek, "Money Matters After All?," *Education Next* (blog), July 17, 2015, https://www.educationnext.org/money-matters-after-all/.

5. Nicholas A. Kristof, "Where the GOP Gets It Right," *New York Times*, April 10, 2014.

6. Randi Weingarten, "Crisis in the Classroom," *This Week* (ABC News, August 15, 2010), https://abcnews.go.com/ThisWeek/week-transcript-crisis-classroom/story?id=11506701.

7. Leo Casey, "The Educational Value of Democratic Voice," in *Collective Bargaining in Education: Negotiating Change in Today's Schools*, ed. Jane Hannaway and Andrew J. Rotherham (Cambridge, MA: Harvard Education Press, 2006): 181–201.

8. Richard D. Kahlenberg and Jay P. Greene, "Unions and the Public Interest," *Education Next* 12, no. 1 (Winter 2012).

9. Diane Ravitch, "Standardized Testing Undermines Teaching," *Fresh Air* (National Public Radio, April 28, 2011), https://www.npr.org/transcripts/135142895.

10. Robert M. Carini, "Is Collective Bargaining Detrimental to Student Achievement?: Evidence from a National Study," *Journal of Collective Negotiations* 32, no. 3 (2008): 217, 226.

11. See Charles Taylor Kerchner, "The Relationship between Teacher Unionism and Educational Quality: A Literature Review" (unpublished manuscript, November 2004): 107–22, http://charlestkerchner.com/wp-content/uploads/2017/12/Kerchner-TUEQ-Review.pdf; Robert M. Carini, "Teacher Unions and Student Achievement," in *School Reform Proposals: The Research Evidence*, ed. Alex Molnar (Greenwich, CT: Information Age Publishing, 2002): 197–216; Joshua M. Cowen and Katharine O. Strunk, "The Impact of Teachers' Unions on Educational Outcomes: What We Know and What We Need to Learn," *Economics of Education Review* 48 (March 2015): 208–23; Joshua M. Cowen and Katharine O. Strunk, "How Do Teachers' Unions Affect Education Outcomes?: Reviewing the Latest Research on the Rent-Seeking Debate," in *Walkout!: Teacher Militancy, Activism, and School Reform*, ed. Diana D'Amico Pawlewicz (Charlotte, NC: Information Age Publishing, 2020).

12. Cowen and Strunk, "How Do Teachers' Unions Affect Education Outcomes?"

13. Cowen and Strunk, "How Do Teachers' Unions Affect Education Outcomes?"

14. See Michael F. Lovenheim and Alexander Willén, "The Long-Run Effects of Teacher Collective Bargaining," *American Economic Journal: Economic Policy* 11, no. 3 (August 2019): 292–324; Caroline M. Hoxby, "How Teachers' Unions

Affect Education Production," *Quarterly Journal of Economics* 111, no. 3 (August 1996): 671–718.

15. For example, as Sarah Anzia and Terry Moe explain: "quantitative studies [of collective bargaining] are almost entirely confined to a small literature—uneven in quality, diverse in method, mixed in findings, and largely dated—that focuses solely on the impact of collective bargaining on student achievement and essentially black-boxes issues of school organization. The aim of most of these studies is to determine whether student achievement is influenced by the existence of collective bargaining or by the strength of the teachers unions (as measured by their density of membership) in the relevant states or districts. Questions of organization, which ask how collective bargaining and its formal rules actually affect important kinds of behavior within schools and districts—and thus, if answered, would help explain why collective bargaining might influence student achievement—have largely gone unaddressed." See Sarah F. Anzia and Terry M. Moe, "Collective Bargaining, Transfer Rights, and Disadvantaged Schools," *Educational Evaluation and Policy Analysis* 36, no. 1 (March 2014): 83–111.

16. See, e.g., Terry M. Moe, "Collective Bargaining and the Performance of the Public Schools," *American Journal of Political Science* 53, no. 1 (January 2009): 156–74; Katharine O. Strunk, "Are Teachers' Unions Really to Blame? Collective Bargaining Agreements and Their Relationships with District Resource Allocation and Student Performance in California," *Education Finance and Policy* 6, no. 3 (July 2011): 354–98; Katharine O. Strunk and Andrew McEachin, "Accountability under Constraint: The Relationship between Collective Bargaining Agreements and California Schools' and Districts' Performance under No Child Left Behind," *American Educational Research Journal* 48, no. 4 (August 2011): 871–903; Bradley D. Marianno and Katharine O. Strunk, "The Bad End of the Bargain?: Revisiting the Relationship between Collective Bargaining Agreements and Student Achievement," *Economics of Education Review* 65 (August 2018): 93–106.

17. See Johnathan Lott and Lawrence W. Kenny, "State Teacher Union Strength and Student Achievement," *Economics of Education Review* 35, no. 1 (August 2013): 93–103.

18. For studies that focus on SAT and ACT scores, see, e.g., Michael M. Kurth, "Teachers' Unions and Excellence in Education: An Analysis of the Decline in SAT Scores," *Journal of Labor Research* 8, no. 4 (1987): 351–67; Morris M. Kleiner and Daniel L. Petree, "Unionism and Licensing of Public School Teachers: Impact on Wages and Educational Output," in *When Public Sector Workers Unionize*, ed. Richard B. Freeman and Casey Ichniowski (Chicago: National Bureau of Economic Research and University of Chicago Press, 1988): 305–22; Sam Peltzman, "The Political Economy of the Decline of American Public Education," *Journal of Law and Economics* 36, no. 1, part 2 (April 1993): 331–70; F. Howard Nelson and Jewell C. Gould, "Teachers' Unions and Excellence in Education: Comment," *Journal of Labor Research* 9, no. 4 (December 1988): 379–87; F. Howard Nelson

and Michael Rosen, *Are Teachers' Unions Hurting American Education? A State-by-State Analysis of the Impact of Collective Bargaining among Teachers on Student Performance*, report, Institute for Wisconsin's Future, October 1996, https://files.eric.ed.gov/fulltext/ED404746.pdf; Robert Carini, Brian Powell, and Lala Carr Steelman, "Do Teacher Unions Hinder Educational Performance?: Lessons Learned from State SAT and ACT Scores," *Harvard Educational Review* 70, no. 4 (December 2000): 437–67.

19. See, e.g., Randall W. Eberts and Joe A. Stone, *Unions and Public Schools: The Effect of Collective Bargaining on American Education* (Lexington, MA: Lexington Books, 1986).

20. See, e.g., John E. Chubb and Terry M. Moe, *Politics, Markets, and America's Schools* (Washington, DC: Brookings Institution Press, 1990).

21. Terry M. Moe, "Teachers Unions and the Public Schools," in *A Primer on America's Schools*, edited by Terry M. Moe (Stanford, CA: Hoover Institution Press, 2001): 151–84.

22. Dan Goldhaber, "Are Teachers Unions Good for Students?," in *Collective Bargaining in Education: Negotiating Change in Today's Schools*, ed. Hannaway and Rotherham, 141–58.

23. Casey argues, "It is useful to think of democratic voice in teachers unions through the image of a three-legged stool, with three distinct, but interrelated and interdependent strategies being employed [by unions]: collective bargaining, political action, and professional development." See Leo Casey, "The Educational Value of Democratic Voice," 183.

24. Randi Weingarten, "Remarks by AFT President Randi Weingarten" (AFT TEACH event, Washington, DC, July 11, 2019), https://www.aft.org/sites/default/files/rw_democracy-education-speech_2019.pdf.

25. See, e.g., Eric Brunner, Joshua Hyman, and Andrew Ju, "School Finance Reforms, Teachers' Unions, and the Allocation of School Resources," *Review of Economics and Statistics* 102, no. 3 (July 2020): 473–89.

26. Kahlenberg and Greene, "Unions and the Public Interest."

27. For the rent-seeking perspective, see the following: Hoxby, "How Teachers' Unions Affect Education Production"; Peltzman, "The Political Economy of the Decline of American Public Education"; Heather Rose and Jon Sonstelie, "School Board Politics, School District Size, and the Bargaining Power of Teachers' Unions," *Journal of Urban Economics* 67, no. 3 (May 2010): 438–50; Jason Cook, Stéphane Lavertu, and Corbin Miller, "Rent-Seeking through Collective Bargaining: Teachers Unions and Education Production," Economics of Education Review 85 (2021): 102193, https://www.sciencedirect.com/science/article/abs/pii/S0272775721001084; Lott and Kenny, "State Teacher Union Strength and Student Achievement."

28. Kahlenberg and Greene, "Unions and the Public Interest."

29. Terry M. Moe, *Special Interest: Teachers Unions and America's Public Schools* (Washington, DC: Brookings Institution, 2011).

30. Leo Casey, "The Educational Value of Democratic Voice," 181.

31. On the costs and benefits of reducing class size see, Henry M. Levin, Patrick J. McEwan, Clive R. Belfield, A. Brooks Bowden, and Robert D. Shand, *Economic Evaluation in Education: Cost-Effectiveness and Benefit-Cost Analysis*, 3rd edition (Los Angeles, CA: SAGE Publications, 2017): 6–7. For a summary of the literature on class-size reduction, see Matthew M. Chingos, "Class Size and Student Outcomes: Research and Policy Implications," *Journal of Policy Analysis and Management* 32, no. 2 (Spring 2013): 411–38.

32. Jo Craven McGinty, "Schools Learn Expensive Lesson on Class Size," *Wall Street Journal*, September 30, 2016.

33. Lorraine Mary McDonnell, *The Control of Political Change Within an Interest Group: The Case of the National Education Association* (PhD diss., Stanford University, 1975): 304, ProQuest document ID 302782553.

34. Dan Goldhaber, "The Mystery of Good Teaching," *Education Next* 2, no. 1 (January 2002): 50–55.

35. See National Council on Teacher Quality, *Restructuring Teacher Pay to Reward Excellence*, report, Washington, DC, December 2010, https://files.eric.ed.gov/fulltext/ED521227.pdf.

36. The narrow exception is when students are taught by a teacher who has earned an advanced degree in a specific subject area (i.e., a student's mathematics teacher earned a graduate degree in math). However, the vast majority of advanced degrees earned by K–12 teachers are not subject specific, but rather general education training (e.g., pedagogy, leadership). For a study that highlights the narrow exception of subject-specific returns to advanced degrees, see Kevin C. Bastian, "A Degree Above? The Value-Added Estimates and Evaluation Ratings of Teachers with a Graduate Degree," *Education Finance and Policy* 14, no. 4 (Fall 2019): 652–78.

37. See, e.g., Kate Walsh and Christopher O. Tracy, *Increasing the Odds: How Good Policies Can Yield Better Teachers*, National Council on Teacher Quality, Washington, DC, October 2004, https://files.eric.ed.gov/fulltext/ED506640.pdf; David N. Figlio, "Can Public Schools Buy Better-Qualified Teachers?," *ILR Review* 55, no. 4 (February 2002): 686–99.

38. Speech by Robert Chanin to the National Educational Association, NEA National Conference, March 13–15, 1992.

39. Terry Moe says much the same in *Special Interest*. See Moe, *Special Interest*, 5–6.

40. Both Goldhaber and Moe have articulated this possibility. To my knowledge, no empirical research has tested this hypothesis in the context of the American states. See, for example, Moe, *Special Interest*, and Goldhaber, "Are Teachers Unions Good for Students?"

41. Kleiner and Petree, "Unionism and Licensing of Public School Teachers."

42. On the variety of ways that unions project power and influence in politics, see, e.g., Leslie K. Finger, "Interest Group Influence and the Two Faces of Power,"

American Politics Research 47, no. 4 (July 2018): 852–86; Michael Hartney and Patrick Flavin, "From the Schoolhouse to the Statehouse: Teacher Union Political Activism and State Education Reform Policy," *State Politics and Policy Quarterly* 11, no. 3 (2011): 251–68; Moe, *Special Interest.*

43. Matthew Chingos, "Breaking the Curve: Promises and Pitfalls of Using NAEP Data to Assess the State Role in Student Achievement," (Washington, DC: Urban Institute, 2015), https://www.urban.org/research/publication/breaking -curve-promises-and-pitfalls-using-naep-data-assess-state-role-student-achievement. The NAEP database is regularly updated and can be accessed at https://apps .urban.org/features/naep/.

44. I focus exclusively on score gains here. However, if I model adjusted NAEP scores as a function of union political power without considering gains, I find substantively similar results. Notably, I do not find a positive correlation between a state's collective bargaining legal regime and adjusted NAEP scores. This finding contrasts with older work that does not adjust NAEP scores and that shows a positive correlation. As such, I take this corrective as part of the explanation for the findings of earlier scholarship that did not have demographically comparable test score data.

45. NAEP was not administered to all fifty states until 2003. While I prefer to focus on the longest-term changes in student performance, the analyses carried out in tables A8.2 and A8.3 are substantively similar if I instead focus on this shorter period of change in NAEP performance.

46. This practice is the conventional one when modeling growth on test scores like NAEP. However, the results of my analyses are not sensitive to this modeling choice. The negative relationships that I observe between union power and states' adjusted NAEP performance remain in place irrespective of whether baseline test scores are included as a control.

47. Chingos calculates performance differences on NAEP that account for gender, race and ethnicity, poverty, English-language-learner status, special education status, accommodations, and a variety of other family-level characteristics of test takers.

48. It is worth noting that when I include state-level measures that account for various differences in states' education inputs (e.g., spending, student-teacher ratios) or differences in their political culture (e.g., Democratic-party vote share), the effects of union power remain robust and substantively unchanged. This finding provides some additional assurance that the effect I have uncovered of teacher-union power on adjusted NAEP performance is not a spurious artifact of other omitted state-level factors that correlate with union power.

49. See, e.g., Eric A. Hanushek and Margaret E. Raymond, "Does School Accountability Lead to Improved Student Performance?," *Journal of Policy Analysis and Management: The Journal of the Association for Public Policy Analysis and Management* 24, no. 2 (March 2005): 297–327.

50. Unfortunately, it is not possible to use adjusted NAEP scores to measure cohort gains between the fourth and eighth grades because the adjustment process is done on grade cohorts in a given year, making the difference in the adjusted scores between different year-grades less interpretable. However, I am able to confirm that the results of the unadjusted cohort analysis is robust to a non-cohort analysis using the adjusted eighth-grade NAEP scores to measure the adjusted performance level of a state's eighth-grade students pre- and post-retrenchment. These estimates are shown in table A8.5 in the chapter appendix. For example, I find a positive relationship between labor-retrenchment laws and adjusted eighth-grade scores in both math and reading. The coefficient on labor retrenchment is 3.0 in reading and 2.4 in math in my preferred estimates, though the point estimate for math is shy of reaching conventional significance levels. The coefficient on reading is $p < 0.05$.

51. For studies examining the nature and consequences of various policy reforms after states curtailed their collective bargaining laws, see Kaitlin P. Anderson, Joshua M. Cowen, and Katharine O. Strunk, "The Impact of Teacher Labor Market Reforms on Student Achievement: Evidence from Michigan," *Education Finance and Policy* (May 2021): 1–43; E. Jason Baron, "Union Reform, Performance Pay, and New Teacher Supply: Evidence from Wisconsin's Act 10," *AEA Papers and Proceedings* 111 (May 2021): 445–49; Barbara Biasi, "The Labor Market for Teachers under Different Pay Schemes," *American Economic Journal: Economic Policy* 13, no. 3 (August 2021): 63–102.

52. See, e.g., Kristin Blagg and Matthew M. Chingos, "Does Gentrification Explain Rising Student Scores in Washington, DC?," *Urban Wire* (blog), May 23, 2016, https://www.urban.org/urban-wire/does-gentrification-explain-rising-student-scores-washington-dc; Thomas Toch, "Disrupted: Public Education Reform in the Nation's Capital," *Education Next* 20, no. 3 (Summer 2020).

53. Moe, *Special Interest*.

54. Kevin Mahnken, "A Turning Point for Union Research? New Study Shows a Negative Relationship Between Collective Bargaining & Boys' Future Earnings, Career Tracks," *The74: The Big Picture* (blog), April 1, 2018, https://www.the74million.org/cornell-study-shows-negative-effects-of-collective-bargaining-on-boys-future-earnings-career-tracks-a-new-era-for-union-research/.

55. Kahlenberg and Greene, "Unions and the Public Interest."

56. See, e.g., Alexander Hertel-Fernandez, "Policy Feedback as Political Weapon: Conservative Advocacy and the Demobilization of the Public Sector Labor Movement," *Perspectives on Politics* 16, no. 2 (June 2018): 364–79; James Feigenbaum, Alexander Hertel-Fernandez, and Vanessa Williamson, "From the Bargaining Table to the Ballot Box: Political Effects of Right to Work Laws" (National Bureau of Economic Research Working Paper no. 24259, revised February 2019), https://www.nber.org/system/files/working_papers/w24259/w24259.pdf.

57. Daniel DiSalvo, *Government against Itself: Public Union Power and Its Consequences* (New York: Oxford University Press, 2015).

58. Robert Maranto, "Engaging Teachers Unions in Education Reform," November 20, 2019, in *EdNext Podcast*, MP3 audio, 28:57, https://www.educationnext.org/ednext-podcast-engaging-teachers-unions-in-education-reform-maranto/.

Chapter 9

1. See, e.g., Sarah F. Anzia and Terry M. Moe, "Do Politicians Use Policy To Make Politics? The Case of Public-Sector Labor Laws," *American Political Science Review* 110, no. 4 (2016): 763–77.

2. See Don Eddins, *AEA: Head of the Class in Alabama Politics: A History of the Alabama Education Association* (Montgomery, AL: Composite, 1997); Dana Beyerle, "Hubbert Leads Lobbying Power in Montgomery," *Gadsden Times*, March 5, 2007.

3. Brian Lyman, "AEA Hits Pause on Political Contributions," *Montgomery Advertiser*, January 20, 2016.

4. See, e.g., Indiana State Teachers Association, *Advancing the Cause of Education: A History of the Indiana State Teachers Association, 1854–2004* (West Lafayette, IN: Purdue University Press, 2004); Scott Elliot, "The Basics of Teachers Unions in Indiana: Facing Tough Times," *Chalkbeat*, December 22, 2013.

5. For arguments against this dominant narrative that the quality of American public education had declined, see David C. Berliner and Bruce J. Biddle, *The Manufactured Crisis: Myths, Fraud, And The Attack on America's Public Schools* (Reading, MA: Addison Wesley, 1995); Richard Rothstein, *The Way We Were?: The Myths and Realities of America's Student Achievement* (Washington, DC: Brookings Institution Press, 1998).

6. "Help! Teacher Can't Teach!," *Time*, June 16, 1980.

7. Haley Sweetland Edwards, "The War on Teacher Tenure," *Time*, November 3, 2014.

8. See, e.g., Editorial Board, "Where's the School Reform? D.C. Deserves Better than the Teachers Union's Counteroffer," *Washington Post*, February 10, 2009; Editorial Board, "Reform and the Teachers' Unions," *New York Times*, January 24, 2011; "Enemies of Progress: The Biggest Barrier to Public- Sector Reform Are the Unions," *Economist*, March 19, 2011; Evan Thomas, "Why We Must Fire Bad Teachers," *Newsweek*, March 5, 2010.

9. April Castro, "Apple CEO Jobs Attacks Teachers Unions," Associated Press, February 18, 2007.

10. See Michael Edwards and Mark Walsh, *More Than a Lawyer: Robert Chanin, the National Education Association, and the Fight for Public Education, Employee Rights, and Social Justice* (Washington, DC: National Education Association, 2010): 228.

11. See, e.g., Steven Greenhouse, "Strained States Turning to Laws to Curb Unions," *New York Times*, January 3, 2011.

12. See, e.g., Davenport v. Washington Education Association, 551 U.S. 177 (2007); Ysursa v. Pocatello Education Association, 555 U.S. 353 (2009); Knox v. Service Employees International Union, 567 U.S. 298 (2012).

13. Edwards and Walsh, *More Than a Lawyer*, 225.

14. Edwards and Walsh, 225.

15. See Terry M. Moe, *Special Interest: Teachers Unions and America's Public Schools* (Washington, DC: Brookings Institution, 2011): 247–48.

16. See, e.g., William Lowe Boyd, David N. Plank, and Gary Sykes, "Teachers Unions in Hard Times," in *Conflicting Missions? Teachers Unions and Educational Reform*, ed. Tom Loveless (Washington, DC: Brookings Institution Press, 2000): 174–210.

17. By having his state pay for teachers' liability insurance, Governor Bush eliminated an important incentive that Florida's teachers unions used to recruit members. See Linda Kleindienst, "Teacher Union Leaders Accuse Florida GOP of Retribution," *South Florida Sun Sentinel*, May 15, 1999.

18. See, e.g., Madeline Will, "From 'Rotten Apples' to Martyrs: America Has Changed Its Tune on Teachers," *Education Week*, September 28, 2018.

19. Katie Reilly, "I Work 3 Jobs And Donate Blood Plasma to Pay the Bills. This Is What It's Like to Be a Teacher in America," *Time*, September 13, 2018.

20. This estimate was derived by using 2018 data on the size of the K–12 teacher workforce in each state as provided by the National Center for Education Statistics, "Public Elementary and Secondary Teachers, Enrollment, and Pupil/Teacher Ratios, by State or Jurisdiction: Selected Years, Fall 2000 through Fall 2018," Table 208.40 in *Digest of Education Statistics*, 2018, accessed November 21, 2021, https://nces.ed.gov/programs/digest/d20/tables/dt20_208.40.asp.

21. See, e.g., John Bailey, *Is It Safe to Reopen Schools? An Extensive Review of the Research*, report, Evidence Project at the Center on Reinventing Public Education, March 11, 2021, https://www.crpe.org/sites/default/files/3-12_is_it_safe_to_re open_schools_an_extensive_review_of_the_research_1.pdf; Kanecia O. Zimmerman, Ibukunoluwa C. Akinboyo, M. Alan Brookhart, Angelique E. Boutsoukas, Kathleen A. McGann, Michael J. Smith, Gabriela Maradiaga Panayotti, Sarah C. Armstrong, Helen Bristow, Donna Parker, Sabrina Zadrozny, David J. Weber, Daniel K. Benjamin Jr., and the ABC Science Collaborative, "Incidence and Secondary Transmission of SARS-CoV-2 Infections in Schools," *Pediatrics* 147, no. 4 (April 2021).

22. See, e.g., Michael T. Hartney and Leslie K. Finger, "Politics, Markets, and Pandemics: Public Education's Response to COVID-19," *Perspectives on Politics* (2021): 1–17, https://doi.org/10.1017/S1537592721000955; Bradley D. Marianno, Annie Hemphill, Ana Paula S. Loures-Elias, Libna Garcia, and Deanna Cooper, "Power in a Pandemic: Teachers' Unions and Their Responses to School Reopening" (working paper, 2021), https://drive.google.com/file/d/1Ay3fTUch_eTu3fTD cuWhU5kRNBdP9R-0/view; Matt Grossmann, Sarah Reckhow, Katharine Strunk,

and Meg Turner, "All States Close but Red Districts Reopen: The Politics of In-Person Schooling during the COVID-19 Pandemic," EdWorkingPaper: 21–355, Annenberg Institute, Brown University, 2021, https://doi.org/10.26300/cb1f-hq66; Corey DeAngelis and Christos Makridis, "Are School Reopening Decisions Related to Union Influence?," *Social Science Quarterly* (March 25, 2021); Douglas N. Harris, Engy Ziedan, and Susan Hassig, *The Effects of School Reopenings on COVID-19 Hospitalizations*, technical report, National Center for Research on Education Access and Choice, January 24, 2021, https://www.reachcentered.org/publications/the-effects-of-school-reopenings-on-covid-19-hospitalizations.

23. Some of the examples that are discussed here and in the remainder of this section draw from an article that I previously published with Daniel DiSalvo at *Education Next* in the fall of 2020. See Daniel DiSalvo and Michael T. Hartney, "Teachers Unions in the Post-Janus World," *Education Next* 20, no. 4 (July 2020): 46–55.

24. Act 10 also required annual certification elections—which pose the question of whether a majority of workers in a bargaining unit want union representation—and limited the scope of collective bargaining to wages with an inflationary cap. Public unions found the former costly and cumbersome. Bargaining also hardly seemed worth the effort if the subjects of negotiation were so limited.

25. See "Gov. Murphy Signs Workplace Democracy Enhancement Act," *NJEA Report* (blog), June 1, 2018.

26. See Larry Sand, "The Janus Decision and Teacher Freedom: One Year Later," *California Policy Center*, July 2, 2019, https://californiapolicycenter.org/the-janus-decision-and-teacher-freedom-one-year-later/.

27. For research that advances this theoretical argument, see James Feigenbaum, Alexander Hertel-Fernandez, and Vanessa Williamson, "From the Bargaining Table to the Ballot Box: Political Effects of Right to Work Laws" (National Bureau of Economic Research Working Paper no. 24259, revised February 2019), https://www.nber.org/system/files/working_papers/w24259/w24259.pdf; Alexander Hertel-Fernandez, "Policy Feedback as Political Weapon: Conservative Advocacy and the Demobilization of the Public Sector Labor Movement," *Perspectives on Politics* 16, no. 2 (June 2018): 364–79.

28. Sarah Rankin, "Virginia Lawmakers OK Limited Public Sector Bargaining Bill," *Washington Post*, March 8, 2020.

29. Tennessee later repealed its mandatory teacher bargaining law in 2011, replacing it with a system that the state calls "collaborative conferencing."

30. See Yana Kunichoff and Samantha Smylie, "Bill to Restore Chicago Teachers Union's Bargaining Rights Could Become Law Soon," *Chalkbeat*, April 2, 2021, https://chicago.chalkbeat.org/2021/4/2/22363391/bill-to-restore-chicago-teachers-unions-bargaining-rights-could-become-law-soon.

31. See, e.g., Aaron Tang, "Life After Janus," *Columbia Law Review* 119, no. 3 (April 2019): 677–762; Aaron Tang, "Public Sector Unions, the First Amendment, and the Costs of Collective Bargaining," *New York University Law Review* 91, no. 1 (April 2016): 144–226.

32. John Maynard Keynes, *The General Theory of Employment, Interest, and Money* (New York: Springer, 2018).

33. See, e.g., Kevin Carey, "The Little-Known Statistician Who Taught Us to Measure Teachers," *New York Times*, May 19, 2017.

34. Edwards and Walsh, *More Than a Lawyer*.

35. Robert Chanin, "Remarks to the RA" (Speech, 88th Annual Representative Assembly Meeting of the National Education Association, San Diego, CA, July 6, 2009).

36. Chanin, "Remarks to the RA."

37. Chanin, "Remarks to the RA."

38. Terry M. Moe and John E. Chubb, *Liberating Learning: Technology, Politics, and the Future of American Education* (San Francisco, CA: John Wiley and Sons, 2009).

39. Terry M. Moe, *The Politics of Institutional Reform: Katrina, Education, and the Second Face of Power* (New York: Cambridge University Press, 2019).

Chapter 10

1. See, e.g., Greg Bishop, "Molded for Success on Clay," *New York Times*, June 8, 2012; Cindy Shmerler, "The Stresses of Playing on the French Open's Clay Courts," *New York Times*, May 24, 2019.

2. See, e.g., Kay Lehman Schlozman and John T. Tierney, *Organized Interests and American Democracy* (New York: Harper & Row, 1986); Kay Lehman Schlozman, Sidney Verba, and Henry E. Brady, *The Unheavenly Chorus: Unequal Political Voice and the Broken Promise of American Democracy* (Princeton, NJ: Princeton University Press, 2012).

3. See, e.g., Alexander Hertel-Fernandez, *State Capture: How Conservative Activists, Big Businesses, and Wealthy Donors Reshaped the American States—and the Nation* (New York: Oxford University Press, 2019).

4. See Paul Frymer, "Teachers Unions and Public Education: A Discussion of Terry Moe's 'Special Interest: Teachers Unions and America's Public Schools,'" *Perspectives on Politics* 10, no. 1 (January 2012): 124–36, at 126.

5. See, e.g., Sarah F. Anzia, "Looking for Influence in All the Wrong Places: How Studying Subnational Policy Can Revive Research on Interest Groups," *Journal of Politics* 81, no. 1 (2019): 343–51.

6. David B. Tyack, *The One Best System: A History of American Urban Education*, vol. 95 (Cambridge, MA: Harvard University Press, 1974): 289.

7. See, e.g., Steven Brill, "The Rubber Room: The Battle over New York City's Worst Teachers," *New Yorker* 31 (August 31, 2009); Joel Klein, "The Failure of American Schools," *Atlantic* 307, no. 5 (June 2011): 66–77.

8. See, e.g., Reema Amin, "New York Legislators Overhaul Teacher Evaluations, Removing Mandatory Link to State Test," *Chalkbeat*, January 23, 2019.

9. See Eliza Shapiro, "New York Joins Movement to Abandon Use of Student Tests in Teacher Evaluations," *New York Times*, February 4, 2019.

10. See, e.g., Alyson Klein, "Here's How Sen. Kamala Harris Wants to Raise Teacher Pay," *Education Week*, March 26, 2019; Louis Freedberg, "Kamala Harris's Plan to Boost Teacher Pay Would Cost $315 Billion over 10 Years," *EdSource*, March 26, 2019.

11. Unfortunately for them, many of the policies that teachers unions support are costly (e.g., lower class sizes, universal early childhood education, salary increases) and local school districts face hard revenue constraints. See e.g., Paul E. Peterson, *City Limits* (Chicago: University of Chicago Press, 1981).

12. Thomas B. Fordham Institute and the American Enterprise Institute, *A Nation at Risk: Thirty Years Later*, April 26, 2013, video, 23:21, https://www.youtube.com/watch?v=R9WMI703WrA.

13. See, e.g., George Tsebelis, *Veto Players: How Political Institutions Work* (Princeton, NJ: Princeton University Press, 2002); Terry M. Moe, "Vested Interests and Political Institutions," *Political Science Quarterly* 130, no. 2 (2015): 277–318.

14. See, e.g., Noel Epstein, ed., *Who's in Charge Here? The Tangled Web of School Governance and Policy* (Washington, DC: Brookings Institution Press, 2004); Jeffrey R. Henig, *The End of Exceptionalism in American Education: The Changing Politics of School Reform* (Cambridge, MA: Harvard Education Press, 2013).

15. See, e.g., Terry M. Moe, "Teachers Unions and American Education Reform: The Politics of Blocking," *Forum*, vol. 10, no. 1 (2012); Stuart Buck and Jay P. Greene, "Blocked, Diluted, and Co-Opted," *Education Next* 11, no. 2 (2011): 26–32.

16. See, e.g., Jeffrey L. Pressman and Aaron Wildavsky, *Implementation: How Great Expectations in Washington Are Dashed in Oakland; Or, Why It's Amazing That Federal Programs Work at All, This Being a Saga of the Economic Development Administration as Told by Two Sympathetic Observers Who Seek to Build Morals on a Foundation*, Oakland Project vol. 708 (Berkeley: University of California Press, 1984).

17. See, e.g., Michael Lipsky, *Street-Level Bureaucracy: Dilemmas of the Individual in Public Services, 30th Anniversary Expanded Edition* (New York: Russell Sage Foundation, 1980).

18. See, e.g., Terry M. Moe, "Vested Interests and Political Institutions," 277–318.

19. See, e.g., Paul E. Peterson, *City Limits*.

20. For an overview of the NEA's federal political advocacy efforts in the 1960s and 1970s, see, e.g., Allan M. West, *The National Education Association: The Power Base for Education* (New York: Free Press, 1980); Wayne J. Urban, *Gender, Race, and the National Education Association: Professionalism and Its Limitations* (New York: Routledge, 2000).

21. Previously, education had been housed under the much-larger Department of Health, Education, and Welfare, known as HEW. See, e.g., David Stephens, "President Carter, the Congress, and NEA: Creating the Department of Education," *Political Science Quarterly* 98, no. 4 (Winter 1983–1984): 641–63.

22. See, e.g., John Hein, "Constitutional Implications of a Federal Collective Bargaining Law for State and Local Government Employees," *Creighton Law Review* 11 (1978): 863–93.

23. See San Antonio Independent School District v. Rodriguez, 411 U.S. 1 (1973).

24. See, e.g., Eric A. Hanushek and Alfred A. Lindseth, *Schoolhouses, Courthouses, and Statehouses: Solving the Funding-Achievement Puzzle in America's Public Schools* (Princeton, NJ: Princeton University Press, 2009); Paul A. Minorini and Stephen D. Sugarman, "Educational Adequacy and the Courts: The Promise and Problems of Moving to a New Paradigm," in National Research Council, *Equity and Adequacy in Education Finance: Issues and Perspectives* (Washington, DC: National Academies Press, 1999): 175–208.

25. On union support for adequacy lawsuits, see Alfred A. Lindseth, "Educational Adequacy Lawsuits: The Rest of the Story," PEPG 04–07, paper presented at conference, "50 Years after *Brown*: What Has Been Accomplished and What Remains to Be Done?," Kennedy School of Government, Harvard University, April 23–24, 2004, https://www.innovations.harvard.edu/sites/default/files/PEPG_04-07Lindseth.pdf; David P. Sims, "Suing for Your Supper? Resource Allocation, Teacher Compensation and Finance Lawsuits," *Economics of Education Review* 30, no. 5 (2011): 1034–44.

26. For research arguing that teachers are under-compensated, see Sylvia Allegretto, Sean Corcoran, and Lawrence Mishel, "How Does Teacher Pay Compare? Methodological Challenges and Answers" (Washington, DC: Economic Policy Institute, 2004). For research arguing against the notion that teachers are underpaid, see Jason Richwine and Andrew G. Biggs, *Assessing the Compensation of Public-School Teachers*, report 11–03, Heritage Center for Data Analysis, November 1, 2011, https://files.eric.ed.gov/fulltext/ED525685.pdf. For a third-party overview of the debate between these two sets of scholars, see, e.g., Carl F. Prieser, "Measuring Teacher Pay," *Monthly Labor Review* 135, no. 2 (February 2012): 39–42.

27. See, e.g., Michael Hansen, "Teachers Aren't Getting Younger, We're Just Paying Them Less," *Brookings Institution: Chalkboard* (blog), September 5, 2018, https://www.brookings.edu/blog/brown-center-chalkboard/2018/09/05/teachers-arent-getting-younger-were-just-paying-them-less/.

28. Frederick M. Hess, "Sketching A Win-Win Solution On Teacher Pay," *Forbes*, May 16, 2018, https://www.forbes.com/sites/frederickhess/2018/05/16/sketching-a-win-win-solution-on-teacher-pay/.

29. See NEA Research Division, *Rankings of the States 2020 and Estimates of School Statistics 2021*, report, National Education Association, Washington, DC, April 2021: 10, https://files.eric.ed.gov/fulltext/ED613033.pdf.

30. Some of this hiring has also been for noninstructional school employees. See, e.g., Matthew Richmond, *The Hidden Half: School Employees Who Don't Teach*, report, Thomas B. Fordham Institute, Washington, DC, August 2014, https://files

.eric.ed.gov/fulltext/ED560006.pdf. See also Benjamin Scafidi, *The School Staffing Surge: Decades of Employment Growth in America's Public Schools*, report, *Friedman Foundation for Educational Choice*, October 2012, https://files.eric.ed.gov /fulltext/ED536674.pdf.

31. Thomas D. Snyder, Cristobal de Brey, and Sally A. Dillow, *Digest of Education Statistics, 2018*, report, NCES 2020–009, US Department of Education, Institution of Education Sciences, and National Center for Education Statistics, Washington, DC, December 2019, https://nces.ed.gov/pubs2020/2020009.pdf.

32. See, e.g., Matthew M. Chingos, *The False Promise of Class-Size Reduction*, report, Center for American Progress, April 2011, https://files.eric.ed.gov/fulltext /ED536071.pdf.

33. See, e.g., Dennis Van Roekel, "Class Size Reduction: A Proven Reform Strategy," NEA policy brief, National Education Association, Washington, DC, 2008, http://citeseerx.ist.psu.edu/viewdoc/download;jsessionid=C8A3027B3545BCBDD1 2F8F80B085DA15?doi=10.1.1.216.5061&rep=rep1&type=pdf; Matthew Chingos, "Class Size Tradeoffs in the Court of Public Opinion," Brookings Institution, January 30, 2013, https://www.brookings.edu/research/class-size-tradeoffs-in-the-court -of-public-opinion/.

34. According to the NEA, in 2021 Washington ranked in the top ten states for both average and starting teacher salaries.

35. See, e.g., Washington Education Association, "Time to Negotiate BIG Pay Raises for All," *OurVoice* (blog), March 28, 2018, https://www.washingtonea.org /advocacy/ourvoice/post/time-to-negotiate-big-pay-raises/; Neal Morton, "Washington Lawmakers Knew School-Contract Chaos Was Coming—and Not Just in Seattle," *Seattle Times*, September 4, 2018.

36. Jami Lund, "Schools Don't Need Another Property Tax Hike," *Spokesman-Review*, March 7, 2019.

37. See, e.g., Editorial Board, "In Our View: Legislature Must Repair Its McCleary 'Fix,'" *Columbian*, April 11, 2019; James Drew, "Education Funding Continues to Bedevil State Lawmakers. Proposed Fixes Have Problems," *News Tribune*, March 27, 2019.

38. See, e.g., Mark Mullet, "My Wife Is a Teacher, but I Disagree with the Teachers Union on Pay," *Seattle Times*, April 10, 2019, https://www.seattletimes.com /opinion/my-wife-is-a-teacher-but-i-disagree-with-the-teachers-union-on-pay/.

39. See Kathleen Bawn, Martin Cohen, David Karol, Seth Masket, Hans Noel, and John Zaller, "A Theory of Political Parties: Groups, Policy Demands and Nominations in American Politics," *Perspectives on Politics* 10, no. 3 (September 2012): 571–97.

40. See, e.g., Sarah F. Anzia and Terry M. Moe, "Public Sector Unions and the Costs of Government," *Journal of Politics* 77, no. 1 (January 2015): 114–27; Sarah F. Anzia and Terry M. Moe, "Polarization and Policy: The Politics of Public-Sector Pensions," *Legislative Studies Quarterly* 42, no. 1 (February 2017): 33–62; Daniel

DiSalvo and Jeffrey Kucik, "Unions, Parties, and the Politics of State Government Legacy Cost," *Policy Studies Journal* 46, no. 3 (2018): 573–97.

41. See Michael Edwards and Mark Walsh, *More Than a Lawyer: Robert Chanin, the National Education Association, and the Fight for Public Education, Employee Rights, and Social Justice* (Washington, DC: National Education Association, 2010): 228–31.

42. See, e.g., Dan Goldhaber, "The Mystery of Good Teaching," *Education Next* 2, no. 1 (January 2002): 50–55.

43. See National Center for Education Statistics (NCES), Schools and Staffing Survey (SASS) 2011–12 https://nces.ed.gov/surveys/sass/.

44. See, e.g., Dan Goldhaber, Michael DeArmond, Daniel Player, and Hyung-Jai Choi, "Why Do So Few Public School Districts Use Merit Pay?," *Journal of Education Finance* 33, no, 3 (Winter 2008): 262–89; Buck and Greene, "Blocked, Diluted, and Co-Opted"; Michael T. Hartney and Patrick Flavin, "From the Schoolhouse to the Statehouse: Teacher Union Political Activism and State Education Reform Policy," *State Politics and Policy Quarterly* 11, no. 3 (2011): 251–68; Leslie K. Finger, "Vested Interests and the Diffusion of Education Reform Across the States," *Policy Studies Journal* 46, no. 2 (2018): 378–401; Leslie K. Finger, "Interest Group Influence and the Two Faces of Power," *American Politics Research* 47, no. 4 (July 2018): 852–86.

45. See Elizabeth Hernandez, "One Year after Denver's Historic Teacher Strike, What Did the Walkout Accomplish?," *Denver Post*, February 9, 2020.

46. See Associated Press, "Denver Teachers Are Heading Back to Class, but Their Strike Revealed a National Divide over Bonus Pay," February 14, 2019.

47. See Zelman v. Simmons-Harris, 536 U.S. 639 (2002).

48. See Espinoza v. Montana Department of Revenue, 591 U.S. ___ (2020).

49. See Drew Catt, "U.S. States Ranked by Educational Choice Share, 2020," EdChoice, October 21, 2020, https://www.edchoice.org/engage/u-s-states-ranked -by-educational-choice-share-2020/.

50. See, e.g., Brian J. Charles, "How Charter Schools Lost Democrats' Support," *Governing Magazine*, April 2019.

51. See, e.g., Jonathan Chait, "Unlearning an Answer," *New York Magazine*, January 5, 2021, https://nymag.com/intelligencer/2021/01/unlearning-democrats-an swer-on-charter-schools.html.

52. Matthew A. Kraft and Allison F. Gilmour, "Revisiting The Widget Effect: Teacher Evaluation Reforms and the Distribution of Teacher Effectiveness," *Educational Researcher* 46, no. 5 (June 1, 2017): 234–49, https://doi.org/10.3102/0013 189X17718797.

53. Emma Brown, "Contentious Teacher-Related Policies Moving from Legislatures to the Courts," *Washington Post*, February 28, 2015.

54. Brown, "Contentious Teacher-Related Policies Moving from Legislatures to the Courts."

55. Brown, "Contentious Teacher-Related Policies Moving from Legislatures to the Courts."

56. See, e.g., Liana Loewus, "Are States Changing Course on Teacher Evaluation?," *Education Week*, November 28, 2017; Michelle Croft, Gretchen Guffy, and Dan Vitale, *The Shrinking Use of Growth: Teacher Evaluation Legislation since ESSA*, ACT Research and Policy issue brief, July 2018, https://www.act.org/content/dam/act/unsecured/documents/teacher-evaluation-legislation-since-essa.pdf; Matt Barnum, "No Thanks, Obama: 9 States No Longer Require Test Scores Be Used to Judge Teachers," *Chalkbeat*, October 8, 2019, https://www.chalkbeat.org/2019/10/8/21108964/no-thanks-obama-9-states-no-longer-require-test-scores-be-used-to-judge-teachers.

57. On the durability of school reform in DCPS post-Rhee, see, e.g., Rachel M. Cohen, "How D.C. Became the Darling of Education Reform," *American Prospect*, April 19, 2017; Thomas Toch, "Disrupted: Public Education Reform in the Nation's Capital," *Education Next* 20, no. 3 (Summer 2020).

58. See Michael T. Hartney, "*A Collective Pursuit: Teachers' Unions and Education Reform*. By Lesley Lavery. Philadelphia: Temple University Press, 2020. 238p. $89.50 Cloth, $27.95 Paper," *Perspectives on Politics* 19, no. 1 (March 2021): 285–86.

59. For an overview of this debate, see Frederick M. Hess, "What Is a 'Public School'? Principles for a New Century," *Phi Delta Kappan* 85, no. 6 (February 2004): 433–39.

60. See, e.g., Paul Manna, *Collision Course: Federal Education Policy Meets State and Local Realities* (Washington, DC: CQ Press, 2011).

61. Sarah Jaffe, "Why Teachers Are Adopting a More Militant Politics," *New Republic*, April 18, 2018.

62. Frederick M. Hess, "Why Can't Politicians Get Out of Schooling?," *Rick Hess Straight Up (Education Week)* (blog), June 5, 2014, https://www.edweek.org/teaching-learning/opinion-why-cant-politicians-get-out-of-schooling/2014/06.

63. See, e.g., Paul E. Peterson, Michael Henderson, and Martin R. West, *Teachers versus the Public: What Americans Think about Their Schools and How to Fix Them* (Washington, DC: Brookings Institution Press, 2014).

Index